Full of specific examples and tools, this compelling boo[k] educational and personal value of mindfulness to all kin[d] tings. Credible and full of common sense, a wonderful res[ource] for every teacher.

   —**Rick Hanson, Ph.D., Author of** *Resilient: How to Grow an Unshakable Core of Calm, Strength, and Happiness*

This book is a beautiful offering to the world. It is filled with powerful stories and learnings from the frontlines of the Mindfulness in Education movement. This book is a must-have for anyone engaged in sharing mindfulness with educators or young people.

   —**Meena Srinivasan, Executive Director, Transformative Educational Leadership (TEL), Author of** *SEL Every Day* **and** *Teach, Breathe, Learn*

A beautifully curated collection of wisdom from experienced practitioners around the country. Kudos to Coalition of Schools Educating Mindfully for facilitating this impactful collaboration!

   —**Dr. Christopher Willard, Harvard Medical School, Author of** *Growing Up Mindful* **and** *Alphabreaths*

With love and rigor, this book highlights the many ways that mindfulness can be a transformative resource to students and teachers alike. Using grounded examples that convey powerful lessons from the field, the book is an essential resource for those in the mindfulness in education movement.

   —**David Treleaven, Ph.D., Author of** *Trauma-Sensitive Mindfulness: Practices for Safe and Transformative Healing*

This is an extraordinary collection, a delicious feast of wisdom and experience from some of the pioneers and leading practitioners in mindfulness in education. As the field enters its adolescence, this book offers an incredible opportunity to share stories, learn from our successes as well as our growing pains, and generate a collective community wisdom. I believe the reader will come away with a clear sense of where the mindfulness in education community has been, and inspiration for the amazing possibilities for the next generation!

   —**Dzung X. Vo, M.D., Author of** *The Mindful Teen: Powerful Skills to Help You Handle Stress One Moment at a Time*, **Board Member, Mindfulness in Education Network**

The collective wisdom is on point in *Educating Mindfully: Stories of School Transformation Through Mindfulness*. I heartily recommend this book filled with narrative that weaves together the history of the mindfulness in education movement.

   —**Gina M. Biegel, Founder, MBSR-Teens, stressedteens.com, Author of** *Take in the Good: Skills for Staying Positive and Living Your Best Life* **and many other books**

I'm very excited as a champion of mindfulness in education to recommend this book. We in New York City know that mindfulness is a powerful tool in helping not just our children but our families, teachers and public servants in other agencies to manage stress, cultivate awareness and realize thriving and compassionate learning communities.

  —**Eric Adams, Brooklyn Borough President, New York City**

Educating Mindfully takes the reader directly into the experience of teachers as they navigate the challenges, successes, heartbreaks, and joys of their profession. And like mindfulness being strengthened through full engagement with the ups and downs of life, this book is an uncompromising celebration of each encounter, from the small and gentle whispers of an opening heart, to the raucous shouts of minds freed to learn. Each chapter author has a unique perspective and context as well, so readers from different areas of the educational environment will find stories to touch them, and the resources to take action.

  —**Ted Meissner, Executive Director, Mindfulness Practice Center**

This is a must read for any classroom teacher or school leader! With so many wonderful stories and ideas from so many inspiring mindfulness teachers, you will find inspiration and ideas to spur your own mindfulness journey and learn about the positive impact that the mindfulness movement is having of children and adults of all ages!

  —**Helen Maffini, Director of MindBE Education and Host of the Preschool Mindfulness Summit**

If you want to know what's actually happening with mindfulness in schools, this is the perfect collection for educators. A superb collection of relevant, robust, and real-life examples to build understanding and capacity. As a school superintendent this will be an invaluable resource for our teams.

  —**Timothy J. Steinhauer, Ed.D., Mt. Lebanon School District Superintendent of Schools, PA**

I have used school based mindfulness as a Principal and now as a Superintendent to transform schools. It is critical for students, staff, and families to process stress, build stress resilience and to create healthy, safe, and inclusive school environments. It is a key driver of improvement in social emotional and academic learning outcomes and staff retention. This book is a wonderful resource.

  —**Itoco Garcia, Ed.D., Superintendent Sausalito Marin City School District, Co-Executive Director HipHop Scholastics**

The field has been waiting for a comprehensive text like Educating Mindfully. It demystifies the practice of mindfulness, acknowledges the needs of the adults, and highlights the need for these practices in Tier One. Real examples of how novices and more practiced teachers can embed this into their daily routine. I am eager to share this with teachers, students, and parents. They have been asking for an answer to the increased need to respond to and navigate the present.

—**Gene Olsen, Director of Student Services, Community Consolidated School District 89, Glen Ellyn, IL**

Mindfulness practices emerge from individual and shared experiences occurring simultaneously. This book models mindfulness practice by offering collective stories of mindful journeys and tales of impact. What a treasure to have regardless of where you may be on your own mindful journey as a companion to inspire, inform, nurture and model mindful practices. The collective voices heard in this rich narrative speak the truth of mindfulness practice and the crucial experience needed by all students and educators in these turbulent times.

—**Vincent J. Walsh-Rock, Ph.D., AP for Counseling and Student Support Services at Downers Grove South High School and Past President of the Illinois School Counseling Association**

This book provides in depth details for many practical and useful approaches for creating mindful classrooms and spaces. When students and adults share mindful practices together, it creates a positive climate and culture that maximizes learning, productivity, and centers students' well-being. The compendium of resources in this book will not disappoint.

—**Dr. Raquel Y. Wilson, Assistant Director for Student Services, Equity & Directions Program, Glenbard High School District 87, IL**

I was so excited to learn about this book! It is a compilation of caring, creative souls in the mindfulness community that I have been following, listening to and taking trainings from over the last few years as I try to gain as much knowledge as I possibly can to bring back to my students and their families. I am in total awe of the passion, knowledge and experience that each one of these contributors brings to this beautiful book. This book takes a little bit of the depth and breath of these wise men and women and packs it all in one peaceful place.

—**Mary Torres MSW, Program Manager, GCJFCS, Good Afternoon Friends and Amigos Afterschool, Hillsbourgo County, Florida, RYT 200, Owner, Mariposa Yoga Tampa**

Mindfulness and yoga in schools can transform teachers, students, and leaders through their lungs, hearts, and brains collaborating to learn. Walking the journey of a mindful educator is one of the best ways to begin your own...learning from others successes and productive struggle is irreplaceable. Many thanks to COSEM for this special book; I look forward to joining you in your next volume!

—**Dr. Lindsay Meeker, EL Director and Mindfulness Thought Partner, Quad City Yoga Foundation Educator, IA**

EDUCATING
mindfully

EDUCATING *mindfully*

Stories of School Transformation Through Mindfulness

A Collaborative Project of
Coalition of Schools Educating Mindfully

Edited by
Tracy Heilers, Tim Iverson, and Barbara Larrivee

Coalition of Schools Educating Mindfully
Saint Charles, Illinois

© 2020 Coalition of Schools Educating Mindfully
523 Monroe Avenue
St. Charles, Illinois 60174
www.educatingmindfully.org

Cover design by Tracy Heilers
Cover photos by Laurie Grossman, Tracy Heilers, Michelle Martin
Back cover photo by Candice Davies; from a North Carolina Chapter Meeting
Interior design and typesetting, Dorie McClelland, Spring Book Design

ISBN: 978-0-578-62722-9

Library of Congress Cataloging-in-Publication Data

Names: Heilers, Tracy, editor | Iverson, Tim, editor | Larrivee, Barbara, editor
Title: Educating Mindfully: Stories of School Transformation Through Mindfulness /
edited by Tracy Heilers; associate editors Tim Iverson, Barbara Larrivee.
Description: St. Charles, Illinois, Coalition of Schools Educating Mindfully, 2020
Identifiers: ISBN 978-0-578-62722-9 (paperback) | LCCN 2019920815
Subjects: LCSH: Affective education. | Reflective teaching. | Stress management for
children. | School psychology. | Social learning. | Meditation for children. | Mindfulness
(psychology). |
BISAC: EDUCATION / General / Classroom Management / Educational Psychology /
Leadership / Professional Development / Teaching Methods & Materials/General. |
PSYCHOLOGY / Psychotherapy / Child & Adolescent. | SOCIAL SCIENCE / Social Work
LCC record available at https://lccn.loc.gov/2019920815

**For information about special discounts for bulk purchases, please contact
Tracy Heilers at hello@educatingmindfully.org.**

Mindfulness Stew

Once upon a time, there was a Trickster, a Sage and an Artist.

Listen to this story about their time in a place called America.

They got together and made a meal called Mindfulness Stew.

Oh yeah, everyone took from their garden and threw something into the pot!

The people ate it and had the vision, planted themselves in the ground;

They turned obstacles into the paths of life-long learning and growth.

They bore fruit in the form of people, places and things–all lessons–all stories

That help us to treat this life, ourselves and one another, this earth and all living things

as the precious gems that they are. Come listen to our story of mindfulness stew.

**By Barnaby Spring, from his keynote at the
inaugural Educating Mindfully Conference**

Contents

Part 3. Create a Schoolwide Culture of Mindfulness

Part 4. Integrate Mindfulness Districtwide and Beyond

About the Editors

Tracy Heilers, Lead Editor

Tracy Heilers is founder and executive director of Coalition of Schools Educating Mindfully (COSEM). She lives in St Charles, Illinois, and is married to Gary Heilers, Department Chair of PE and Health at Glenbard North High School in Carol Stream, IL. Since 2003, Tracy has taught yoga and mindfulness to a wide range of student groups. She is appreciative and eager to serve and has a strong desire to use her unique talents to help the field of mindfulness in education grow in momentum, connecting educators with mentors as well as with all of the great mindfulness-based resources now available. She completed her 200-hour yoga teacher training in 2003, two of Mindful Schools' online courses in 2016 and a Mindfulness-Based Stress Reduction (MBSR) training in 2019. She grew up in Dubuque, Iowa, and has a degree in Civil Engineering from the University of Iowa.

Tim Iverson, Associate Editor
Tim Iverson is a former art and humanities teacher from Minnesota. After training in MBSR, he began sharing mindful practices with teachers and students in the Mounds View Public Schools and elsewhere in Minnesota. He currently serves on the board of the Mindfulness in Education Network (MiEN). In addition, Tim is an award-winning artist, and a former writer and contributing editor for *The Artist's Magazine.* Tim's blog: highviewtest.blogspot.com

Barbara Larrivee, Associate Editor
Barbara Larrivee, EdD, is a COSEM board member, author, researcher, and former teacher education professor at Rhode Island College and California State University. She is the author of eight books and more than 25 articles in education, psychology and counseling journals. She translates research into strategies to help teachers become more mindful, self-reflective and socially-emotionally literate so they can then be models for their students. Her books for educators include *Cultivating Teacher Renewal: Guarding Against Stress and Burnout, Authentic Classroom Management,* and *An Educator's Guide to Teacher Reflection.* Her latest book is for a general audience, *A Daily Dose of Mindful Moments: Applying the Science of Mindfulness and Happiness.* She is a longtime mindfulness practitioner and yogi. Visit dailydoseofmindfulmoments.com.

EDUCATING
mindfully

Introduction

Tracy Heilers

Founder and Executive Director, Coalition of Schools Educating Mindfully

IT'S HARD NOT TO BE SHAKEN by the current mental health statistics. Stress and trauma impact how our brain functions, making it harder to regulate emotions, focus and learn. More and more, school communities are learning about mindfulness when it is briefly brought up in professional development sessions on social-emotional learning (SEL), adverse childhood experiences (ACEs), resiliency, trauma-sensitive teaching, stress management or the neuroscience of learning. The emergence of mindfulness in education is giving children AND educators the tools to overcome ACEs, manage the stresses of modern living, and be part of an educational system that doesn't yet fully value well-being. Mindfulness practices provide healthy coping strategies, ground our nervous systems and get our brains in a ready-to-learn state . . . just for starters.

The community of Coalition of Schools Educating Mindfully (COSEM) was formed to be your next step in learning and a "joining forces" organization within the mindfulness in education field. Schools are now looking for trusted mindfulness-based programs, curricula, trainings, and other resources to lay the foundation for whole school community well-being and social-emotional learning. They are quickly finding that when they prioritize mental health with mindful practices, then compassion and connection flourish, and their school culture transforms.

This book is one of our collaborative projects and is a collection of inspiring stories where passionate educators share their life experiences which brought them to mindfulness and the steps they took to bring mindfulness into their classrooms, schools, districts and beyond. They share what has worked and what has not, as well as details of their favorite practices, programs, books, and trainings. You will be empowered to investigate mindfulness further and explore the resources put forward, perhaps using one or more to strengthen your personal practice and help create a culture of mindfulness at your school.

Together, the stories in this book make a solid case for mindfulness as a catalyst for healing and for supercharging all learning. But this book is meant to be more than just a resource and qualitative evidence. Stories are what move the heart. Hero's journeys are what inspire us to action. You'll get goosebumps as the chapter authors tell their personal journeys that led to discovering mindfulness, you'll cheer them on as they share how they overcame resistance when bringing it to their classrooms and schools, and you'll get teary-eyed when they share letters from their students and other large and small victories. And as I did, I think you'll leave the book feeling enormous clarity that we are on the right path.

This book is for all of the school mindfulness champions out there—from parents to school nurses to social workers to superintendents, as well as educators who are just starting to investigate mindfulness. It is also a great book to gift your administrators to show them examples of schools already having successful transformations with mindfulness. We hope when you read it, whether you are a caregiver, administrator, teacher or other, you are inspired to join us as school mindfulness champions.

How this Book Unfolds

In Part 1, we cover some of the history of mindfulness in US schools and some essential knowledge for getting started. These chapters are by educators involved with long-standing organizations that have played an important role in the growth and momentum of the field of mindfulness in education. Chapters are not in any chronological order and do not give an exhaustive recounting of the history; instead, through our storytelling genre, our intention is to give a sense of the roots of mindful education and the deep dedication of the pioneers of this work—which there are many, many more than included here.

COSEM has been inspired by two other organizations: Association of Mindfulness in Education, founded by Amy Saltzman, and Mindfulness in Education Network, founded by Richard Brady. Amy and Richard both edited similar books in the past and organized similar conferences. We begin Part 1 with chapters by them; Amy starting us off because in her chapter she also explores in detail the converging of multiple fields and how there is a growing number of people entering the shared room of mindfulness from different doors. And because readers are entering through different doors, her chapter is a perfect lead-in for the other chapters.

Stories in Part 2, 3 and 4 involve bringing mindfulness to classrooms, schools, whole districts and beyond, respectively. You'll hear from school mindfulness champions such as Monica Claridge, an elementary school PE teacher in Alaska, Matt Dewar, high school Well-Being Coordinator in Illinois, James Butler, District SEL Mindfulness Specialist in Texas, and Lillie Huddleston, Executive Director of Equity and Student Support in Georgia. They bring us into the nitty-gritty details of their work as well as the vulnerabilities of their hearts.

We'll end with two special chapters, the first by Barnaby Spring, Director of Mindfulness in Education at New York City Department of Education (NYCDOE); I consider Barnaby an honorary co-founder of COSEM as you'll learn in my personal story coming next in this introduction. Barnaby provides us an insightful report into the emergence of mindfulness in the NYCDOE and in the western model of education. Then we hear from COSEM President Tovi C. Scruggs-Hussein, who shares how mindfulness and mindful leadership can start to close the achievement gap and begin the process of racial healing, making us all leaders of equity for the diverse populations we serve.

At the very end of the book is a section with chapter author biographies, contact information, websites and more. In case you want to reach out to any of them.

We decided to independently publish this book so that we could get it to the world more quickly and create future volumes to hear from even more voices. We plan to use a portion of the proceeds to create a fun video-sharing grant program, where we'll regularly and randomly select winners from those who have submitted informal videos detailing ways they practice mindfulness in their classrooms and schools. We'll all be winners from the shared learning and those selected can use the grant to support their personal practice with a training or on resources for mindfulness integrations. We will also take what we are learning from publishing this book to help more educators get their mindfulness-based books to our growing community.

How Coalition of Schools Educating Mindfully Came to Be

Since this book is story-based, I'd like to start with mine. Like many others, I learned about mindfulness during a time of challenge. Starting a family was the first goal I had ever set that I couldn't accomplish, and after six years trying different medical interventions, a book by Thich Nhat Hahn caught my eye at the library. Every word in *Peace Is Every Step* felt like a truth being re-remembered, and it led to the non-stop reading of other mindfulness books, as well as yoga books, starting a daily meditation practice and taking yoga classes.

Mindfulness empowered me to witness and look differently at the unhelpful thoughts flooding my mind that were zapping my zest for life and causing depression. Daily practice helped me focus on the present and less on the future, allowing me to more fully embrace my imperfect, yet beautiful life. Over time, I was able to befriend my uncertain future, even if it meant not having biological children. It was so life-changing that I decided to take a month-long residential yoga teacher training in Sedona, Arizona in 2003. Within weeks of coming home, my husband Gary and I conceived naturally.

As our three boys grew up, I was very proactive regarding their mental health because I had family members who struggled at times with ADD and other mental health challenges. I also wished I had learned mindfulness as a child, and I wanted to gift that to my children through my example. I kept up with the growing mindfulness in education movement from afar and started teaching yoga and mindfulness to kids and their parents in my in-home studio, as well as at my kids' and husband's schools every chance I got. He is Department Chair of PE and Health at a high school, and also a coach, so I had lots of access to student groups.

In the 2017–2018 school year, my kids' school district had both an 8th and 9th grader die by suicide. That winter I checked in to see if they'd be interested in integrating mindfulness as a proactive universal/Tier 1 mental health strategy. They wanted to move beyond putting out fires and were open to suggestions. I began researching mindfulness programs and at my suggestion, they started piloting Inner Explorer in some classrooms at several different schools. That process made me think that there were probably hundreds or even thousands of other schools also in search of and researching mindfulness programs, and how time-saving it would be if there was one spot for schools to learn about them all.

In late February, I led a mindfulness session at a multi-county teacher institute day, and in March, I tried to sign up for an SEL conference at Wolcott School in Chicago that had some mindfulness sessions, but it was sold out. It seemed that the timing was right for a bigger conference in the Chicagoland area and I toyed with the idea of organizing one. I had previously organized a mind-body summer sports camp, as well as several school wellness fairs and summer activity fairs, and I learned that I enjoyed and excelled at event planning, promotion, and web design.

Then came a huge tragedy in our lives when Gary's best friend and colleague, whom our kids called Uncle Bado, died by suicide. We spent April helping his family with the details and grieving together. Although mindfulness is not a magic bullet, I couldn't help but think that if he had learned as a child how the mind and brain worked, along with mindfulness and other healthy strategies for managing ruminating thoughts stemming from the trauma of his childhood, and later the stresses of being a high school English teacher, his life may have turned out much differently.

In between observing and feeling the normal waves of what-ifs, grief, and guilt, I tried to focus on the silver linings, such as the gift Mike was to our marriage, and I started feeling a deep desire to live the rest of my life as joyously and courageously as possible. I had been having so many great-feeling ideas that I knew could impact the well-being of many, and within a few weeks, I became energized to see where they might lead. In May, I started drafting a website, which was just a vision board at the beginning; it included my idea for a web-based community to learn about mindfulness resources, as well as my idea for organizing a large Mindful SEL Conference that aligned with DuPage and Kane counties' Teacher Institute Day.

I shared my ideas with Marjorie Cave, SEL Specialist at DuPage Regional Office of Education, as well as several other local school educators. Their responses and offerings to help boosted my confidence. The conference idea quickly expanded to a coalition that summer when I reached out to Barnaby Spring, Director of Mindfulness in Education at New York City Department of Education, to see if he could do the keynote for it. He suggested that we broaden our vision and brought up how impactful it would be if schools educating mindfully joined forces to support and learn from each other, moving forward together in our collective vision. Doing so would create even greater momentum for what he called the emergence of mindfulness in education.

I reflected on whether I was the person to launch a coalition; I was a parent with a passion for mindfulness in education and I had the skills needed to serve such a coalition . . . AND I had lots of time on my hands, which educators are lacking. I decided to trust my intuition and brush aside my limiting belief of, "I'm not important enough to do this." I researched existing mindfulness and SEL organizations and conferences, and picked the brains of more educators and mindfulness resource providers, creating an advisory team and piecing together their ideas and mine to mold a unique educators-supporting-educators nonprofit, with an annual conference and regularly-held local chapter meetings at its heart.

First-Year Accomplishments

Once our vision was clear, I created branding, filled out our 501(c)(3) application and designed a website that articulated the vision. In September, I reached out through the Mindfulness in Education Network (MiEN) and Association for Mindfulness in Education (AME) email groups to gather an all-educator board of directors. They helped fine-tune our mission and organize our inaugural Educating Mindfully Conference on February 28–March 2, 2019 in St. Charles, Illinois; 330 people from 18 states and 4 countries attended. DuPage Regional Office of Education provided CEUs and CPDUs for attendees.

After the conference, we focused on recruiting state chapter coordinators, creating chapter goals and guidelines together. We currently have 24 US states and 3 countries represented with chapters, each growing slowly in their own way, grassroots style. They are essentially communities of practice where educators meet regularly to support each other's personal practice, learning together and mentoring each other as they integrate mindfulness in their classrooms and schools.

In the spring, we also started this book collaboration with a call for chapter proposals and we created an online Mindful Learning Center. It sustains our mission and provides extremely affordable professional development through access to our growing video library of conference session recordings, interviews, equity-based conversations, webinars and more.

In the summer, we secured a conference venue closer to O'Hare Airport in Itasca and partnered with DuPage Regional Office of Education and Illinois Special Education Leadership Academy, receiving federal grant funding to design an Administrator Academy on Implementing Schoolwide Mindfulness for Well-Being, Equity and Inclusion. Illinois State Board of Education approved it for three years as an in-person and online course that meets the annual requirement for administrative license renewal. Any educator from any state can take it, and we recommend wellness teams take the course together. It includes six hours of instruction and two online mentoring sessions.

We hope to keep collaborating on impactful projects like this in Illinois and then help other state chapter coordinators create partnerships in their states to co-design similar projects. We'd also like to continue sharing mindful educator voices with more books, blog posts, video sharing, in-person gatherings, and free online learning summits.

We are starting as a small volunteer team, but in time and with funding partners, we'll bring all of our ideas to fruition, working together with others to create mindful schools, mindful cities, mindful states, and a mindful nation. We invite you to join our coalition community as we assist each other in implementing holistic approaches to education, equipping the world's educators and youth with skills to thrive and creating a more equitable, inclusive, safe and compassionate world.

PART 1

ROOTS,

RESEARCH,

AND

RESPONSIBILITIES

CHAPTER 1

Emerging of a Unified Field

Amy Saltzman, MD

Co-Founder and Director of the Association for Mindfulness in Education, Author of Multiple Books on Mindfulness including *A Still Quiet Place*

To BEGIN, THE EDITORS HAVE ASKED ME to share a bit of my story. And I notice a bit of hesitation. While the snippets below convey some of the doing, this format does not easily lend itself to sharing the depths of my work and play with my long term mentor, Georgian Lindsey, and my devoted personal practice which infuses this doing. That said, I will begin.

I am a holistic physician, mindfulness coach, and devoted student of transformation. In 1993, during my residency in internal medicine, my persistent outrageous requests—to both Jon Kabat-Zinn and my residency director, ultimately created a life-changing opportunity for me to study mindfulness at the Stress Reduction Clinic at the University of Massachusetts, now known as the UMass Memorial Health Care Center for Mindfulness. Shortly after I returned to my residency, I designed a study assessing the benefits of offering mindfulness to patients with long-term chronic pain and illness.

In 1997, when I became a parent, I began offering mindfulness to parents. And when my son was three, he asked to meditate with me and I began sharing mindfulness with him. For the last 20 years, I have had the privilege of sharing mindfulness with youth and the adults who support them in a wide variety of settings: high risk, underserved public schools, affluent independent schools, middle-class community organizations such as churches and after school programs, in my private medical practice, and with child-parent pairs through the Center for Applied Affective Neuroscience at Stanford. There is no reason to wait until someone is 40 and having a heart attack or going through a divorce to teach them these skills. Children as young as three can benefit from practicing mindfulness.

In the mid to late '90s, pioneering educators and allied professionals devoted to offering children and adolescents essential life skills instinctively understood that individual students, entire classrooms, schools, districts, communities, and society as a whole would benefit if young people received mindfulness. These professionals sought simple, usable, comprehensive, trustworthy interventions to offer to their students, clients, and patients. Thus, I began sharing my curriculum with those seeking training in these practices. I offered the first Still Quiet Place workshop at the annual conference hosted by the UMass Center for Mindfulness in 2005, and subsequently via a cumbersome online platform, with as a spiral-bound manual.

Fortunately, with the support of my mentor and my publisher, the manual has been refined and transformed into a practical, step-by-step guide, *A Still Quiet Place: A Mindfulness Program for Teaching Children and Adolescents to Ease Stress and Difficult Emotions*, and online platforms have evolved, becoming extremely user-friendly, even for technophobes. It has been and continues to be a great privilege to support devoted professionals from literally all over the world in developing a daily personal practice (the foundation for sharing mindfulness with youth) and the specific skills for doing so.

Co-Founding Association of Mindfulness in Education

In 2005, I co-founded the Association of Mindfulness in Education (AME; mindfuleducation.org), which is a collaborative association of organizations and individuals working together to provide support for mindfulness training as a component of K-12 education. In 2007, Jon Kabat-Zinn was the keynote speaker for our inaugural gathering, which was the first large, international, public dialogue on mindfulness in K-12 education. For the next several years, AME hosted national conferences in the Bay Area, while our sister organization Mindfulness in Education Network (MiEN; mindfuled.org) hosted conferences on the east coast.

In 2011, AME partnered with UCSD Center for Mindfulness to co-host the Bridging Hearts and Minds of Youth Conference. From 2012–2018 I had the privilege of chairing this conference. A devoted committee (Steve Hickman, Allan Goldstein, Chris Willard, Randye Semple, Amy Eckhart, John Rettger) shared the daunting task of choosing each year's inspiring speakers, from an ever-growing number of high-quality submissions. In 2018, Dr. Steve Hickman, founder of the UCSD Center for Mindfulness and the Bridging conference, took a new position and UCSD chose to stop hosting the conference. Fortunately, the MiEN Conference continues, and COSEM's Educating Mindfully Conference is filling a long-standing need in the center of the country. There are also now many wonderful free online summits that people can participate in from the comfort of their own home. As discussed below, conferences, no matter how inspirational, are not substitutes for developing a committed personal practice and participating in in-depth, ongoing training.

In the spring of 2010, when I offered the keynote at the MiEN Conference at

Lesley University, I found myself repeatedly forming circles with both hands and moving them toward one another. Over and over, I spoke of circles beginning to converge. As a mindfulness educator, I continue to see a coalescing or "coming together" of this field's previously "separate" parts, perspectives, approaches, and philosophies into a more unified and spacious whole.

In my 2014 closing keynote for the Bridging Hearts and Minds of Youth Conference in San Diego, I described some of the many circles that continue to converge as the field blossoms. The editors of this book felt this would be a great place to share these observations again. My intention is for us to look mindfully, with kindness and curiosity, at these different perspectives, approaches, and philosophies, appreciating the unique and interconnected elements of the field.

For clarity and ease, the term teachers will refer to classroom teachers and the term educators will refer to all of us involved in the shared work of bringing mindfulness into education. The pairings below may initially seem like opposites. However, my experience is that while we may each enter the "room" of mindfulness in education from different doorways, we are all in the same room, devoted to offering our youth essential life skills, in the most compassionate, meaningful ways possible.

Teaching to Students and Teaching to Teachers

Most individuals and organizations involved in offering mindfulness in educational settings have a primary focus, *either* offering training to students *or* to teachers. Regardless of whether a given program emphasizes teaching to students or to teachers, most educators recognize that the greatest benefits will be realized when students and teachers *share* the practice of mindfulness. Thus, many programs that teach primarily to students offer in-services or trainings for teachers. Many programs designed to reduce teacher stress, burnout and compassion fatigue, and enhance teacher well-being, empathy and effectiveness include basic suggestions to support teachers in sharing mindfulness practices with their students.

As programs develop, many are expanding their curricula or partnering with sister programs to create mutually supportive interrelated offerings for students and teachers. Most mindfulness educators agree that ideally 1) teachers would receive mindfulness training for their own self-care during their pre-service training, and 2) schools and districts would offer comprehensive integrated programming to the teachers, administrators, students, *and* parents. On the occasions when I have had the privilege to provide such comprehensive programming, it has been transformative. Unfortunately, due to the limitations of funding, staffing, scheduling and expertise, this ideal is not yet frequently realized and most of us find our niche teaching what is truest for us and where we are invited.

Who Teaches? Mindfulness Practitioners or Classroom Teachers?

Most of us who entered our shared room through the mindfulness doorway feel strongly that only those with an established long-term mindfulness practice should share the practices with K-12 students. Those who entered the room through the K-12 teacher doorway feel equally strongly that only those with significant classroom teaching experience should share the practices with students. Given that currently, the number of classroom teachers with long-term mindfulness practice is relatively low compared with the number of classrooms throughout the country and the world, a middle path seems optimal.

Research has demonstrated that students benefit if a teacher develops a personal mindfulness practice, even if the teacher never formally offers mindfulness to their students. Additionally, in almost every research study showing that students benefit from direct mindfulness instruction, the people offering the mindfulness instruction have had devoted long-term mindfulness practices. Thus, nearly all educators doing this work agree that a classroom teacher should have an established personal practice before sharing mindfulness with their students.

Sharing the practice with students includes offering formal practices, games, songs, interactive exercises, and most importantly encouraging students to use their developing mindfulness skills to respond with creativity and kindness to circumstances in daily life. If you are called to do this work, please begin by cultivating a daily, ongoing, personal practice, and *then* only when you are truly ready, formally share the practices with your students (see the chapter "Am I Ready?" in *A Still Quiet Place*).

The question of how much practice is enough practice to begin offering age-adapted practices to children remains unanswered. For me, the absolute bare minimum for those who wish to offer mindfulness to youth is that you have participated in an 8-week mindfulness course *and* committed to an ongoing daily practice. Preferably you would have a year or more of personal practice, including retreat experience. As a corollary, most mindfulness practitioners, who are not also classroom teachers, can benefit from formal instruction in classroom management/responsiveness and creating engaging, supportive learning environments.

Secular Mindfulness and Buddhism

When we bring these practices into public school classrooms across the country, it is essential that we—individually and collectively—offer the practices in ways that are completely universal, secular and accessible.

In public schools, separation of church and state requires that we offer these essential life skills independent of any religion, philosophy or belief system. Some well-intentioned educators deeply immersed in this work occasionally forget that many people in the US have tremendous fear of well-proven aspects of psychology and are terrified of "meditative" practices. On more than one occasion, a frightened parent has sued (unsuccessfully) to end a local program and this has sent ripples of resistance through our increasingly interconnected and internet-connected world.

When we offer mindfulness to children, the fears of their parents must be met with respect, understanding, compassion, clarity, and reassurance. I find the best way to do this is to share the practices with the parents, either offering an introductory evening specifically for parents and/or inviting parents with concerns to join a classroom session. This approach increases the odds that concerned parents and inquisitive decision-makers will discover through *their own direct experience* that they can practice just as they are, within the context of their current opinions and beliefs—including religious, atheistic, scientific and agnostic paradigms.

Still, it is important that we respond with integrity to the loving, concerned parent who asks, "Is mindfulness Buddhist?" My answer is, "Mindfulness and compassion are innate human capacities; one does not need to be Buddhist to practice mindfulness and compassion any more than one needs to be Italian to enjoy pizza." This statement acknowledges one of its historical lineages as well as the universality of the practice.

As the field continues to evolve, those who learned the practices in Buddhist settings are coming to understand the absolute necessity of offering them in a secular, accessible form. And those who learned the practices in more secular settings are discovering ways to honor the multi-faceted origins of the practices with wisdom and integrity. As we move forward, it is essential that secular is not translated as devoid of ethics, and that we continue to emphasize that the intention of mindfulness is to cultivate wise and compassionate ways of relating to ourselves and others in our fragile, imperfect humanness.

Mindfulness and Yoga

Movement is an ideal doorway into mindfulness and can be particularly beneficial for students who have experienced trauma and those with learning differences. And all children, adolescents, and adults need to move. Thus, most mindfulness programs incorporate movement practices in their curricula. Many of the practices come from yoga traditions and others have been borrowed from dance and improvisational theater or are created spontaneously. Children also need stillness and quietness so many yoga and physical education programs are infusing mindfulness into their programming.

As with SEL and mindfulness, some educators enter our shared room through the mind door and others enter through the body door. However, most in the field recognize that the mind and body are inseparable, and educators are actively incorporating best practices from multiple disciplines.

Social Emotional Learning (SEL) and Mindfulness

In the early days, I experienced a confusing, and to me, false separation between proponents of social emotional learning and mindfulness. In April of 2005, Garrison Institute hosted a gathering of pioneers in the field. The intention of the gathering was to create a Mapping Report, documenting and describing programs utilizing contemplative techniques in K-12 educational settings. The Mapping Report detailed similarities and differences in program pedagogy and methodology, and explored the degree to which such programs foster love and forgiveness among students.

Even now, it is difficult to convey the palpable sense of separation, attachment and even righteousness about "our way" between those who entered our shared room through the mindfulness door and those who entered through the SEL door. We were all involved in the transformative work of offering mindfulness and contemplative practices to enhance students' social, emotional and academic skills, yet the language of the final report reflects subtle divisions of "us" and "them" within the group.

When one reads CASEL's (Collaborative for Social, Emotional and Academic Learning) definition of social emotional learning, the overlap with mindfulness is apparent. Let's pause here and consider our working definition of mindfulness. When I share mindfulness with school-age children, I offer the following definition: *Mindfulness is paying attention here and now, with kindness and curiosity, so that we can choose our behavior.* However, in the Mapping Report, mindfulness-based contemplative programs were defined as emphasizing attention training and primarily fostering academic success. For me, this definition represented a frustrating misunderstanding of the practice of mindfulness, and a false division.

Although mindfulness curricula vary in their format—15-minute sessions 3 times a week for 5 weeks, 30-minute sessions twice a week for 8 weeks, 45 minutes once a week for 6 weeks—the primary content of the courses is fairly similar. In my curriculum, students learn to look inward and attend to the breath, the body, the five senses, thoughts, feelings, impulses, wants and needs. Additionally, they are supported in looking outward and becoming aware of others' thoughts, feelings, impulses, wants and needs. They practice cultivating an attitude of friendliness or loving kindness toward themselves and others. These skills are taught in combination to support students in developing the ability to *respond,* rather than react, to situations in daily life. Students are encouraged to respond to their own experience and to the experience of their classmates, friends, family members and people in their communities with compassion and wisdom.

CASEL.org defines social emotional learning as "recognizing and managing our emotions, developing caring and concern for others, establishing positive relationships, making responsible decisions, and handling challenging situations constructively and ethically." Additionally, CASEL identifies many of the same desired outcomes that are emphasized in mindfulness curricula. "They are the skills that allow children to calm themselves when angry, make friends, resolve conflicts respectfully, and make ethical and safe choices."

Over the years, proponents of various SEL and mindfulness curricula have grown into a deeper appreciation of each others' strengths and our shared intentions. Those entering the dialogue through the doorway of SEL have come to understand that mindfulness provides a student with a foundational awareness of their internal and external experience, as well as the shared human experience. These awarenesses allow the child to choose to act with integrity, respect, and compassion. Pamela Seigle, the creator of the Open Circle SEL curricula (open-circle.org), told me that, "Incorporating mindfulness into my SEL curricula has greatly enhanced its effectiveness."

At the same time, those entering the dialogue through the doorway of mindfulness have come to a greater appreciation for the activities, skills and years of refinement offered in many of the SEL curricula. At the end of the mapping initiative meeting, I noted somewhat pleadingly, "We are all *here, now,* in the *same* room, working together to bring these valuable skills to children and adolescents, and it doesn't matter which doorway we entered through." Now it is beginning to feel, that as a field, we are more respectful of the wisdom various perspectives bring to the table and more appreciative of our shared intentions.

Flowering of the Field

My description above of the ongoing emergence of a unified field details how far we have come in a short time. And by writing my description, in what some might still view as opposing pairs, I also show the shortening distance yet to be covered to create a truly unified field that is inclusive, non-dual, secular, accessible, rigorously researched, and which supports students' and teachers' social, emotional and academic development.

I do not mean to suggest that the desired endpoint is the coalescing of the various viewpoints into one homogeneous circle or blob. Rather, I recommend that we continue to strive mindfully to appreciate the distinct gifts of each perspective and remain grounded in our shared intention to bring these essential life skills to young people. We are all in the same room, blossoming together with a shared commitment to relieving suffering, enhancing compassion and creating peace.

Schoeberlein, D. (2005). *Contemplation and education a survey of programs using contemplative techniques in K-12 educational settings: A mapping report.* Garrison, NY: Garrison Institute.

CHAPTER 2

Growing the Mindfulness in Education Network

Richard Brady, MS

Former High School Mathematics Teacher, Co-Founder, Mindfulness in Education Network, Co-Editor *Tuning In: Mindfulness in Teaching and Learning*

THE WINTER OF 1999–2000, I'M READING *The Seven Stages of Money Maturity* by George Kinder. A stage called *vigor* gets my attention. Kinder explains that work contains vigor if it returns as much or more energy as you put into it. He then invites his readers to meditate on work that has this quality. Two instances immediately come to mind—teaching problem-solving at St. Mary's residential summer center for Maryland gifted and talented junior high students and conducting a senior seminar on conflict resolution at Sidwell Friends School in Washington, DC, where I've been teaching Upper School mathematics since 1973.

Does my math teaching have *vigor*? I enjoy it, do a good job, and have no signs of burnout, but at the end of each year, I'm tired. Summer vacations recharge my batteries. I could continue in this vein until I'm ready to retire, but do I want this repeated pattern? Or do I want to go for *vigor*? I make an appointment to talk with Sidwell's Headmaster Bruce Stewart and explain that I want to refresh my spiritual life through a one-year leave of absence. Bruce asks if I plan to return next year and I say yes. I do plan to return, but I honestly have no idea whether a year away will change my mind.

As the spring wears on with no plans for my leave, I start to feel uneasy. What if the year passes and I discover no passion? I get the idea to go to Parker Palmer's new Center for Teacher Formation and train to be a facilitator. My partner Elisabeth tells me, "That's Parker's work, Richard. You need to find your own work." I know she's right, and I continue to live with uncertainty. Later in the spring, my friend Sue-Anne calls from upstate New York, lamenting the tremendous pressures experienced by students and teachers. "Someone ought to teach them meditation," I tell her. As I hear the words come out of my mouth, I know that someone is me. I've hit on my new direction. I'll offer mindfulness retreats to teachers.

The sum of my retreat-leading experience is co-leading two Quaker retreats with Elisabeth in the '90s. Elisabeth is an experienced retreat leader, undergirded by a strong Quaker foundation. At our retreats, I share mindfulness exercises and lead guided meditations. By spring 2000, I've practiced mindfulness in Thich Nhat Hanh's tradition for eleven years, but feel far from confident about teaching it. The mindfulness practices I've shared with an algebra class and with a colleague arose spontaneously; they seemed natural. Now I need to devise a curriculum. Where do I begin? I have no idea how to organize such a program.

Pendle Hill, the Quaker center near Philadelphia I've visited regularly since 1984, seemed like the perfect place to host a retreat of this kind and their extension secretary agrees. They have an open weekend in October. Looking for a co-leader, I consider the mindfulness practitioners I know. Susan Murphy would be ideal. She's a Quaker, like me a member of Thich Nhat Hanh's Order of Interbeing, and a professor of nursing at San Jose State University. I leave a message on her phone. When I arrive at school the next day, there's an email from Susan, brightly accepting my invitation.

Although Susan and I have both practiced mindfulness for some years, neither of us has taught it. There are no mindfulness curricula or guidelines that we know of. We decide to offer a menu of practices and exercises for reflection and sharing. Since our Pendle Hill students will range from kindergarten teachers to university professors whose mindfulness backgrounds vary, we give the course an inclusive approach.

It comes as no surprise that participants most appreciate the eating and walking meditations, which can be carried out anywhere during the day. Since we practice these meditations together as a group, each participant is supported by the others. They also enjoy sitting individually outdoors for twenty minutes with their eyes closed, just listening. When we gather indoors, one teacher excitedly reports hearing a leaf fall for the first time in his life. The results are so gratifying that we reprise the retreat for educators the following spring at Ben Lomond Quaker Center, near Susan's home in California.

Mindfulness Lessons Ideal for Students

I'm invited by several schools to teach mindfulness. Following an after-school workshop for interested teachers at a Friends school in New Jersey, several faculty invite me to visit their classes. The teachers' retreats boost my confidence. Now I'm sure I can come up with mindfulness lessons ideal for students. The teacher of a 12th-grade religion class currently studying events leading up to the Holocaust asks me to help prepare students for what they'll soon encounter. I tell the class that mindfulness practice can provide a way to be present with our suffering without becoming overwhelmed.

Describing the process of holding emotions in our awareness with great tenderness like a mother cradling a crying infant, I invite students to choose personal experiences of "small" suffering from their own lives—an argument with a friend or a disappointing test result. The event needs to be small, I explain, so that our mindfulness will be strong enough to hold it. After leading them through a guided meditation focused on the breath, I ask them to bring their small suffering into awareness, then to hold it gently for five minutes. The room falls silent. Afterward, several students share with the class. Overall the group is surprised by how useful the practice has been. One boy tells us he discovered his suffering isn't as small as he thought.

I go on to a 3rd-grade class where we mindfully eat chocolate chip cookies. I've no clue as to what approach to use with a 9th-grade English class. So I start by introducing myself, letting students know I teach high school math as well as meditation for students and teachers. Then I ask, "Why would your teacher have invited me to teach you meditation?" A number of hands shoot up. I take notes as students respond, and let them guide me in shaping my remarks and choice of visualizations. One student suggests I might have been invited because his class tends to be restless. I follow up on this great opening with a guided meditation:

> *Breathing in, I know I am breathing in.*
> *Breathing out, I know I am breathing out.*
> *Breathing in, my breath grows deep.*
> *Breathing out, my breath grows slow.*
> *Breathing in, I feel calm.*
> *Breathing out, I feel ease in my body.*
> *Breathing in, I smile.*
> *Breathing out, I release.*
> *Dwelling in the present moment,*
> *I know it is a wonderful moment.*

On my return to Sidwell, I teach a stress reduction class as part of the health unit in Freshman Studies. Sidwell can be stressful. Families who send their children here hold high expectations. Four US presidents have enrolled their children at Sidwell. The environment at New Trier, my own high school in Illinois, was similar. I read somewhere that during the 1960s, when I attended high school, the rate of teenage suicides on Chicago's Northshore was the highest in the country. I wonder if my brother's emotional and physical disorders are stress-related. I think of him as I plan the class.

Freshman Studies: Mind as a Stage

Freshman Studies is an ungraded one-semester course required for all ninth graders. I plan to base the class on mindfulness. It will not be easy to engage them. I recall the book *Teacher Man* where author Frank McCourt writes about connecting with his unmotivated New York City high school English class. "What is it they're interested in?" he asks himself. The answers are immediate: *sex* and *food*. He introduces a hugely successful unit in which students collect and recite family recipes, some with musical accompaniment by classmates. My classes are not as challenging as McCourt's. However, asking kids to attend fully to anything with nonjudgmental awareness and an attitude of curiosity is asking them to care.

Extending care requires a vulnerability some resist; to care involves taking a risk in the face of possible scoffing and ridicule in the ever-judgmental peer atmosphere. I carefully select what I ask them to focus upon while considering McCourt's question "What interests them?" At their age young people are figuring out who they are. They're interested primarily in themselves, their peers, and their bodies. For them, the mind is a fresh frontier. Inviting them to watch what their minds do at rest becomes the basis of my exercise, "Mind as a Stage." I begin the lesson by suggesting that our minds play a significant role in our well-being:

> *When I talk about mind, I'm talking about awareness. It will help to think of your awareness as a "stage." On your stage, a succession of actors will make their appearance: thoughts, feelings, perceptions, physical sensations.*

Once they're comfortable in their seats, we conduct a short experiment to look at our personal stages. I ask students to close their eyes and tune into whatever might appear on their stage.

> *Just watch. Whatever thoughts, feelings, perceptions, or sensations arise during the next few minutes, continue observing. Don't get carried away by anything you see.*

After five minutes students slowly open their eyes. The room feels gathered in silence. I quietly begin a series of questions. How many were aware of physical sensations—sounds, smells, tastes, contact with their seat, heartbeat, breathing, feet, other body parts? How many were aware of emotions? Thoughts? Who saw a thought arise? A thought end? Who experienced negative thoughts or feelings? Of these, how many had to do with events that have already happened, incidents you feel upset or guilty about? Many hands go up. How many negative thoughts and feelings have to do with the future, things you're anxious about? This also gets a big response. Finally, I ask how many of their negative thoughts and feelings have to do with the present. I see one or two hands in the air.

I point out that what our minds do during any particular five-minute interval of our waking life is repeated about 70,000 times each year. If we multiply the number of negative thoughts and feelings we observe by 70,000, we can understand why the mind plays such a significant role in creating stress and tension. If we're aware of the negative thoughts and feelings that fill our minds and if we can develop ways to replace them with positive thoughts and feelings, we can live happier, less anxious lives in and out of school. As we will soon see, I tell them, meditation is one means of helping our minds turn to wholesome thoughts.

I then describe a school assembly where I told of reading Thich Nhat Hanh's book *The Miracle of Mindfulness* to my math classes and later hearing about meditation experiences from Sidwell Friends senior Chris Anderson. I concluded that assembly with a two-minute sitting meditation. Several days after the assembly Audrey, a 12th-grader, shared the following message at our all-school Meeting for Worship:

I've been thinking about the fact that the main change Mr. Brady's student noticed in himself after he had been meditating on a regular basis was that he was less angry. Lately, I've been so angry myself because I've had all this resentment building up inside over responsibilities that I have to fulfill. I really want to let it all go, but I can't. This makes me even more resentful and angry. The other night I was sitting at my desk around 12:30 a.m., completely stressing because I had so much work to do. I was on the verge of breaking. But I just closed my eyes and took in ten deep breaths, concentrating on inhaling and exhaling the whole time. When I opened my eyes, I was so relaxed. If any of you are stressed out or angry, just take ten seconds to close your eyes and breathe. The action is so little, but the reward is tremendous.

This story—coming from a peer—provides a good opportunity for me to invite my freshmen to move from learning about meditation to doing meditation. I lead them in a ten-minute guided visualization using Thich Nhat Hanh's mindfulness verse focusing on the positive:

Breathing in, I know I am breathing in.
Breathing out, I know I am breathing out.
Breathing in, I see myself as a flower.
Breathing out, I feel fresh.
Breathing in, I see myself as a mountain.
Breathing out, I feel solid.
Breathing in, I see myself as still water.
Breathing out, I reflect things as they truly are.
Breathing in, I see myself as space.
Breathing out, I feel free.

It's but a brief introduction, yet it underlines the importance of tuning the mind to positive channels.

Honored by Thich Nhat Hanh

In the fall of 2000, I hear via the grapevine that I'm being considered for lamp transmission, a ceremony in which Thich Nhat Hanh transmits the authority of *dharma* teacher in his tradition, as successor in an unbroken lineage of teachers and disciples, a spiritual ancestry traced back to the Buddha himself. I receive this news with mixed feelings. Lamp transmission would be a great honor. Yet I'm committed to teaching mindfulness in educational settings. I wonder if *dharma* teachers are expected to focus on teaching in Buddhist settings. The next fall, the invitation comes. Will I come to Plum Village in December 2001, to receive lamp transmission? Of course, I will!

I understand that the ceremony will include my offering of an insight poem to Thich Nhat Hanh (Thây, meaning *teacher*, as his students call him) and the ancestors, as well as receiving a personal poem from Thây. I'm daunted. On occasion I've been inspired to write a poem or two, none with the expectation that they contain special insight, much less that I'd read them aloud to Thich Nhat Hanh and the assembled Plum Village monastic and lay community. I can't see myself just sitting down and writing such a poem.

However, as I continue to think about it, the subject of *freedom* pulls me in. I recall how, after my father was diagnosed with Alzheimer's and was living only in the present moment, a kind of freedom developed in our relationship. Old knots that bound me were untied. I don't feel this depth of freedom in other close relationships. Old knots still remain. For weeks I think about freedom and talk about it with friends, but no insight comes.

Finally, I take the subject of freedom to my therapist. The conditions for insight ripen, leading to the poem I offer to Thây and the ancestors:

> *This freedom—not freedom from,*
> *from childhood habits,*
> *from childhood fears;*
> *not freedom to,*
> *to open to the love enfolding me,*
> *to know and live my truth.*
>
> *This freedom—freedom with,*
> *with habits, with fears,*

with heart protected,
truth hidden deep inside.

This freedom—freedom with this moment,
just as it is.

Thây, as is traditional with a new *dharma* teacher, presents me a poem he has written:

A dharma rain penetrates the realm of the heart.
A great Bridge helps reestablish deep love.
Tending the precious flowers every day
helps purify all layers of society.

Dharma Bridge, the *dharma* name Thây had given me in 1992, appears in the first lines of the poem. I'd receive this name as a confirmation of my calling to share the *dharma* in non-Buddhist settings. After reading the poem aloud to me, Thây explains that "precious flowers" refers to my students. Moved by his understanding, I weep. But what exactly is Thây thinking I teach? Mindfulness practice isn't just about relieving stress. It leads to deep insights about life.

Launching the Mindfulness in Education Network

While it may not appear so, I'm by nature introverted. So, it was a giant leap for me to venture forth from Sidwell Friends, lead retreats and teach mindfulness in new schools. I'm encouraged during several of Thây's retreats to organize meetings for educators in which we introduce ourselves with a few words about our work with mindfulness. In 2001, with a special appeal to educators, Thây offers two five-day retreats—one in Massachusetts and one in California. At the start of one of his *dharma* talks at the University of Massachusetts, Thây invites the educators to the front of the hall to sit around him. He begins by advising the fifty of us to turn our classes into *sanghas*, mindfulness communities.

Inspired, I reserve a large classroom for two teacher get-togethers during the retreat, where we gratefully meet other pioneers on this new frontier. Mindfulness isn't yet a buzz word; it isn't yet featured on the covers of national magazines. Mindfulness training for teachers doesn't even exist. Most of us know no other educators who share our mutual interest. Suddenly we are a community! We want to stay in touch. I collect names and email addresses, then contact two West Coast friends to suggest they do the same at Thây's retreat in California. On October 18, 2001, the Mindfulness in Education Network (MiEN) is born as an email listserv with 78 participants. Soon MiEN launches a website, mindfuled.org, for sharing our new movement worldwide.

Because I manage MiEN's listserv, I often get requests for advice. "I suggest you share your problem on the listserv. There are folks out there with more relevant experience to draw on than I," I often respond. Eventually, I post an appeal for advice myself. Two friends in one of my classes, both good athletes, have gotten in the habit of kicking and tripping each other like a couple of puppies. Discipline is rarely a problem at Sidwell. Is there a way, I want to know, to employ mindfulness here? Humbled to reach out for help, I know I'll receive good advice.

Of four thoughtful replies, one related to the Japanese martial art of aikido turns out to be ideal. I meet with the young men individually and explain the principles of this martial art. "When your attacker comes at you, you gracefully stand aside and turn his energy back on him rather than oppose him and give away your power," I explain. Each boy understands right away and agrees not to respond to his friend's provocations. The three of us then meet and seal the agreement. There are no further incidents. MiEN's listserv whets my appetite for an in-person community of mindful educators. This is only a taste. I want a whole meal.

In 2006, Amy Saltzman, founder of MiEN's sister organization, the Association for Mindfulness in Education (AME), invites Rob Wall (a fellow student of Thây's), Irene McHenry (my educator retreat co-leader following Susan Murphy), and me to present at AME's first conference in San Francisco. The day before the event, we join the West Coast presenters for practice and conversation. We are invigorated. Amy suggests MiEN offer a similar conference on the East Coast, but who among us has the time to coordinate such an event? I need to wait for retirement in 2007.

With the support of Irene, Rob, and Amy, I organize a one-day conference at Sidwell Friends in February 2008, attended by 160 people, which becomes an annual gathering. Held on college campuses, MiEN's conference expands to three days with a full-day opening workshop, an evening keynote talk, a symposium, and a closing day of mindfulness practice for conferees. With an international reach, MiEN invites people with mindfulness backgrounds from diverse areas of education to join our listserv and attend the conference. By 2019, MiEN's listserv has grown to more than 1,700. Hundreds more visit the website to watch videos of plenary speakers from past conferences, examine resources, related links, and articles on mindfulness with students.

A few years prior, the mindfulness in education movement is in its infancy. Around the country, individual teachers who are students of mindfulness begin to incorporate their learning into the classroom and programs in schools begin. Many of the teachers who have attended Irene's and my workshops and weekend retreats are among them. As no books are available to assist teachers who wish to do likewise, Irene suggests we collect and publish a book of stories. In 2007, we begin to edit *Tuning In: Mindfulness in Teaching and Learning*. When published two years later, *Tuning In* is the first book on mindfulness for educators. The book includes diverse pieces by eighteen educators from all levels of teaching.

Stopping and Looking Deeply

Mindfulness practices involve both stopping and looking deeply. In the years just prior to retiring from Sidwell Friends, I wanted to share the latter, insight practices, with my students. In February 2005, I attend a conference at Teachers College, Columbia University, sponsored by the Center for Contemplative Mind in Society, aimed at teaching contemplative practices. Nearly two hundred people from all levels of education attend. I'm inspired. This is just what I've been looking for. I leave the conference hopeful about the future of education.

During the conference, I learn about a week-long summer workshop on contemplative curriculum development at Smith College. I'm drawn to attend—eager to develop contemplative methods for one of my math courses, to see where this leads. Math II, my honor's geometry course, seems the best candidate. If we behold geometric figures in a mindful way, will we uncover new insights? I hope so. What other methods might I employ? I'm still in the dark. I later chronicled the contemplative component I developed for Math II in Learning to Stop, Stopping to Learn: Discovering the Contemplative Dimension in Education, *Journal of Transformative Education*, Vol. 5, No. 4, 372–394 (2007), available on the Resources page on mindingyourlife.net.

Just prior to the workshop, I attend a retreat with Thây near Boston. Besides helping me slow down and settle more deeply into a contemplative frame of mind, this retreat gives me another chance to participate in a special interest group with other educators. In one of our sharings, several teachers say they dread the coming school year. Referring to the No Child Left Behind Act and state-mandated testing, they question the possibility of ever teaching "the whole child." Then, one of the group shares a verse from Woody Guthrie's "This Land Is Your Land,"

> *As I was walking, I saw a sign there*
> *And that sign said, "No Trespassing"*
> *But on the other side, it didn't say nothing*
> *That side was made for you and me!*

He goes on to suggest we look at the other side of No Child Left Behind. Its intent—for all children to learn—is an ideal we all support. If we teach with integrity, addressing the whole child, our students will meet any mandated standards and much more.

With the calm of the retreat I seamlessly enter curriculum development at Smith College. During an evening of poems, stories, and music, I read Martha Graham's advice to her sister and dancer, Agnes de Mille:

> *There is a vitality, a life force, an energy, a quickening, that is translated through you into action, and because there is only one of you in all time, this expression is unique. And if you block it, it will never exist through any other medium and will be lost.*

These words speak with passion to my own aspirations and hopes. Let it be so.

Recalling the True Purpose of the Mindful Life

I retired in 2007 after my two most fulfilling years of teaching, thanks to sharing mindfulness with my students—five minutes of journaling, meditating before tests, mindful stretching when the students were tired. Since then I've watched mindfulness become an industry, selling cures for ADHD, emotional dysregulation, stress, and so on. Those of us who practice mindfulness know it's much more than a cure—it's being present to life, with all its ups and downs. Practicing equanimity in the face of affliction has become an important part of my continued work with educators—how important that they, in turn, equip their students for a world beset with suffering. I've also begun to focus on relationships—deep listening, loving speech, and mindful action, seeing our profound connection with all of life. The educator's vocation has never been more sacred.

*Parts of this chapter were previously published in 2004 in *Independent School*, Vol. 64, No. 1, 82–87.

CHAPTER 3

The Support of Community: An Important Kind of Self-Care

Elizabeth Kriynovich

English Teacher, Delaware Valley Friends School, Paoli, PA, Board President, Mindfulness in Education Network (MiEN)

I WRITE THESE WORDS ON A BRIGHT, CRISP FALL MORNING, aware of a pleasant sense of spaciousness and ease at having successfully completed one of those frenetic cornerstones of any teacher's life: report card writing week. I welcome the chance to pause this morning and reflect on what mindfulness has meant to me, both in my teaching and personal life, and also how I appreciate its role in the broader world of education. As I contemplate the steam rising from my teacup in the morning sunlight, I feel a sense of gratitude for the work of the countless individuals working to support both new and experienced educators in sustaining a mindful approach to their personal and professional lives, and to those who are sharing that benefit with students.

I came to full-time teaching after several years of counseling work in higher education and secondary schools. I had the good fortune to begin my teaching career in a Quaker School, one of several dozen schools around the world founded by people in the manner of Friends (another name for Quakers). Quakerism has a long history of silence and contemplation, and has traditionally embraced contemplative practices to help community members feel centered and connected—both to one another and to a greater spirit. It was in this community, which valued the experience of gathering as a group to sit in silence, that I developed my teaching career.

During my first year of teaching, as I navigated the challenges faced by any new teacher to grasp the day-to-day demands of the job and also somehow meet the needs of my students, I came to realize that my students responded better, the classroom ran more smoothly, and learning was much more meaningful when I felt centered and calm. I drew frequently on my personal yoga practice, an eight-week Mindfulness-Based Stress Reduction (MBSR) course I had taken to help manage anxiety, and the Quaker tradition of centering silence.

In the winter of 2010, fresh into the second semester of my teaching career and searching for any sources of support and guidance I could find, I became aware of a workshop offered by Irene McHenry, a Quaker educator and leader, and then-director of the Friends Council on Education. Irene was offering a six-week workshop drawing on practices described in the newly published book *Tuning In: Mindfulness in Teaching and Learning,* which she had edited along with another longtime Quaker educator, Richard Brady. The book featured stories written by teachers at a variety of levels, describing how they were using mindfulness practices in their classrooms. Attending the workshop, I immediately realized the power of this practice to both sustain my energy as a teacher and potentially help me support my students in the classroom.

As the years went on, I continued to develop my practices of mindfulness, yoga and teaching high school students. As the field of mindfulness in education grew, I grew in my practice with it, eagerly reaching for new books as they were published, attending meaningful conferences and presentations by a multitude of transformative speakers, and attempting as best I could to maintain a personal practice of yoga and mindfulness.

Something was Missing

My personal mindfulness practice deepened, and I could feel its benefit while at the same time growing more skilled as an educator. But for many years, these still felt like separate things. I viewed mindfulness as a tool that could enhance my teaching, and while I did see some benefit to opening each class with a chime and a few moments of breathing, these practices did not feel as meaningful as I knew they could. I was using mindfulness intellectually and practically, yet it felt incomplete. Looking back, the quality that was missing was a true sense of compassion for myself and empathy for my students.

In 2014, I learned of a "Day of Mindfulness" being offered by Irene McHenry and Richard Brady as part of a three-day conference held by the Mindfulness in Education Network (MiEN). I attended the day of silent practices, mindful walking, mindful eating, and mindful listening, and came away from the mostly silent day feeling incredibly nourished. In particular, the practices of lovingkindness and deep listening resonated most deeply. During those times of connection, I could very clearly feel the presence and compassion of the others in the room. For the first time, I felt the powerful support of a practice community, and this spoke to something I had been missing in my own practice. I learned that mindfulness *is* a personal practice, but not a *solitary* one.

The support I had been seeking began to click into place. I subscribed to the MiEN listserv as a way of virtually participating in this community in an ongoing manner. That fall, I attended another weekend-long mindfulness retreat for teachers offered by Richard Brady, which felt transformative for my personal mindfulness practice and reinforced the feeling of support and connection to other educators I had felt at the MiEN conference. Richard's teachings about mindfulness, with their emphasis on compassion, ease, and joy, spoke to me in a way that other trainings and readings I had encountered had not. I learned that his teacher was Thich Nhat Hanh, the Vietnamese Zen Buddhist monk noted for cultivating mindfulness throughout the world.

Embodying Mindfulness Practices

In 2015, desiring a chance to deepen my practice in the tradition of Thich Nhat Hanh (who is known to his students as Thay, the Vietnamese word for teacher), I attended a retreat at Plum Village, the practice center founded by Thay in France in the 1980s after his exile from Vietnam. The week I spent there solidified and furthered my mindfulness practice in a way that nothing else had to at that point. I finally grasped what it meant to *embody* mindfulness practices, instead of simply using them as another layer or tool.

In *Happy Teachers Change the World*, Thay writes,

Mindfulness is a kind of energy that helps us to be fully present in the here and the now, aware of what is going on in our body, in our feelings, in our mind, and in the world, so that we can get in touch with the wonders of life that can nourish and heal us. The practice of mindfulness is the practice of joy. It is an art of living.

Of the many gifts I received in that week's teachings, one of the most fundamental and transformative was Thay's instruction not to simply 'do' mindfulness, but to 'be' mindful, to tap into those sources of joy and happiness that are always present in life.

But what does it mean to be mindful? As I have continued on my journey as an educator and a meditator, I have found that the practice of mindfulness is inseparable from the word that is at its root, the Pali word *Sati,* meaning awareness. Mindfulness, whether expressed outwardly through movement, breathing, awareness of speech, or other practices, is a practice of holding space for awareness of everything that is in any given moment. In education, that moment usually contains a complex combination of many people's experiences, emotions, and truths. Maintaining a full awareness of the present moment—to be able to respond fully and compassionately to that multitude of needs—is a skill that we must continually cultivate.

However, this cultivation is not an easy task; it benefits from the support of others on the same path. I have experienced mindfulness to be most transformational to relationships and to communities when it is shared by a community, not attempted by individuals alone. To be mindful, you need the support of a community, or sangha, as it is known in some traditions. The trip to France and Plum Village was a life-changing experience, but as a secondary school educator, that trip was not something I could access regularly. I knew that I needed to draw upon resources closer to home.

In 2017, after several years of membership and several conferences attended, I was invited to join the Board of MiEN. The Mindfulness in Education Network grew from Richard's and other educators' deep commitment to nurturing the seeds of mindfulness in both teachers and students. MiEN has grown tremendously since its founding in 2001; we now have almost 2000 educators around the world as members of an online community frequently used to support queries around using mindfulness in schools, and offer celebrations and encouragement of accomplishments shared. Hundreds of people have attended MiEN conferences over the years to feel the power of that in-person connection, and the warmth, lovingkindness, and sense of welcome it offers.

An Important Kind of Self-Care

At its deepest level, the power of mindfulness in education lies in its ability to help us build empathy and connection; both for and with ourselves, and for and with those with whom we are in community. Mindfulness enables us to cultivate a classroom community where all feel seen, recognized and loved. All humans experience suffering in some form throughout their lives, and children are no exception. With mindfulness, we see that everyone can be supported in some way.

The non-judgment aspect of my mindfulness training helps me to notice when I am reacting out of judgment rather than out of openness, allowing me to see when a student is speaking out in some way for more support due to whatever they might be facing, whether emotional, behavioral or academic. I have found many misunderstandings, discipline issues and problematic interactions can be resolved when we check in on whether our judgments, biases or other limiting beliefs are preventing us from seeing a situation clearly. When we let go of judgment, we open up space for understanding.

Through this practice, I have also found my connection to and compassion for fellow teachers deepening. Cultivating a relationship with others who practice mindfulness is not merely a form of professional development; it is an important kind of self-care. The support of a community can strengthen and nurture us in both our mindfulness and teaching practices, giving us the space to tune in to our own needs and to those of others.

Being an educator demands a great deal from us. It can be unspeakably rewarding, but it can also introduce its own unique forms of suffering. A personal practice of mindfulness and the use of mindfulness-based strategies in teaching can help meet the suffering and stresses students face, but may not on their own help resolve the emotional demands on the teacher. This is where the community comes in. Connecting regularly with fellow mindful educators strengthens and nourishes our deepest selves so that we can be present with calm and love—for ourselves and all those who we encounter.

The Mindfulness in Education Network was founded on the belief in the power of connection, whether in the resource of the MiEN listserv, (where participants can reach out for conversation and support from one another), to the annual conferences and Days of Mindfulness. In-person meetings can nourish individual practice in a space that also allows for connection, build awareness of nonviolent and mindful communication, and simply offer a space to recharge. This mission is shared by COSEM, and it is encouraging to see growing opportunities for educators to connect in person and strengthen the community of educators practicing mindfulness.

Today, MiEN continues to be a space for mindful educators to nourish one another, nurture our community and support other educators to approach their work with love and joy. By doing so, we can be present for the needs of the students we teach, whatever their ages, and spread calm, openness and ease to those we encounter. When that happens, patience can be nurtured, and openness to fully supporting our students can grow. This leads to greater happiness for ourselves, our families, and for those we teach. This is how, in the words of Thich Nhat Hanh, "Happy teachers will change the world."

CHAPTER 4

A Lifetime Search for Social Justice and Educational Equity: Mindful Schools to Inner Explorer

Laurie Grossman

Laurie Grossman, Co-Founder, Mindful Schools, Director of Social Justice & Educational Equity, Inner Explorer, Co-Author, *Master of Mindfulness* and *Breath Friends Forever*

In February 2007, after hearing therapist Kathy Grayson say, "The kids at that school live with lots of turmoil," the following words popped out of my mouth, "They need mindfulness." Luckily for me, since I knew virtually nothing about mindfulness, Kathy replied, "My husband teaches that."

Within a few days, her husband Richard Shankman and I were sitting down at a local café discussing how we could bring mindfulness into the classroom. He'd never taught kids so he reached out to his friend Diana Winston from UCLA who sent him a kids' curriculum. Since 1992, I had been sharing social and emotional curricula and resources with dozens of Title 1 public schools in Oakland, California. When we sat together, I said, "Sessions have to be short; teachers' days are packed. Lessons need to be interactive and include getting feedback from the kids."

Richard and I were on the same page. I told him we would pay him from my community outreach budget at Park Day School. He said he'd be happy to volunteer to which I replied, "This isn't a volunteer gig. We need you to be there 15 whole days in the next five weeks and we're going to pay you $2,000 to do this." We agreed.

While Richard developed lessons, I contacted five principals from Title 1 schools that were part of the Park Day School partnership and with whom I had over a decade-long relationship of collaboration and mutual learning. I asked if they would be willing to try something that was still in the development stage, but which I believed would be valuable for their students. I told them we would need 15 minutes per class, 15 times over a five-week period. By the end of the next day, all five principals responded positively. I asked my boss at Park Day School if we could launch the pilot outside of our school before bringing it in-house. He agreed and we began our adventure at neighboring Emerson Elementary School in North Oakland.

The Very First Lesson Went Like This

"Hi, I'm Mr. Richard and I'm going to come to your class three times a week for the next five weeks to teach you something you may never have heard of before called mindfulness. Let's not talk about it, let's just do it. I'm going to ring this bell, and please just listen to it." Kids responded with gigantic smiles because the bell sounded cool and its sound was long.

After a short conversation soliciting responses from the students about their experience, Richard asked the kids to listen to the bell a second time with their eyes closed, and asked, "Was there a difference?"

The third time he said, "This time, please close your eyes and when you cannot hear the bell anymore, raise your hand." Many kids raised their hands before the sound ended. Impulse control is not something many of us instinctively possess.

The fourth and last time, Richard said, "This time let's listen to 'no bell'; just listen to whatever sounds you hear." I was observing the first class's first lesson and when I heard a 3rd-grade boy comment, "I think if we do this every day we won't fight anymore," I almost fell over. It will stay with me forever.

Launching The Community Partnership for Mindfulness in Education

For 15 years I had worked at Emerson School, where 70% of the students in a 5th-grade class knew people in prison and 40% knew someone who had been killed on the street. While students were enthusiastically engaged in literacy, service-learning, and anti-bullying programs, nothing I'd ever witnessed had had this kind of impact.

That first day, Richard and I visited 12 classrooms. Students were attentive and their responses were nothing short of astonishing: "I feel like I'm on a cloud floating. I feel so calm. I've never felt that way and when I opened my eyes, everyone's faces looked different. I felt like there was a rainbow in my heart."

I could barely contain my excitement when I returned back to Park Day School that first day. Tom Little, my boss, and principal, listened with interest when I relayed what we had experienced. Tom had his own mindfulness practice, knew me well and was not the least bit surprised when I told him I had to quit to pursue whatever this mindfulness stuff was. I made this proposal, "We look for someone to replace me as Community Outreach Coordinator and I find money to fund this new work so we can bring this to more kids." He agreed and we were off and running towards launching The Community Partnership for Mindfulness in Education, an outreach program of Park Day School, later known as Mindful Schools.

The Team Grows

Towards the end of our first program at Emerson Elementary School, Richard suggested I attend a conference where people were beginning to talk about how to bring mindfulness into schools. There I had the pleasure of meeting Megan Cowan and Gina Biegel. Megan, a long-time mindfulness practitioner, was excited about our work and immediately joined our team. She taught the same curriculum at our second Title 1 school, Piedmont Avenue Elementary, driving two hours each day to bring mindfulness into the classroom. With her deep mindfulness practice, superb organizational skills and love of children, she brought creative ideas to the table. Piedmont's principal, Dr. Angela Haick, was enthusiastic about what she observed in classrooms and asked us to provide training for teachers and parents.

I asked Angela if I could invite the press to witness what we were seeing in her classrooms. Low and behold, the New York Times showed up. While their article brought me to tears mischaracterizing what we were doing, it spread the word and we began hearing from people all over the world. It occurred to me that we should be teaching others about the power of this work. In the summer of 2007, we advertised a workshop at Park Day School thinking 10–15 people would show up; we had over 50. The following summer we had over 100 attendees and in 2009, we held the workshop off-campus in an auditorium with 240 people.

The movement was taking on a life of its own and people wanted to help us. Megan and I became co-directors. I was raising money from old funders of Park Day. Richard volunteered and met with us weekly to plan strategy and hire mindfulness teachers like Daniel Rechtshaffen, Martina Schneider, Kevin Griffin, and Oren Sofer. Dr. Haick joined our meetings bringing the perspective of a seasoned and committed educator.

People were coming out of the woodwork to make this movement happen and they volunteered with their hearts and skills. Someone made us a beautiful brochure and another photographed our program in action. Randy Fernando attended one of our conferences and approached us about volunteering to help us build a basic business plan, website, and strategy. After about two years of volunteering and driving from the South Bay, he took a substantial pay cut, leaving his full-time Silicon Valley job. He officially joined Mindful Schools in January 2010 as the Director of Operations.

Word continued to spread. I spoke at an event and a young woman named Kate Janke asked me if she could volunteer. She was so excited about the work and brought important technology and mindfulness skills. I still tell Kate's story about how she got into mindfulness. A friend dragged her to a mindfulness class she didn't want to go to. When she got there and realized she couldn't count ten breaths without her mind wandering, she said, "Boy do I need this stuff. I have no control over my mind." She is a fantastic mindfulness teacher and eventually became the Director of Curriculum. It was Kate who eventually created the mindfulness and curriculum trainings that were put online.

Gina Beigel and Jon Kabat-Zinn Support Our Efforts

Shortly after launching our first school, Gina Biegel, a therapist and founder of Stressed Teens, immediately took me under her wing. We became friends as well as colleagues, meeting and speaking regularly.

A few months into our relationship, Gina insisted that I attend a Sunday morning meeting with some guy named Jon Kabat-Zinn in San Jose. Having returned to Oakland at 10 pm after a trip with my elderly parents, the last thing I wanted to do was wake up early on a Sunday morning to drive an hour to go meet some guy, but Gina made me go. Little did I know that Jon Kabat-Zinn was the founder of Mindfulness-Based Stress Reduction (MBSR) in 1979. Jon and Bob Stahl held meetings annually to gather MBSR teachers in Northern California. Jon asked all attendees to each say how they were using mindfulness. No one was doing anything in schools. When it was my turn, I mentioned what we were doing in Oakland and I begged everyone to join me. No one volunteered to do so except Jon, who said, "I need to talk to you when we break for lunch."

Jon has been a mentor and ally from that very first moment. Excited about our work in Oakland schools, he encouraged me to sign up for an MBSR class and to begin practicing daily. A few days later, I received a package with three of Jon's CD series. My husband and I took an MBSR class at Kaiser and I began practicing every day. Months later, I invited Jon to Park Day School to meet the director and to visit our classrooms and the classrooms at Emerson Elementary School next door.

The night before his visit, I received an uncharacteristically late call at 10:30 pm from my boss. Tom told me that he had been reading one of Jon's books and wanted me to know Jon wrote that we should not proselytize about mindfulness. I had been a self-proclaimed zealot since day one, so at lunch, I said to Jon, "Tom said you wrote people shouldn't proselytize about mindfulness." He replied, "I wasn't talking about you. You are a mindfulness activist. Please continue doing what you are doing."

During his tour of Park Day School, a school-based on social emotional learning, Jon remarked, "This is mindful education." A few years later I asked Jon if he would do a fundraiser for Mindful Schools. He said, "I no longer do this, but YES, I would love to." Jon was 100% committed to helping us bring mindfulness into schools. A few years later I asked if he would write the foreword for *Master of Mindfulness, How To Be Your Own Superhero in Times of Stress*, a mindfulness book I facilitated that was written by students in East Oakland. I got a similar response, "I don't have time to do this anymore, but here's my foreword if you'd like to use it." Jon's commitment to kids has always been crystal clear.

Several months later Gina invited me to present with her at the MBSR headquarters in Worcester, Massachusetts. Jon and his wife, Myla were active participants in our workshop. Attendees, over the top excited about our work, wanted to spread the word. John Meiklejohn and Catherine Phillips took the helm and hosted several meetings. Our small group eventually published a white paper called Integrating Mindfulness Training into K-12 Education: Fostering the Resilience of Teachers and Students.

While a few big-name educators and psychologists told me what we were doing wouldn't work or was unconscionable because we didn't have the research, I replied, "The kids I care about are hemorrhaging, and this is the first thing in 32 years that I have found that stops that." Needless to say, we are all now on the same page.

The Community Partnership for Mindfulness in Education literally had a closet full of thousands of surveys with teachers and kids which all showed the same thing. Students and educators loved the program. Academic achievement went up, behavioral issues went down, stress was relieved and community was built.

However, we had no formal research; so I invited Gina to do a research project on a school in Oakland. Gina and a colleague from Virginia Tech, Kirk Warren Brown, did the study with 2nd and 3rd graders at Berkley Maynard Academy, a Title 1 Charter Elementary School. Computerized assessments measuring attention, teacher evaluations and students' self-report showed favorable results. The white paper describing the study and results can be found here: https://www.mindfulschools.org/pdf/Mindful%20Schools%20Pilot%20 Study%20Whitepaper.pdf

How Mindfulness Leads to Educational Equity

As someone who had been looking for social justice and educational equity my entire life, I was in heaven. I now began to understand why brilliant kids from vulnerable communities frequently didn't do well. For many, trauma impacts their nervous system, precluding them from doing well in school. Emotions get the better of most of us; add a little trauma to the mix and emotions take over. Kids who had impulse control issues and were often in trouble were now able to calm themselves down and pay attention in class. A teacher in a Title 1 school said how much the program was helping her; she found herself yelling at her students a lot less. A high school student at a party recognized a dangerous situation, took a few breaths, took his friend's gun away, and left the party! This was not just a program to increase academic success. I began seeing mindfulness as a way to save lives.

So why was this effort of bringing mindfulness into the classroom so effective? Our society is a very noisy place, and kids and teachers found quiet within the intensity of the school day. Some children had never experienced quiet. A 2nd grader said, "I love this; do you think this is real?" Mindfulness provides a vital respite from the pressure so many teachers and children feel in schools.

In the classroom, we quickly identified four benefits of practicing mindfulness. First, we were teaching children to pay attention, arguably the most important skill in school. By asking students to listen to sound or by directing them to return again and again to their breath, we actually taught them how to pay attention. Secondly, mindfulness promotes self-regulation, without which classrooms can become chaotic environments. As educators, we know how easy it is to lose our cool. Children's emotions are like the weather and change quickly. Accidental moves, like pushing crayons on the floor or bumping into someone in the hallway can create mayhem when students have little self-regulation. By slowing down and listening to quiet, we are more able to recognize our emotions and respond rather than react to them.

Thirdly, mindfulness reduces stress. This has been evident since Jon Kabat-Zinn's first MBSR class forty years ago. Since then, millions have experienced the calming of the sympathetic nervous system and the stimulation of the parasympathetic nervous system. I often noticed that although students are in their seats, their minds are not necessarily with them. Worries about friendship, family, academic or athletic pressure, social media, gun violence, poverty, the environment, and immigration are only some of the issues that preoccupy the minds of our youth. If their minds are not with their bodies in their chairs, how can they possibly learn?

Finally, mindfulness creates community. A principal at Franklin Elementary School in Oakland used to say, "When the day ends and the bell rings, mindfulness goes home with the children." In our thousands of surveys, we found that 70% of the children in Title 1 schools teach mindfulness to their families. In other schools, 40% do. I'll never forget a parent at Park Day School saying to me, "I can't believe your program. I took our son to the dentist yesterday which has always been a very traumatic experience. This time he was calm. Leaving, I asked him what changed. His reply: "I just practiced my mindfulness."

Racism, economic injustice, and school and healthcare inequities are primary drivers of a broken society. While mindfulness will not fix all societal ills, it is the tool with the greatest possibility for school and societal transformation. Building calm and peace provides space for excellence. Empowering students to discover their best selves and find their purpose, fostering a positive outlook and a sense of gratitude, enabling youth to find their personal humanity and kindness to build positive connection, and improving teacher performance all lead us towards educational equity and social justice.

Teaching Teachers

The 15 sessions for students included awareness of the breath, the body, sound, sight, movement, thoughts, emotions, kindness, and others. Lessons were delivered in classrooms three times over five weeks. Soon we realized that it would be best to offer an eight-week series, so we began offering 16 sessions twice a week for eight weeks. Having been a kid that stressed out over tests, I wrote a test-taking lesson.

Two years into this magical ride, a teacher I met from East Oakland begged me to come teach her classroom of 5th graders, primarily boys. By that time I had taken the MBSR course three times and watched hundreds of lessons taught by our teachers, but I told her I didn't have enough experience. She finally convinced me and I was amazed at how much fun it was to teach mindfulness; I was hooked. I still remember many amazing stories from kids in that classroom. One student shared that when their grandma had a diabetes attack, she asked them to ring the doorbell so they could start practicing mindfulness. Another shared that they and their mom used to get really mad when the neighbors upstairs made noise, but it doesn't bother them anymore; it's just sounds.

So who gets to teach mindfulness? This question is often debated in the mindfulness in education movement. At Mindful Schools, we believed that only people with years of personal practice could teach it. After all, if you don't know how to play the piano, how could you teach it? Early on I told Megan that I thought we needed to teach teachers. Many teachers were excited about what they were witnessing, but almost none had a personal practice. Megan agreed and began offering a weekly class at Park Day School after school. In some cases three teachers showed up, other times there were ten.

Megan and Kate taught the first courses offered at Park Day School. I enthusiastically attended every session to continue learning. One of my very favorite stories came from that first formal class. Between week one and week two of the class, Megan asked, "Did anyone notice anything this week?" A teacher raised her hand and said, "I've been teaching at my school for ten years. Every day I walk back and forth from the office to my classroom many times. Do you know we have birds on our campus?" This teacher had walked back and forth thousands of times over the years. Preoccupied with lessons, to-do lists, and parent meetings, she never noticed the trees or birds on her campus. A single two-hour mindfulness class made her aware of her surroundings. Could it get any better than this?!

We launched our first pilot in February 2007. By June 2009, we had taught 7,000 students in 26 schools in the Bay Area, mostly in Oakland. Our website launched about 20 months after our first lesson and had hits from people in 47 states and 49 countries. We received constant inquiries. Mindfulness in education was here to stay.

In the early days, we were just attending conferences, but by year two, we were being invited to present at conferences. In our second year of the program, we presented to all of the psychologists and language therapists in the Oakland Unified School District, the California Association of Independent Schools, the University of California Berkeley Psychology Ph.D. conference with Dan Siegel, the Center for Mindfulness in Massachusetts, the Omega Institute in New York, and at Georgetown Medical Center, where we were brought in to talk to doctors who were considering using mindfulness with pediatric oncology patients.

One-on-One with the Most Vulnerable

At the end of 2011, I left Mindful Schools to work exclusively in vulnerable communities. For decades I had been interested in working with the most challenged students. I felt students who acted up during mindfulness sessions needed mindfulness the most and often derived the most benefit. A 1st grader who had been suspended multiple times for behavioral issues was the only student in the class who knew how to lead the others with no help. When I began whispering the words as I did with all the "Littles," he said, "You don't need to tell me; I know it!" Despite his crawling under tables and never sitting still, he was the only one who needed no help. He asked the students to stand up and put their hands on their hearts and say, "I have the power to make wise choices." Then he asked them to sit down, do the Shark Fin, listen to the bell and practice mindfulness for two minutes before he rang the bell to close the session.

I wondered what would happen if I worked with him regularly on a one-on-one basis. I spoke with the principal and asked her if I could work with him and a few others in a quiet place in the school. She happily agreed. The young boy, described above answered my question, "Do you want to sit for one minute or two today?" with "I want to sit for 10 minutes." I told him I didn't believe he could do that. After letting a loogie drip down his chin, he slurped up his spit and sat for ten minutes. The following year his 2nd-grade teacher said he was one of his best students. One-on-one work with the children who have faced significant trauma is some of the most meaningful of my career.

In the fall of 2012, I ended up at Reach Academy in East Oakland to discover the principal was a teacher I had worked with ten years earlier in our partnership programs. Thrilled to see each other, I began teaching mindfulness in classrooms, to the staff, and to the parents. Because of the success of the work I had done the prior year, I recruited mindfulness volunteers to work one-on-one with the most vulnerable students at the school. Volunteers spent 20 minutes with each child engaging in a variety of mindfulness activities. When I no longer had time to organize the program, other volunteers, equally committed, stepped up to organize the troops, and now, like ten others, I am simply a volunteer.

My favorite story from this one-on-one work was when I was working with two 2nd graders together. I had known one of them since kindergarten. He had been referred to the program because he had very little ability to pay attention. In kindergarten, he would wander around the class and did not respond when the teacher called his name. The second student was a child whose trauma resulted in his crawling into a corner in the hallway to scream and cry a few times a week. In one session I asked which of the two boys would like to ring the bell. The one with attention issues said, "I would." He picked up the bell and looked at his classmate. He said to him, "It looks like you want to ring the bell, is that true?" The boy replied yes and got handed the bell. The boy with significant attention issues read his friend's disappointment and answered it with kindness. This is the power of mindfulness.

Master of Mindfulness: The Making of a Student-Authored Book

In early 2014, Mr. Musumeci, a 5th-grade teacher at Reach Academy, pulled me aside during Spirit Week and told me that one of his most challenged students suggested the class create a mindfulness superhero. That made me smile. Several weeks later during my mindfulness practice, it occurred to me that maybe his class could write a book. When I proposed the idea, telling him it would take several hours each week, Mr. Musumeci jumped at the opportunity. The next day, I showed up and asked the students if they liked mindfulness. 100% of the hands went up. When I asked why, the answers were all meaningful. Then I asked if they thought other kids should know about mindfulness. Again, 100% of the kids raised their hands to explain why.

As a class, we determined the structure of the book, the main ideas, and how we'd get those across. In small groups, some kids delved into the story, others worked on illustrations, and some wrote mindfulness scripts. The kids named the book *Master of Mindfulness: How To Be Your Own Superhero in Times of Stress*. Things were going well, but having no artistic instinct whatsoever, I had no idea how we were going to turn the kids' words and pictures into a book.

Then I met Angelina Alvarez (now Manriquez) and learned that she was an artist. She was ecstatic at the opportunity to share mindfulness with children through art. School ended in mid-June and we needed to finish the project before the kids dispersed for the summer. A day before school ended, we made 30 colored copies for the authors, after which we discovered it was full of typos! The publishing party turned into an editing lesson. Red pens were distributed with the books and everyone was delighted with the finished product.

For over eight months I sent the book to dozens of publishers to no avail. Then sitting at the opening of the Wisdom 2.0 Conference in February 2015, the speaker asked us to introduce ourselves to the person next to us. As luck would have it, I was sitting next to the Acquisitions Manager at New Harbinger Publications. When we introduced ourselves, I told her she had turned down our book. She said, "No we didn't." I said, "Well actually you did." She asked if I had a copy and I handed her one. After looking through the book, she said she wanted to publish it.

Almost 50,000 copies have been sold and proceeds from the book sit in a scholarship account for the authors. Monies will be distributed when the authors finish high school in a few years. The sequel, *Breath Friends Forever*, written by Ms. Moses' 4th graders at Reach Academy, is a story about two best friends who share a birthday. One is calm and the other often frustrated. Leo gives Nessa mindfulness for her birthday.

Inner Explorer Solves a Problem

Shortly after finishing *Master of Mindfulness*, I received a call from Laura Bakosh, co-founder of Inner Explorer who, with her childhood friend Janice Houlihan, had developed a K-12 mindfulness audio program delivered through iPods and docking stations. I told her that I didn't think her program would work, but agreed to listen to all 90 elementary practices—they have four programs; preschool, elementary, middle and high school. I realized that Inner Explorer had solved the problem of how to get mindfulness to kids. The program, based on Mindfulness-Based Stress Reduction, could be easily delivered. It was effective and scalable. My only suggestion was to increase the diversity in narration, which we soon did.

Though I wasn't looking, I had a new job. I've been traveling around the country for several years promoting Inner Explorer, now delivered through the internet, accessible through an app on any device. The push-button program is incredibly simple to use. With no training, teachers learn mindfulness with their students from a diverse group of narrators with decades of mindfulness experience. One of the most fabulous parts of bringing mindfulness into the classroom is that teachers benefit as much as their students; with Inner Explorer, both the student and teacher can practice together daily.

The power of Inner Explorer can be demonstrated with this anecdote. Eighteen months ago, I read an article in The Nation Magazine about Kaiser Elementary School, a K-2 school in Ravenswood, West Virginia where kids were watching their parents die from opioid use. The last line of the article was the principal Amber Hardman saying, "We just need help." Because we had the financial support of LG

Electronics, I was able to call her and offer her the program at no cost. After one 45-minute conversation, she began to implement the program schoolwide. Though she mandates almost nothing with her teachers, she made the use of Inner Explorer a "non-negotiable" because she felt the teachers and kids needed it desperately.

Because of busy school schedules, I did not speak to Principal Hardman until almost a year later when I learned the program had made a significant impact on Kaiser. One child who had been to the office 4–5 times a day (700 visits!) the previous year, visited the office only one time once they began using Inner Explorer. A 31-year veteran teacher said she had "had it" with student behaviors and was about to quit. By May, she said she was in tears about having to leave her students. She is still teaching.

Experience Happiness! LG Electronics Joins Inner Explorer To Spread Mindfulness

About four years ago, LG Electronics began looking for new ways to support the community. LG's Division of Corporate Social Responsibility looked at hunger and homelessness and wondered about their root causes. What they found were mental health problems. They pondered what could be done about that. Continuing their exploration, they discovered that happiness skills counter depression and mental health issues and those happiness skills were, in fact, teachable. Recognizing the challenging mental health issues among youth, and since the company's tagline is Life is Good, LG launched an initiative called Experience Happiness to help teens thrive.

While promoting happiness, Inner Explorer and LG recognize that life is full of ups and downs. Well-being does not mean we won't experience the downs, it means that we recognize that life is good, even when it's hard sometimes. Well-being occurs when our well of resilience is deep. Our ability to bounce back gracefully from difficult experiences makes the journey of life so much more pleasant.

With the guidance of The Greater Good Science Center at UC Berkeley, LG identified six sustainable happiness skills they wanted to provide to 5.5 million youth. Those skills are mindfulness, human connection, gratitude, purpose, positive outlook, and generosity.

Incredibly, practicing mindfulness promotes each of those skills. When we slow down enough to be in the present moment, we feel our feelings. When we do so, we are much more able to notice how others are feeling. Much research indicates that practicing mindfulness fosters kindness. A principal in Killeen, Texas called us and said, "I get that Inner Explorer improves academics and helps with discipline, but why are kids nicer to each other?" It's that human connection!

Research on gratitude is plentiful and indicates that practicing it daily actually extends one's life (David Snowdon's nun study, 2001). Since practicing mindfulness gets us out of our heads and into the present moment, we are available to appreciate nature, smiles, goodness, and when we focus on that appreciation, it transforms into happiness. "I have never been thanked so much by so many teachers in such a short time."—Middle School Vice Principal, Georgia

Since mindfulness helps us focus by teaching us to return again and again to the breath, sound, and to a variety of other sense doors, it is logical that students' academic achievement improves with the practice of mindfulness. That focus enables students to appreciate more of what they learn and to find what excites them. When one is excited about learning, one is much more likely to find a purpose in pursuing that excitement inside and outside of school. In this way, mindfulness promotes purpose in teens. "These students are experiencing really dramatic learning gains as well as developing increased confidence, perseverance, and focus."—Principal

Positive outlook does not come naturally. Early human brains were wired with a negativity bias for the purpose of survival. Looking out for danger kept our oldest ancestors alive. Our brains are still wired this way even when we are not in danger. By practicing mindfulness, we stimulate neural networks that promote positive thinking. Sara Lazar's research from 2005 indicates that practicing mindfulness increases the density of gray matter in several parts of the brain and decreases it in others. Thicker prefrontal cortexes result in higher optimism, and smaller amygdalas produce less anxiety. "Because of mindfulness, I'm not a negative person anymore."—Student

Generosity is another attribute fostered by mindfulness that educators frequently witness when practicing with their students regularly. Students become more helpful and considerate of one another. "Our students have become more helpful, more concerned about each other and go out of their way to engage when someone is hurt or in need."—Principal

Inner Explorer was very fortunate to be approached and vetted by LG Electronics to be a partner in this initiative. Because of Inner Explorer's research, track record, scalability, and sustainability, with LG's support, we have brought our mindfulness program to over 250,000 students in eight locations where LG has business enterprises throughout the US. Other partners in the initiative include Discovery Education, Project Happiness and CASEL. Together we are helping students, educators and families Experience Happiness!

I believe mindfulness should be taught to all students from preschool to grad school. I'll repeat the same plea I made at the MBSR meeting 13 years ago: we need your help. In my opinion, this work is even more important now than it was in 2007. If you are not already involved in this movement, please join us. Students and educators need mindfulness. Please find your niche and come aboard. You will be glad you did. I promise.

CHAPTER 5

Mindful Schools' Transformation Over Time

Megan Sweet, EdD

Director of Training, Mindful Schools

WHEN THINKING ABOUT THE HISTORY OF MINDFULNESS IN SCHOOLS, I was reminded that I was actually taught mindfulness when I was in 5th grade—almost 40 years ago. Every day after lunch, our teacher would have us sit at our desks and breathe, eyes closed or looking down, while she walked around the room speaking in a quiet voice. I can still see her, holding one hand on her throat and saying "whisper" and other centering prompts.

My teacher was from Georgia, so her "whisper" sounded more like "whiss-paa" and she'd say that word over and over again as she snaked the rows of desks. While she said other things, that *whiss-paa* stands out, as well as the fact that I got into some of the worst trouble in my young life while passing notes during our breathing practice.

Flash forward to my senior year in high school, and I found myself in another mindfulness class. I chose this class because I thought it would be easy and figured there couldn't be a lot of homework for a class dedicated to mindfulness! On those accounts, I was right. Rather than sitting behind a desk and taking copious notes, we explored different mindfulness practices including breathing, yoga and walking. Our homework was to practice the techniques we learned at school. Clever me. What I hadn't bargained for, however, was how much I loved those practices and how noticeably better I felt at the end of them. While I hadn't planned on it when I enrolled, that was the beginning of the mindfulness journey that I continue on today.

I offer these anecdotes because capturing the history of mindfulness in schools is tricky. Until now, I had written off my experiences with mindfulness as examples of the unconventional social and educational experiences I had growing up in the San Francisco Bay Area post-1960s. As I reflect now, however, I find it difficult to tell how unique my experiences actually were. We do not have a national curriculum in the United States, and no way of capturing the nuances between instructional practices school-to-school in many districts, so identifying when and how mindfulness has emerged and grown is difficult. If we add-in the reflective practices that are inherent in different faiths and that have been practiced in private schools for decades, I feel hard-pressed to root mindfulness in schools to a specific moment in time.

These stories are also noteworthy because they are examples of teacher-initiated mindfulness programs. Both of my teachers had their own practices and felt compelled to bring them to their students. These weren't school-wide programs in which everyone participated, nor were they supported by a curriculum or standard set of exercises. My teachers created their mindfulness curriculum on their own, based on their personal experience.

Finally, these stories are significant for the impact they had on their students. My 5th-grade troublemaking notwithstanding, I gained many benefits from practicing mindfulness in school. It helped to calm me down and to focus when I was younger, and in high school, it served as a counterbalance to the other demands in my life, including friendships, college applications, challenges at home, and a rigorous course schedule. I have turned to mindfulness practices ever since, especially when times have been hard.

Fundamentals, Personal Practice, and Educator Well-Being

Mindful Schools' beginnings share the grassroots nature that my teachers' programs had—it began with people who had deep personal practices and who understood that those practices would be beneficial to students. In 2007, we brought our inaugural mindfulness program to an elementary school in Oakland, California. It was a direct service program, led by Mindful Schools staff as guests in teachers' classrooms. Our program quickly picked up speed and within just three years, we were in 50 schools.

In 2012, to more effectively meet the growing demand for our programming, we transitioned from providing direct service mindfulness instruction to students, to bringing mindfulness instruction to teachers. This shift—ensuring educators have a mindfulness practice of their own *before* teaching mindfulness to their students – still guides our approach—and is what sets Mindful Schools apart to this day.

Once teachers were familiar with the fundamentals of mindfulness, our trainings then followed up with a course on how to bring mindfulness to students from preschool through high school. We continue to add to both our online and in-person trainings today. Promoting educator well-being through the practice of mindfulness remains at the heart of our approach because we believe that the most effective way to grow mindfulness in education is one committed educator at a time.

On a practical level, we believe this to be true because mindfulness cannot be effectively taught by people who do not have an embodied practice themselves. Without having the lived experience of its benefits—increased focus, calmness, and compassion—it is difficult to appreciate the impact that mindfulness can have on students. *Even more difficult is creating the conditions that will make a mindfulness lesson truly beneficial to students when we do not know how those conditions look and feel ourselves.*

On a transformational level, a growing body of research reinforces the positive effect that mindfulness has on individuals. More regulated, self-aware, and balanced teachers lead to calmer and more welcoming environments for students. When students feel seen, safe, and supported, they are able to learn at a deeper level. Even if we stopped right there, the impact would be profound. When students practice mindfulness themselves, the impact is even greater, and like me, they walk away with tools that last a lifetime. This is the ideal.

Our Strength Lies in Our Community

As we have transitioned to offering mindfulness via online courses, we have learned a lot about the strengths and drawbacks of that model. The great advantage of online courses is that our participants are able to access the content when it is convenient to them, any time and anywhere. Because mindfulness in schools still tends to begin with grassroots efforts by individual teachers, it can be difficult for teachers to access professional development on mindfulness in their schools or even local communities. For busy, oversubscribed educators, online is often the only way that they can access mindfulness content.

As service providers, online teaching allows us to reach people we never could have if we remained direct service providers in schools. Our reach has been profound. Today, Mindful Schools is one of the key players in the movement to integrate mindfulness into the everyday learning environment of K-12 classrooms. To date, we have trained over 50,000 educators, parents, and mental health professionals who work with youth. These graduates, spanning 100+ countries, from Myanmar to Colombia, have reached over 3 million children worldwide. Much of this is due to our online coursework.

While online courses are a great modality for teaching mindfulness, mindfulness is a practice that deepens when shared in a community. We provide some of that community within the online courses themselves. Every class we teach has at least one live webinar that allows students to connect with one another. We also offer an intensive year-long program where a group of educators learns how to teach mindfulness with others. This program begins and ends with residential retreats where we practice, build community, and learn from one another. Throughout the year, we deepen that community via small and large group practice sessions, live discussions on topical issues, and via online coursework and discussion boards.

Many of our participants remark that they feel as though they've "found their people" once they meet and practice with others in our retreats and year-long programs. This is true because while mindfulness can be done alone, there is a great benefit when practice is shared with others. Through shared practice we deepen our connection to other people and feel a level of grounding and support that we do not always feel on our own.

To deepen the opportunities for our educators, we are developing even more ways to connect. In addition to our courses, we also offer monthly interactive workshops and sits. We have also built a community platform that allows our participants to connect in small affinity groups as well as to share lessons and learnings to a wider audience.

Mindful Schools' strength lies in our community. We continually engage with our participants about how we can improve our offerings and identify the needs they have as they bring mindfulness to their various contexts. The feedback we get from our participants directly impacts our content, and in this way, we use our community to help shape the trajectory mindfulness is taking in education.

From a Hand Full of Adopters to a School-Wide Strategy

Finally, while I said that tracing the history of mindfulness in schools is difficult, if we use Mindful Schools' growth over the past decade as an example, *it is* safe to say that mindfulness is taking off. Educators by nature learn from one another and are ever-striving to improve outcomes for their students. Our anecdotal evidence suggests that many school-wide mindfulness programs, therefore, grow through word of mouth. As teachers notice the difference in the classroom environments of their peers, they want "in" on the action, and they adopt mindfulness programs in their rooms.

Sometimes, it's the students that spread the practice—they experience the benefits of mindfulness in one class, and start asking for it elsewhere—on the yard, or in other classes when they are feeling overwhelmed. Either way, it is introduced, and we have seen time and time again that directly witnessing mindfulness' impact leads to more widespread adoption of mindfulness school-wide.

On a national scale, it makes sense that mindfulness has spread in a similar way. In recent years, this growth has been supported by an ever-widening foundation of scientific research about the benefits of mindfulness. The more we know how our brains work and how mindfulness impacts the way we cope with difficult emotions, the more mindfulness has moved from a fringe activity used by a handful of early adopters to a core school-wide strategy.

This makes sense. We live in a complex world where the demands on our time, energy, and attention can feel never-ending. Add to that the challenges we face as individuals to find peace within our own lives, and as educators to support students who come to school with trauma and dynamic needs that can feel overwhelming to address, it is understandable that mindfulness has been gaining ground. We see the need for system-wide implementation of mindfulness as the next logical step for our programming, and we will launch our first school-wide mindfulness certification program in the summer of 2020.

While mindfulness is not a panacea, as someone who has experienced its benefits first as a student and now as a leader at Mindful Schools, the positive impact that mindfulness can have should not be discounted. Mindfulness is a powerful strategy that can stand alone but that also complements many other social-emotional learning strategies, promotes safer classrooms and schools, and supports deeper student learning. I am gratified to see mindfulness spread, and as one of our elementary school students recently said, "If everyone in the world practiced mindfulness, there wouldn't be as many problems."

CHAPTER 6

Yoga Calm and Trauma-Informed Mindfulness

Lynea Gillen, LPC, RYT
Jim Gillen, ERYT-500

Co-Founders, Yoga Calm

THE SEEDS OF YOGA CALM WERE PLANTED in both of us years ago when we were teens. Jim was 16 when introduced to yoga through his study of the martial arts. An energetic and highly active young man, he found that the practice helped him achieve focus and discipline. At the same age, Lynea discovered yoga at a church camp on the shores of beautiful Lake Tahoe. Having experienced some crucial losses early in life, she found through the practice a place of healing and inner peace.

When we met in a dance class in 1995, we were both excited to have found a partner who shared a love of yoga, and we set out to pursue a practice together. At the time, Jim had just left the business world for a more fulfilling job that blended his lifelong interests in science and the outdoors: directing a National Science Foundation-funded environmental education program for youth. Lynea had been working with children of all ages for years, as an educator in a variety of settings and then as a counselor in the public schools. As she continued this work, Jim decided to act on our shared desire to bring yoga to others. He built our studio, Still Moving Yoga, and began teaching yoga full time.

"Help me! Can anyone please help me!"

Yoga Calm sprouted early in the new millennium when Lynea began to see an increasing number of students with extreme behavioral issues. Some had been diagnosed with severe attention deficit hyperactivity disorder (ADHD), while others had been diagnosed with autism or oppositional defiant disorder. Some came from traumatic backgrounds. As their counselor, Lynea observed how hard it was for them to sit in a group and share. She felt they needed opportunities to manage and direct their strong feelings and impulses—like those of the young boy she saw one day crouched under a table in a fetal position, screaming, "Help me! Can anyone please help me!" This child's obvious pain touched her deeply. She wanted to help him find peace in his small body. She could see the trauma he physically held, how his instinct to protect himself drove him under the table—a common way for wounded children to self-soothe.

Through her own yoga practice and counseling work, Lynea had learned to listen to the body and the heart to find a path toward healing. When the body opens, emotions can be released, and the body and heart grow strong together. She wanted to help her students experience these benefits. She believed that a practice that was both physically and emotionally supportive could help these children and others like them.

At home, Lynea would share with Jim her concerns about the children. We would have long talks about how we could use yoga to help them learn the things that have helped us in our individual journeys toward healing and inner peace. Lynea began to incorporate yoga activities into her work with the kids, reporting on the effects each evening. Jim was a good listener and creative in developing games and activities. Occasionally, he'd come out to the school, and together we'd try out these activities with the kids. The students loved Jim's playful nature, strength, and enthusiasm as he showed them new poses—"yoga tricks," as they called them.

Persistence Starts to Pay Off

Still, it wasn't easy. In fact, teaching yoga to behavior-disordered children started out as a nightmare. The kids didn't listen. They fought over the mats. They whined that it was too hard. At one point, Lynea wanted to give up, but thanks to teacher encouragement and support, we kept on. And after a while, we began to see a change in the students. They started to show a greater ability to be still. They began to show compassion and support for one another. Some students would come into the classroom to practice yoga during their lunch recess. Something was beginning to shift.

It took time to learn how to effectively and successfully blend the two practices of yoga and social/emotional skill-building. Some days, the yoga would stimulate a great deal of emotion, and the children would spend most of their time processing their feelings. Other days, the students wanted only to do physical poses, and little emotion was addressed. Lynea began to trust the group process and found ways to direct the poses to help students maintain a sense of control when emotions emerged.

Over time, a sense of community developed in the yoga class. The students gradually became more skilled at managing their emotions and helping one another through tough times. Lynea recalls one day when they asked to do a series of poses in complete silence and insisted that this meant that she had to stay quiet as well. It was a beautiful experience, watching them all move together mindfully. They had come a long way.

When Mindfulness Can Become Triggering

When we have the privilege of observing the fragile beauty of children's open hearts and minds, we understand how important it is to provide them with a safe and supportive environment, the tools for self-discovery, and the skills they will need to maneuver successfully through life. Unfortunately, not everyone in our culture holds children's lives sacred. As counselors, teachers, and parents, we regularly encounter the negative effects of shattered and chaotic environments.

It's easy to think that if something works for us, it will work for anyone. How could the action that brought us peace or joy not bring that same good feeling to everyone who tries it? We come to each moment from our own history, our own tastes, our own habits, our own way of understanding the world. While there is so much that we share, so much that connects us with each other, there's no one-size-fits-all way of pursuing anything.

For those who have experienced trauma, the practice of mindfulness can become emotionally and physically intolerable. Closing one's eyes in a group can feel unsafe, and watching our thoughts can lead back into habits of rumination. For others, the past experience of physical trauma has meant that they have learned to dissociate themselves from feeling anything at all, and focusing on the physical sensations in body scans or other mindfulness processes can become overwhelming to a point where intense agitation, physical pain or illness occurs. The benefits of mindfulness then become inaccessible.

Therefore, when we introduce mindfulness to the classroom, it's important to remember that roughly half of all students have experienced at least one adverse childhood experience (ACE). A good number may be experiencing one right now—from parents separating, to homelessness, substance abuse in the family, or sexual abuse.

Typical mindfulness practices, such as body scans and observing sensations, can be triggering for such students. They may "act out" or otherwise resist what we're asking them to do.

Where trauma is in play, such "bad behavior" may be better understood as a trigger or coping mechanism, however ineffective or even destructive it may seem. It's a way to protect oneself when feeling threatened—even by something as seemingly benign as closing one's eyes.

Trauma-Informed Mindfulness

It's interesting to note that in the yoga tradition, meditation practices weren't the first skills to be taught. Instead, they often followed training in social mores, physical movement, and breathing practices. We think there is wisdom to that, especially when it comes to teaching mindfulness for trauma recovery.

Before anyone with trauma can close their eyes in a group, they must first feel safe. There needs to be a sense of community, rules of conduct, structure and a strong leader. As kids work together in a positive, supportive environment on social and emotional skills, they are in the process of building relationships and this trust is a foundation critical for all—especially for those who have experienced trauma.

Secondly, trauma is held in the body, and that needs to be addressed early on. The world's foremost trauma researchers, including Bessel van der Kolk, Ph.D., and Dr. Bruce Perry, recommend yoga and other "bottom-up" (sensory-motor and brain-stem-based) approaches as a beginning treatment for traumatized children.

Dr. Bruce Perry reports that brain stem-related activities that emphasize patterned, repetitive, rhythmic somatosensory activities. like yoga, singing, drumming, and running, help regulate the nervous system and make the brain more accessible to relational (limbic brain) reward and cortical thinking.

Occupational therapists, too, have similarly been using balance activities and "heavy work" that emphasizes physical effort, to provide vestibular and proprioceptive input. That's because these systems help regulate our nervous system, calm our bodies, and help us feel more oriented (safer) in space.

Lynea has made similar observations through her counseling practice, especially in working with children who have experienced trauma early in life. Often, they had been diagnosed as having ADHD, but the cause was trauma. Traditional children's counseling techniques were much more effective after kids learned how to safely release energy and regulate their nervous systems through simple yoga flows and breathing exercises.

The following physical activities can promote a sense of safety and help students release, regulate and relate:

- *Whispering*; teacher and students spend two minutes whispering;
- *Slowing the breath down* through Hoberman sphere breathing or playing a game where children hold their breath for five seconds;
- *Slow repetitive standing yoga flow* sequences (e.g., Upward Mountain, Star, Warrior 2, Star, Upward Mountain) or simply having students stand up and sit down from their chairs to provide "heavy work" and to restore sensation in the body;
- *Roots* (while standing, rock forward and back or around in a circle, feeling the weight shift in your feet, eyes open or closed); follow this activity with Tree pose;
- *Trust Walk*; where one student leads another student with their eyes closed around the room, fingertip to fingertip.

Safe, slow, physical movement helps with the discharge of tension and calms the amygdala, turning on the "thinking brain" (prefrontal cortex), which is not only key for trauma survivors but useful for all students to help them regulate their nervous systems, build resilience and inoculate them from the effects of stress.

Body-based practices also help trauma survivors explore present-oriented experience in the context of playful and safe sensory-motor experiences, further developing arousal regulation skills and expanding their "Window of Tolerance" (Siegel, 1999). And these activities are just as beneficial for the adults who teach them to help keep us regulated too!

Third, combining physical movement with supportive cognitive themes, like our Yoga Calm "strength principle," as well as students choosing and leading the activities, can help kids develop a sense of control and self-efficacy—another key aspect of trauma recovery.

Additional cognitive integration can occur through the strategic use of relaxation stories to not only echo and reinforce the class themes of strength, safety, and community, but to generally reframe and give meaning to life's challenges as a "hero's journey."

The routine of all these activities provides the structure and reliability they need as well. Often, trauma survivors are coming from environments where chaos was or is the norm, where stability may be fleeting. Yoga Calm then becomes something they learn they can rely on and use anywhere. Our research in a low-socioeconomic status Detroit elementary school indicated that over 70% of students were practicing Yoga Calm at home, unsolicited and in response to stress.

Over time, they may find it easier to close their eyes during one of our Mindful Moment Card contemplations or during a guided relaxation. Or they may choose to keep their eyes open. There are, as we've noted, many ways of doing mindfulness.

Creating a Culture of Wellness

In challenging times, new opportunities for growth arise. And the good news is that creating trauma-informed classrooms—where students' physical and emotional needs are honored—benefits all students. Indeed, many of our trauma interventions show that the reduction of stress through physical activity, the development of social-emotional skills, and the creation of safe environments that support a sense of well-being, improve academics and have wellness benefits for both students and staff.

Having worked in education for over 40 years and as providers of school professional development (PD) training for the last 15 years, we have seen many initiatives come and go due to changes in staff, short-term grant funding and budget cuts. Meanwhile, student health, stress, and behavioral issues continue to mount and teachers are leaving the profession in alarming numbers. That's why we developed a comprehensive suite of services to help schools create a culture of wellness that's sustainable.

In addition to our in-person Intensive training retreats and school-based staff trainings, we have created a suite of online, college-accredited Certification and professional development courses. These courses and in-services give teachers and counselors the tools they need and the flexibility to learn anywhere—in fact, teachers in over 20 countries are studying with us online.

Our latest development is a video-based classroom curriculum that makes implementation as simple as pressing the "play" button. Our new EMPOWER Health & Wellness program is a whole-child education approach that integrates brain science, movement and SEL education—in 5- to 20-minute lessons. It not only supports staff needs and meets education standards, but it's also flexible, sustainable, and low cost.

Our new TeleTraining staff coaching services provide ongoing customized live staff training and support—the crucial and often missing link to successful program implementation. Depending on their needs, schools and their staff can mix and match the above services to choose the best-fitting professional development approach while providing long-term support for systemic change.

Yoga Calm is our gift to our teachers, families, and friends. It is an offering of hope and support to children—and to those who work to protect and enhance their lives.

CHAPTER 7

Keep Your MindUP

Dido Balla, MEd

MindUP Regional Lead, Speaker, Entrepreneur with Mika Jain, Assistant Director of Education Partnerships, MindUP l The Goldie Hawn Foundation

I AM A MINDUP REGIONAL CONSULTANT LIVING IN SOUTH FLORIDA. I lead schools and organizations around the US in year-long professional development, focusing on understanding the core pillars of the MindUP curriculum. I scaffold the content to best meet the needs of students in each unique environment and make sure the program is implemented with fidelity both short and long-term.

I begin my story with the memory of a middle school teacher, whose favorite two words to me were: "Calm down!" As a middle schooler, I had positive, tenacious energy—but when told with a menacing finger to calm down, I had little knowledge of what that meant or *how to calm down*. As a result, my teacher often resorted to punitive measures, such as having me write the sentence "I will learn how to be calm in class" one hundred times.

Reflecting back on this time, I wish my teacher had the resources to teach and model strategies on how to calm an overactive amygdala. When I set off to become a teacher, I made a commitment to learning about the factors that affect the adolescent brain as well as acquire concrete ways to help students take control of their emotional wellbeing.

An Approach to Building Classroom Culture

My teaching journey began 9 years ago in Miami in a high school English class for ESOL students—English for Speakers of Other Languages. While the English language was new to my students, hard work, resilience, and creativity were not. Some of my students worked full-time jobs to help support their families; others were part of immigrant families who had to walk hundreds of miles and live in detention centers prior to making a home in the United States. As a new teacher, I committed to creating a positive classroom culture that respects, encourages, and celebrates learning through mistakes. My students felt safe in my class and were willing to take risks in learning, trusting their classmates and teachers to support them.

Unfortunately, this culture of responsible risk-taking was, on its own, not sufficient in creating a mindful and positive classroom culture. My students had limited, if any, understanding of how the brain works and struggled to recognize and respond to emotions such as frustration and test anxiety. This is where my growth as a teacher really began. I decided to pursue a Master of Science in Education, which was instrumental in helping me learn tools and strategies to teach students about brain science and emotional regulation. I took influential classes such as Brain-Targeted Teaching, a class focused on the effect of *external stimuli on the classroom environment,* learning that stimuli such as background music, colors on the wall, and the scent of the room impact not only student focus, but teacher instruction.

I began to use a more mindful approach to educating students about the brain, its function, and its impact on everyday emotions. I witnessed instances where the tools I learned in graduate school allowed students in my ESOL classes to perform better during an exam, avoid getting into trouble in the school environment as well as at home, and even prevent fights from breaking out. By the end of my fourth year teaching in Miami, it became clear that cultivating and fostering emotional intelligence was essential for student success.

Resistance in the Education System

As with many schools in the US education system, my school in Miami measured student success solely through academic achievement and state-wide assessment scores. Unfortunately, there was minimal focus on social and emotional development, which made it very challenging for me to justify utilizing instructional time to teach mindfulness, breathing techniques, gratitude, and kindness, despite being regarded as noble goals.

My job was put in jeopardy as I continued to teach SEL in direct opposition to my school administration—a problem that still persists today in schools all over the country. Even when administrative teams are supportive and inclusive, teachers are pressured to reach certain academic results. Student test scores often directly impact teacher evaluations, performance reviews, and even salary raises, but their emotional intelligence has no impact on a teacher's performance. This professional and financial impact too often leads to SEL being put on the backburner.

Revelations and Information Overload

The more I listen to my former students, the more I see the impact of mindful awareness and SEL on academic, social, and emotional success. My students have told me that brain breaks have lessened their anxiety before important interviews and auditions, and that understanding *how the brain works* have helped them resolve conflict in a variety of scenarios. If my students from 9 years ago have been able to lessen their anxiety by focusing on mindful breathing and listening, students today should have access to the same tools.

In today's "attention economy," consumers are overloaded with information through smartphones and computers, and we are constantly exposed to content that is often chosen by someone else. This, in turn, impacts our brains and affects the way we behave and how we feel. Mindfulness allows us to recognize the over-exposure to content as well as gives us tools to better manage what and how we receive information.

As humans, we are motivated to live lives full of purpose and peace. We know now that mindfulness is universally attainable and requires minimal external tools, and that together we can bring our world one step closer to being more peaceful and fulfilled by providing these basic truths and understanding to the future of tomorrow.

Targeting Executive Function with the MindUP™ Program

MindUP™ is the CASEL-SELect, signature social-emotional learning program of The Goldie Hawn Foundation (TGHF). The foundation was created in 2003 by Academy Award-winning actress Goldie Hawn who, after the terrorist attacks in New York on September 11, 2001, was alarmed by the state of the world and set out to create a curriculum that would help children learn how to manage the increased stress and anxiety of everyday life. Hawn brought together neuroscientists, positive psychologists, teachers, and other experts to create MindUP™, a neuroscience-based curriculum that targets brain fitness activities to stimulate and prime the brain for learning.

The MindUP curriculum is a Scholastic-based 15-lesson series for PreK-8thgrade students (ages 3–14) that aims to increase prosocial behaviors, breath control, self-regulation, social competence, and executive functioning. MindUP supports children's working memory, self-control, and cognitive flexibility. Executive function is the primary target of MindUP, as it is the main building block of cognitive capacity and can directly impact a child's ability to learn. No matter how talented the teacher, if a student's executive function capacities are underdeveloped, a sole focus on subject matter instruction may not be effective or helpful.

Research Outcomes that Matter

MindUP is a recognized evidenced-based program. It is accredited by the Collaborative for Academic, Social, and Emotional Learning as a CASEL SELect program, meaning it meets high design quality and evidence-based criteria. Most recently, MindUP has been recognized as 1 of 10 top brain fitness SEL programs in the US, as it meets the evidence-based standards of the federal Every Student Succeeds Act (ESSA). In December 2015, ESSA passed into law, replacing the No Child Left Behind Act (NCLB). This reauthorization of the ESSA of 1965 raised the bar for school interventions from research-based in NCLB to evidence-based through ESSA's "Evidence of Effectiveness" criteria.

MindUP has more than 10 years of independent research, including four randomized control trials. Findings have shown that students participating in the MindUP curriculum have demonstrated reduced aggression and increased prosocial behaviors and have shown gains in executive function skills, math, and language arts. Specifically:

- Children in 4th–7th grades improved in optimism along with teacher-reported improvements in social emotional competence and reduction in aggression and oppositional defiant behaviors.
- Students gained 15% in math achievement.
- PreK and kindergarten students improved in teacher-reported attention and had higher vocabulary and reading scores.
- MindUP was adapted for the Uganda educational context and research found the program can be successfully adapted into an African context with children who have been traumatized by war.

These are just some of our findings. Most recently in 2018, Portland State was awarded a $3.3 million federal grant to study MindUP's impact on kindergarten readiness in 100 preschools around the greater Portland area.

MindUP Program Services

Today, MindUP is being offered in schools across the United States, United Kingdom, Canada, China, Hong Kong, Serbia, Australia, Uganda, Portugal, Finland, and in various countries throughout Latin America. In the US, MindUP Consultants have formally trained over 350 schools, impacting over 32,000 teachers across the country.

The formal training program consists of year-long professional development, coaching, and mentorship for schools and organizations around the US. MindUP

Consultants lead face-to-face trainings for staff, on-site coaching, and mentoring sessions, as well as virtual video conference calls, providing continuous support throughout year one of implementation. The formal training program also includes a parent/family workshop for adult stakeholders in a child's life to learn the tools and techniques to use MindUP in the home environment.

Shared Goals and a Vision for the Future

In my role as a MindUP Consultant, I have worked with educators around the United States as well as in Brazil and Jordan. I have come to realize that the brain is what unites us. We are triggered in similar ways, affected by the same general stresses, anxieties, and fears, and have the same ultimate goal: to live peaceful, fulfilling lives. I truly believe that learning to regulate emotions, appreciate the present moment, witness the power of kindness, and practice gratitude are all part of the journey to living more peaceful, fulfilling lives.

As founder and president Hawn looks to the future, her call to action is even louder. She intends to continue expanding the reach of MindUP, focusing on research and evaluation, accessibility to professionals in different fields, and long-term sustainability of the program.

"Life can have many chapters, and I can say MindUP may be the greatest of my life."—Goldie Hawn

CHAPTER 8

Mindfulness Without Borders: Compassion Education for a Better World

Theo Koffler

Founder, Mindfulness Without Borders

MINDFULNESS WITHOUT BORDERS (MWB) WAS BORN out of my own personal journey while living in Israel. It was the late seventies and I was thirty-two years of age. I had moved there with my brother as part of a group of corporate professionals invited by the Israeli government to bring best business practices to a country just beginning its ascent into the global economy. Coming from careers in drugstore retailing, our vision was to develop Israel's largest national drugstore chain —just as our father had done in Canada.

In many ways, I was at the top of my game. I had successfully transitioned from university into my first corporate job in Toronto and then moved to Israel to further my career. At the time, Israel was reshaping itself to be a player in the global economic scene. But as determined as I was to succeed in my professional life, underneath the surface I found myself struggling to deal with the stress associated with living in a country divided by conflict. The longer I was there, the harder it became to watch the 'us versus them' paradigm in action. The violence, cultural divide, biases and social injustices were seemingly impenetrable.

Furthermore, as a Canadian, and having grown up in a country of peace in which cultural and religious diversity was part of the fabric of society, I had little, if any, experience with the complexities inherent in living in a country of war. As hard as I tried to deal with the differences, in the end, I just couldn't. Eventually, the stress caught up to me, the country's divide became mine and shortly after the birth of my second son, I crashed.

I was diagnosed with Lupus. My world turned upside down and everything changed. It truly stopped me dead in my tracks. I went from an active, career-driven, athletic, ambitious mother of two to a woman dealing with a serious health condition. The more I learned about Lupus, the more I realized how much my internal stressors and personal choices contributed to my overall well-being. It soon became apparent that if I wanted to get better, I would have to figure out a new way of living.

Thankfully, around that same time, a friend gave me a book written by Thich Nhat Hanh called *Peace Is Every Step*. The book introduced me to meditation and mindfulness and truly changed my life. The wisdom in those pages put me on a path toward healing and laid the foundation for the values that guide me and the choices that I make day, after day, after day.

Envisioning Systemic Change in Education

My professional life also turned 180 degrees. I left the very company that I helped to build and focused on my mental and physical health. As I regained strength, I began to inquire about the missing piece in my education that would have equipped me with the skills I needed to manage the challenges I faced while living in Israel. With time and exploration, I discovered social and emotional learning (SEL)—and before long I'd set my sights on a new goal.

In 2005, I ventured into what would prove to be an incredibly rewarding second career. For two years, I volunteered as program advisor for the Garrison Institute's first-ever Contemplation and Education Initiative. Under the leadership of Diana and Jonathon Rose, the Institute explored the wisdom of contemplative practice and its impact on personal and social transformation. As a co-researcher for their Mapping Report on the *Current Status of Contemplative Techniques in K-12 Educational Settings*, I had the unique experience of interviewing the leading thought-providers, visionaries and luminaries in the field of mindfulness and SEL.

As a result of the growing interest in mindfulness-based interventions, I helped organize the Institute's first-ever symposium in which 40 key players attended a 3-day retreat to explore the role of contemplation in education. Jon Kabat-Zinn, Richard Davidson, Daniel Segal, Daniel Goleman, Tobin Hart, Mark Greenberg, Susan Kaiser Greenland, and Goldie Hawn were among the many participants. These relationships have been foundational to my growth as well as my professional development. In fact, as the Ubuntu saying goes, "I am who I am because they are who they are."

Envisioning a vital role for mindfulness and SEL in education, I gathered a small team of practitioners and educators together to create the vision and mission of a charitable organization that would bring SEL and mindfulness practices to society. We dedicated ourselves to developing a curriculum that would equip young people, and the adults that surround them, with the social and emotional skills and attention training (secular mindfulness practices) they need to effectively navigate daily challenges. That curriculum is known as the Mindfulness Ambassador Program and was originally implemented in select locations in

Rwanda, Uganda, and Nigeria. The intention was to work in countries that were reshaping themselves—out from under the trauma of violence and war.

Known as Between4Eyes, our small charitable organization worked solely in conflict and post-conflict communities. Our workshops and school programs focused on developing an intelligence of the heart. The questions we seeded ignited conversations around becoming caring, ethical citizens, capable of providing leadership that catalyzes positive societal change. Whether in small or large groups, we honored the wisdom in the room and focused on conversations that unite people. As a result of our programs, we witnessed that, while the conditions change from country to country, people everywhere are thirsty for a sense of belonging. Social and emotional intelligence, kindness, and compassion had a definitive role in the peacebuilding process.

Addressing Research and Growth

Four years after working in Africa, we decided that we needed research if we were to become a major contributor to the field of mindfulness-based SEL. We collaborated with a research team at the Faculty of Social Work at The University of Toronto, and our objective was to receive meaningful data around where student learning outcomes. The research results confirmed a lot of what we had witnessed firsthand. The findings demonstrated that our programs enabled participants from all walks of life to build self-esteem, better cope with challenges, communicate effectively with others and manage stress.

With this new development, we changed our name to Mindfulness Without Borders and centralized our activities out of Toronto and San Francisco. Founded on the premise that peacebuilding and co-existence are possible when individuals have the skills to lead compassionate, caring and ethical lives, we turned our sights to a revised working model that trained and certified individuals to facilitate our evidence-based programs in the communities in which they served. As a result, we could curtail our travels and devote more human and financial resources to program development. We realized that through training others to facilitate our programs, we could reach more diverse populations—not exclusively in under-developed or developing countries. Our growth became steady, thoughtful and paced.

Since 2007, we've worked diligently to create inclusive learning environments in which everyone feels welcome and where it feels safe to be themselves. Our three curriculum pillars of secular mindfulness, SEL, and the Council process continue to create a solid foundation on which every person's experience, identity, and gender are valued equally. Rather than taking a didactic approach to learning, our programs continue to focus on building upon each individual's gifts and talents as well as the cultivation of positive virtues—making the conversation around how to cultivate an intelligence of the heart all the more dynamic.

Our program content focuses on conversations that ignite self-reflection and human connection. It is fueled by seeding questions that encourage the understanding of our individual similarities and differences. It is through acknowledging and valuing our differences that a more compassionate understanding of our world is created. Developing and making peace with our internal world is not an extravagance if we want to create peace in the world. It's a necessity.

Training Attention

Fundamental to our curriculum design is the practice of mindfulness as a tool to train attention and raise awareness. With a secular approach, we are able to focus on the basic understanding that mindfulness exists inside every one of us, and is not something we need to create. Rather, it is a practice that we need to cultivate. By deliberately slowing down and bringing more awareness to the mind and body in the present moment, we can more accurately observe our thoughts, feelings and sensations and act on them with discernment, kindness and compassion. One mindfulness practice we teach program participants who are challenged by slowing down is called TAKE FIVE.

In this breathing practice, we use the five fingers of one hand to count each breath cycle, hence the name TAKE FIVE. We notice the body expanding with each in-breath and contracting with each out-breath. In so doing, we withdraw our attention from distracting thoughts that can cause restlessness or anxiety. Over time and with practice, our mind becomes calmer and our emotional states more balanced. Here's how:

> Sit in a comfortable position. Allow both soles of your feet to connect to the floor and rest your hands on your lap. Gently close your eyes or look for a point somewhere on the floor where you can return your eyes when you get distracted.

> Turn one hand palm-up to the ceiling. This will be your counting hand. At the end of each breath cycle, you will fold one finger on this hand into your palm until all five fingers are folded.

> Gently take a breath in to fill your lungs. Notice the pause that happens naturally once the in-breath is complete. Gently breathe one long breath out until you notice the natural pause again. Fold your first finger. This is TAKE ONE.

Gently take another in-breath to fill your lungs. Notice the pause that happens naturally once the in-breath is complete. Gently breathe out until your breath comes to a pause. Fold your second finger. This is TAKE TWO.

Breathe in again, filling up your lungs until you feel the pause. Breathe out to empty the lungs until you feel the pause. Fold your third finger. This is TAKE THREE.

Breathe in; notice the pause. Breathe out; notice the pause. Fold your fourth finger. This is TAKE FOUR.

Now, breathe in following the whole length of the breath. Breathe out, following the whole length of the breath. This time, turn your counting hand palm down. This is TAKE FIVE.

Continue to breathe in and out. Remember: You don't need to breathe in a special way. Your body knows how to breathe. When you are ready, slowly bring your attention back to the room, and take a moment to notice how you feel.

Ever-Evolving as Our Collective Wisdom Grows

In 2015, we celebrated our tenth year of operation. As part of their Next Ten Campaign, *The Huffington Post* specifically acknowledged Mindfulness Without Borders as an organization positioned to make a significant impact over the next ten years. We have accepted this great honor and continue to develop and advance our work around the globe.

At the core of it all, our mission remains the same. MWB's primary focus centers on helping people develop skillsets that will enable them to better cope with the emotional ups and downs of daily life. Over the years, our in-person and online Facilitator Certification model has become the most efficient way to expand our programs' reach, internationally. Whether from English or Spanish-speaking countries, our certification process attracts individuals from all walks of like that recognize the essential role social and emotional intelligence and mindfulness plays in overall health. After successfully completing this training process, graduates are able to take our evidence-based programming into the communities that they serve. In turn, they join thousands of other program participants from around the world who stand for kindness and compassion—driving positive impact in our world.

Our most recent initiative, The RETHiNK Kit, extends a hand to parents, homeschoolers, educators, and health professionals interested in short fifteen minute, SEL-based activities. These activities are meant to provide adults with new and interactive ways to catalyze conversation among young people to discover their core values, discuss issues that matter, connect with their peers and fully engage in their communities as curious, responsible, and caring of the world in which they live.

At the end of the day, no matter where we are working or who we are working with, our main purpose holds steady. We acknowledge that our programs and content are ever-evolving—making it critical for our growing team and certified facilitators to grow and evolve as well. We are grateful to the staff, researchers, facilitators, volunteers, board members, advisors and communities that have contributed their unique talents to our growth. And, as our collective wisdom continues to grow, we envision that we will discover more about the world that surrounds us and create more space to fully explore who we are as individuals, communities and engaged global citizens.

See Chapter 32 for MWB's work in action with the Decatur School Systems.

CHAPTER 9

Social, Emotional, and Ethical Learning: Can We Build a Safer, Happier World?

Brendan Ozawa-de Silva

Associate Director, SEE Learning, Center for Contemplative Science and Compassion-Based Ethics at Emory University with Lobsang Tenzin Negi, PhD, Emory University

TAKE A MOMENT TO THINK ABOUT THE KIND OF SOCIETY we want to have in the future, the kind of world we want future generations to be able to live in. What would it have that our current world lacks? What problems do we have now that we would want to see resolved? What good things do we have now that we would want to continue and have more of?

Then consider the following question: Do we have everything in our current education system that is going to prepare our children and our children's children to create and sustain that better, happier world?

This isn't just a philosophical or abstract question. It's an empirical question as well. Since 2012 the United Nations has invited countries to submit data for the World Happiness Report, an annual study analyzing what factors are most important for the happiness and well-being of societies. To the surprise of many of the economists involved in the beginning, it wasn't economic factors that showed the most influence on happiness, but things like trust and social support. In the most recent report of 2019, generosity was one of the six key determinants of the happiness of a society.

Is our education system cultivating children's capacity for generosity, trust, and social support? Is it teaching them how to think about complex problems like international conflict, immigration, and climate change? Do we have a framework for what such an education and such a society would look like? Can such things even be taught?

Fortunately, in the past several decades, our scientific understanding of the human condition has advanced tremendously. Thirty years ago, it would have been unthinkable to speak of the science of mindfulness, the science of compassion, the science of happiness. Yet now these have become legitimate domains of scientific inquiry and research. We have entirely new disciplines like contemplative science and positive psychology, and other already established disciplines, like affective and social neuroscience, psychoneuroimmunology, epigenetics, and trauma physiology, that have resulted in groundbreaking new discoveries. We know more than ever before about the interrelated workings of stress, emotions, rumination, inflammation, and the nervous system. We have made important new discoveries regarding what promotes and what compromises our health, both physical and psychological. We know that even very young children can be taught in ways that enhance their innate capacity for systems thinking.

And yet very little of this new knowledge has made its way into schools for the benefit of children and our future society. For this reason, a few years ago noted scholars Daniel Goleman and Peter Senge called for a new form of education that would have a "triple focus." Children should develop an "inner focus" through understanding their own minds and emotions and cultivating the skill of attention. They should cultivate an "other focus" by cultivating compassion, empathy, and social skills. And they very much need opportunities to develop their "outer focus" by learning about and cultivating their innate capacity for systems thinking: the ability to understand interdependence and the workings of complex, interrelated systems. Goleman and Senge argued that this new approach to education, which would bridge the worlds of Social and Emotional Learning (SEL) and systems thinking, should be based on the best science.

Forty years ago the Dalai Lama was also calling for a new approach to education: one that would teach the cultivation of basic human values like compassion on the basis of science, common sense, and common experience—not on the basis of one particular religion or another. He calls this approach "secular ethics"—not because it is opposed to religion, which it is not, but because it is non-sectarian and open to people of any, or no, religious tradition. Like Goleman and Senge, the Dalai Lama emphasized that the cultivation of attention and what he calls "ethical mindfulness" could play a central role in such education. This is because coming to a deep understanding of one's mind and transforming emotional and relational habits is hard work, and this work is greatly aided by meta-awareness and the ability to focus attention on one's own mind, body and behavior.

The Call for a New Approach in Education

In 2015, these various streams came together to give rise to the SEE Learning program. The Dalai Lama invited Emory University to develop a program that could contribute to a global movement to bring the cultivation of basic human values into education. A group of us convened as a core team to start developing the framework for this program. The Dalai Lama had laid out in his writings and talks—such as in books like *Ethics for the New Millennium and Beyond Religion: Ethics for a Whole World*—what the theoretical basis of this program could be and what content areas it could involve. The basis should be our common humanity and our interdependence, which the Dalai Lama called "the two pillars" of secular ethics. By basing an approach to ethics on these two pillars—things we all have in common—the program could be open to anyone. It could serve as a way to bring people together, rather than divide them. In terms of the content, the program should involve the cultivation of basic human values like compassion, forgiveness, integrity, generosity, kindness, and love. And it should include the tools necessary to facilitate that cultivation, such as ethical mindfulness, heedfulness, and awareness.

At the same time, Goleman and Senge's book *The Triple Focus* provided us with a structure for the framework. The program should have three domains: Personal, Social, and Systems. And drawing from the Dalai Lama, it should have three dimensions: Awareness, Compassion, and Engagement.

All we needed now was a name, and that was provided by our senior advisor Daniel Goleman himself. Because we were taking the best that SEL had to offer and adding the ethical component, he dubbed the program *Social, Emotional and Ethical Learning*, or *SEE Learning*. He then went so far as to say that because of the new components it was adding to the traditional SEL framework, SEE Learning represented SEL 2.0.

The SEE Learning Framework and Program

2015–2019 saw the development of the SEE Learning program and its global launch in April 2019, in the presence of the Dalai Lama and other dignitaries, as well as over 1,000 educators and supporters of education from 32 countries. The program materials are all free and are being translated into 15 languages at present. They consist of the *SEE Learning Companion*, which contains the framework and an implementation guide, as well as curricula for early elementary, late elementary, and middle school—with the high school and college curricula in development. There is also an online platform, *seelearning.emory.edu*, that contains a free orientation course open to anyone. While sample materials and the *SEE Learning Companion* are available without taking the course, completion of the course unlocks the ability to download all the materials in full. There is also now a dedicated team of staff for SEE Learning at Emory's Center for Contemplative Science and Compassion-Based Ethics, where the program is housed, as well as a large international community of institutional and individual collaborators.

The SEE Learning framework builds on the innovative work done in SEL and other educational initiatives, such as mindfulness in education, that seek to introduce holistic education into schools. Where schools already have existing SEL or mindfulness programs, SEE Learning can be used to complement these programs.

One innovation of SEE Learning is to integrate mindfulness and SEL. As Goleman notes, "Because it is such an essential element of helping children better manage their inner worlds and enhance learning, training in attention seems an obvious next step for SEL." Despite the flourishing of SEL and mindfulness programs in schools, only a few programs have tried to integrate the two approaches in a single program.

Importantly, SEE Learning does this integration in a trauma- and resilience-informed way, by teaching students about their nervous systems and how to regulate them using simple body-based techniques before beginning formal practices of mindfulness or focused attention. It does so through a strengths-based resiliency lens, meaning that it is appropriate for all students, including both those who have suffered from trauma and those who have not. Because all students, and indeed all human beings, experience varying levels of safety and threat, all students can benefit from learning about their nervous systems and how to regulate stress through body-based practices and the cultivation of "body literacy."

We have found that students report that they use these simple strategies of grounding, resourcing, tracking and Help Now! on a daily basis. In fact, one teacher reported that her students wouldn't allow her to administer a test without first allowing them to ground and resource for a few minutes. Having taught them these skills, she was forced by them to practice what she preached!

SEE Learning also adds to SEL a more comprehensive focus on ethics and basic human values. SEE Learning begins with an exploration of our common humanity and our interdependence. This leads to an understanding that we all commonly prefer kindness from others to cruelty or meanness. And since we are interdependent, share spaces with each other, and depend on others for all our needs, it only makes sense that we should commit to helping others just as we would want them to help us; or at a minimum not harming others, since we would not want them to harm us. As Goleman has pointed out: "It's not enough just to know how other people think or feel; we also need to be concerned about them and be ready to help. . . . Such an addition to SEL would be an important next step for schools."

Lastly, SEE Learning includes a focus on increasing awareness of interdependence and systems thinking. In our shrinking world, our students' and children's individual and collective flourishing requires that they recognize how interdependent we are. SEE Learning both includes explicit teaching of systems thinking to students and adopts a systems thinking approach itself.

By incorporating systems thinking and recognizing the importance of cultivating resilience at cultural, structural, interpersonal, and individual levels, the SEE Learning framework also contributes to our understanding of equity. Equity is the idea that people should have fully sufficient opportunities to succeed and to meet the basic requirements for survival and flourishing in our societies, and that systems should reflect this principle by ensuring that no particular group is comparatively disadvantaged and that inequities are not perpetuated systemically.

If we are to bring about systems that are more equitable in lasting, sustainable ways, we cannot stop at the level of policy recommendations. We also need the cultivation of basic human values, such as a recognition of common humanity and a recognition of our interdependence. By demonstrating how the structures that ensure equity or allow for inequity connect with basic human values, and by teaching skills to cultivate those values further, SEE Learning provides an approach for addressing the root causes of inequity, and its perpetuation, in ways that can involve students and can be explored along with them.

What It Means for Educators and Students

It was about ten years ago, in 2009, that we began piloting lessons on teaching compassion in schools here in Atlanta with elementary students and adolescent foster children. In one of those classes, one of our colleagues and team members at the time, Brooke Dodson-Lavelle, was teaching a class of 5th-grade students the practice of mindfulness. When all the kids were supposed to be mindfully sitting and watching or counting their breaths, one boy would hear another child making a sound and would suddenly shout in a loud voice, "Be quiet!"

Naturally, all the kids lost their concentration and would start to laugh. Then he'd shout again, "Be quiet! You're supposed to be quiet!"

This went on for a few weeks until one day Brooke took the boy aside for a one-on-one talk.

"You know when we are all practicing mindfulness and we're trying to be quiet so as not to disturb anyone else? If we're doing that and you feel like saying something, what could you do?"

The boy looked back at her. "If I feel like saying something? Then I say something!"

Brooke smiled. "Yes, but what else could you do?"

The boy was thoughtful for a moment. Then he slowly said, "I could . . . not say something."

Brooke smiled again. "Really? Do you think you could do that?"

The boy nodded.

If this scene had been in a cartoon, we would have seen a light bulb go off over the child's head. The ability to recognize impulses, thoughts, and emotions and deal with them constructively, rather than being pulled along with them, is at the heart of emotional intelligence. It's also at the heart of what the Dalai Lama calls "ethical mindfulness." It's at the heart of SEE Learning. And it's at the heart of an approach to education that we need to bring about the happier, safer world that we want for future generations.

What has been so exciting for us to see over the past few years since SEE Learning started is how educators and students around the world are taking up the program and putting it into practice. Little "a-ha" moments are sparking every day in classrooms, and as that happens, our growing international SEE Learning community becomes increasingly able to share what works best and what doesn't, for our collective benefit. Collectively, we still have a lot to learn about how to bring ethical mindfulness, compassion, trauma and resilience skills, and systems thinking into education in the most effective ways. Quality research and ongoing assessment will be critical. But we feel fortunate to be on this journey together with so many around the world.

CHAPTER 10

Transforming Education with Mindfulness and Anti-Oppression Framework

Jersey Cosantino

Doctoral Student and Former Middle School English Teacher, NY

Akira Gutierrez and Sara Krachman

Transforming Education

Mindfulness Research and Practice to Support Whole Child Development

Akira Gutierrez Renzulli and Sara Krachman, Transforming Education

SARA FIRST BEGAN PRACTICING MINDFULNESS AS A WAY TO COPE with stress around the time she founded Transforming Education. In addition to traditional seated meditation, Sara practices embodied mindfulness through yoga, dance, and singing. As her personal practice deepened, she began to see the obvious intersections between mindfulness and Transforming Education's work on whole child development. The opportunity to study the impact of mindfulness for students through a researcher-practitioner partnership was an exciting chance to bridge her personal and professional interests in this field.

Akira has been exploring approaches to developing positive mental health and well-being for well over a decade. She first started practicing mindfulness in community with health professionals through a Mindfulness-Based Stress Reduction course that also engaged participants in discussions about the science and promise of the practice for overall health promotion. What began as a personal journey towards practicing acceptance, self-compassion, and learning how to live in the present has joyfully collided with her professional path towards supporting the mental health of youth, families, and educators.

Mindfulness has also shaped parenting for both Sara and Akira, who enjoy exchanging ideas about teaching mindfulness to their toddlers using modeling, books, and sensory practices. For example, Akira guides her toddler in belly breathing by placing her own hand on her daughter's belly and modeling deep breaths. Sara encourages her toddler to pretend she is smelling flowers and blowing out birthday candles to practice mindful breathing. These daily practices have shaped our lives at home and at work, and they are deeply connected to the mission of our organization, Transforming Education.

Transforming Education (TransformEd) partners with school systems to support educators in fostering the development of the whole child so that all students, particularly those from underserved populations, can thrive. One of our partnerships, the Boston Charter Research Collaborative (BCRC), is a multi-year research-practice partnership between six Boston-area charter management organizations (CMOs), Harvard University, MIT, and TransformEd. These partners combine their expertise to conduct research and improve practice to support students' social-emotional development. Both researchers and educators in the BCRC have expressed interest in mindfulness strategies as a tool to support students' social-emotional development, so we worked together to conduct a randomized controlled trial to study the impact on students of a mindfulness-based intervention.

During the study, 6th-grade students spent eight weeks either learning about and practicing mindfulness, or learning to code (which served as the control condition). The mindfulness program took place in 45-minute sessions four times per week, during which students learned about the concept of mindfulness and engaged in guided practice. For example, in one session, students learned about focus and attention, then tried to focus on a rock for one minute and discussed what happened in their minds during this activity. Students were also encouraged to practice for 5–15 minutes each day outside the classroom. Anecdotally, students reported that they practiced before falling asleep at night, before playing sports, or before/during tests at school (Gutierrez, Krachman, Scherer, West, & Gabrieli, 2019).

Compared to students in the coding group, students assigned to the mindfulness intervention reported a reduction in their perception of stress and demonstrated modest (but significant) improvements in their ability to maintain their attention on a particular task—even when they were not actively engaged in a mindfulness practice. Brain imaging of students who participated in the mindfulness intervention also showed a reduced response of the amygdala (a brain structure associated with emotion and stress) when looking at images of fearful faces. These findings suggest that school-based mindfulness programs have the potential to help students build attention skills and cope with stress (Bauer et al., 2019).

Learning to cope with stress may be especially useful for students who are experiencing adversity, which can trigger a stress response in the body. However, as Alice Pettway noted in a 2017 edition of Teaching Tolerance Magazine, "Implementing mindfulness programs without integrating culturally responsive practices is akin to treating the symptoms of inequitable education without addressing the cause" (Petway, 2017). In other words, all students (and adults) can benefit from developing strong coping skills, but we must also simultaneously challenge the systemic inequities that create disproportionate levels of stress for students of color, students living in poverty, refugee and immigrant students, LGBTQ students, and other students who experience social marginalization.

When used effectively—and in conjunction with efforts to address systemic inequities—mindfulness can be a powerful tool for creating an inclusive school community in which students experience a sense of belonging. Engaging regularly with a mindfulness practice may encourage students and educators to be more accepting of those who differ from themselves with respect to race/ethnicity, gender, and other facets of their identities. The power of this idea came to life for us when we met Jersey Cosantino, a trans/non-binary educator and doctoral student who focuses on using mindfulness practices to create more inclusive academic environments for transgender, non-binary, and gender non-conforming students and staff using an intersectional, anti-oppression framework. Jersey was teaching in one of the BCRC partner schools when we began our mindfulness study, and they shared the following reflections on the Transforming Education blog (http://bit .ly/2Ct3cNM).

Supporting Our Trans, Non-Binary, And Gender Non-Conforming Students Through Mindfulness And An Anti-Oppression Framework

Jersey Cosantino

During the winter of 2018, in the middle of the school year, I came out as trans and non-binary. Navigating the highly binary-gendered world of our educational system, I struggled deeply with daily misgendering. When others were unable to see me for who I declared myself to be, I felt my newly realized identity invalidated and erased. I knew that this was largely not the result of any mal-intent on the part of my students or colleagues, but rather the direct result of society's oppressive normative structures seeping into the fabric of our academic institutions.

As a 31-year-old with a strong queer community, various support networks, and a plethora of coping mechanisms to help me survive this experience, I worried about the journeys of our trans, non-binary, and gender non-conforming (GNC) youth in schools across the country who are denied access to similar resources.

Therefore, I began to look into ways that school communities could better support students' social-emotional well-being during their identity evolution process.

As reports from The National Center for Transgender Equality's 2015 Survey (James, Herman, Rankin, Keisling, Mottet, & Anafi, 2016) and GLSEN's 2017 National School Climate Survey (Kosciw, Greytak, Zongrone, Clark, & Truong, 2018) show, the impacts of sustained discrimination on the academic outcomes and psychological well-being of trans, non-binary, and GNC youth are dire and disturbing, to say the least. Additionally, these effects are compounded when trans-identifying students have additional intersecting marginalized identities (Kosciw et al., 2018).

With this knowledge in mind, I probed more deeply the intersectional complexities of identity development and explored the coping mechanism that seemed to have the most powerful impact on my own transition: the study of mindfulness. Each time I was incorrectly called "Ms," or felt dysphoria hearing my voice congratulating a student, or experienced disgust seeing my reflection in the mirror of the school bathroom, I turned to the non-judgmental present-moment awareness of mindfulness to help calm the encroaching despair. Thinking of all of the students and educators across the country trying to thrive within persistently unjust systems, I wondered if mindfulness could provide a similar beacon of hope for them as it had for me.

Scholarly literature and a new, but growing, body of research show that mindfulness can indeed help trans, non-binary, and GNC students cultivate a positive relationship with their gender identity, self-acceptance, self-pride, and resilience in the face of daily discrimination. An additional necessary component of this is teaching students to contextualize their emotions and experiences in relation to the ways in which society affirms and stigmatizes certain identities. For me, each time that I was misgendered I tried to remind myself that the pain I felt was not a result of my physical self being inherently wrong, but rather a terrible consequence of society's oppressive binary views of gender identity and expression. Although this understanding did not eradicate my unhappiness, it was a vital tool in helping me affirm my own identity despite continuous microaggressions. Therefore, if teachers choose to bring mindfulness into the classroom, as in the valuable ways that Janice Houlihan describes, it is critical that teachers offer this practice through a social-justice, anti-oppression lens (2018).

By teaching mindfulness in conjunction with an analysis of internalized oppression, trans, non-binary, and GNC students will have a framework for unpacking the harmful narratives that have been ingrained inside of them by society. According to Beth Berila in her article, "Mindfulness as a Healing, Liberatory Practice in Queer Anti-Oppression Pedagogy," many of these students have already developed the qualities of mindful present-moment awareness through the process of discovering their own identities and determining what aspects of themselves are safe enough to express in a given situation (2016). Explicitly incorporating anti-oppression work into mindfulness practice builds on the skills these students have already refined by providing a scaffold to dive deeper into this liberating, but oftentimes triggering, introspective process. By joining the skills of mindful awareness with the language to name and address heteronormative and cisgender systems that oppress them, students are better equipped to confront society's potentially harmful messages and begin to process the ways in which these narratives may have created internal barriers to self-acceptance (Berila, 2016).

As Iacono Gio demonstrates in his recent case study entitled "An Affirmative Mindfulness Approach for Lesbian, Gay, Bisexual, Transgender, and Queer Youth Mental Health" (2018) educators must offer these students not only the remarkably beneficial tools of mindfulness practice, but also the framework necessary to nurture the compassion, lovingkindness,[1] and non-judgmental awareness that is central to survival and resistance of pernicious normative systems. Specifically, trans, non-binary, and GNC students sometimes falsely blame themselves and their identities for their own suffering, thinking they are somehow deficient or lacking in self-worth (Vosvick & Stem, 2018).

This can be further intensified when considering the oftentimes incongruent relationships trans, non-binary, and GNC students might have with their own bodies, something that can surface and become triggered in complicated ways when participating in body-scans and body awareness exercises that lay the foundation for mindfulness practice. Thus, using mindfulness to recenter students' blame onto oppressive systems rather than themselves can foster the self-acceptance and healing necessary for academic success and positive emotional well-being. As Thich Nhat Hanh states, "If you can see how your suffering has come to be, you are already on the path to release from it" (1999).

Although the research backing the interconnection between mindfulness, social-justice, non-normative identities, and adolescent development is still emerging, the findings are optimistic and promising.[2] There is a distinct call to action right now for us as educators to teach mindfulness from an intersectional standpoint, thus helping this centuries-old practice have the most profound impact possible on all of our students, particularly those with marginalized identities. By teaching a mindfulness practice rooted in an anti-oppression pedagogy, we are fortifying our trans, non-binary, and GNC students with the skills necessary to actively disrupt systems that oppress them while simultaneously cultivating a sense of empowerment and resiliency that ensures that their identities can never be erased and are, in fact, honored and celebrated.

1. Lovingkindness, as mentioned here, is in reference to a form of meditation called metta meditation which involves silently repeating phrases that wish happiness and well-being for oneself and others. During metta meditation, an individual is planting the seeds of kindness in the form of intentions that opens one's heart to compassion and love.

2. Due to the necessity for brevity, it was not possible to reference all of the studies, scholarly literature, and current practices that address the interconnections between mindfulness and anti-oppression pedagogy. If access to further examples of research and scholarly literature is desired, please feel free to reach out to the author directly for links to various forms of content promoting this particular framework at jersey.cosantino@gmail.com.

Bauer, C. C., Caballero, C., Scherer, E., West, M. R., Mrazek, M. D., Phillips, D. T., . . . & Gabrieli, J. D. (2019). Mindfulness training reduces stress and amygdala reactivity to fearful faces in middle-school children. *Behavioral Neuroscience,133*(6), 569–585.

Berila, Beth. (2016). Mindfulness as a healing, liberatory practice in queer anti-oppression pedagogy. *Social Alternatives, 35*(3), 5–10.

Gio, I. (2018). An affirmative mindfulness approach for lesbian, gay, bisexual, transgender, and queer youth mental health. *Clinical Social Work Journal,* 1–11. https://doi.org/10.1007/s10615-018-0656-7

Gutierrez, A.S., Krachman, S.B, Scherer, E., West, M.R. & Gabrieli, J.E. (2019). *Mindfulness in the Classroom: Learning from a school-based mindfulness intervention through the Boston Charter Research Collaborative.* Retrieved from https://www.transformingeducation.org/wp-content/uploads/2019/01/2019-BCRC-Mindfulness-Brief.pdf

Hanh, T. N. (1999). *The heart of the buddha's teaching: Transforming suffering into peace, joy, and liberation.* New York City, NY: Broadway Books.

Houlihan, J. (2018, October 15). It's time we outsmart stress and take a stand for teacher wellbeing [Blog post]. Retrieved from https://www.transformingeducation.org/its-time-we-outsmart-stress-and-take-a-stand-for-teacher-wellbeing/.

James, S. E., Herman, J. L., Rankin, S., Keisling, M., Mottet, L., & Anafi, M. (2016). The Report of the 2015 U.S. Transgender Survey. Washington, DC: National Center for Transgender Equality.

Kosciw, J. G., Greytak, E. A., Zongrone, A. D., Clark, C. M., Truong, N. L. (2018). The 2017 national school climate survey: The experiences of lesbian, gay, bisexual, transgender, and queer youth in our nation's schools. New York, NY: GLSEN.

Pettway, A. (2017). Mindful of equity. Retrieved from https://www.tolerance.org/magazine/fall-2017/mindful-of-equity

Vosvick, M., & Stem, W. (2018). Psychological quality of life in a lesbian, gay, bisexual, transgender sample: Correlates of stress, mindful acceptance, and self-esteem. Psychology of Sexual Orientation and Gender Diversity. https://doi-org.ezproxyles.flo.org/10.1037/sgd0000303

CHAPTER 11

Secularity: Guiding Questions for Inclusive Mindfulness and Yoga in Schools

Jennifer Cohen Harper

Founder, Little Flower Yoga

Catherine Cook-Cottone, PhD, MA
Traci Childress, MA, MEd

In 2013, the parents of two students filed a lawsuit against Encinitas Union School District (EUSD) claiming that yoga was a religious practice and should not be taught in schools. Around the same time at national conferences on yoga for children, a discourse was taking shape that reflected the concerns, tensions, and hopes for the field of yoga in schools and secularity. By 2015, an appeals court in California upheld the previous court decisions ruling that the health and wellness program that integrated yoga at EUSD was not religious and therefore was not a violation of the Establishment Clause in the First Amendment of the United States Constitution. Yet, the discussion among yoga teacher trainers, yoga teachers, school personnel and demonstrators, parent groups, and yoga researchers continued.

There was no white paper upon which to anchor these discussions and there was a growing concern that if we did not take ownership of the conversions as a field of practice, the court system would. The authors of this chapter, integrating input from a passionate group of professionals and educators, dedicated two years to research, reflection, and contemplation creating a series of guiding questions and areas for contemplation for those choosing to offer yoga in schools. The resulting article that was the basis for this chapter is a result of that effort. The hope is that this work will provide a starting point for an ethical perspective that honors both the practice of yoga and the US Constitution and an architecture for the ongoing conversation.

MINDFULNESS AND YOGA ARE BEING TAUGHT in schools at growing rates. An increasing number of schools nationwide are offering formal programs, and the popularity and success of training programs specializing in school-based mindfulness and yoga are expanding (Butzer, Ebert, Telles, & Khalsa, 2015). With this growth, we've seen substantial variation in content and form of programming, and in particular variation in how programs and teachers address the issue of secularism and spirituality in relation to programming. This chapter explores the topic and offers guidance for offering school-based programs ethically, sustainably, and in accordance with legal mandates.

Mindfulness and yoga are related practices and depending on who you ask, yoga is a mindfulness practice or mindfulness is an aspect of yoga. Generally speaking, mindfulness is the practice of being mindfully aware, in the present moment, with an attitude of curiosity and kindness and mindfulness practices help you cultivate mindfulness (Cook-Cottone, 2017). The word yoga means "to yoke" or "integrate." In school-based yoga, this refers to the integration of mind and body to enhance well-being and student engagement. Specifically, school-based yoga is generally described as a set of mind/body practices and tools for well-being and student engagement including awareness and attention training, postures, breathing, relaxation, and meditation (Butzer et al, 2016; Cook-Cottone, 2017; Khalsa & Butzer, 2016; Serwacki & Cook-Cottone, 2012).

Neither yoga nor the notion of mind-and-body learning are new. For example, the use of mind/body tools in learning can be traced to theoretical work in the field of educational psychology (i.e., Lev Vygotsky in his book *Thought and Language*, 1962). Consistent with school-based mindfulness practice and research, the primary rationale for teaching yoga in educational settings is based on evidence from cognitive and affective neuroscience as well as biopsychosocial research suggesting outcomes salient to school success (Jennings, 2016; Mind and Life Education Research Network MLERN, 2013).

The larger fields of yoga and mindfulness have long and complex histories and are remarkably heterogeneous with substantial variation across schools, applications, context, and types (see Cook-Cottone, 2017). School-based programs have evolved from this varied field through an organic and practical process, so they can look rather different from district to district, and even school to school, depending on the teacher and program. Despite the emergence of specific training programs designed to guide teachers on how to best offer mindfulness and yoga in schools, there is no standardized protocol or set of guidelines for school-based training or teaching. There are also no specific regulations related to the provision of mindfulness and/or yoga in schools from state-to-state or federally. To address this need for guidance and structure, Childress & Harper published *Best Practices for Yoga in*

Schools (2015) to offer a set of guidelines for the field. Yet a wide range of practices continues to be taught today as the field strives to define what is best and most appropriate for students in the school setting.

The issue of secularity has emerged as a point of discussion within both the educational world and the fields of yoga and mindfulness. Childress and Harper (2015) posit upholding the principles of secularism in schools as an ethical and legal obligation of providers. The ethical concern relates to access and inclusion for all students. The legal concern centers on whether or not school-based mindfulness or yoga practices constitute religious activities that cross the boundary between church and state as specified in the first amendment of the U.S. Constitution (e.g., Jennings, 2016; Sedlock v. Baird, 2015; Cook-Cottone, Lemish, & Guyker, 2017). We address this issue by asking two questions: "What does it mean to be secular?" and "Why is it important to be secular?"

What Does it Mean to be Secular?

Secularity means "not pertaining to or connecting with religion" (Jennings, 2016, p. 176). *The Merriam-Webster Dictionary* defines religion as "the service and worship of God or the supernatural, commitment or devotion to religious faith or observance, a personal set or institutionalized system of religious attitudes, beliefs, and practice, or a cause, principle, or system of beliefs held to with ardor and faith." It is important to draw a clear line between secular and religious practices (Greenburg & Mitra, 2015). School-based mindfulness does not include worship of a supernatural being or deity, devotion to a religious faith, or adherence to any beliefs or set of beliefs (Jennings, 2016), nor do school-based yoga programs. School-based yoga has evolved from traditional forms of yoga with roots in Indian philosophy and religion (Cook-Cottone, 2017), and most school-based mindfulness has evolved from practices taught in Buddhist, Jesuit, and other traditions.

Consider how the modern clock evolved from religious to secular: from a tool originally created exclusively to time prayer to a tool for maintaining academic schedules. Another example is the distinction between choral reading of prayer in religious settings and the use of choral reading of poetry or drama in English class. The tools of yoga and mindfulness can be practiced in schools in a distinctly secular manner (Cook-Cottone, 2017; Jennings, 2016). Secular school-based programs utilize effective methodologies (e.g., awareness and attention training, physical postures, breathing techniques, relaxation, and meditation) without integrating religious dogma and philosophy (Cook-Cottone et al, 2016; Cook-Cottone, 2017; Masters, 2014).

As providers create programming for schools and consider their secularity, they can ask the following critical questions:

- What is the educational purpose of the program?
- How does the program enhance student learning and well-being?
- Do I have evidence that this practice is effective for the intended purpose?
- Does the type of practice I am offering include, or allude to, a set of non-empirical beliefs?
- Does the content I am teaching conflict with, or have the potential to conflict with, students' religious beliefs?

What Does it Mean to Be Aligned with Secular Ethics?

Secular programming aligns with secular ethics. By definition, secular ethics is a branch of philosophy in which moral ethics are separated from religion. A secular teacher can address important social-emotional values that enhance emotional and relational well-being within the context of a secular program (Greenburg & Matri, 2015; Jennings, 2015). Secular ethics do not come from a spiritual or religious source, and they include concepts such as gratitude, integrity, self-inquiry, loving-kindness, honesty, hope, caring for others, compassion for others, self-compassion, equanimity, non-harming, and joy (Greenburg & Matri, 2015; Jennings, 2015). Many of these constructs are currently being studied in the field of positive psychology (Boiler et al, 2013). Within the context of a secular mindfulness or yoga practice, teachers can share positive principles and concepts without making religious connections or using Sanskrit words (Cook-Cottone et al., 2016).

Programs and teachers should consider the following questions when integrating ethical concepts into yoga programming in schools:
- What is my intention in teaching these concepts?
- Does the secular ethics content I am delivering enhance student social and emotional learning?
- If there is an overlap between secular and religious ethics, am I delivering the content in a secular manner designed to enhance emotional and relational well-being?

Are Cultural Tools Appropriate in a Secular Environment?

While we have discussed mindfulness and yoga as a set of practices, they also have particular cultures and histories. Yoga culture is often associated with specific artifacts reflecting its long history, may be infused into religious and spiritual practices of yoga, and, at times, pays homage to the roots of these practices. Yoga culture often includes language (e.g., Sanskrit), rituals (e.g., use of incense, mala beads, and mantras), and other symbols (e.g, deities, use of the prayer mudra, Om symbol).

Many current forms of yoga embrace yoga culture and symbolism without a sense of its history or meaning, a phenomenon that is debated and challenged as cultural appropriation (a conversation beyond the scope of this chapter).

Integrating yoga culture into programming can give the impression that the practice is religious and/or spiritual (Jennings, 2015; Masters, 2014). It is important to share histories as histories within the appropriate developmental and educational contexts. But a growing body of research shows that using cultural artifacts or descriptive stories from historical cultures is not necessary for a school-based program to be effective. Anything that suggests religious significance in a practice should not be used without the appropriate context (Jennings, 2015). For school-based programs, cultural artifacts that are not exclusively historical (and presented as such) may create confusion regarding the secularity of a program or threaten to undermine secular programming. For example, teaching students about the use of mala beads within the context of a history class is significantly different from using them in practice.

Providers should consider the following questions related to cultural artifacts when planning and implementing school-based programs:

- Do any of the items I'm using have a spiritual or cultural significance that may be interpreted as connected to a religious tradition?
- Am I using language (such as Sanskrit) or music that contains religious references, or could be perceived as the language of a specific religion?
- Am I using items that are superfluous to the intended outcomes of the program, but are being retained for the sake of tradition or custom (such as mala beads), or items that have been overlooked (such as clothing with deities or religious symbols)?

Discovering vs. Prescribing Meaning

Secular programs can invite students to explore personal experience(s) with the practices while remaining aligned to legal mandates. But doing so successfully requires careful consideration and understanding. At the heart of a democratic education is the invitation to engage with a subject and to explore what it means to the learner. Vygotsky, whose theories underlie much of modern education, names the individual learner as an active agent in constructing meaning (Smidt, 2009). He points out that all people use tools to understand the world, and that we benefit from new tools when seeking to understand ourselves, our thoughts, and the world around us. We need new tools, such as painting, music, and language "in order to make clear to ourselves what we are thinking or contemplating" (Smidt, 2009, p. 34). Yoga and mindfulness can be such tools for learners.

Secular mindfulness and yoga programs *acknowledge, invite, and include the experience of the student*, rather than prescribing the meaning of the experience. Sharing the practices as a tool encourages learners to use them to discover meaning about themselves and the world they live in; this is a process of introspection and reflection.

When practices are non-secular, they can create barriers for student participation, decreasing or impeding access. While there is a common misconception that secularism promotes non-belief, an important distinction to make is that rather than promoting a position of *non-belief*, a secular approach invites students to bring their own belief system to the educational experience (Childress & Harper, 2015).

If we are to offer students the full benefits of programming, we must acknowledge yoga in particular as a practice of integration, not just a practice of physical exercise. Horton (2016) acknowledges the risk of speaking about the mind-body connection in schools, and the parallel need to find meaningful and accurate ways to do so. Individual practitioners and programs discussing the experience of yoga and mindfulness often use the word transformation. Providers of school-based programs may shy away from this conversation, feeling ill-equipped to explore this personal process in a reliably secular way. But failure to acknowledge the introspective experiences students may have can limit learning and positive outcomes, create confusion, and send mixed messages, diminishing the capacity to ensure secular programming. While finding the right language can be challenging, considering and expanding conversation on the topic of personal transformation is valuable.

Finally, secular programs can welcome the personal experience by positioning yoga and mindfulness as contemplative practices. Hyde and LaPrad (2015) point out that the goal of contemplative practice is to know through personal inquiry, not by being told what to believe. This acknowledgment of the role of and inclusion of personal inquiry into meaning is aligned to a secular approach to sharing practice.

Secular mindfulness and yoga invite inquiry into the meaning of the experience, just as a music course invites students to consider the meaning and significance of a discovery made while creating or listening to music, or as the study of history can invite students to explore their own experiences in a new context of understanding. The field of education provides a solid foundation for a secular framing in which to discuss transformative experience. Teaching mindfulness and yoga must provide the student agency in the creation of meaning, just as viewing art or reading powerful literature does. *Secular programs provide tools for inquiry and contemplation, not a set of beliefs, artifacts, or tools that unveil a prescribed truth.*

Do School-Based Programs Prioritize Access and Inclusion?

The first section of this chapter explored what it means to be secular. This second section addresses why it is important to be secular and explores the issues of access, inclusion, and legal imperatives.

Inclusive and accessible school-based programs respect diverse religious and nonreligious beliefs, maintain separation of church and state in principle and practice, and recognize religious equality before the law (Childress & Harper, 2015). This is consistent with the legal requirements of the First Amendment, which maintain religious neutrality in public schools and their associated activities (Childress & Harper, 2015; Jennings, 2016). Secularism maintains a separation between state and religious institutions recognizing religious equality before the law.

School-based mindfulness and yoga programs empower youth to embrace effective mind-body integration, self-regulation, and physical fitness using practices without the stress of negotiating religious and cultural values. Secular classes are equally appropriate and engaging for those of varied religious backgrounds, and for those coming from a position of non-belief. Because secularism maximizes inclusivity, this approach is recommended for private as well as public schools (Childress & Harper, 2015).

Providers seeking to create or expand programs in schools must consider how to maximize access and inclusion. Important questions to ask include:
- Will all students regardless of their religious background feel comfortable with the content in my class? If no, why?
- Would parents and family members, regardless of their religion, feel free to embrace practices without feeling conflict with their own beliefs?
- What specific aspects of my program might act as a barrier to participation for students and families from a variety of religious and cultural backgrounds?

How Can We Be Sure Our Teaching is Aligned with Legal Imperatives?

There is a legal imperative for school-based programs and teachers to comply with federal law. There is a growing body of case law that informs practice. Publicly funded schools in the United States must practice separation of church and state. Specifically, the Establishment Clause of the First Amendment prohibits public schools from advancing any particular religious belief over another, or over non-belief. The Free Exercise clause requires public schools to accommodate the religious beliefs and practices of teachers and students when such practices do not interfere with the daily operation of the school.

In 2013, a group of parents unsuccessfully sued the public school system in

Encinitas, California, because they believed that its district-wide yoga program was inherently religious and, therefore, unconstitutional (Cook-Cottone, et al., 2016; Childress & Harper, 2015; Masters, 2014). In 2015, the California Court of Appeals upheld the lower court's ruling that the Encinitas program was constitutional, stating "while the practice of yoga may be religious in some contexts, the classes in question were "devoid of any religious, mystical, or spiritual trappings" (Sedlock v. Baird, 2015).

It is important to note that in order to be considered constitutional, a government practice must pass the following requirements of the Lemon test:

1. the governmental practice must have a secular purpose,
2. the program's primary effect must be one that neither advances nor inhibits religion, and
3. the program must not foster an excessive government entanglement with religion (Lemon v. Kurtzman, 1971).

The following questions will help yoga providers reflect on the content and intention of their teaching to ensure their programming is consistent with legal imperatives:

- What are the intended outcomes of the programming? Is the purpose entirely secular?
- Does the programming have the effect of advancing or inhibiting religion? Does it pass the Lemon test?
- Are any of the teachers leading the programming giving the impression of supporting or inhibiting any religion?

Conclusions

Mindfulness and yoga providers working in schools have an obligation to recognize and uphold the principles of secularism and respect the diverse religious and nonreligious beliefs of the school community, both in principle and in practice (Childress & Harper, 2015). Secular mindfulness and yoga programming should be informed by and responsive to research, prioritize access and inclusion, not be religious or comprised of religious symbols, practices, or narratives. Secular programs must be aligned with legal imperatives and secular ethics.

Research shows that the effects of secular contemplative practices—postures, breath exercises, relaxation, and meditation—enhance the mind-body connection and give students tools for facing stress, enhancing their capacity for control over the physical body, emotions, and thoughts, and supporting overall physical well-being (Butzer, et al., 2016; Felver, et al., 2015; Khalsa, et al., 2012; Serwacki & Cook-Cottone, 2012).

Secular programming invites students to create meaning of their own as they learn and use the tools of the practice. Such transformative experiences have obvious merit. Failure to adhere to the key components of secularity in publicly funded schools threatens to undermine the success of the field and hinder access to practices that have positive effects on young people (Cook-Cottone et al., 2016).

This chapter is adapted with permission from work previously published by the International Journal of Yoga Therapy

Albrecht, N. (2014). Wellness: A conceptual framework for school-based mindfulness programs. *International Journal of Health, Wellness & Society, 4*(1), 21–36.

Baron, A., Evangelou, M., Malmberg, L. E., & Melendez-Torres, G. J. (2015). *The Tools of the Mind Curriculum for improving self-regulation in early childhood: A systematic review.* The Campbell Collaboration.

Bauder, D. (2015, April). Is yoga a religion? Courts say it is, but Encinitas schools have scrubbed their yoga programs clean. *San Diego Reader.*

Bolier, L., Haverman, M., Westerhof, G. J., Riper, H., Smit, F., & Bohlmeijer, E. (2013). Positive psychology interventions: a meta-analysis of randomized controlled studies. *BMC public health, 13,* 1.

Butzer, B., Bury, D., Telles, S., & Khalsa, S. B. S. (2016). Implementing yoga within the school curriculum: a scientific rationale for improving social-emotional learning and positive student outcomes. *Journal of Children's Services, 11*(1), 3–14.

Butzer, B., Ebert, M., Telles, S., & Khalsa, S. B. S. (2015). School-based yoga programs in the United States: a survey. *Advances in mind-body medicine, 29*(4), 18.

Cook-Cottone, C. P. (2017). Mindfulness and yoga in schools: A guide for teachers and practitioners. New York, NY. Springer

Cook-Cottone, C. P., Lemish, E., & Guyker, W. M. (2016). *Yoga is religion lawsuit: Phenomenological analysis of the Encinitas Union School District experience.* Yoga in the School Symposium (March, 2016). Kripalu, MA.

Childress, T., & Harper, J. C. (2015). *Best practices for yoga in the schools.* Rhinebeck, NY: Omega Institute, Yoga Service Council.

Crowther, J., & Martin, I. (2005). Twenty-first century Freire. *Adults Learning, 17*(2), 7–9.

Douglass, L. (2010). Yoga in the public schools: Diversity, democracy and the use of critical thinking in educational debates. *Religion & Education, 37,* 162–174.

Felver, J. C., Butzer, B., Olson, K. J., Smith, I. M., & Khalsa, S. B. S. (2015). Yoga in public school improves adolescent mood and affect. *Contemporary School Psychology, 19,* 184–192.

Freire, P. (2005). *Pedagogy of the oppressed* (30th anniversary ed.). New York, NY: The Continuum International Publishing Group.

Greenburg, M. T., & Mitra, J. L. (2015). From mindfulness to right mindfulness: The intersection of awareness and ethics. *Mindfulness, 6,* 74–78.

Harper, J. C. (2010). Teaching yoga in urban elementary schools. *International Journal of Yoga Therapy, 20,* 99–109.

Horton, C. (2016). Mind-body integration and progressive education. *Yoga, the Body, and Embodied Social Change: An Intersectional Feminist Analysis, 109.*

Hyde, A. M., & LaPrad, J. G. (2015). Mindfulness, democracy, and education. *Democracy & Education, 23*(2), 1–12.

Jennings, P. A. (2016). Mindfulness-based programs and the American public school system: Recommendations for best practices to ensure secularity. *Mindfulness, 7,* 176–178.

Karpov, Y. V. (2014). *Vygotsky for educators*. New York, NY: Cambridge University Press.

Khalsa, S. B. S., & Butzer, B. (2016). Yoga in school settings: A research review. *Annals of the New York Academy of Sciences, 1373*(1), 45–55.

Khalsa, S. B. S., Hickey-Schultz, L., Cohen, D., Steiner, N., & Cope, S. (2012). Evaluation of the mental health benefits of yoga in a secondary school: a preliminary randomized controlled trial. *The Journal of Behavioral Health Services & Research, 39*(1), 80–90.

Lemon v. Kurtzman (1971). 403 U.S. 602 [29 L.Ed.2d 745, 91 S.Ct. 2105].

Levenson, M. R., Aldwin, C. M., & Igarashi, H. (2013). Religious development from adolescence to middle adulthood (pp. 183–197). In Eds. R. F. Paloutzian & C. L. Park. *Handbook of the Psychology of Religion and Spirituality, 2nd ed*. New York, NY: The Guilford Press.

Religion. In *Merriam-Webster's Online Dictionary*. https://www.merriam-webster.com/ Retrieved 12/2017.

Mind and Life Education Research Network (MLERN), Davidson, R. J., Dunne, J., Eccles, J. S., Engle, A., Greenberg, M., Jennings, P. A., Jha, A., Jinpa, T., Lantieri, L., Meyers, D., Roeser, R. W., & Vago, D. (2012). Contemplative practices and mental training: prospects for American education. *Child Development Perspectives, 6*, 146–153.

Parker, P. (1999). Evoking the spirit in public education. Retrieved from http://www.couragerenewal.org/parker/writings/evoking-the-spirit

Palmer, P. (1997). *The courage to teach: Exploring the inner landscape of a teacher's life*. San Francisco, CA: Jossey-Bass.

Sedlock v. Baird, (2015). 235 Cal. App. 4th 874 (Ct. App. 2015).

Serwacki, M., & Cook-Cottone, C. (2012). Yoga in the schools: a systematic review of the literature. *International journal of yoga therapy, 22*, 101–110.

Stephens, M. (2010). *Teaching yoga: Essential foundations and techniques*. Berkeley, CA: North Atlantic Books.

Smidt, S. (2009). Introducing Vygotsky: A guide for practitioners and students in early years education. New York, NY: Routledge.

Smidt, S. (2014). Introducing Freire: A guide for students, teachers, and practitioners. New York, NY: Routledge.

Stuchul, D. L. (2006). The soul of education: Helping students find connection, compassion, and character at school. *Encounter, 19*(3), 54–56.

Tanyi, R. A. (2002). Towards clarification of the meaning of spirituality. *Journal of Advanced Nursing, 39*(5), 500–509.

Vygotsky, L. S. (1962). *Thought and language*. Russia.

PART 2

GET STARTED

FROM YOUR ROLE

WITHIN A SCHOOL

CHAPTER 12

Working on Your Mental Game in Physical Education Class

Monica Claridge

Physical Education Teacher, East Elementary, Kodiak, AK

ON A SUMMER NIGHT IN JUNE OF 2013, while driving home exhausted from a basketball tournament with a fellow referee, my heart began racing. My hands were shaking while tightly clutching the steering wheel and fear shot through me like a lightning bolt. Sweat began to form on my brow, my hands were clammy, and I felt faint. I guzzled my diet Mountain Dew hoping it would revive me enough to power through the last few miles home. When my field of vision narrowed, I began to think I was having a heart attack. I pulled over and called 9-1-1. My entire world caved in, never to be the same.

The arrival of the EMTs was momentarily reassuring. They ran a battery of tests and determined I was experiencing a panic attack. One of the men slyly remarked that I should reserve 9-1-1 calls for "real emergencies" as he walked away. Those words still sting as much today as they did six years ago.

My friend took over driving and when she dropped me off, I collapsed on my bed. I was exhausted, but did not sleep more than a few minutes at a time for days on end. My doctor prescribed different medications to help me sleep, one after another. When the last pill led me to such despair that suicidal thoughts began to creep into my mind, I knew I needed help.

At my mother's suggestion, I met with a psychiatrist and was diagnosed with generalized anxiety disorder and prescribed purposeful medication. That night, I slept soundly for the first time in nearly a month. I also began seeing a therapist and told her I just wanted to "be me" again. It was as if the real me had been kidnapped and I was having an out of body experience. I was a former collegiate basketball coach who had to be driven by my parents to and from a teaching job I could barely hold onto.

The therapist recommended, *Wherever You Go, There You Are* by Jon Kabat-Zinn. I delved into it wholeheartedly, willing to try anything at this point as I did not want to be on high-powered medication. To my surprise, as I began to implement the mindfulness practices and suggestions, I slowly began to feel "human" again. Completing simple tasks such as brushing my teeth, washing the dishes, and playing with my sweet pup, utilizing all my senses, slowly led to more time spent in the present moment. As my personal practice developed, so did my peace of mind, and I gradually began to "return to me" and was able to wean off the medication.

Taking What Helped Me to My Students

It was at this time one of my elementary students was diagnosed with a stress-related illness and was no longer medically cleared to participate in my physical education classes. Also, I began to become aware of unsolicited comments in conversations with other students—words and phrases indicating stress they were facing from academic, peer, and family pressures and challenges.

This got my wheels turning. Wouldn't it be great if I could teach my students stress management skills they could pull from their toolbox when needed? Through my research, I found Mindful Schools, a fabulous organization that provides training to teach mindfulness to students. I enrolled in their Mindfulness Fundamentals and the ensuing Mindful Educator Essentials Courses.

My challenge then became how could I, an elementary physical education teacher, teach my students the practice of mindfulness while also doing justice to my required curriculum? And would my administrators be open to this?

Mindful Schools has a presentation and curriculum I shared with my administrator, who was open to the implementation in bite-sized lessons. Soon after though, I left that Florida school for one on Kodiak Island, Alaska. Over 70% of my students (215) receive free and reduced lunch and many have experienced trauma because of absentee parents, addiction, and deployed caretakers (the largest Coast Guard base in the country is on Kodiak Island). My students needed the tools, but they needed them to be taught in a trauma-informed manner.

I started out cautiously, initially simply ending my PE classes with a mindful minute. These short activities help my students transition from physical activity back into the classroom. I facilitate them at their squad spots after our drink and before lining up. I created a list of various deep breathing techniques for children and randomly pick ones for them to try. Student favorites include Blowing Out the Candles and Hot Chocolate Breath. I also encourage my students to create their own deep breathing techniques based on their interests. Two books that provide additional breathing techniques are *AlphaBreaths* and *Breathe Like a Bear*, which my students here on Kodiak Island, home of the Kodiak Brown Bear, find very relatable.

Expanding the Practice

I came across two resources to facilitate my mindful minute with activities beyond just breathing:

- *The Mindful Games Activity Cards: 55 Fun Ways to Share Mindfulness with Kids and Teens* created by Susan Kaiser Greenland and Annaka Harris; these cards offer playful activities that improve student focus and attention skills.
- *Mindful Kids: 50 Mindfulness Activities for Kindness, Focus and Calm* written by Whitney Stewart and Mina Braun; these cards are more tailored to younger children ages 4 and up. They contain simple scripts for activities that engage students in practice, providing multiple options with minimal prep.

Transitions to the classroom became increasingly positive as a result of the mindful minute and teachers became curious about mindfulness. Many borrowed my resources to use in their classrooms. After continued comments, questions, and general interest, I approached my administration and was given permission to implement the Mindful Schools curriculum as part of my physical education classes.

I presented an overview of the curriculum to the staff and PTA, led them in some practices, and provided them with resources to supplement the lessons I was using. I focused on the secularity of the practice, making sure to use the word "practice" or "sit," as well as various bells and a vibratone instead of a singing bowl. I also shared articles about mindful parenting and the research behind the practices.

As I teach the curriculum, I work to make it my own and relate it to physical education as well as to life. Using real-life examples, such as videos about sports figures like Lebron James, Kobe Bryant, Derek Jeter, and teams like the New York Knicks, Seattle Seahawks, Chicago Cubs, and the US Women's National Soccer Team, helps my students embrace the practice.

I have a specific mindfulness day for each class. On that day, we skip our warm-up and play one of their favorite games for half of the class, get drinks, and meet at the middle circle to do our mindfulness lesson. I don't force the issue with my students. As long as they are respectful and allow others to focus, I ignore other behaviors. Disengagement does not necessarily mean they are not benefiting from the time and practice.

Some Student Favorites

My students love props and the opportunity to lead exercises themselves. The Hoberman Sphere is a great tool to help students breathe—breathe in as the sphere expands and breathe out as it retracts. Different bells and a vibratone provide renewed enthusiasm for mindful listening.

The Eerie Orb/UFO Ball (a ping-pong-sized ball that lights up and makes a warbling sound when both electrodes are touched simultaneously) is an excellent tool to teach how our words and actions affect each other and the importance of being kind and caring. When everyone is connected (holding hands or even just touching pinkies), it lights up and makes the warbling sound. When one student lets go, it stops, showing that the words and actions of one individual can impact the entire class, positively or negatively.

I incorporate practices from *Master of Mindfulness: How to be Your Own Superhero in Times of Stress*, written by Laurie Grossman, Angelina Alvarez, and Mr. Musumeci's 5th-grade students in Oakland, California. The students share examples of how mindfulness helps them be confident, calm, focused, and to rely on their own inner strength to handle challenging situations in everyday life. Hearing about when and how those students used mindfulness helped my students transfer the practice from the classroom to the playground and beyond.

In the book, the students share the shark fin to help them focus on something or start a mindfulness practice. To do the shark fin, you place your thumb on your forehead with your fingers all together pointing up like a fin. Then you move your hand slowly down the middle of your face to the center of your chest while whispering, "Shhhhh." The shark fin is also a reminder of the five Ss: sit/stand up straight, sit/stand still, sit/stand silently, softly breathe, and shut your eyes if that feels comfortable. (Grossman & Alvarez, 2016, p. 6).

Students can be seen using the shark fin throughout school and many teachers commented on the impact it has on their students. Prior to the performance of our school-wide play, one teacher saw students in the green room putting on their shark fins to calm and center themselves for their production.

A 2nd-grade teacher, Peggy Demmert, said this about the shark fin: "Using deep breathing with my students to calm and refocus them wasn't new to me, but the shark fin was a new approach. I liked the way it brought everyone together in a more uniform way. It also gave independence to the students so they could do the shark fin without my direct leading. Definitely worked with my class when we needed to refocus." Several parents mentioned to me that their child uses the shark fin at home, most of whom acted "too cool" for the practice in class.

My Learning

Just as mindfulness is emerging in the field of education, the practice is emerging in my gym/classroom. Brené Brown suggests we, "Lean into the discomfort of the work." Last year was my first year teaching mindfulness to my students so I leaned in often. The individuals who are a part of Mindful School's Mindful Educator

Community Facebook group were invaluable resources when I had questions, or needed additional resources, as I am one of only a few individuals on the island with any experience of the practice.

Often, I was unsure of how the concepts and lessons were going to be received and questioned myself. In times like this, my personal practice is what centered and focused me, enabling me to do the work and lead by example. As I continue teaching mindfulness practices, I believe my presence is as powerful as the lessons; my students get to witness mindfulness in action. My awareness continues to increase as I become even more cognizant of my thoughts, words, and actions. This teacher is truly learning right along with her students.

Moving forward, I'm planning to record and share my lessons with staff so everybody can view them at their leisure. I will be expanding my basic mindfulness lessons to cover topics like "I" statements, coping skills, the growth mindset, and setting goals mindfully. We will be referring to this as 'working on our mental game'. I will shift my focus to a more school-wide approach.

I will be offering Mindful Mornings once a week for staff members prior to the start of the day. Our daily morning announcements will begin with a script for a mindful moment. I will schedule Family Mindfulness Nights periodically so caregivers can learn and practice these skills alongside their children. It is the hope that, in time, we can create a truly mindful community in which administrators, staff, students, and caregivers alike, embrace the practice.

As I ponder advice for those just starting down this beautiful path, I say keep on trekking one step, one breath, one minute, one practice, one conversation, one meeting, one presentation, one lesson at a time. Be kind to yourself. Often our biggest victories and acts of courage emerge from our greatest struggles.

I used to curse that fateful day I had my first panic attack and beat myself up for not being able to "overcome" my anxiety, but today I am forever grateful. It is because of my personal struggles, including that panic attack, that I am now equipping my students with the skills they need to succeed with self-compassion. The journey has not been an easy one, but it has led me right where I need to be.

Grossman, L., & Alvarez, A. (2016). *Master of mindfulness: How to be your own superhero in times of stress*. Oakland, CA: New Harbinger Publications.

CHAPTER 13

Speech and Language Pathology Meets Yoga and Mindfulness

Candice Lynn Davies

Former Speech and Language Pathologist, Owner, Integrity Movement Studio, Cary, NC, Author/Illustrator, *DharmaDinos*

MY NAME IS CANDICE DAVIES AND I'M A YOGA TEACHER, owner of Integrity Movement Studio and the creator of DharmaDinos. I work with all ages in North Carolina, but the bulk of my caseload has been with youth, many of whom have sensory processing, ADHD and/or anxiety disorders. This is my second career.

My first? A Speech & Language Pathologist (SLP) who worked primarily with the public schools. It was a wonderful career, but in my 26th year, I became an unhappy casualty of teacher burnout. I was not alone, joining a depressingly long line of many fine but exhausted peers.

You've heard the stories and may even be facing these scenarios in your own work: tsunamis of paperwork, pressure-cooker testing demands, hour-gobbling IEP meetings, unmanageable caseloads, an increasing number of hats to wear, and too-often bruising social and emotional encounters. Not surprisingly, the U.S. rate of teacher burnout is currently at unprecedented and epidemic proportions. This is a heartbreaking and unsustainable reality.

During my final year in the schools, the brightest spots involved my integration of rudimentary yoga forms, basic breathing techniques and other mindfulness practices into my therapy. Admittedly, it began as much for my own rattled mind as for my students, but I quickly realized that they and their teachers needed it as much as I did. Here are three simple examples as well as two uncomfortable questions that led me away from schools for a bit.

Fill & Chill

I began with very simple breathing techniques. An immediate favorite was Fill & Chill: Pretend your hand is a balloon. Begin with a fist, then inhale slowly while extending your fingers. Slowly exhale while gradually pulling in one finger at a time, back to the fist. This easy technique quickly calmed the room, and students began reminding their teacher, or lecturing their friends, "Hey, let's Fill & Chill." This demonstration of kids independently attempting to modulate their state, was powerful. And it beautifully flipped the narrative that mindfulness is a way for teachers to calm down their students. These youngsters were intervening on their own behalves! And I learned later, delightedly, that my pull-out students were asking their regular classrooms for Fill & Chills!

> Relative to therapy: I began using this at the beginning of all of my sessions and letting kids call for it as they needed. The shift was significant in terms of both my students' attention and application, and my own engagement. Therapeutically, this activity can be exploited in all the lovely ways SLPs do: What does 'inhale' mean (vocabulary). What happens to our body when we breathe in? (concepts/ research and problem-solving, organizational thinking). What would it be like to have balloons for hands? (imagination, deduction, hypothesis). What are three things that start with the same first letter as 'balloon'? (literacy).

B3

A breath management technique that also engages gross motor and state management is B3 (Balloon, Bounce, and Bees).

Capitalizing on the balloon analogy, our entire body is mobilized. Students gather on a mat or in a circle, standing, but drooped into a boneless forward fold. The leader calls out *INHALE SLOWLY* while modeling a slow inflation toward standing as they breathe in. As kids follow, the leader calls out *EXHALE* while quickly emptying most of the air and drooping partially back down.

This cycle repeats with the body becoming increasingly upright each time. On the final breath, everyone has full balloon bodies with their arms outstretched, standing tall, and on tip-toes. Balloons begin to lift off and float slowly around their mat.

As kids demonstrate emotional regulation and respectful body awareness, they can float around the room, very gently bouncing off of each other. To end the exercise, the leader plays the part of a bumblebee, gently popping balloons, which then zig-zag slowly back to their mats, onto their backs, and ready for relaxation. Once kids get this, they will want to lead!

> Relative to therapy: I began by closing sessions with this and it proved to be a huge motivator. If we weren't moving quickly enough through our work, I would note it and ask, "Do you think we're gonna need a shorter Fill and Chill, instead of 3B?" The answer was most often, "No!" with an increase in effort [grin]. Eventually, it became an actual lesson frame.

Again, it's endless the ways in which you can press home objectives in this activity: How does the world look from way up here? (hypothesis, abstract thinking). Can you repeat that using the smooth speech skills we've been practicing? (fluency). Tell me three reptiles you spy from the air? (categorization). How are balloon and globe alike/ different? (analysis, compare/ contrast). When you begin allowing students to lead, wonderful social communication skills begin to emerge.

Yo-yo Roll

A significant part of my caseload with the schools was in Special Education classrooms, largely comprised of kids with sensory processing issues. I got the idea of Yo-yo Roll from the works of Temple Grandin, who turned our ideas about Asperger's upside down.

Students lay down at the end—and perpendicular to—their mat, and allow you to slowly roll them up inside. Some like it loose and some like it tight. They can stay inside as long as they like and you'll be surprised how long some stay. When they signal that they're ready to unspool, the teacher slowly pulls the open end of the mat, allowing the student to roll out. Some like it fast, some like it slow, and some like it back and forth like a yo-yo before finally unspooling.

> Relative to therapy: A lot of communication is involved in this activity including making requests, clarification of communication breakdown and giving directions, and the experience is exquisite for students' grounding into the moment and their immediate sensory experiences: How tight do you want it? Why? What feels best? How long do you want to stay? How fast do you want to unroll? Yo-yo or no? Why do you like it that way better? Where did it feel hottest/ coolest/ tightest? Kids are developing body and kinetic awareness as they learn to communicate how to get their individualized sensory needs met. In addition to putting the onus of communication on the students, it puts kids in the position of dictating to YOU what's going to happen and that is always a win-win.

> Again, uber-easy to deploy communication goals while kids are cocooned. Just get on with your goals: What is wrong with this sentence: Five dogs comed to my house? (irregular past tense). Tell me three things that start with the letter 'r' and be sure to curl your tongue as we've practiced (articulation). You may find, like me, that you do entire sessions with your students cocooned.

Two Uncomfortable Questions

The not-so-surprising result was seeing a myriad of benefits in my augmented therapy: improved and maintained attention for longer periods of time, improved emotional regulation, expanded self-awareness, faster acquisition of goals and objectives, and more joyful engagement—for both me and my students.

The unanticipated result was that questions began pestering me. Were my kids showing this more joyful engagement because they were making greater gains on their communication skills or was it the other way around? While I was increasingly content in my actual sessions, I continued to struggle with my overall public school experience. Was my discontent because the workload and institution of the schools were increasingly toxic or was it the other way around?

Concurrently, in my studio, I was witnessing some startling responses by students. Several children who began sessions with a diagnosis of selective mutism were unfolding in spectacular ways. Ditto with kids with a diagnosis of Asperger's and most strikingly, anxiety disorders. Certainly, this was explainable to a significant degree by the longer intervention periods, the engagement of parents in the actual classes and their carryover at home, the low language-loading of the yoga and mindfulness experiences, and the equalized playing field of a non-competitive arena.

But here's the thing: We were not doing communication therapy aside from the ways it may have leaked into my can't-help-being-a-SLP presentation. Studio classes were just yoga and mindfulness yet communication and social skills were sky-rocketing. Not only were the kids responding in grand ways, but they were forming friendships with each other, and so were their parents. That moved out of the studio and into their everyday lives. My public school therapeutic interventions, generally limited to two 30-minute sessions a week, never cranked up that kind of transformation.

Knocking on Doors to Find a School Mindfulness Champion

So I retired from the public school and devoted my time to studio work, which was awesome and gave me time to play, observe, refine and study. The results were rewarding and gratifying in uncountable ways, but I kept coming back to teacher burn-out statistics and the social and emotional deficits that are at crescendo levels across our schools, our nation, the world. The World Health Organization has now formally recognized worker burnout as a legitimate medical condition (ICD-11). Among their recommendations are practices like yoga and mindfulness. It doesn't matter what our bailiwicks are, these practices are going to make us happier, more resilient and more productive.

So in 2015, I began knocking on the public schools' doors and after nearly two years I met my first school mindfulness champion, an inspiring woman who also happened to be the superintendent of a local school district. She invited me to do an educational presentation for her area principals. The presentation was 2.5 hours long and introduced the history of yoga and mindfulness, tightly aligning to educational impacts while stressing the science and research. Sixty-three principals attended, many arriving with arms folded and eyes rolling. Yeah, some left unconvinced, but several wanted more information, inviting me to present on their campuses. And the ball was rolling.

Within two years we had six schools, elementary through high school, actively pursuing yoga and/or mindfulness programs and we organized our first mindfulness conference. We have a district-wide professional learning network (PLN), folks in training to lead their campus mindfulness teams. The ride's been FUNtastic, albeit plenty bumpy.

Yoga and mindfulness have really only gained credibility traction in the last decade and integrating them into the public schools is a fledgling venture, too often led by a single individual, not seasoned educators, and based on personality and anecdotal information. It is rare to find folks with the necessary educational and personal practice experiences. At the same time, mindfulness is a new hot topic and folks are crawling out of the woodwork purporting to be experts in a field they likely knew nothing about six months ago. I counsel my schools to put program implementation on the back burner and to first cultivate a cohort of folks with strong educational underpinnings and developed, personal practices.

To that end, we now have over thirty teachers pursuing the Mindfulness Fundamentals course with Mindful Schools. I am a HUGE advocate for this organization and actively promote their work. Their resources are phenomenal, research-driven and educationally focused, and they are leaders in the field.

Because I am a graduate of Mindful Schools and a mentor for the schools I work with, I'm fortunate to be able to offer significant discounts to our local cohort on what are already remarkably inexpensive trainings. That has helped us and I rest happily in the knowledge that our leaders will be well educated and cultivating strong personal practices. It's already yielding dividends as our cohort members report shifts in their thinking and more skillful ways of dealing with the stressors of school.

Next Steps and Final Observations

The next and larger task will be to choose a mindfulness-based SEL curriculum and implement a school-wide, curriculum-integrated, mindfulness, yoga and SEL program. My guess is that it will begin in a few classrooms, with our cohort members leading. There are strong curriculum candidates out there, immediately imple-mentable and not requiring our already-overworked teachers the lengthy task of re-inventing wheels. After two years of research, my personal favorite and current recommendation is Empowering Education.

Empowering Education is a nonprofit organization that offers an inclusive cur-riculum that blends the best of mindfulness, cognitive behavioral theory, and neu-roscience. It includes guided lesson plans that are directly aligned with Common Core Standards, 21st Century Student Learning Outcomes, and CASEL's 5 Core Competencies. In addition to clearly articulated lessons, they provide academic extensions for other school content areas, video tutorials featuring classroom foot-age and modeled instruction, topic links and resources, and daily take-home liter-ature for parents.

In summary, we're in the nascent phase. We've got a great cohort, all currently in training with an excellent organization. We've been lucky in that our principals are fully on board. I am currently chewing on how we can bring community leaders and parents into the training and implementation. We are constantly refining and adjusting. As I was once told by a lovely Tanzanian many years ago, as I struggled with altitude sickness, "Pulee pulee, mamma." One step, one step.

I'll leave you with a few final observations and some links to mindfulness and SLP literature.

1. First and foremost, do your practice. Your practice is what, ultimately, makes you an authentic communicator and model for your students and clients, not to mention the myriad benefits that your practice will bring you!

2. Study, read, learn. Research in these domains is exploding and we should all be in download mode. You will be staggered by all that research is revealing.

3. Do not fall prey to the common practice of overstating what yoga and mindful-ness practices can do. Excitement is grand. Outrageous and uninformed claims are toxic.

4. Critically important and perhaps the most challenging as we talk to educators: please avoid peddling these practices as behavior control programs for kids. Mindfulness is not about controlling our or others' behaviors. Ever. It is about empowering folks with the skills to more skillfully and compassionately face life. Yeah, behaviors will likely improve, but our goal is skillful, mindful, com-passionately realized lives.

5. Don't stop knocking. You never know where you'll meet your champions.

Mindfulness practices for communication science and disorders students:
https://www.ncbi.nlm.nih.gov/pubmed/28776062

Mindfulness and stuttering:
https://www.sciencedirect.com/science/article/pii/S0094730X11000386

Mindfulness and aphasia:
https://content.iospress.com/articles/neurorehabilitation/nre1323

Mindfulness and voice therapy:
https://www.sciencedirect.com/science/article/abs/pii/S0892199705802395

CHAPTER 14

A Mindfulness-Based Alternative to Detention

Jennifer Haston-Maciejewski, RYT-200

Special Education Teacher, Greenfield-Central High School, Greenfield, IN, Founder, Stop.Breathe.Be

"You never know what a kid is dealing with, this class could teach him to calm down and really help him with his mind. If he's like me, it will help him shut up his noisy mind."—Student after attending mindfulness classes

I JUMPED UP FROM MY DESK, trying to catch him in the act just like last week. He hurriedly clicked away from his virtual comic book, "What?! I'm working on my paper!" I looked over his shoulder to see a blank document with a blinking cursor —just as blank as it was thirty-five minutes ago. "Just focus and get to work!" I said sternly. "Focus on what? I'm not here because I don't get my homework done, I'm here for punching a kid. I'm here, why can't I do what I freaking want?"

He was here last week for yelling at his teacher.

I slumped back in my desk thinking about this form of discipline and how there had to a better way. Ideally, three hours of detention on a Friday night should work. And it does work . . . on some kids. But what about those frequent flyers- kids who keep coming back? The kids who spend every Friday at the school staring at a wall or pretending to do work?

In order for us to decide that a form of discipline like detention is working and making a difference in a student's life, we must look at its effect. In order for us to say it works, the rate of referrals should decline. The student should be learning from their mistakes. If this form of discipline is working—why are the same kids sitting in the same seats week after week?

This was the birth of my interest in bringing mindfulness into schools for kids who had discipline issues. And when I started at an ED-Alternative school and saw a student spit on a teacher and scream, "FU, IDIOT. I DON'T CARE ABOUT YOU," it solidified my desire to try another tactic.

A Revelation and Some Research

What works for one student, doesn't necessarily work for all students. Sometimes we meet that one kid that makes us wonder why we even decided to go into teaching to begin with. But then we remember that this kid is just a product of his environment. He has been through trauma and, as we know, trauma has certain neurological effects on a brain—especially a young one. Before we can expect any learning to take place, we have to regulate the nervous system.

More often than not, negative responses to stress are unconscious, impulsive and automatic responses born out of anger, anxiety, or sometimes simply boredom. Stress can often manifest itself in physiological responses. Any kid who has suffered from the toxic stress of trauma can quickly and inexplicably become either hyper-aroused (reckless, explosive, and irritable) or hypo-aroused (go into shutdown mode or become zombie-esque).

Many teachers can relate with pulling out their best calm teacher voice saying something like, "Hey, I know, buddy, let's play with this stress ball," or trying to coax a student into a timeout, calm-down corner. But what happens when you're all out of ideas and your student isn't responding to anything you do—no matter how creative and "Pinteresting" it is?

It was in that moment it hit me. I had been teaching yoga and mindfulness meditation to adults for years. I even had my own yoga studio and a slew of Instagram followers. I was already teaching older kids who got themselves into trouble. What if we taught our youngest members of society the emotional regulation and coping skills needed to be successful students and successful people? What if we taught kids how to pay attention and how to focus? What if we taught kids how to be kind to others and themselves? What if we taught kids how to take that pause between stimulus and action? What if we taught our kids how to just be alone in their own minds?

Some of our kids learn these things over the course of growing up with attentive, loving adults in their lives; other kids don't. Traditional education teaches important skills such as literacy and numeracy; however, it doesn't necessarily create compassionate members of society and/or mindful leaders. Working in schools—and now specifically with students that have emotional disabilities—I realize that kids don't know what they haven't been taught. As educators, adults, and parents, we often expect, tell, and even demand that young people "sit still," "settle down," "pay attention," "take a deep breath," and "focus." However, they've never been taught to do these things—even adults struggle with these ordinary skills.

So I went home that night and dug in. What I found was surprising: here I am thinking I am on to something great and it turns out there have been studies going on for years! Research suggests the benefits of adopting a mindfulness-based curriculum for classrooms are profoundly transformative because students learn to focus their attention, become less reactive, and learn to be more compassionate with themselves and others – ultimately leading students to a more engaging and fulfilling life of lower stress and anxiety.

I came upon these statistics from the Children's Defense Fund (2010),

- once every second, a child is suspended;
- every eleven seconds, a high school student drops out;
- every twenty seconds, a student is corporally punished;
- every three hours, a child or teen is killed by a firearm;
- every five hours, a child or teen commits suicide;
- and every six hours, a child or teen dies of abuse or neglect.

These statistics are alarming. Parents, teachers, and schools must do better. Students are not being taught the adequate skills to help alleviate the normal stress of their everyday modern lives. Mindfulness cannot stop stressful events from happening, but it can aid in students' abilities to cope.

I Had the Power, Permission, and Program. Now What?

I went to my administration with as much information, courage, and positivity that I could muster. I had a whole speech prepared. I walked in and after a few minutes of talking, I had the go-ahead. They were going to let me start a voluntary mindfulness program!

During my research phase, I came across a mindfulness program by Amy Saltzman called *A Still Quiet Place*. I looked at so many other options, but hers just kept speaking to me. It has sample dialogues, worksheets, and different exercises so there was no need to reinvent the wheel. I especially appreciated the focus on kindness and curiosity.

As a teacher of students who struggle with emotional regulation, I really believe in allowing kids the freedom to have different moods, but also in giving them the tools to help them not be *overcome* by their moods. My students' ability to think before they act is limited, and mindfulness is a tool that helps improve this ability. Teaching mindfulness in schools trains the brains of students to be less reactive. With training, students are better able to regulate their emotions—to take that pause before reacting and find out the why behind their moods and often destructive outbursts.

My plan was to systematically teach young adults coping strategies, time management skills, anger management/self-control, how to value themselves and others, and empathy. Often I would come in with a plan and it would just turn into allowing students to talk about their feelings. Sometimes just getting them to name their true emotions was the difference-maker. Like my hero Fred Rogers, the OG of SEL, said, "Anything that's human is mentionable, and anything that is mentionable can be more manageable. When we can talk about our feelings, they become less overwhelming, less upsetting, and less scary."

Participation in the program was voluntary and in many cases, we were able to reduce the initial severity of the discipline if students opted into the class. Office referral rates went down by 40%. It also took the place of a student staring at a wall pretending to work; aka, traditional detention. We received praise from parents for finding solutions instead of just placing blame and doling out punishments. Teachers noted that the students who were frequent office referrals were using breathing techniques and asking to take a mindful walk to cool down.

Student Buy-In

I was quite aware that these kids were just saying yes to my program to get out of work or detention, and I was okay with that. The hardest hurdle was taking a bunch of tough, sad, angry, sometimes emotionally-disturbed teenagers, who rarely trusted adults, and getting them to buy-in. I had to gain their trust before they would even begin to take me seriously. When I said, "Close your eyes, inhale through your nose and exhale with a sigh while you allow your body to sink into the floor," they snickered and looked around to see if anybody was laughing at how dumb they looked. After a gentle reminder to be open and respectful, students would one by one start to settle in.

Since participation in class activities was voluntary, some students were using it as a way to get out of the boring, more traditional detention. Quickly, however, students started to realize how calm they felt after they took part in our mindfulness meditations. Students were talking about the class in their other classrooms. Parents were emailing me asking if their students could sit in on the next class. Kids were coming to the class after school just to "chill out" before they went home for the weekend.

With a targeted curriculum, proper communication, and selected implementation, we were able to offer classes such as time management, empathy, anger management/self-control, and valuing yourself and others. The assistant principal would often assign students the class that corresponded with their negative behavior choices. Instead of getting an in-school suspension for punching a student, he would sometimes assign the student the next three anger management mindfulness classes.

At the beginning of each Friday Night School (3-hour detention on Friday nights), the assistant principal and I would go into the room and tell them a little about the mindfulness class and invite them to come. Each class was an hour-long.

Occasionally, I would offer one-on-one classes for students who agreed to take the class in lieu of suspension. After a couple of months, the "detention frequent flyers" were changing their behavior and students were asking if they could come to the class without getting in trouble!

Each class starts with a reminder that the only rule we have is to be open and respectful—we then discuss as a group what that looks like. Students are then given a half sheet of paper with prepared questions on them that have to do with our lesson – sometimes this is as simple as: why are you here and what do you hope to get out of this class? We then move into a quick 3–5 minute meditation just to set the stage and calm our minds. Then we begin our lesson for the day.

Some days lessons look like group time just chatting, other times we do yoga or an activity. We close with another 3–5 minutes of meditation. We then fill out the backside of the half sheet of paper, which has a survey: What would you do differently knowing what you learned today? I want students to reflect on their behavior and theoretically be able to apply what they learned. I always end the survey with the yes or no question: Do you need to talk more? Some students just need to feel heard. As we know, negative behavior can sometimes be a cry for help or a student reaching out, I didn't want to miss any opportunity to help a kid in need.

> *"Many of our students and parents appreciated that we were trying to help instead of just punish. The time a student told me she learned breathing techniques that helped her when she got angry reminded me that sometimes we assume kids know coping mechanisms, but in reality, they were never taught and we shouldn't assume they were taught. I know some of our kids like Tina* appreciated the ability to talk through things. That's how she deals with issues, and it gave her an open safe place to do so."*—James Bishir, Assistant Principal, Manchester Jr/Sr High School

The Place to Start is With Yourself

Teachers are confronted, sometimes daily, with disruptive behaviors in the classroom. Some of us work with students who are kicked out of school for flipping tables and punching other teachers. If we haven't been cussed out or had to dodge a flying textbook—it's likely been a good day. Our calm demeanor, compassion, loving-kindness, and willingness to see the good in even the most volatile of students may be the difference between a student who has hope and learns resiliency, and one who continues to hate himself and his whole world.

If you are reading this, you are obviously ready to dive into the world of mindfulness. Or maybe you already have and you are ready to pioneer a program in your school. Remember the place to start is with yourself. It's hard to teach something we know nothing about. Trust me, there have been times in my life that I have had to "fake it til I make it." Teaching mindfulness cannot be one of those times.

Until you have come face to face with the emotions that live inside you; until you know how rage, anger, sadness, jealousy, excitement, and anxiety can fester and manifest inside your body; until you know the physical sensations each emotion brings; until you've visited that calm inside your own mind, and you're familiar with the voice of peace and reason within yourself, you cannot teach others about it.

A dysregulated adult cannot calm a dysregulated child. Start with yourself so you can model that regulation for your students. This includes sharing in the moment when you are self-regulating so that students can see the power of the tools you are teaching them in real-time. Sometimes you'll even find that your students become your teacher.

Recently, I was frustrated because technology was failing, yet again, and one of my students with emotional disabilities and Autism, told me to take a deep breath because I was starting to get grumpy. When I took a weak inhale, he looked at me compassionately and calmly said, "No, look at me, that wasn't a deep breath, you need to breathe deeper, into your belly, like you taught us," and then he modeled a belly breath. This kid, who I was told would probably never learn the skills he needs to be in a general education setting with his peers, saw what I needed to cope with my frustration and coached me through it.

As I said at the start, in order for us to decide that something is working and making a difference in a student's life, we must look at its effect. In order for us to say it is effective, it has to work. At The Catamount Center in Greenfield, Indiana, we have found that mindfulness works.

CHAPTER 15

Creating a Semester-Long High School Course in Mindfulness

Michelle A. Martin, MEd, IMTA

Certified Mindfulness Teacher and French Teacher, Brebeuf Jesuit Preparatory School, Indianapolis, IN

As a child of seven, I clearly remember my teacher asking me what I wanted to do when I grew up. I proudly and confidently replied, "I will be a teacher." As I grew up and went through the difficult adolescent years, my desire to teach never wavered, but I did add a disclaimer to my passion for teaching: "Not in high school." Life has a funny way of leading you to where it wants you to make your mark because I just happily completed my twenty-sixth year of teaching—in high school.

Those twenty-six years of teaching French have flown by and I have had the privilege of working with a beautiful rainbow of teenagers from differing socio-economic levels, racial, ethnic, religious and spiritual backgrounds, sexual orientation and gender identities, and personal life experiences. Currently, I work in a Jesuit Catholic college preparatory school in Indianapolis, Indiana. We have a population of approximately 800 students and a student-teacher ratio of 12:1. In keeping with the mission of a Jesuit education, our students are encouraged to develop their own individual gifts and talents in an academically rigorous setting with the goal of using those gifts to serve others, specifically, pursuing justice for those who are marginalized in society. Approximately 25% of our student body is Black, Asian or Hispanic and the school awards $2.8 million in financial aid to students each year.

There are many outside the private school community who might have the misconception that students who attend private schools don't have as much "need" as those who attend public schools. I was one of those skeptics. Having worked in public education for 13 years before coming to my current position, I had serious doubts about why I was being called to a new school. It didn't take long for me to understand that the majority of my new students had just as many needs as my former students. The needs just differed.

Student Stress is Universal

Many of my students were stressed, anxious, and extremely hard on themselves with respect to their academics. Students are expected to achieve and/or maintain a high grade point average, to be involved in extracurricular sports, clubs, and the arts, in addition to actively engaging in community service and mission trips. But internal and external pressures have contributed to a decline in our students' physical, mental, and emotional health. Having developed a personal meditation practice of my own, I knew that sharing these same tools and life skills with my students would not only be beneficial for them while in high school, but that they could also take these skills with them into college and beyond.

In my tenth year of public high school teaching, and with class sizes growing to 30+ students per class, I noticed a distinct change in the way that my students were behaving and I knew that I had to find some way of connecting with them. At the time, I had very little knowledge of meditative techniques and asking some students to "meditate" might come off as being "religious," something that was to be avoided in public school.

One class of particularly squirrely, hard-to-focus freshmen whose 90-minute class was split by a 30-minute lunch, was to be my first endeavor into mindfulness. The Wednesday before Thanksgiving break was my target date, and when my energetic cherubs finally settled into their seats, I said to them, "I am really concerned for you all. When you come to class, I can see that you are having trouble focusing or you are tired. I have a feeling that you have quite a few responsibilities at home that are weighing on you. Would this be an accurate description?" Of course, they all shouted yes.

As they began to elaborate, I learned that some of my students were care-givers for siblings at home and others were working a part-time job in addition to trying to keep up with their school work. I asked them if they would like to try a 3-minute relaxation exercise. And thus began my attempt to help my students ground themselves, to be present in the moment, and to be kinder to themselves. Students took to the short relaxation exercises quickly and within a week, all of my classes were asking for a chance to de-stress. If I ever forgot to begin a class with breathing or music, the students would be quick to remind me that they needed a moment to re-focus.

I'm not sure that any of the administrators or other teachers knew that I was doing this. I didn't talk about it because I thought that the techniques I was teaching the students would be viewed negatively or as a "waste of time." So the students and I continued to quietly "relax" together and their overall focus and effort in my classes increased. What was equally important to me, however, was that the *connection* I had with my students deepened and they came to trust me. I was their teacher, yes, but I had also become someone they knew they could trust and with whom they could talk. That, for me, was more important than anything I had ever done in the classroom.

When I changed jobs and went to my current (private) school, I discovered that these students also needed this same personal time to re-center themselves. I began to explore and develop my own personal mindfulness practice formally and discovered how beneficial it was to my own well-being and I knew that I needed and wanted more preparation so that I could provide helpful tools to my students. I formally trained with Gina Biegel (MBSR-T) and Todd Corbin (Mindfulness for Student Athletes) through Stressed Teens. And I recently completed Inbody Academy's 200-hour online Mindfulness Certification Program to earn my CMT-P; this stands for Professional Level Certified Mindfulness Teacher through the International Mindfulness Teachers Association.

A Mindfulness Class is Born

Two years ago, my school began to acknowledge that we needed to do something to help our students address their own anxiety and stress and so we ordered a climate survey to be conducted by a third party. The student response to the questions posed supported that which faculty and staff had anecdotally seen and discussed amongst each other—that our students were experiencing greater incidences of worry, stress, anxiety, and depression. The iron was hot, so to speak, so it was then that I shared with my administrative team my desire to teach a one-semester, one-credit course on mindfulness. The proposal was accepted for the fall of 2018.

I wasn't sure how well the mindfulness course would be received in a school where students were strongly encouraged to enroll in "academically rigorous" coursework, but I was pleasantly surprised when I learned that there would be three sections of the course being offered during the 2018–19 school year. Many students who completed the Mindfulness 1 course that year clamored for a second semester to help them go deeper into what they had learned. This fall (2019), we will offer one class of Mindfulness 2 and we have enough students signed up for three sections of Mindfulness 1!

Many colleagues have asked me about the results of the course. I am in the process of compiling the data that I collected during this first year to report back to my administrative team, but I can safely say that students' written feedback has been positive. I have no hard data at this point to demonstrate that the course helped any of the students improve their grades—which seems to be the number one question I receive. But to be honest, *how my students handle the stress and anxiety of school* is as important as the letter grades they earn.

My hope is that in sharing my story with others who teach in public or private schools, this will encourage them to, at the very least, begin incorporating basic mindfulness skills into their classes. Perhaps as interest grows and school communities begin to realize that mindfulness and meditation enhance student life and support the curriculum, more for-credit programs like the one in my high school will be adopted. I'll end by sharing my syllabus and some details about the curriculum to give you a feel for what is included, as well as some student testimonials for the class.

Course Curriculum Details

For the student community that we have at our school, I chose to use Gina Biegel's *Stressed Teens* program (MBSR-T). My classes meet 200 minutes each week, which includes two 40-minute periods and two 60-minute periods.

Course Rationale

This course is designed to help students establish mindfulness techniques as a way to increase their physical, emotional, and psychological well-being.

Course Objectives

At the end of this one-semester course, students will have developed techniques to increase awareness, focus, and concentration, decrease stress and anxiety, respond instead of reacting to challenging emotions, enhance a sense of calm, increase self-care, and expand their circle of love and acceptance to also include others.

Format and Procedures

Students will use a series of readings, reflections, videos, and guided mindfulness practices to develop techniques to cope with stress in healthy ways, manage difficult emotions and make better decisions. Each class will consist of formal and informal practices, class discussions, and self-reflections which will allow students to develop an understanding of awareness (or mindfulness).

Scope and Sequence

The Stressed Teens curriculum covers all of this, but in general, these are the units:
    Introduction to Mindfulness
    Effects of Stress; Beginning a Personal Mindfulness Practice (PMP)
    Developing and Strengthening a PMP; Increasing Present-Moment Awareness
    Cultivating Self-Care; Becoming Aware of the Good
    Noticing, Being and Working with Thoughts; Becoming Aware of the Unpleasant
    Improving Awareness; Positive Coping Strategies and Behaviors

Developing Mindful Resilience; Building Mindful Relationships
Making Mindfulness a Part of Your Daily Living

Practices include, but are not limited to mindfulness of the five senses, mindful breathing, mindful eating, body scan, sitting practice, mindful walking, mindful movement, heartfulness practice, yoga, mindful stopping, mindful pause, gratitude practice, letting go practice, and dropping-in practice.

Assessments include: journal, workbook activities *from The Stress Reduction Workbook for Teens* by Gina Biegel, mindful quality, class participation, and discussions.

Student Testimonials

I ask my students for written feedback every month. By giving them simple, open-ended questions, I gain quite a bit of formative information which helps me guide the lessons and practices in the direction my students need to go. Among some of the questions I ask my students:

- What is going well for you in class?
- What are you struggling with in class?
- What can I do as your instructor to make this class work for you?

From all of the feedback I have read, the following are statements that are repeatedly shared.

> *"The information and practices in this course help to keep me grounded, focused, and calm. I now have beneficial tools that help me address my stress and anxiety."*

> *"My biggest take-away from this course is that I can choose to change my perceptions of how I see things. That was a big struggle for me before the class—that I wanted to control everything and every little thing that didn't go my way upset me."*

> *"This class is the most applicable class that I have ever taken. I will take everything I learned into my life—college and beyond. Mindfulness isn't just something to think about and reflect on. It's real-life skills to use for personal and social reasons."*

> *"In reflecting on this semester, I have grown so much! I'm a healthier person and because of that, I am more patient and caring with others. My parents have said so!"*

"One of the biggest things I appreciate about the class is that you create an environment where I feel comfortable to share my thoughts. This allowed all of my classmates to share too and I didn't feel so alone in what I was going through because I found they are going through some of the same things"

"Every time that I leave mindfulness class, I feel as if a weight has been taken off of my shoulders. I'm more awake in my other classes and, honestly, it didn't feel like a "class"—it was an experience."

Currently, I am working on designing a more scientific feedback system to obtain concrete data which demonstrates the effect that this mindfulness course is having on our students. The pre- and post-course survey I currently give indicates an improvement in each of the course objectives in the case of *every single student* who has taken the Mindfulness 1 course. Because this semester (fall 2019) is the first semester I have offered the Mindfulness 2 Course, the final surveys have yet to be completed. However, the ongoing feedback that I ask for throughout the semester currently indicates that the course is equally popular with and beneficial to the students.

CHAPTER 16

Using Mindfulness and Poetry to Build Relationships and Writing Skills

Laura Bean, MFA

Mindfulness and Writing Curriculum Developer and Consultant, and Founder, Mindful Literacy, Former English Language Development Teacher, San Pablo, CA

WHEN I WAS THIRTEEN, MY OLDER BROTHER DAVID had a psychotic break and was diagnosed with schizophrenia. I don't remember ever talking to any teacher or counselor at school about what was going on at home. My family was ashamed of David's mental illness and angry at him for his rambling monologues at the Sunday dinner table. The tension in the room was palpable. I silently prayed for things to return to normal.

I wonder how life might have been different if I'd been able to share the sadness, fear, and confusion I felt with my parents, teachers, classmates, and other caring adults. What if I'd been offered compassion and encouraged to express my conflicting emotions through poetry, storytelling, or some other form of creative expression? I believe it would have "normalized" what was happening and provided me a pathway to the support I needed.

Just like me back in my school days, we teachers only see the tip of the iceberg. There's so much about our students we don't know—where they've come from, their home life, how they rank in the fierce social order of their peers. Before becoming a mindfulness and writing consultant, I taught English Language Development for three years at Helms Middle School in San Pablo, CA, a full-service community school in an impoverished neighborhood, where students are provided with three meals a day, and free medical and counseling services—if they're lucky enough to secure an appointment in the overburdened department.

When a therapist would knock on the door to take a student out of class, it left me wondering what was going on. Because of confidentiality, the therapist couldn't tell me. Still, I had a gut sense that whatever the issues were, they were standing in the way of that student and I developing an authentic relationship, as well as taxing my classroom management skills.

I simply needed to know more. The opportunity presented itself in October. "The Day of the Dead" is an ancient Mesoamerican (Mexico and northern Central American) holiday honoring those who have passed away in a celebratory way including sugar skulls, "pan de muerto," a sweet bread shaped like a skull, monarch butterflies, marigolds, and traditional paper banners. I used the occasion to share another family tragedy.

In his early twenties, my oldest brother Jeff had a motorcycle accident while driving drunk that left him a paraplegic. He spent thirty years in a wheelchair before dying at the age of fifty-six from smoking-related bladder cancer. To lighten the storytelling a bit and create audience participation in my class of newcomers, I used gestures to indicate his drinking, motorcycle riding, smoking, and wheeling his chair, while the students filled in the missing action words. Allowing myself to be vulnerable with my students by sharing this story gave them permission to tell their own tales of loss.

We'd already begun using mindfulness in our classroom—anchoring our attention to sounds, our bodies, and our breath. Compassion was an integral part of our practice. For example, I appreciated students' efforts to come to school every day and acknowledged that, in truth, sometimes *I* didn't want to come to school either. In challenging classes after lunch, I'd remind them in a calm and empathetic tone of voice—"Just a few more hours." In this way, I normalized the desire many had to go home already.

Training Myself First

Taking part in Mindful Schools' Year-Long Mindful Teacher Certification Program changed the way I thought about mindfulness in education. Mindfulness stopped being a thing to do on Mondays—just because it made sense to start the week with a positive intention, and the alliteration sounded good. The most important thing was not to teach my students mindfulness, but rather to become an embodied, mindful teacher.

Training myself meant developing a moment to moment practice that required pausing, breathing, and when necessary, naming whatever was going on inside me and around me in the room. "Wow! It's really wild in here right now, isn't it?!" I'd remark when the energy in the room seemed to be bubbling over. However, my tone was not accusatory or judgmental. Instead, I simply verbalized what I was noticing and feeling in the moment. By regulating my own nervous system in this way, I could help students regulate their own.

The Mindful Literacy curriculum sprung out of my work with English learners, many of whom had multiple "adverse childhood experiences" (ACEs) and needed a lot of support, both with self-regulation and writing. It's designed to help teachers build authentic relationships with their students and help young people build their writing skills as well as deepen their connections with themselves and each other. Each lesson introduces a new mindfulness concept and provides a script for a short, guided awareness practice paired with a poem that reinforces the theme. Listening activities and poem templates support students to appreciate the artistry of the works and create their own poem.

A poem I often share to inspire compassion is "Kindness" by Naomi Shihab Nye. It begins: "Before you know what kindness really is /you must lose things, /feel the future dissolve in a moment /like salt in a weakened broth." It's an evocative image that reminds us of how ephemeral and vulnerable our lives really are. It also helps young people open up: we've all lost someone dear to us, and acknowledging our shared humanity builds safety and trust in the classroom.

The line "Before you know kindness as the deepest thing inside, /you must know sorrow as the other deepest thing" reminds us that true empathy and compassion are built upon acknowledging our own suffering. At the end of the poem, the speaker shares the insight one gains from this journey, as kindness "raises its head/ . . . to say/ it is I you have been looking for/ and then goes with you everywhere/ like a shadow or a friend."

A shy, soft-spoken student named Karina wrote the poem below, which echoes the transformative power of acknowledging our suffering:

What Kindness Is

Before you know what kindness really is, you must lose things.

Feel the future dissolving in a moment like sugar in strong coffee.

If you lose a family member like me, you will know.

One day the people you love and have in your hands

will never come back. That is very sad

and you start knowing what kindness is.

Writing these lines gave her an opportunity to express the sadness that was in her heart. She "named it to tame it," which helps develop emotional intelligence and connection with others. Along with writing poems, another option is to have students write a personal narrative reflecting on a significant loss and its meaning.

Toward the end of the school year, students' poems were collected in an anthology entitled *This Being Human: Poems to Help Us Remember*. One student commented on the process, saying, "By writing poems, I've learned to be calm and patient, especially when I get mad about something dumb." Another student showed pride in having her writing published: "I feel good because other kids can use it for calming down when they're angry."

Reaping the Benefits

To see how creative writing lessons grounded in mindfulness impact students, I invited them to rate their resilience through a self-compassion survey at the start of the school year and again in the spring. Dr. Kristen Neff, pioneering educational researcher, teacher, and author of the book *Self-Compassion*, created this survey to measure how we relate to ourselves when confronted with difficulties, failures, or a sense of our own inadequacies. The survey can be found at self-compassion.org/test-how-self-compassionate-you-are.

Two-thirds of students surveyed increased in self-compassion. The program also works at developing their reading and writing skills. At mid-year, forty percent of my students advanced to the next level of ELD (English Language Development), compared to twenty percent the previous year.

"Meet students where they're at" is a wise adage in education. Having the strength and courage to learn about students' whole lives is our task as educators, today more than ever. Creating a safe space where students can open up, drop their defenses, and write about experiences of loss or trauma requires that we show our own vulnerability. Reflecting on the impact of traumatic events from our own childhoods and generating compassion for ourselves allows us to bear witness to our students' trauma instead of getting triggered by it. Then true healing can begin to happen.

Lesson Plan

Here is an excerpt from the lesson on the theme of loss and self-compassion based on the poem "Kindness." You can find the full lesson plan at mindfulliteracy.com/sample-lesson-plan.

Step 1: Quickwrite (5 min)

Prompt: Write about a time when you lost someone or something dear to you.

Step 2: Guided Practice (5–7 min)

Script excerpt:

> *Now, grounding your body, your feet rooted in the earth, your back supported by the chair. (pause) Taking a few deep breaths and letting go of any remaining tension in the body (pause). . . . Now calling*

*to mind a moment of sadness or disappointment from this week
... maybe you felt left out or unseen by somebody or somebody said
something unkind to you or maybe it was your own voice of disap-
proval and blame. ... (pause) Touching in to where you notice the
emotion in your body, maybe in your heart center or your belly or
throat. Allowing whatever sensation you're experiencing to just be
there, knowing that, in time, it will change.*

*If you feel comfortable, placing your hand on your heart. (pause)
And recognizing that you're not alone in feeling this way. Everyone
experiences sadness, frustration, anxiety, whatever emotions have
come up for you ... and offering yourself some kind words like you
would to a friend who was going through a hard time. "I'm so sorry
this is happening right now" or "It's okay to feel sad." Whatever words
feel right to you. (pause) Then gently, returning to your breath, taking a deep inhalation and exhalation and opening your eyes when
you are ready.*

Step 3: Read "Kindness" by Naomi Shihab Nye (2 min)

See above or full lesson plan.

Step 4: Making Connections (5 min)

What words or phrases do you remember?
What images stand out in your mind? Colors? Sounds? Textures?
What is this poem saying to you?

"Kindness" Poem Writing Play Sheet

Students fill in the blanks with their own creative responses to the lines of the poem
using the suggestions given. I encourage you to try it!

Before you know what kindness really is you must lose things,
Feel the future dissolve in a moment
Like _____
(something that dissolves)
...
Before you know kindness as the deepest thing inside

You must know _____
(something difficult you've had to endure)

Then it is only kindness that_____
(a realization or insight)

Only kindness that _____
(how kindness comforts you)

DID YOU KNOW?

Mindfulness is about befriending ourselves. To acknowledge our own sorrow is to awaken self-compassion. Dr. Neff explains that by simply placing our hand on our chest, we're able to tap into the mammalian care-giving system, triggering the release of oxytocin. This feel-good hormone increases feelings of safety and trust, calms stress and anxiety, and lowers the harmful effects of elevated cortisol levels.

CHAPTER 17

Mindfulness in the Department of Defense Schools

Jana York, MS

Former Health Promotion Educator, U.S. Army, Founder and Author,
The Vowels of Mindfulness

GROWING UP AS A DAUGHTER OF MILITARY PARENTS, I was assured of one truth: change is constant. My place to cuddle with my family, share my toys and call home was uprooted three times before I turned nine. It was the norm, but certainly didn't feel normal. The poetic words of the wise sage Oogway to Po in the movie *Kung Fu Panda* were unbeknownst to me as a child, yet certainly resonate today, "Yesterday is history, tomorrow is a mystery and today is a gift, that is why it is called the Present."

My name is Jana York and I had the honor of serving as a civilian in the role of a Health Promotion Educator for the U.S. military for over 28 years. I was the mindfulness champion for the U.S. military community in Japan for several years, and this is where my journey to awareness began. Mindfulness has guided me to fully experience what is happening now with a greater appreciation, whether it is joy, sorrow or holding compassion for others. I claim it as my superpower.

I was first introduced to mindfulness by an Army Physician, Dr. Michael Brumage in 2010. He had a deep interest in the adverse childhood experiences (ACEs) study and its role in health and disease. He was looking for effective and proven treatments for post-traumatic stress (PTS), suicide prevention, and improving well-being in the military community. He shared his meditation practice with me and inspired me to start my own. This helped me immensely with awareness and my appreciation for the present moment. What began as a conversation about his research, and his training with mindfulness mentors at the University of Massachusetts Center for Mindfulness led to offering mindfulness sessions to military and civilians working on the Army base.

We began offering 8-week courses strongly based on the well-known Mindfulness-Based Stress Reduction (MBSR) curriculum, which consisted of inquiry and experiential practice. We were fortunate to have Jon Kabat-Zinn and Saki Santorelli share their teachings and insights with us. Their wisdom evoked a passion in me to share the potential for mindfulness within all of us.

We used community calendars and on-base information exchange protocols such as base newspapers, command television stations, flyers and posters, and word of mouth to promote a two-hour introduction to mindfulness orientation session. Participants in the orientation were offered an opportunity to register for the eight-week course. The initial response was very encouraging, and classes filled-up rapidly. We feel that co-teaching worked very well for our situation as we each taught to our strengths of meditation and mindful movement.

Eventually, I took courses from two highly accredited organizations: Mindfulness in Schools Project (MiSP or .b) and Mindful Schools. I have been trained to teach the .b mindfulness curriculum since 2014. I have also been trained by Mindful Schools to teach mindfulness to students in K-12, since 2015.

Three of the graduates from our 8-week course were inspired and carried their enthusiasm to their schools. One of the graduates, a middle school principal, saw the importance of mindfulness and made a commitment to incorporating it into her school. She gathered teachers and school counselors and they began introducing mindfulness to their students, which led to a "Mindful Minute" where the entire school pauses in stillness during morning announcements. Subsequently, mindfulness techniques were taught in Physical Education and Health Departments and used throughout the classrooms by many. This spread to the use of mindfulness throughout the school community.

An elementary school teacher began immersing herself in mindfulness courses, using her own resources to become trained by Mindful Schools to teach mindfulness to students in K-12. Mindfulness is now flourishing within classrooms at her school.

Another teacher developed a mindfulness program for athletes, teaching them concepts like flow, present-moment awareness and how to be in the zone. Her team won the championships and they attribute part of their success to Mindfulness! She also is currently enrolled in the certification program through Mindful Schools.

I taught at the same schools as two of the course graduates, one was an elementary school and one was a middle school. I was allowed 15 minutes, two times a week for eight weeks in order to teach the mindfulness curriculum in the elementary school and 40 minutes once a week for nine weeks in the middle school. My position, as mindfulness champion, was funded as part of my regular duties as a health educator and not part of a grant.

On average, military families move every three years, so there is a potential for a host of stressors: like separation from the United States, adjusting to life in a foreign country, being without familiar friendships, facing possible military parent deployments, and reintegration into the family upon return from military commitments.

Students in these situations face the daunting task of making new friends and finding acceptance in their new community, along with the more common realities of test anxiety, lack of self-confidence and emotional dysregulation. Being aware of how mindfulness has helped me face adversity and become more resilient, I saw mindfulness as a perfect tool to help deal with these challenges.

Presenting our Case and Receiving a Grant

The three graduates mentioned above saw the importance of the practice and had the courage to move forward, bringing mindfulness to their students. As most military programs are data-driven, the only way for mindfulness to be sustainable was to show results. We successfully collected data and presented it to leadership.

Our school pilot program consisted of me introducing an eight-week mindfulness program to elementary students in one classroom. Due to the success of the pilot program, we expanded to include middle school students as well as other elementary school classes.

Our pilot was so well received that it led to funding in the form of an operational grant. Student self-reports and subjective data demonstrated highly satisfactory results. Testimonials proved that students grasped the concept of mindfulness and saw the value in applying techniques for focused awareness and emotional regulation. The teachers reported that students showed an increase in respect and compassion for others with less bullying. In addition to the data, seeing a child calm themselves with finger breathing, sharing a hug with a buddy or creating an art piece expressing what mindfulness means to them provided evidence that the goal had been met.

I encourage teachers to solicit feedback from their students by using the Mindful Attention Awareness Scale-Adolescent (MASS-A) or by developing their own questions such as: What did you find helpful and not helpful; Would you recommend mindfulness to other students or your parents, etc. Students can also be interviewed and recorded, and you can share their authentic words in your presentations.

Here are a few testimonials from our students:

> *"One night, I was trying to go to sleep but couldn't. Then I used mindfulness, and what do you know, I slept like a baby."—6th grader*

> *"My friend pushed me in the mud, and it got my new pants dirty. I was so mad; I was about to yell at her! Then I took deep breaths and she said she*

was sorry. If I would have yelled at her, we would have lost our friendship. Mindfulness helps!"—4th grader

"Sometimes, when I eat out at a restaurant or at home, I eat slowly and savor every bite, so I don't eat as much and love the dish I am eating."—8th grader

"My favorite thing about mindfulness is when I'm mad, I could do finger breathing or mindful walking, so I don't get mad at all. It also takes away all my worries."—7th grader.

The Vowels of Mindfulness

This experience led me to create a guidebook called *The Vowels of Mindfulness*. It is designed to support teachers in following a simple and flexible curriculum with lots of activities. The guidebook may be beneficial to parents as well. Here are a few examples of each:

Vowel A stands for Attention, and it aims to bring you into the present by giving students permission to be still. Activities include feeling your feet on the floor, listening to sounds, and focusing on your breathing. Any of these short practices take you away from "thinking" mode and into "sensing" mode.

Vowel E stands for Experience, and its aim is to enjoy the present moment using all your senses of taste, touch, see, smell, and listening.

Vowel I stands for Investigate, and its aim is to explore the physical sensations in the body and what they are trying to tell you. A few examples include 'a trip around the body' scan, slow motion movement, and squeeze and relax activities.

Vowel O stands for Observe and its aim is to notice your thoughts, feelings and emotions and how to respond to them. Firefly catch, S.T.O.P. practice, and Count to 10, are just a few activities to help create space between thought and action.

Vowel U stands for Understanding, and has more discussion-type activities, reflecting compassion and appreciation. An example activity is what I now call Grapeful. Each student is given a grape and we trace its path from a seed, observing with a sense of appreciation for all of the people, nature, love and nurturing it took to bring a piece of fruit to their plate.

The first time I did this activity, I placed a grape in each student's hand and told them this was a lesson on gratitude. I was a little nervous thinking about how I could convince them to be grateful for one silly grape. One student blurted out, "I get it, we need to be grapeful." To this day, I am not sure if he misspoke or if it was a profound epiphany. We all had a laugh and attention soared.

Vowel Y stands for You and its aim is finding fun ways for YOU to use mindfulness every day.

Unexpected Learning Along My Journey

While teaching, you have to let whatever transpires in the classroom be your teacher. Once I was asked to spend 15 minutes with 3rd graders and share an activity about using your senses. I chose what I thought would be the perfect activity. In this particular session, I was attempting to illustrate sound. I started by asking the class, "Did you know we can make sounds with our bodies that sound like other sounds?" In my naïve mind, I never fathomed that flatulence sounds would fill up the room. "Ok," I thought, "You got me."

Next, without telling them what the sound was that we were going to create, I asked students to follow my instructions. I divided the class into three groups. Group one was to snap their fingers, group two was to rub their hands together lightly, and group three would pat their hands on their thighs. I pointed to group one, then group two, and finally group three. I was bursting with enthusiasm in anticipation for them to be able to identify the sound. To add some flair to our handmade sound bite, I blurted, "Ok, all together now. Make it rain!" At once, they all started with the motion of sailing dollar bills toward me like I was an exotic dancer. I turned three shades of red and realized that was the animation for making it rain.

Choose your words wisely and find humor in your journey. This is part of what mindfulness is all about. Along with seeing the value of being authentic and vulnerable, this journey has also brought me a sense of validation for encouraging students to develop a growth mindset and curiosity about mindfulness through the introduction of both formal and informal mindful practices. They now have these tools and hopefully, they will revisit them. I felt a close connection to the students in and out of the classroom as well as a deeper sense of well-being in the community in which I served.

If I could offer a piece of advice, it is to trust that there is value in planting the seeds of mindfulness. Set a clear intention and know that it is okay to stay small and simple, focusing on just one group or class. When we react to the need for quantity over quality, before you know it, we are overwhelmed. Introducing mindfulness will begin to flourish on its own and you will see the ripple effects, especially when students grasp the concepts and tools. They will begin sharing it with their peers, parents, and friends. Other teachers will see the results and want to engage in mindfulness with their own students.

Lastly, remember to take some breaks from all of the distractions of daily life to balance and center yourself; pause for 5–10 minutes to observe your thoughts without judging them, feel your heartbeat and notice your body breathing. These pauses are the goodness of mindfulness and it is time well spent!

CHAPTER 18

Bringing Storytelling, Performing and Visual Arts into the Classroom

Andrew Jordan Nance

Founder, Mindful Arts San Francisco, Author, *Puppy Mind*, *Mindful Arts in the Classroom*, *The Lion in Me*, and *The Barefoot King*

AS VETERAN EDUCATOR PARKER J. PALMER SAYS, "Whoever our students may be, whatever subjects we teach, ultimately we teach who we are." This adage is most true in the elementary school classroom, where students are highly sensitive to the quality of presence in the adults around them. Our own ability to self-regulate is crucial for teaching mindfulness, so I want to invite you to remember that leading mindfulness lessons is an opportunity to deepen and extend your own practice.

I created the first version of *Mindful Arts in the Classroom* after just six months of teaching mindfulness to students, partly because I was interested in finding lesson plans that were creative, effective, and fun—and at that time there were no such books available.

The road to this point starts as a child studying drama at San Francisco's Attic Theater. Then I went on to train at the American Conservatory Theater, eventually receiving my Bachelor of Fine Arts in theater from New York University's Tisch School of the Arts. I furthered my studies later in life traveling to Umbria, Italy, to study with Ellen Stewart and the teachers of the celebrated La MaMa. Over the years, I have had many brilliant teachers, including David Mamet, Linda Hunt, W. H. Macy, and Anna Deavere Smith.

I eventually became the conservatory director of an innovative theater called The New Conservatory Theater Center (NCTC) in San Francisco. For almost 20 years I headed NCTC's youth and adult training programs, growing the program from seven classes a year to nearly eighty. Additionally, I performed and directed frequently, winning awards and nominations for various performances, including for two one-man shows.

With a feeling of gratitude, accomplishment, and pride, I left NCTC in the summer of 2013 to find out what my next life chapter might be and seek out a new passion. I just did not know what that passion would be.

Mindfulness and Theater Trainings Converge

I began taking classes in topics such as the Science of Happiness and attended UC Berkeley's Greater Good Science Center's week-long Summer Symposium for Teachers. There I learned about something called "mindfulness" or "the act of paying attention to the present moment, on purpose, without judgment." Little did I know that in just five years, I would be teaching young people this very skill. The definition we use in the Mindful Arts curriculum to teach our young people is: "Mindfulness is the practice of using our breath to focus our minds and bodies to make good choices."

At the GGSC symposium, I heard many inspiring speakers including Rick Hanson and the co-founders of an organization called Mindful Schools, Megan Cowan and Chris McKenna. Megan and Chris took turns teaching the group how to go inward, guiding us through the fundamentals of mindfulness. They taught us how to meditate and helped us label our emotional states in ways that seemed familiar to me; after all, as a theater performer and director, I had practiced analyzing emotions to be able to reproduce them on stage. Then they started using theater games that I had played at university and in countless classes and rehearsals. That is when the light bulb went off: theater training and mindfulness training have a great deal in common!

Both encourage the participant to understand their inner world, witness what is going on around them in the moment, notice what feelings arise, and proceed with skillful intention. How does the body convey feelings, and how do we stay present in the moment, even when we are fearful or jittery, or in other emotional states that might prevent us from acting skillfully? Both trainings ask us to use our breath so that the body and the mind perform optimally. Both trainings ask us to be in the present moment, noticing the given circumstances, so that we can truly inhabit the experience, and be fully present for ourselves and others.

Here is where the two trainings diverge: when we are on stage we want to *react*. If someone says something distasteful to us, the most dramatic course of action would be to react with a clever, funny, or biting retort, that possibly escalates into a fistfight—or better yet, a duel with swords or pistols, à la *Hamilton*.

In off-stage life, however, reacting can get us into a lot of trouble. With mindfulness we learn how to *respond* wisely, rather than reacting blindly to stimuli. With mindfulness training we soon know that there is always a pause between a stimulus and what happens next. With theater training we are taught to ignore that pause, and just react instinctively ("Acting is reacting") to give our performances a sense of realism and spontaneity. With mindfulness training we are taught to be more measured, intentional, and responsive about what we say or do directly after any given stimuli.

So with this new realization of the similarities and differences between mindfulness and theater training, I signed up for my first online course through Mindful

Schools, a certification program to teach mindfulness. It was inspiring to take the course with people from all over the world who were teaching young people this life skill or were about to do so. I was eager to teach a mindfulness class of my own.

As soon as I completed the course, I reached out to my dear friend and theater colleague, Michelle Holdt. Michelle runs an organization called Arts Ed Matters, whose mission is to train teachers how to incorporate the arts into other subjects, such as math, English, and the sciences. At one of these trainings, I asked her to mention that I had just completed a mindfulness course and was looking for an interested teacher to allow me to try out my newfound mindfulness skills in their classroom. Two teachers reached out to me right away and off we went, supplied with the Mindful Schools curriculum. They both taught kindergarten! *Yikes! I thought. What if such young children were too rambunctious to follow the instructions?* I had years of teaching, mentoring, and directing under my belt, including at preschools, but truthfully, I was a bit scared.

Thankfully, it went well. Each lesson brought a new understanding for the kids and for me. Most of them were surprisingly receptive to a mindfulness curriculum. Even in these two kindergarten classes, I had a few "eye-rollers"—those students who thought mindfulness was silly—but when I encountered their resistance, I tried to create learning opportunities for both the child and myself: "Where in your body do you feel bored?" I would ask them. And then I would ask myself, *how does it feel to you that a five-year-old is bored by what you have to say?* And I took a lot of deep breaths.

The semester went by quickly. I moved through the curriculum rather fast, because I was presenting twice a week to those two classes. Perhaps too fast, as I finished the curriculum well before the end of the semester. With my new focus on mindfulness, I started testing out theater games that I had taught or remembered from my years of theater training. The children *loved* my mindfully-adapted theater games, such as Mindful Museum, Emotional Musical Chairs, and What Are You Feeling?

Bestselling Books and Mindful Arts San Francisco

Then I started looking for mindfulness books for kids—picture books. At that time, I did not find a lot to choose from, and the ones I did find did not resonate with me. But I eventually found one and read it to one of my classes. It was, to put it mildly, a disappointment. I saw the glow in these kindergarteners' eyes dim and I knew that I might have to take matters into my own hands. That day I went home, sat down at the dining room table, took a deep breath, and began writing a children's book on mindfulness. That story was *Puppy Mind*. Before I knew it, I had written three more: *Just STOP and Breathe, Find the Pleasant in the Present* and *The Lion in Me.* *Puppy Mind* and *The Lion in Me* have gone on to be bestsellers for one of my publishers, *Parallax Press*, founded by Thich Nhat Hanh.

That summer of 2015, buoyed by my success with the Mindful Schools curriculum and those adapted theater games, I wrote ten more stories and incorporated performing arts, drawing, and poetry into a curriculum that was uniquely my own. When I finished, I had a teacher's manual of almost 300 pages that highlighted twenty-plus practices with many supplemental activities.

That fall, working under the auspices of the San Francisco Education Fund, I began training volunteers in this new curriculum, which I named Mindful Arts San Francisco (MASF). Our mission: to provide volunteer-facilitated mindfulness instruction to students of the San Francisco Unified School District through a partnership with the San Francisco Education Fund. Using focusing techniques, storytelling, and performing and expressive arts, participants get the opportunity to cultivate the skill of present-moment awareness to improve attention, self-regulation, and social-emotional learning, so that all students can excel.

As I write this, MASF is gearing up to hire a Program Coordinator that will help bring on more volunteers and do outreach to schools so that we can continue to reach more and more students. My mindfulness practice has allowed me to broaden my own skills, write books, and teach both kids and adults in various settings around the globe. I am honored to be permitted, in my own small way, to contribute to its continuation and I hope that my books spark your imagination, inspiring you to bring your own creativity to this work, to your students, and to yourself.

I want students and adults to look forward to learning the principles of mindfulness. Those principles are all in *Mindful Arts in the Classroom*, practice by practice: the breath, our senses, our emotions, gratitude, kindness, compassion, courage, and curiosity. Each practice lesson guides the student and the teacher in learning the principles of mindfulness in a fun and playful way that meets these young minds where they are, at the most imaginative and receptive stage of their lives. It is my wish that through mindfulness young people and we, the adults who support them, can learn the tools to navigate our lives skillfully, safely, joyfully; to cultivate empathy for ourselves and others so that we can build communities that are more safe and loving, giving young people the opportunity to learn in the most conducive environment possible.

As I tell my students, just keep at it—practice makes progress.

A Cherokee Story About Mindfulness: The Wise Man and the Two Wolves

There is also a great animated version of this story on YouTube.

> One evening the wisest of men,
> Gathered together his children.
> He said, "The battle of two wolves is inside us all,
> Whether we may be quite big or very small."
>
> One wolf is angry: full of hate, meanness,
> rage, disgust and weakness.
> The other wolf is kind: full of joy, generosity,
> love, gratitude, and curiosity.
>
> The children thought about it and then one grinned,
> asking his father, "Which wolf will win?"
> The old Cherokee simply replied,
> "The one we feed inside."
>
> The story is simple but true,
> There are two wolves in each of you.
> Our thoughts feed the wolves each and every day,
> Which wolf will you feed, and in what way?
> We can choose to feed our kind wolf positivity,
> or feed our mean wolf with toxic negativity.
> So the question to always ask each day,
> is "Which wolf will I feed today?"

Instructor:

You are good listeners. Who can tell me what the wise man said lives inside each of us? That's right: two wolves! Which wolf did he want us to feed? That's right he wanted the children to feed their kind wolf.

Now let's play a game to see if you know when you are feeding your kind wolf or your mean wolf. Are we feeding our kind or our mean wolf when we . . . (alternate from examples below of feeding our kind or our mean wolf).

Examples of feeding our kind wolf:

When we eat healthy foods, get enough sleep, brush our teeth, do our homework, be a good friend, do our chores. Being helpful to our teacher, our family? Help students, share our things, say "Good Morning," "Good-bye," Please," and "Thank you."

Examples of feeding our mean wolf:

When we are bullies, hit people, scream and shout, break the rules, don't clean up after ourselves, yell out in class, and say mean things.

Which wolf do you want to feed? That's right—the kind wolf! Because we can feel unsafe around a mean wolf, can't we? So we all have to keep remembering to feed our kind wolf, don't we? We can make being kind a habit, like brushing your teeth! And be gentle with ourselves when we make mistakes because we all make mistakes. Remember, when we do good, we feel good.

Stop Walk Game

This is a fun and challenging game that requires focus and a pause before responding. Have participants begin walking around the room by saying "Walk." Then have them stop when you say "Stop." Practice this a few times. Then switch it so "Walk" now means "Stop" and "Stop" means "Walk." Next, add "Clap" (participants clap) and Name (say their name). Then switch it so "Clap" means "Name" and Name means "Clap."

Depending on their ages and how well the class is doing, add the prompts "Jump" and "Jiggle." Then switch it so "Jump" means "Jiggle" and "Jiggle" means "Jump." Get creative and add other prompt pairings such as "Punch to the Sky" and "Take a slow deep breath."

Check-in Questions: Was that hard? Easy? What did you learn? Did you have to think before you made a decision? Respond, rather than react?

*Reprinted from *Mindful Arts in the Classroom* by Andrew Jordan Nance, courtesy of Parallax Press, Berkeley, California

Palmer, P. J. (2017). *The courage to teach guide for reflection and renewal.* San Francisco, CA: Jossey-Bass.

CHAPTER 19

Caring for the Whole Student in the Nurse's Office

Mary McCarter, BS, RN, MEd, PEL-CSN

Former Certified School Nurse, IL

AS A CHILD, I EXPERIENCED MANY ACES (adverse childhood experiences). I struggled. Finding a youth service program with outreach counselors helped me to realize that I had everything I need inside of me. This led me to college, and to the belief that as a social worker I could heal not only myself, but others. Fast forward four years and I became an outreach counselor at the same agency that helped me to begin my healing journey.

The job, however, paid poorly and required at times 60 or more hours a week without overtime compensation. This just didn't feel right. I left and went to work as a customer service rep and then as an administrative assistant, but my desire to care for people remained strong. A few years after getting married, I moved to a flexible position as an office manager and returned to school to become a registered nurse.

Upon graduation, I was hired as a staff nurse at a suburban Illinois hospital. I was in a fast-paced department where I dealt with life and death. Moving to a retirement community as the nurse clinician-case manager was a delight because I was actually able to get to know my patients. During this same time, I struggled with infertility. The day I found out I was pregnant, I was placed on bed rest. I had to resign my position as there was no short-term disability at that point for pregnancy-related work leave.

I was overjoyed when I gave birth to twins. Returning to work when our kids were six months old, I worked in all areas of the retirement community. When my kids entered school, a friend suggested I explore school nursing. "What does a school nurse do?" I thought. I spoke with one at my childrens' school. She informed me of the depth of skill that a school nurse required. As the only medical professional in a building, any medical or unusual physical need that arises becomes the nurse's responsibility. All IEP related paperwork, including vision and hearing, health history, emergency care, and plan initiation and implementation, are provided by this single soul. In addition, each child that felt ill or got injured at school came to see the nurse for care.

Working part-time in a special education cooperative with the medically fragile was an initiation into caring for children with special needs. I learned to provide care that was not taught in nursing school. Each child had their own needs and required individualized care. Although I enjoyed this role, I needed to return to work full-time. Moving to an elementary school district, responsible for two buildings and having a classroom in each of special needs students, was a challenge. Without the help of a second nurse, I would not have been able to handle this busy role. When an opportunity presented itself to work at the local high school, and in just one building, I made the switch.

The Impact of Stress Leads to a Mindful Response

The busyness of the elementary role, along with two active middle schoolers of my own, and a husband gone 12 hours a day, caused stress in my life. I was drawn to yoga and began attending classes, eventually entering a hatha yoga teacher training program. I enjoyed learning about the physiology of asana (yoga postures) and was empowered with many tools for stress management.

During this time, I recognized that I was already practicing some mindfulness with my students. The tummy aches in the grade school became the chest pain or shortness of breath in the high school. When I took time to look past the physical symptoms, which often included normal vital signs, I saw that children were experiencing many of the same feelings that I had as a child.

Honing in on what was going on in their life enabled me to assist students in recognizing their own fears and anxieties. I began asking them to take a deep breath and to allow their shoulders to relax. From here I added a simple grounding activity, like the following sequence:

- *Place your feet on the floor.*
- *Sit upright.*
- *Roll your shoulders up and back and down.*
- *Take a breath.*

I began to add a head-to-toe relaxation exercise similar to this:

> *Place your feet on the floor. Sit upright, pull in your core and roll your shoulders up, back and down. Take a deep breath in. Release. Close your eyes if you are comfortable. Relax the muscles of your forehead. There are no more lines between your eyebrows. Unclench your teeth, relaxing your jaw.*

Allow the relaxation to flow down the front and sides of your neck. It continues to your shoulders, through your biceps, elbows, forearms, wrists, palms, fingers and fingertips. Pull your next breath in through your fingertips, through the tops of your hands, your wrists, your forearm, past the elbows through the triceps and back to your shoulders. Allow your shoulders to sink more deeply down into your back.

Inhale, and as you fill your lungs notice how the chest expands. As you exhale allow the muscles of your chest to sink between your ribs and down to your spine. As your abdomen relaxes, the hips and pelvis follow. It sinks to the front and sides of your thighs, past your knees, your shins, to your ankle, feet, and toes.

Take your next breath in through your toes, and as you exhale send any thoughts, worries or stresses out the bottoms of your feet. Take this time just for you. (I pause here and if they are engaged in breathing, allow a few breaths.) Pull the next breath in through your toes, past the soles of your feet, through your calves, thighs, buttocks, your lower back, middle back, and upper back. Bring the breath through the curve of the back of the neck, to the head, and finally to the crown of the head.

Only when you are ready, wiggle your fingers and wiggle your toes, bringing awareness back to your body. When you are ready, open your eyes.

It never fails to amaze me when I see a student relax before my eyes. Students began coming to my office and asking me to walk them through the exercise. Their attendance improved and they were no longer calling their parents to go home 'sick'. It not only benefited the students, but also the parents.

As this practice grew, the students became adept at their self-calming techniques. I created a mindful corner in my office that was darker and had an electric waterfall. Kids would ask if they could sit in the corner. Then they would take the time they needed to gather their thoughts and return to class. We added calm music to the waiting area and several mindful toys. My office took on a more serene feel. I took an online mindfulness certification course for nurses through Dr. Susan Taylor, which helped to ground my practice and gave me further ideas to use in my office.

Expanding Mindfulness to Other Students and Staff

A physical education teacher asked me to teach yoga to her life-style class. This class was for students that don't enjoy the typical PE class. I became a regular. Then by student request, we also started an after school yoga program. The class ran for 45 minutes so that students could catch the activity bus home. The movement of the body with the relaxation at the end of class was beneficial for all. Students took ownership of recruiting other students.

Teachers then asked me to teach them yoga. I led a one-hour yoga class for teachers after school once a week on a different day than the student class. We began with a relaxation exercise, practiced asana for about 45 minutes and ended with a guided mindful exercise or quiet reflection lasting about five minutes.

I realized that the teachers were as stressed about their roles as I was about mine. In schools, there is never enough time or hands to complete all the tasks that are required. My stress came from seeing 80–100 students per day, managing an office for 2000 students and caring for all of their individual needs, as well as completing the IEP paperwork (plans for special needs students).

Teacher stress was evident in that they felt they could not fail students, as it would impact their job review. In addition, all students are strongly encouraged to take an AP (advanced placement) class. Are freshman ready to take a college-level class during their first semester of high school? Some yes, but many struggle. Should all students learn to be mindful of their needs? Should they learn the physical symptoms of stress and how to manage it? This seemed more important to me than an AP class.

I found Integrative Yoga Therapy (IYT) around this time, which focuses on health through the integration of body, mind, and spirit, and I completed the teacher training program. This program not only taught asanas, but it taught mindfulness in a way that the hatha yoga program had not. We discussed the different styles of yoga, Ayurveda, body awareness, pranayama, mudras, and bandhas. We spent time talking about stress management, energy, and the mind-body connection. We practiced meditation, imagery, relaxation and yoga nidra. This program showed me that everyone has their own way to practice mindfulness. In our crazy-busy, stressed out world, some people have difficulty sitting for five minutes in a silent meditation.

Following the Advice I Have Given Others

Also about this time, I transferred to our School of Specialized Learning Programs. This was a new full-time role supporting students who were not successful at their home school. In the beginning, I was able to teach two weekly yoga classes and a yoga group for students with emotional and behavioral challenges. As the learning programs grew, the medical needs of the students took more of my time. I was the nurse first, so the yoga practices decreased, and last year completely dissolved.

A few years ago, another teacher asked me to teach a course on mindfulness for our internal university program. It was certified through Quincy University and the staff earned graduate credit. The content included a discussion of what mindfulness is, as well as current research. We practiced breathing exercises, body movement and yoga, relaxation activities, mindful eating, and walking meditation, including a visit to a walking labyrinth. We had guest speakers that spoke on nutrition, animal therapy, reiki and the history of the labyrinth. Acupressure was discussed and practiced.

The homework started as choosing any mindfulness activity and practicing it 10 minutes per day, six days per week. I quickly realized that asking the students to sit for 10 minutes a day would result in additional stress, and not completing the homework. The teachers instead kept a journal of what they tried and the time of day. It was a pleasure to read the journals and see the different practices they tried. The goal was to find a mindful practice that they could sustain. The final project included a lesson plan that they would use in their classroom or at a staff in-service. These lesson plans now make up a toolkit that is available to all of the students that have taken the class over the last three years.

I decided to retire from my school nurse role last year. The position had become so demanding that I was constantly spinning. I covered five different special needs learning programs in two schools, by myself. My requests for assistance were denied and it became too much. I didn't have the time to teach self-care skills. So, I did what I have encouraged the staff and students to do for years: I decided to take care of me. I realized once again that I already have everything that I need inside of me. My practice of mindfulness will support this new chapter of the journey that I am on. Sometimes it is not enough to work with what is; sometimes you have to change what is.

CHAPTER 20

Mindful Check-ins with the POP Chart

Carla Tantillo Philibert

President and CEO, Mindful Practices; Co-Founder, Class Catalyst; Author, *Cooling Down Your Classroom,* **Everyday SEL,** **and** *Everyday Self-Care for Educators*

I WAS APPROACHED BY ROUTLEDGE IN 2014 to write a Social and Emotional Learning (SEL) book, *Everyday SEL and Mindfulness,* which was practical for educators. My editor wanted strategies and tools that would be accessible to teachers of all stripes and backgrounds. The POP Chart was born.

The field of Social and Emotional Learning up to this point was strongly rooted in theory and, although important, many educators did not have the time to read a meta-analysis or scholarly journal. Teachers needed practical tools to implement in only a few minutes each day. Having founded Mindful Practices in 2006, I knew that yoga and mindfulness were perfect vehicles for cultivating SEL competencies like self-awareness and self-regulation. So, I developed the POP Chart, a simple bulletin board with space for students to take a breath and Pause, then Own their emotions, and Practice a yoga or mindfulness strategy that would help them get focused, centered, and ready to learn. The trick to successfully implementing a POP Chart is to include practices that are accessible to all students and educators, even those who might not be apt to strike a tree pose or get on all fours to give downward-facing dog a try.

To remedy this question of accessibility, my husband, a Senior Creative Director at a Fortune 100 Company, and I developed an online platform, Class Catalyst (www.classcatalyst.com) to deliver the SEL, yoga, and mindfulness content in those classrooms where the educators believed in the practices, but did not feel comfortable implementing them without help. When we started Class Catalyst in 2016, I had been working arm and arm with Dr. Kiljoong Kim at Chapin Hall at the University of Chicago to study the impact of Mindful Practices' professional learning programs. By applying those findings to Class Catalyst, we were able to create an online resource that paired nicely with *Everyday SEL and Mindfulness,* but was also accessible to those educators who had never read my book or taken part in a professional development workshop with Mindful Practices.

Included below are stories from Anne-Marie and Kate, two amazing educators at Berlin Public Schools in Berlin, New Hampshire, whose school communities have been negatively impacted by the opioid crisis. To help their students center, focus, and get ready to learn, both educators used the POP Chart and Class Catalyst. I am honored and excited to share their stories with the hope that educators in similar circumstances will be empowered with the SEL, yoga, and mindfulness tools they need to succeed in today's classrooms.

I Hear You and I Love You

Katharine Moore, M.Ed, CYT 95, Grade 2 Teacher

Every once in a while you have that kid, the one who is a success despite the world around her, the one that you scratch your head and wonder, "How does she keep it all together?" Recently, in my class of 24 second graders, I had that child. Let's call her Kaylee. With one parent incarcerated, Kaylee was removed from her abusive home, sent to a foster family with new siblings to adjust to, and was attending a new school. Despite all this, she thrived.

She was at school every day, interacted beautifully more often than not with her peers, and had the ability to rectify it when she didn't. She excelled in all academic areas and was a true joy to be around—and not just the quiet "do-what's-asked" type of joy teachers of large classes appreciate, but the witty, crack-a-joke, chat-about-your-day, accidentally-drop-an-f-bomb and immediately-own-up-to-it type of way that is rare among second graders.

I pride myself on making connections and relationships with my students. That is my strength. Reading and math instruction are necessities, but it's the bonds I forge with students that keep me coming back every day, every year. Kaylee and I forged a bond that was tight; we had a great connection and a strong foundation of trust. Coming from a life of chaos and too much responsibility for a 7-year-old, she immediately took to the SEL skills and strategies that were taught in my classroom.

She loved gross motor movements and the freedom to take a moment of space for herself before talking to myself or peers when disagreements arose. She was a writer and loved using the online POP Chart through Class Catalyst. She would take time each morning to type me a note about her day or what was happening. While I realize not every school may be fortunate enough to have Class Catalyst, I want to recognize the power of nonverbal communication for students who may not be willing or ready to verbally share their thoughts, worries, or problems. Kaylee felt safe at school through this online messaging system and knew through this communication that she could be heard, validated, and loved, and I truly believe this is why she was soaring.

One Friday in early spring, I was informed that she was being removed from her foster home. They were losing their foster license. She was being placed with another foster family who already had four children and could not take her two younger siblings. Kaylee came to school that day with her backpack busting with all her possessions, ready for the move. As she showed me her photo album, she shared her fears about not being able to comfort the younger brother she was leaving behind. At the end of the day, I walked her to the office and watched her get introduced to a new woman who would be her foster mother, and Kaylee was taken away to meet her new foster family.

That next week, she also began visits with her birth mother whom she had not seen nor had contact within over a year. The changes were immediate. There were outbursts and tears, which was not surprising for any child considering what she was going through, but this was certainly new for her. She became withdrawn from her peers, started yelling at other kids and teasing them, and she started shouting insults about their behaviors. She refused to participate in activities and questioned everything I said to her as an individual or to the class as a whole. She shouted insults at me when I requested she do things such as sit with the class or line up for a specialty. It quickly became a volatile relationship.

As much as I could look at her behavior as an outsider and empathize with this small child who was going through things no child should have to, I struggled personally with this change since we had been so close. The energy and effort I put into the following days was exhausting. Her behaviors were scary and upsetting to her peers. I was beginning to neglect the rest of my class, and the energy in the room had changed. I felt like a failure, and my classroom was no longer this fun, creative space for learning I had worked so hard to build. It became difficult for me to get up and go to school each day.

Despite the negative trend in our relationship, there was a glimmer of positivity that allowed Kaylee to stay connected to me and to the rest of the class. My students always had access to Class Catalyst, the online POP Chart we use in our classroom. The software has a messaging feature that continued to be a safe outlet for Kaylee to share her thoughts or emotions with me. Our relationship had changed so drastically that my spoken words were like poison to her. She didn't want to hear what I had to say if the message was delivered orally.

In those tough days, Class Catalyst saved me. It was the only place where I could get this child to hear me, and if I am being honest, for me to hear her as well. In our messages, she was able to explain to me things she could not in a face-to-face interaction. One day she would yell in all caps and tell me she hated me and couldn't wait to be out of my class or that I was a liar and she could never trust me. I would respond simply, "I hear you, and I love you," and the next day she would apologize in a message.

Through these interactions, she was able to tell me in a safe way that when she was taken from her mother, it was easier to be angry at her and push her away than to feel the pain of the loss, and that this was what she was doing to me because it worked with her mom. She said it was easier to push me away than have to deal with losing me as summer approached.

Having this online POP chart gave us a space to remain connected when all of the face-to-face interactions were difficult and messy. Despite what was being said, screamed, or cried at me out loud, there was a written piece of truth and honesty that was able to remain and ultimately salvaged our relationship.

Though we were both sad to see each other go, on the last day of school I got a note on my desk. It said, "Thank you for helping me when I needed it." Underneath, she had written this poem for me:

> *You twinkle like a star*
> *Over the summer sea*
> *You sink into my heart*
> *So it is so hard to let you be*
> *That is why I love you so much*
> *—Sincerely, Kaylee*

Supporting SEL Competencies

Anne-Marie Gagne, RYT 200, CYT 95, SEL Behavior Interventionist

I'm entering my 24th year in education, and I can say with certainty that I am now working my dream job. By year 20, I had reached that point of burnout that is so evident in education. Then, three years ago I began a journey with Mindful Practices. Our school board adopted SEL and mindfulness as one of their three-year-plan goals. The Office of Student Wellness initiated a contract with our district for a three year training with Mindful Practices, and I hit the road running, boots to the ground, diving into SEL and absorbing the approach.

Within that three year span, I completed the Mindful Practices SEL Certification Cohort, a Yoga Teacher Certification, and a Child's Yoga Teacher Certification. I also developed a six week long Tier II SEL intervention plan based on SEL competencies and on the *Everyday SEL in Elementary School* approach, primarily using the beloved POP Chart.

I've been privileged to present nationally and at many SEL Summits within New Hampshire. A colleague and I have shared the SEL and Mindfulness approach developed by Carla in neighboring school districts throughout Northern New

Hampshire. I presently work as an SEL Behavior Interventionist, and I truly enjoy and believe in this work.

It wasn't easy to choose which POP Chart success story to share, but there is one I am going to share that is dear to my heart. It's a story about a 6-year-old boy and how the POP Chart helped to foster a relationship between him and his mother. First, let me tell you a little about CE, a delightfully good-natured child. At the time, he was kind, jolly, and had a solid build that he hadn't quite grown into. Therefore, he struggled with spatial awareness, and in conjunction with his size, caused other children to be wary of him. He was getting written up frequently for inadvertently hurting other children by bumping into them and knocking them about. Due to the amount of Office Disciplinary Referrals he had received, it was recommended he attend an SEL small group Intervention.

CE joined a group of three students to practice SEL skills with a focus on social awareness. I based the structure of the intervention on the use of the POP Chart. The acronym POP is explained as: P–pause and take a breath while thinking of how you are feeling in the present moment, O–own your feeling by naming it, and P–practice a strategy to help you get in the zone where you are ready to learn and be present.

The use and introduction of the POP Chart provided an organized and well-managed environment. The plan included providing consistency in expectations for behavior management and student choice. After teaching and modeling skills that students could practice to get them ready for our group time, the expectation was that as they arrived, they went directly to the POP Chart to check-in. Being familiar with the process, they took one to three breaths, then took a post-it note with their name on it and placed it next to the emotion they were feeling. Lastly, they chose a practice that they had been taught from the list under P-practice and proceeded to engage in that activity or breathing exercise.

On that particular day, CE appeared exceptionally tired. As he meandered over to the chart, he proceeded as expected, and when he moved his name, he placed it next to the choice of feeling hungry. Up until that moment, no one had ever chosen hungry before. So I was alerted to approach CE and inquire further about his choice, to which he divulged that the previous night, his younger brother had kept him up running about and jumping on him, and he didn't get any sleep. We later learned that his brother had autism and oftentimes did not sleep through the night. CE continued to explain that he was so tired that he only fell asleep just before it was time to go to school and he did not get to eat breakfast.

Although most of his story was true, after a phone call home to his mom, we further learned that she was working on changing the family's eating habits in the hope to address the family's need to lose weight and to help the little brother sleep better. The fact of the matter was that CE chose not to eat the healthy breakfast she had prepared for them that morning, and yes, that he did indeed fall asleep.

This interaction initiated some supportive conversations with CE about healthy changes and honesty, and it also gave me and the classroom teacher an opportunity to support the mother with her son during this difficult transition. CE also learned that school and home were working together, and that helped create a sense of safety. His mom agreed that CE could have something to eat that morning, and CE agreed to start eating his healthy breakfast at home.

All of this would not have been possible if it were not for the use of the POP Chart, which was the primary reason for learning of the hunger and other family factors the family was facing. We were much better prepared to support this family, and it opened the door for this single mother and full-time nursing student to feel safe in building a home-to-school relationship.

This is just one example of the value of the POP Chart tool in supporting SEL competencies and our students. It teaches students not only how to self-regulate but also how to develop self-awareness. Additionally, it proves its value in aiding educators in learning more about our students and building relationships. The POP Chart is instrumental in helping to foster relationships as well as addressing decision-making and social-awareness competencies.

PART 3

CREATE A

SCHOOLWIDE

CULTURE OF

MINDFULNESS

CHAPTER 21

The Mindfulness-Based Preschool that Found Me

Renee Metty, MEd

Leadership Development Consultant and Executive Coach, Founder, The Cove School, Founder and CEO, With Pause

"Mindfulness is both a skill and a way of being."

MINDFULNESS TRANSFORMED MY LIFE. My journey is not the typical mindfulness journey that you may hear about. In fact, I thought mindfulness was for hippies. I was an east coast, high performing, Type A perfectionist that didn't need mindfulness. I had this life thing down and slowing down was not the direction I wanted to go. As an entrepreneur, with a background in tech and education, I had strong conditioning regarding what success looks like. I could face any challenge that came my way and I didn't need help from anyone. As the saying goes, "I got this!" Now, I live much differently and relate much differently to my experience, the people around me and how I engage with work and life.

I never had any desire to build, found or create a school. I left teaching in 2006 vowing to never teach again and never look back. Long hours, lack of resources and drained from the physical and emotional toll that working in schools brings, burned me out. I became an entrepreneur and started my wedding planning business during my last year of teaching. Shortly after, I became pregnant with my first child and left the teaching field for good after he was born. Two children later, I found myself opening an in-home daycare at the encouragement of a former parent of one of my students. I needed childcare for my two children, didn't like what was available and had strong ideas about what daycare could and should look like. It was strictly a means to an end. I was taking my wedding planning full time. My in-home daycare took off, but I quickly realized I was not a daycare person. Within 18 months, I knew I wanted to transition to a preschool model for the fall of 2010.

I often joke that the preschool found me. In the fall of 2009, I began planning for the transition from daycare to preschool for the fall 2010, but life had other plans.

With a crashing economy and daycare enrollment being cut in half virtually over-night, I had to let go of my staff of three, be the full-time lead in the classroom and run the business myself. In 2010, nine months pregnant with my third child, I transitioned what was once a wildly successful in-home daycare to a preschool. I was a mom of a three-and-a-half-year-old, a 22-month-old and due to give birth in three weeks when I opened the doors to The Cove School in the daylight basement of our home. Our family of five lived upstairs in 900 square feet and two bedrooms, with the family room and 3rd bedroom set up as classroom space with French doors out to the backyard.

For the next two years, due to the success of our program, my husband and enrolled families encouraged me to grow the program. I resisted and didn't imagine myself running a school. Through a series of serendipitous events, a beautiful craftsman home came up for rent in the winter of 2012. It was perfect for The Cove School. I would then spend the next 8 months figuring out how to make it all work so we could be ready to launch a new space that fall. When I combined my love for learning, mental wellness, children and business with my deep desire to transform what education and learning could look like, The Cove was born and brought to new levels.

From a Traditional Preschool to Fully-Embodied Mindful Preschool

At first, the preschool model I built was a fairly traditional, play-based, high perform-ing, let's get my kiddo into Harvard type school. Within 6 months, I knew I wanted to go another direction. Simultaneously, due to the real estate crash, I had close family and friends going through rough times. I was helping people through anxiety, mild depression and just a whole lot of stress. Despite families at our school struggling, and my own family wondering if the day would come when my husband would lose his job, I wondered what I could provide these incredibly curious and open 2- and 3-year-olds that would help them through times like these when they were adults. With a quick Google search, I came across mindfulness; and many searches later, still mindfulness. So I picked up the cheapest and quickest online curriculums I could implement right away: A Still Quiet Place and Mindful Schools.

Little did I know that what started as a curriculum for children would end up transforming the way I live, work and do business. Amy Saltzman of A Still Quiet Place and Mindful Schools would end up being the foundation of not only my school and what I wanted to offer in education, but my greatest supporters and lifelines. Dr. Amy saw my gift long before I ever could and her course was my first step into the mindfulness in education field. I also dove right into Mindful-ness Fundamentals offered by Mindful Schools and soon after was fortunate to be in Mindful Schools first-ever online curriculum training with Megan Cowan and Chris McKenna, a couple of years before their Year-Long Certification program was available. These would be the stepping stones needed to build the foundation for The Cove School.

As I built my school—implementing things like growth mindset, positive psychology, mindfulness, and some early childhood trends—led me to the root of all these philosophies and methodologies. It didn't take long to realize that the best curriculum in the world would never surpass the importance of my own personal practice in mindfulness.

I spent the first year just using mindfulness curriculum in the classroom with children. At the time, there were lots of conversations in the field around the necessity of having a practice in order to teach mindfulness. My type A, do it yesterday attitude, wanted to hear nothing of the sort. I didn't want to put the "time" in because I was already having success with the curriculum in the classroom. It wasn't until I began the Mindful Schools Year-Long Certification and completed my first silent retreat as part of the program, that I understood the impact of my own personal practice and of having embodiment at the core of delivery. That week was transformational and the beginning of a life-long journey.

The Clearer Your Why, the Clearer Your Path Becomes

Building a school did not come without its struggles. On top of teaching, managing staff, running the school and working with the city and state around regulations, I was trying to find the right staff with the heart and hustle necessary to execute my vision. It took years of attracting, training and retaining the right people to get where we are today. In all transparency, much of it was trial and error with some skillful—and not so skillful—moments. Implementing a mindfulness program in a school and making it part of the fabric of the culture requires intention, commitment and practice.

Once I knew that my purpose was to create a school and a program that could be a model for the future of education, my path became very clear. My relationships shifted, my goals changed and I articulated the school differently. One of the first things I did was get very clear with my why. Why does this world need a mindfulness-based preschool? Why does mindfulness need to be part of education? My why goes beyond the benefits from learning the techniques of mindfulness practices. I have a deep knowing that we, as humanity, need to be different. I know that deep in my core, mindfulness has offered me a different way of being in the world and that this way is available to everyone. So, let's start with the children who are naturally this way already and continue to nurture their mindful awareness.

Our program begins with hiring the right facilitators. Our facilitators are open to learning and developing a practice. They have a positive attitude, are open to trying new things and are willing to push boundaries and question the status quo. We provide them with the tools, courses, and environment that promotes well-being, creativity and a genuine penchant for curiosity. When I first started, one of the requirements of paying for staff to take a mindfulness course was they had to commit to stay with The Cove for a full school year after completing the course. All facilitators take the Mindful Schools Fundamentals course as part of their training as a Cove facilitator. This is to create the foundation for practice and a common language among our staff. Those that seemed to be highly interested could then continue to do the Educator Essentials.

After the first year, I no longer required a length of time for facilitators to stay in order for me to pay for the courses. My invitation to anyone that took these courses was just to have the intention to bring it into the next place they go, whether they stayed with us 6 months or 6 years. This aligned more with my why and the kind of impact and reach I wanted to have in the world.

How to Prepare Children for a World that Does Not Yet Exist

In creating a mindfulness program for both adults and children, the question that is the core of everything is: How do you prepare children for a world that does not yet exist?

Children starting preschool or kindergarten this year will be applying for jobs in 13–15 years that don't yet exist today. When I taught kindergarten back in 2003, one of the standards that we had to make sure each kindergartner knew was what a computer mouse was. Less than 5 years later that question was almost obsolete. Those kindergartners, now all grown up, have jobs in artificial intelligence or social media, as an example, and at that time those positions were not even on our radar.

Our focus really starts with the end in mind. The question becomes what kind of global citizens do we want in the world? Then we reverse-engineered from there. With my deep interest in human behavior and how the mind works, combined with my understanding of learning and development, and the neuroscience of mindfulness, what was always clear to me is that the current education system was not providing an optimal environment for learning. As I looked at how humans needed to show up in the future, a key tenant became Napoleon Hill's quote, "Whatever the mind can conceive and believe, it can achieve."

So, what does this look like and how is it implemented in the culture of The Cove School? We began looking at where the breakdown happens from childhood to adulthood. What I found is that it happens way sooner than we think and it is we, the adults, that get in the way. I often pose this question in my talks, "How many of you can draw?" The response I often get is, if I am lucky, 25% of the room raises their hand, but often it is less. Of those 25% hands that are raised, at least half of them are half-hearted hand raises, hovering in the middle with a distinct look of "maybe?" on their face. So then I pose the question, "What happened between preschool and now?" Because if preschoolers were sitting here right now, 100% of their hands would be raised.

Mindset and language is the first place we start with our facilitators and parents. We recognized that although we have good intentions for the children, the language we use unconsciously limits their beliefs. One idea that I share often is that we do not allow the phrase "I can't" from anyone. When a child or adult says "I can't," it automatically puts a stop to any other option. It takes choice away from someone. Instead, we replace it with "How can I?" For example, Jenny says, "I can't put on my shoes." Our facilitator would respond, "How can I put on my shoes? I can try a different way, I can ask a friend for help, I can ask an adult for help." This begins opening the mind to various possibilities.

Another mindset shift that is powerful for parents and facilitators is bringing awareness to how we react or respond to children. Every year by the end of September, I get an email from a parent (often upset) that they picked up their child with their shoes on the wrong feet. After explaining our rationale behind it, they are often grateful for the shift in perspective. Once a child puts their shoes on independently, we celebrate the fact that they did it on their own.

What the unconscious mind tends to do though is to focus on the negative. The first thing we want to do as an adult is correct them and say, "Oh, but they are on the wrong feet." Now, if this happened to us at work when we set out to do something new and the first thing our boss says is, "Oh, but you did this wrong," you can imagine the lack of motivation we may feel to try something creative or new again. I use this just to illustrate the importance of bringing awareness to our language and how we engage with people. It is the foundation of the culture at The Cove School. As we are building a child's confidence, one of the easiest things to do for 2.5- and 3-year-olds is to show them how to do things that they can do for themselves like putting on their shoes and coat.

Reflections on This Journey

I learned so much personally and professionally throughout my journey. Here are a few of the realizations, insights, and lessons that have made the biggest impact in my life.

- Embodying the practice is everything and everything starts with the adults (facilitators and parents). This way of being will have more impact and sustainability than any program or curriculum. It becomes about how you relate to others and your experience.

- Relationships are pivotal. I am not able to do what I am doing without key people in my life. I did not go at this alone and many of you reading this are likely part of my journey and for that, I am eternally grateful.
- I realize that I can do seemingly hard things with ease. Instead of ignoring or resisting difficulties and negatives, I find ways to appreciate the contrast and see the potential, clarity or opportunity it provides. I have learned to lean into what is difficult; as Ryan Holiday says, the obstacle is the way.
- I create my own stress. I learned that my reaction to situations causes the stress in my life. By slowing down and developing presence and patience, the next actions unfold naturally without tension or strain. There is more space for allowing instead of controlling or directing.
- It takes a systemic approach because nothing operates in a silo. What I set out to do started with children and I quickly realized the importance of our facilitators and parents practicing as part of the process. It is all of us working together that allows the work to take root and have a ripple effect in the world around us.
- I originally set out to create the best preschool in Seattle. That created a competition mindset and had me looking at all the preschools around to see how I could be better than them. Once I shifted and began creating from my own unique perspective, there was no competition. I realized I was just facilitating the creation of The Cove and it was a place our community needed.
- The mindfulness in education community is tight and supportive. I love the connections I have made with people all over the world and I have been blown away by the generosity, heart, and connection I have experienced. My mentors and mentees play a huge part in this journey and without them, The Cove wouldn't exist.

Favorite Practices

These are a few of our favorite practices because they are helpful for adults and you can do them with children as young as three. I encourage doing these practices often and when the children are calm and in good spirits; that way when emotions get big, they can access these practices more easily.

Pinwheel Breathing

Breath can be abstract for the little ones, so we always start an introduction to breath using a pinwheel. When we give the children a pinwheel, we start by asking them to play with it and then ask what they notice. We scaffold learning and see if they can come to the understanding that the breath is being used to move the pinwheel. Then we play with our breath by using fast, slow, long and short breaths. This gives them a more tangible experience around understanding the breath and sensations around the breath.

Cotton Ball Breathing

The first part of this activity is to have one cotton ball for every two children. They pair up and play catch with the cotton ball by using their breath. They can do it on a table, floor or with their hands without throwing it. You can start asking them to notice their breath and any sensations that arise as they play the game. This amps up their energy and they have a really fun time with it.

The second part is to help their nervous system begin to rest and digest. They each have their own cotton ball and place it in the palm of their hand closest to their wrist. The invitation is to use their breath to blow the cotton ball across their flat palm facing up to the end of their fingertips without it falling off. This will allow for them to slow their breathing down and activate their parasympathetic nervous system.

Drawing Emotions

Have the children close their eyes, if it is comfortable for them, and see if they notice what they are feeling. It is important to do this at different times of the day and with different emotions. You can offer different options for naming them if they are not coming up with them on their own, like silly, happy, sad, frustrated, scared. You can ask them to assign it a color or draw a picture that represents the emotion. This is helpful for adults to do as well.

Eating Mindfully

You can choose a meal or a treat and have children explore their food in their hand, noticing closely the taste, texture, smell. Have them take a small bite and chew slowly so they can begin to notice the taste and texture in their mouth.

Noticing 5 Things

At any given moment, have a seat and notice 5 things around you in the environment. Start by modeling it, then have the child do the same. This is something they can learn to do by themselves, especially when feeling nervous or scared. Orienting to the environment is helpful to support nervous system processing and strengthens self-regulation.

Nature and The Senses

Nature is a great way to connect children to their senses and being outside in nature is one of the best ways to improve physical and mental wellbeing. When taking a walk outside or in the woods, choose one of the senses like touch and begin noticing different textures and how they feel, like bark on a tree, stones, blades of grass, leaves, and sidewalks. Each walk can focus on one sense or you can incorporate sight, smell, and sound.

Transitioning from Facilitating Learning with Children to Adults

What we need to be thinking about and talking about is understanding the perspective of those that are skeptical, fearful and just flat out against mindfulness in schools. What are the beliefs and values that they hold that put mindfulness in education in question? By understanding the other side, we can learn what can be improved, how we can talk about it and implement it in a way that can be universal and make the necessary shifts if it makes sense. Listening to the criticism will only strengthen the field and if we are embodying the practice, then all thoughts are welcome.

Also, long term sustainability and creating a mindfulness-based culture has to be a systems approach and it starts with the adults. The Cove School is in its 10th year with approximately 34 students a day, 50 plus families a year and 6 of us on staff. Ms. Claudia, the director of The Cove, runs the day to day operations and started as my assistant 10 years ago, so has experienced all iterations from when I began creating the program. She is an instrumental part of our program and loved by all.

My facilitators are amazingly dedicated to mental well-being and supporting the optimal conditions for learning at The Cove. Many ask how I go about hiring our facilitators and the main things I look for are a positive attitude, growth mindset and love of learning. I do not require a degree in education and in fact, prefer they do not have an education degree. We do things so differently at The Cove, I often find that experienced teachers have to unlearn some of the traditional ways of teaching they picked up along the way.

My involvement with The Cove is more high level these days. I still do admissions with Ms. Claudia—which I love—meeting the families, talking about our program and making sure it is the right fit all-around for everyone. I manage our private Facebook group for enrolled families and alumni and provide research, activities, musings and live videos for Q&A or other concepts families want to learn. This still gives me a little presence at the school since I am usually their first point of contact when they come across The Cove. The biggest difference from when I opened is that I am not on-site daily or involved with the day-to-day.

Children are so easy for me to work with and facilitate learning. I had no idea I could have the same experience facilitating learning with adults. Creating a mindfulness-based preschool led me to work with the parents who wanted to learn more about mindfulness and what their children were learning. After providing several Mindful Parenting workshops, parents began experiencing the benefits and seeing the value, so they brought me into their workplaces. Strictly through word of mouth and connecting with people in the mindfulness in education community and the mindfulness at work community, I now work primarily with adults.

Most of my time is working with leaders, teams, and individuals both in business and education facilitating workshops, coaching, consulting and speaking across the country. I am also humbled by the opportunity to co-facilitate a well-being circle for educators called the Millennium Forum. It is a beautiful, healing and support-ive environment bringing together and developing whole educators so they can educate the whole child. My latest projects involve building online courses, so I can have more impact and reach helping others to manage change with greater ease. I'll have one for parents, teachers, leaders and middle school athletes. What started as teaching mindfulness is now also using mindfulness as the lens in which I help organizations, districts and schools earn trust, build culture and manage change.

CHAPTER 22

Shared Vision and Collaboration by a Principal, School Counselor, and School Social Worker

Julie H. Chamberlain, MEd, MS

Erica L. Herrera, MSW

Jennifer M. Perilla, MEd

Tyler Elementary School, Gainsville, VA

As a school counselor, I have always used mindfulness with my students, both individually and in small groups, and it has been very beneficial. It has also been my personal path to maintaining balance. Despite this, it had not occurred to me to share it school-wide until my principal, our school social worker, and I formed our collaborative team.

Jennifer Perilla is our school principal. In the midst of her many demands, mindfulness has been essential to bringing a calm and kind approach to herself, her staff, and especially her interactions with our students. She believes in approaching the children through compassion and kindness, modeling mindfulness and helping them regulate their emotions.

Erica Herrera is our school social worker, as well as a yoga instructor. She works at both the elementary and middle school levels. She was the initiator of implementing a schoolwide mindfulness practice at our school, Tyler Elementary. She secured a grant of $1000 that made it possible to purchase many of the tools used. Her background, knowledge, and experiences have been an incredible resource on this journey.

All three of us have taken the Mindfulness Fundamentals and Mindful Educator Essentials courses through mindfulschools.org. Erica is currently in a mindfulness educator certification program, and I plan to begin the certification program in 2021. I am also the Virginia State Chapter Coordinator for the Coalition of Schools Educating Mindfully. Each of us is very passionate about mindfulness and its importance in the school setting.

Our Why

At Tyler Elementary School, teachers, administrators, and support staff noticed a trend in our students that was mimicking the national increase of mental health challenges. Students were entering kindergarten without the ability to manage their emotions and displayed behaviors that were more disruptive and severe. Older students reported being anxious about tests and their school performance, which resulted in frequent trips to the nurse, school counselor, and social worker, as well as to administrators. Discipline infractions were noted by a student's inability to recognize anger and use positive coping strategies, and teachers were showing signs of burn-out. We knew we had to implement more than a program or an idea- it had to be a total philosophical shift, from reactive to proactive. Offering students, families, and staff the skills to use any time, in any situation, could be transformative.

Surprisingly, according to the VA School of Education Journal, anxiety affects over 40% of students in the United States today and is the leading mental health issue among youth. Educators experience stresses comparable to emergency room physicians and up to 61% of mental health providers experience symptoms of burnout. With increased suicide attempts and completions, and anxiety and stress at higher levels than ever before, we knew that something monumental needed to change.

Studies show that adults who learn mindfulness report reduced stress and burn-out and greater efficacy in doing their jobs. Students who learn mindfulness show improved cognitive outcomes such as reduced attentional problems, enhanced focus, improved social skills, along with emotional regulation and increased compassion.

Simply, mindfulness changes the brain, emphasizes focus on the present and leads to happier people. Therefore, a mindful centered school made sense. We will share our journey, the neuroscience and benefits of practicing mindfulness, how to engage your community, and mindful practices that will help you to begin your own, and your school's journey.

Concerns and Resources

Since mindfulness is included in Buddhist teachings, it is necessary to educate the community, and always from a place of kindness and compassion. Share that it is also a secular practice that focuses on present moment awareness and emotional recognition and regulation. We shared what our program looks like with our parents, our school board representative, and on social media through our school district's videographer, who did a feature story on mindfulness at our school.

The concern is also very real about whether or not the teachers will buy into the concept of mindfulness and feel comfortable using it in their classrooms. To help with this, once a month we taught, and continue to teach, mindfulness classes in each classroom to model what it looks like and give them ideas for how to proceed.

Educating the staff and the community is an integral component of the success of mindfulness in schools. Besides Mindful Schools, resources we've used so far include the MindUp curriculum, Empowering Education curriculum, Mindful Activity Cards, Mindful Life Project, and JusTme videos. We have many books and links included in our resource list as well.

We were very fortunate to have administrator support, involvement, and enthusiasm right from the start. Our principal has been instrumental in initiating, building and reinforcing mindfulness throughout every aspect of our school. This makes a monumental difference.

First Year: Growth Mindsets, Mindfulness, and Empathy

Initially, the three of us brainstormed ways to become a mindful-based school in the summer of 2017. During the teacher work-week in August we presented to the faculty, and during the first day of school to all of the students, on Growth Mindsets, Mindfulness, and Empathy, realizing that mindfulness really encompasses the other two. Following that, each team of teachers brainstormed and shared ways mindfulness could be implemented in their classrooms. Most of the staff were on board and at least willing to implement mindfulness a little bit, and some were gung-ho. At each subsequent faculty meeting, teachers shared incredible ideas, inspiring others to follow suit.

By the end of the first year, every teacher in our school did at least one daily mindful practice with their students. For a resource, we taped some practices that they could access and play at any time. Some did one first thing in the morning, some did one following recess to help their students calm down, and some did one in the afternoon to refocus their students for the subjects taught later in the day.

Throughout the year, students and staff were engaged in many experiential mindfulness activities and school-wide events were implemented including a Family Mindfulness Night and the Great Kindness Challenge. We gave presentations to parents at our school, counselors in our county, and at the Equity and Excellence in Education Conference, Student Leadership Conference, Virginia Counselors Association Conference and American School Counselor Association Conference.

Mindfulness Implementations Expand

During the second year of implementation, we had more of an organic approach. We experienced growth from many angles—teachers, staff, and administration. Mindfulness was taught in all of the classrooms and for targeted small groups. Besides classroom teachers incorporating a daily mindfulness practice, other elements that were implemented the first year, and continued or were added the second year, include:

- Beginning each faculty meeting with a mindfulness practice and dedicated discussion time for the "Teachers as Readers" selection from *Happy Teachers Change the World* by Thich Nhat Hhan and Katherine Weare
- Grade level teams presenting ideas of implemented mindful practices in their class
- The Mindful Minute (Moment of Silence)
- Weekly class meetings that include discussion of student concerns and how to address them mindfully
- A calming corner (some have corner tents) in each class with a class calming bottle
- Calming boxes in each classroom with many mindfulness tools
- Groups for students at risk academically or emotionally
- Student mindfulness clubs (before school)
- Staff mindfulness clubs (after school)
- Monthly in-class mindfulness lessons
- Mindful journaling
- Yoga
- Student-led mindful practices taped and accessible for staff to use with their class
- One-word mindful messages painted on rocks lining the school entranceway
- Mindful ambassadors: Two students are selected from each class to lead and be an example of mindful practices

Additionally, there is a dedicated committee to lead the continued integration of mindfulness in the school community. The four core areas that we focus on are awareness, focus and attention, emotions, and acceptance. Through the above mindfulness implementations over two years, we have seen an increase in test scores, a decrease in referrals and lowered anxiety. Qualitatively, a significant difference in how students acknowledged and took control of anxiety was observed.

Examples of Practices, Activities and Lessons

Mindfulness is about noticing whatever experience you are having in the present moment, including all thoughts, feelings, or physical sensations. That way we can change the way that we relate to them, particularly the challenging ones, and how we are relating to one another.

The mind generally wanders between the past and the future, which can lead to stress and unhappiness. The Chinese philosopher Lao Tzu shares a very powerful quote: "If you are depressed, you are living in the past. If you are anxious, you are living in the future. If you are at peace, you are living in the present." Our hope is that the following activities will enable more moments in the present. Best of luck on your journey to mindfulness, both professionally and personally, and may you have many moments appreciating and being in the present.

> *"I close my eyes and take deep breaths, and I let the butterflies in my stomach stop flying."*—3rd-grade student.

During a "kind wishes" mindfulness activity with a 2nd-grade class, the students were asked how the activity made them feel. One student said, "My anger felt like fire and mindfulness felt like a bucket of water being poured onto it!"

Mindfulness Club Activities

Mindful scavenger hunt, creation of classroom calming boxes, breathing cards, shape breathing wheels, breathing beads, sensory playdough, therapy dog visit, calming bottles, mindful bingo, and mindful sitting practice.

Understanding How the Brain Works

Students are taught that the amygdala is where the fight/flight/freeze reaction occurs. When a perceived threat approaches, the amygdala goes on high alert. A great example of this is the sea turtle. If he is swimming close to the surface of the ocean, and a shark approaches, his instincts kick in, he turns his hard shell toward the predator, and high-tails it to the bottom of the ocean. This is an automatic reaction.

Reptilian brains do not have a conscious level of awareness. They run on instinct. That is why we refer to the amygdala as the "lizard brain." The instinctual "lizard brain" can be demonstrated by shaking a calming bottle showing what happens to the brain when frightened, making it difficult to make good decisions. When the "lizard brain" is activated, information cannot pass through to the prefrontal cortex, the "wizard brain" (the wise decision-making part of the brain) because it is blocked by the emotions of the "lizard brain" and held captive.

The amygdala is great for protection but does not allow one to focus, decide, and reason—essential skills needed in school. Through the practice of mindful activities, students build their capacity to respond consciously, instead of reacting instinctively. They can train the "lizard brain" to de-activate, and not see perceived threats as real. The sea turtle has actually adapted its heart rate to one beat per minute, allowing it to only have to come up for a breath every 6 hours! Students can learn to use their wise "wizard brain" to regulate their emotions, and create new neural pathways. The brain can actually stretch and grow the more we use it, so we want to encourage growth in all of the most beneficial parts!

Mindful Breathing

One practice that is central to mindfulness is breathing. By giving our full attention to our breath, we heighten our awareness, notice the present moment, and choose what thoughts and feelings to hold onto and for how long, and what to let go of. Spending time in stillness mindfully breathing, just "being," is a counterbalance to all of our to-do lists, activities and other "doing."

When stressed, breathing can come to the rescue. Deep, full breathing calms the amygdala and helps the "wizard brain" to think clearly. One technique is to turn down the lights, play calming music, or use a variety of guided mindfulness apps. Students sit in a comfortable position and are invited to close their eyes or focus on something in the room, such as a calming bottle. The students are instructed to focus on breathing slowly. If their thoughts wander, it is okay; the purpose is not to keep the mind from wandering, but to recognize when it does, and bring it back to focus on their breath or focal point.

It is wise to start with a short period of time, increasing as the students become used to the technique, and debrief together what was easy and what was challenging. If there are students who have difficulty sitting still, they can be encouraged to use other strategies such as a focal point, or introduce another sensory component like tapping their leg as they inhale or exhale. They can also place their hand on their heart as they breathe.

Belly Buddies

Students choose a small stuffed animal or squishy that they designate as their 'belly buddy' to use when they practice breathing. Students lay on their backs and place the belly buddy on their abdomen. The belly buddy will rise when they inhale and fall when they exhale.

Five Finger Breathing or Shape Breathing

The hand is held upright, each finger is traced around one at a time, breathing in as the finger traces up, and breathing out as the finger traces down the other side. This is done with each of the five fingers or around designated shapes.

Five Senses

A few deep breaths are taken and then participants think of five thoughts they are thinking, four things they hear, three emotions they feel, two things they see, and one thing they can touch.

Mind Bubbles

The book *Mind Bubbles,* by Heather Krantz, is read to demonstrate that we all have thoughts that come and go. Students are allowed to pop bubbles and it is pointed out that this is a natural reaction. Next, they just watch the bubbles as they float around, and recognize the desire to pop them, but are encouraged to just observe, rather than react. Help make the connection that we always have the choice to observe and respond thoughtfully and kindly to our thoughts and emotions instead of just acting on instinct, autopilot or how we have in the past. This is a great exercise to build self-control.

Anchoring

Picture yourself on a sailboat riding the waves of your emotions. Some days the waters are calm and your boat gently bobs with the change of the waters. Other days they are rough and toss your boat around. If you had to choose a captain for your boat, would you choose your "lizard brain" or your "wizard brain"? Your "wizard brain" is wise and knows when to drop an anchor to keep your boat steady, despite the choppy waters. An anchor is a word, phrase, symbol, or technique such as breathing, that brings one back to the present moment, a core mindfulness practice.

Brain Dump

Participants are asked to write down all of their thoughts, completing a 'brain dump'. Once the list is complete, participants are asked to review it and indicate which thoughts are related to the past, present or future. Open a discussion about what they recognize about their thoughts. Being aware of them, without judgment, is an important exercise in mindfulness.

Mindful Eating/Tasting

Incorporating the brain dump, along with a mindful tasting exercise, is a great way to introduce two mindfulness practices together. Each participant is given a piece of gum. They are instructed to break it in half and chew the first half. While chewing, they are asked to follow the directions above for the brain dump. Following the examination of their thoughts, they chew the second half of the gum mindfully-paying attention, on purpose, just to chewing the gum. They debrief the difference between the first experience with the gum and the second.

Mindful Listening

Fill a carton of plastic eggs with pairs of the same objects. Students shake the eggs to hear the noises they make, using mindful listening skills to match the eggs by sound only.

Four Rock Meditation

Each child is given four rocks. They represent the freshness of a flower, the solidity of a mountain, the calm reflecting nature of still water, and the freedom of space. The book *A Handful of Quiet* by Thich Nhat Hanh is read and participants follow along through the guided practice. Rocks are kept as a reminder that we all have these qualities within us.

Mindful Movement

Yoga and mindful walking are simple ways to include mindful movement during the day. Students listen for new sounds and record them. A 'rainbow walk' is a fun way to see how many things they can find from the colors of the rainbow. Great books include *Yoga Bunny* by Brian Russo and *Good Morning Yoga* by Mariam Gates.

Mindful Body

Being aware of how and where emotions are felt, allows one to respond mindfully. A good way to do this is to create a body map identifying emotions with colors, symbols, and words and where they physically happen in the body. Process that it is normal to have uncomfortable emotions, but realize that they come and go. To demonstrate further, participants close their eyes and are told that an uncomfortable object such as an ice cube or prickly pine cone will be placed in their hand. They are instructed to pay attention to how the object feels and fully explore it. They sit with the uncomfortable feeling and are directed to focus on their breath. This activity is great to pair with the books *Angry Octopus* by Lori Lite, *Shubert Learns to Be a S.T.A.R.* by Dr. Becky Bailey, and *Listening to My Body* by Gabi Garcia.

Calming Bottle

Individual or classroom calming and feelings bottles can be created. After reading aloud *Moody Cow Meditates* by Kerry Lee Maclean, students can be directed to listen to the feelings that Moody Cow experiences and how he is able to calm down.

Each student is encouraged to choose colored glitter to place in the bottle to represent a feeling they have. Emphasize the idea that feelings are not good or bad, but they can be pleasant or unpleasant. Using a calming bottle as a focal point during mindful breathing is a great tool.

Mindful Practice for School Counselors

Here is a script that I created for the school counselors when we presented at the ASCA Conference:

> *I would like to take you through a short mindful practice that will help you to experience present moment awareness and free your mind of the worries and responsibilities that you have to focus on every day.*
>
> *Sit in a comfortable posture, with your spine upright and your shoulders rolled down and back. Close your eyes, if that feels comfortable for you, or just lower them to a soft gaze.*
>
> *Allow your breath to be natural. . . . As best you can, bring your attention to your breath, noticing when you are breathing in . . . and when you are breathing out . . . .*
>
> *See if you can notice what your breath feels like in your nose, as the air goes in your nose, and then comes out over the lips . . . . (pause) . . . .*
>
> *Notice what your breath feels like in your chest, perhaps sensing the gentle expansion of the chest on the inhale, and the fall of the chest on the exhale . . . (pause) . . . .*
>
> *You may find yourself thinking about breathing, but see if you can focus on the actual physical sensations of breathing. . . . What does it feel like, right now, in your body as you breathe?*
>
> *Next, see if you can notice what your breath feels like in your belly, noticing how the belly expands as you inhale, and softens as you exhale . . . . (pause) . . . .*
>
> *You may also be able to notice the sensations of the breath elsewhere in your body. . . .*
>
> *For a few more moments, just try to let your attention rest on your breath, wherever YOU notice it most . . .*
>
> *Thoughts may float through your mind, just like clouds across the sky, just watch them, observe them, without feeling a need to do anything.*

Continue to breathe, in through your nose and out through your mouth . . . .

Breathe in one positive thing that you know about yourself, breathe out a negative thought that you may be holding.

Breathe in another positive thought that you know to be true about a student you helped, breathe out a negative thought that may be judgmental.

Place your hand over your heart and allow your thoughts and feelings to meld together into compassion. Say to yourself, "I am awesome!" Say out loud, "I am awesome!" Say loudly, "I am awesome!" As you go through each day, allow kindness and compassion toward yourself and others to be your guide.

When you're ready, bring your focus back to your surroundings. Spending a few moments deliberately attending to your breath each day, lowers your heart rate, and has a calming effect on the mind and body. You deal with so many stressful situations each and every day, for so many different people.

Research indicates that when you consistently practice mindfulness, present moment, non-judgmental awareness, it lowers rates of anxiety and depression, leads to better sleep, stronger relationships, and increased self-awareness, all of which can go a long way toward changing your relationship with stress, which is a gift you can give to your students and family.

CHAPTER 23

Yoga and Mindfulness for All Students with an Onsite Yoga Studio

Jessica Janowsky, MEd, RYT-200

Creator, Y.O.G.A. Program, Founder of Yoga m.a.g.i.c. LLC, Yoga and Mindfulness Instructor, Elmira City School District, Elmira, NY

I'm a teacher in the state of new york for grades Pre K-6th and I began my mindfulness practice as a young person. My mother would invite me to share her yoga practice with her. My favorite instructor on video was Rodney Yee because he had a playfulness about him that didn't make yoga seem as serious as the other instructors. I would occasionally visit my yoga practice, but did not commit to my practice until about 5 years ago when I began to struggle with keeping calm and centered in the classroom.

I've been teaching for the Elmira City School District for 14 years. The Elmira area is a low-income community. One unique feature of our community is that we have two maximum security state prisons within a five-mile radius of each other. Currently, I am on special assignment as a full-time yoga and mindfulness instructor for the students at Parley Coburn Intermediate School. It is a Title 1 school with 475 3rd–6th grade students, 71% of them White, with 6 sections at each grade level.

The program began through grassroots introduction during the 2017–2018 school year and then was approved to be a full-time pilot program during 2018–2019. This school year is the second full-time pilot year. My special assignment as a yoga and mindfulness teacher was approved because Elmira City School District has a "Community Schools" focus. We are seeking to improve social-emotional learning and provide sound strategies promoting good mental health and attention to the "whole child."

Additionally, I am qualified to teach in such a capacity. I completed a 200-hour yoga certification, am a certified Kidding Around Yoga Teacher, and hold a certificate in Trauma-Informed Yoga for Children through Childlight Yoga. I have several other certifications and have also been trained in Breath, Body, Mind by

Dr. Richard P. Brown and Dr. Patricia L. Gerbarg. My qualifications, along with the district's vision to develop a curriculum which enables students to better self-regulate and calm themselves in the face of adversity in a positive, prosocial way, was the premise for the program I am developing. My program is titled Y.O.G.A. (Your Objectives Get Accomplished).

Be Part of the Solution

After being in the classroom for 12 years, I was becoming mentally and emotionally weary. There are many studies documenting the challenges of teaching low-income populations. Although I love teaching curriculum, I was not finding much enjoyment in the rest of my job. Behavioral problems were a continuous struggle. Grading papers, analyzing data, and never-ending paperwork seemed to be the main focus, not instruction.

My outlook was becoming increasingly negative. Before school even started, I anticipated a tough day ahead. After years of not seeing any significant changes in students' attitudes, despite various programs, I started to get back on my own yoga mat. I engaged in a daily practice before school. Resuming my practice more faithfully made me feel better, more grounded. I was more resilient to the difficult situations and the emotional roller coaster that often comes with teaching young people. I decided to pursue a yoga certification since I was already a fitness professional. Becoming a yoga teacher seemed to fit in perfectly with who I already was and who I was seeking to become.

Within a few weeks of committing to my yoga practice, I had a revelation as I was meditating—I could be part of the solution! My negative energy was adding to the problem. Parley Coburn students tend to have a negative work ethic, poor self-regulation, limited focus, and explosive or violent tendencies when they are emotionally upset. The reports on yoga and mindfulness programs in schools really got my attention. Many studies have shown improvement in students' self-regulation skills and focus. I read reports saying how it could help calm and focus people, but in terms of understanding *what* a mindful practice consisted of, I was clueless.

It was through my yoga teacher training in 2017–2018 that I was introduced to mindfulness. I immersed myself in dozens of books to expand my knowledge of the practice. Some books that I've found especially helpful are *Coming to Our Senses* by Jon Kabat-Zinn, *The Way of Mindful Education* by Daniel Rechtschaffen, *Mindfulness for Teachers* by Patricia A. Jennings, and *Mindful Games* by Susan Kaiser Greenland.

From Initiation Period to Full-Time Pilot

I shared my findings with my principal, asking that I be allowed to introduce yoga and mindfulness to the entire school. My principal and superintendent allowed me to present my case in a private meeting. I relayed current research in educational trends and demonstrated the need for our school to improve students' self-regulation strategies. I made the case for how implementing the Y.O.G.A. program could be instrumental in helping our students with promoting social-emotional learning and good mental health practices. The district agreed to provide a Y.O.G.A. program "initiation" period.

At that time, I met with one homeroom a day for 40 minutes, providing instruction on calming and breathing practices, yoga poses, mindfulness and meditation techniques. Classroom teachers were required to stay for the Y.O.G.A. lessons, but could choose to participate or just observe. Additionally, an aide was assigned to my 5th-grade classroom to monitor my students in literacy stations while I taught yoga in our in-school yoga studio. At the end of the introductory period, my principal and superintendent believed our initial findings were promising, especially in helping students self-regulate when faced with challenges. The program has been evolving ever since.

In 2018–2019 I was placed on special assignment and permitted to teach Y.O.G.A. full-time in my building. Y.O.G.A. ran as a special area, along with PE (physical education), art, music, computers, and library. I had five, 40-minute classes a day. I also had one 40-minute period we termed "Intensive" where teachers sent me the students in need of the most support for self-regulation skills. We are modifying the program again for 2019–2020 in that I will use the "Intensive" times to push into classrooms for mini-lessons with teachers present. In this way, we hope to build a more cohesive school culture.

My personal practice of mindfulness has not been without challenges. It was a requirement of my yoga school that we practice a minimum of 10 minutes a day. At first, I found meditation difficult. I'm a highly active person and I was not used to sitting still. For months I practiced meditation with a non-judgmental attitude and I worked on accepting whatever happened in my practice without worry or self-criticism. Once I was able to master the mindset, I was better able to meditate. Now I can typically meditate for 20 minutes or more without feeling restless. I can rest my thoughts and let go of expectations not only of myself, but of the present moment experience. I love to meditate now and practice daily.

Adapting the Lessons for Different Grade Levels

Every lesson I teach, despite the grade level, has a mindfulness component. Students in 3rd- and 4th-grade love mindfulness and most 5th graders also love the practice. They have been open-minded, allowing the practices to be as they are, whatever they are, in the present moment. The program has provided them with strategies to calm and self-regulate. One 5th grade student wrote me a note in which she stated, "I like the program because it makes me feel powerful, relaxed. It makes me feel like my true self. It makes me see a better life for me."

Sixth graders, on the other hand, have been very resistant to the lessons. Many of them have a fixed mindset with regards to health—if it isn't PE class, they cannot see its value. To overcome this issue, I have been implementing more community circles. A community circle is a restorative practice in which a group of people sit in a circle and focus on a topic. One person holds a talking tool, and they are the only person allowed to speak. No one is permitted to interrupt, comment or even ask a question when someone is sharing. All others in the circle are mindfully listening.

An example of a mindfulness community circle would be asking students to describe something that makes them angry. Then I set a timer for one, two or three minutes, depending on the energy and focus of the group. Wait time is always given for students to have an opportunity to think deeply about their responses. Once the time is up, the talking tool is passed around, giving each person an opportunity to express themselves. We have a rule that they are not allowed to name names or call out another student. They need to replace names with "someone" or "people."

After everyone has shared, I ask a second question, "What does anger feel like in your body?" Then, "What do you typically do or how do you usually react when angered?" To conclude this lesson, I provide them with three to four strategies they can employ as a conscious response to anger, such as deep breathing, fist squeeze/release and using finger taps—whereas each finger touches the thumb in succession as you say one word of an affirmation such as, "I can choose wisely."

The lesson is disguised mindfulness because when I ask them to think quietly on one question before responding, they are employing a short, focused meditation. Then they are asked to think about how their body feels in a situation, leading to increased mind-body awareness. Finally, they reflect on how they usually react. Reflection and acknowledgment of "what is" is important if you want to consciously change your patterns. With awareness comes the opportunity to teach students that they have the power to consciously choose a path of appropriate action, instead of just reacting.

I've learned that sixth graders have a lot of issues and sometimes just want to be heard. They like to hear themselves talk, but not necessarily listen to others. They also tend to want to talk about how others have wronged them, rather than about their feelings. I've intuited that some mock meditation or mindful practices because they are afraid of their own feelings. By not taking mindfulness seriously, they can protect themselves from having to reflect and feel their deep, sometimes uncomfortable emotions. The community circle helps them practice their mindful listening skills and expand their awareness to include being compassionate to others.

Effectiveness Despite Colleague Resistance

A handful of teachers don't believe the program has value. They make comments, often in front of the students, that Y.O.G.A. is "just an extra prep," and that no true learning is happening. These classes are the most difficult to teach. Those teachers allow their students to come to my room with cell phones, tablets, and toys. It becomes a challenge to get students to "unplug" for the lesson.

Because Y.O.G.A. is a pilot program, I am required to report data as to its effectiveness to my superintendent, but I haven't yet been able to get data from the Planning Room—a designated room in our building where students are sent when they are being so disruptive that they are creating an unsafe environment. Data, such as which students are visiting the planning room, the reasons, how often, and for how long would help me know if the Y.O.G.A. program is making a difference and helping students self-regulate in difficult situations. It is very challenging to rely on others, whose information is so crucial. I have worked with the teacher in that room to show her many of the "go-to" calming techniques we employ, even creating a binder for her to use as a reference tool.

Since the start of the program, to show program effectiveness and to get feedback to improve the program, I have constructed several teacher surveys. My most recent one was administered during April of 2019 with the following results:

- 45% of the teachers participated (18 of 40)
- 94% believe the Y.O.G.A. program is beneficial to students' social-emotional development
- 89% reported observing students using Y.O.G.A. strategies independently
- 100% believe the program has helped at least one student in their classroom
- 100% encourage the Y.O.G.A. strategies within their own classrooms to promote a cohesive school culture
- 78% admitted to relying less on outside resources (Resource Officer, Planning Room, or Administrative Interventions) to help manage student behaviors since Y.O.G.A.

"My students learn to find their voice and use it to encourage themselves to make positive choices. Often, their lives are very chaotic, leaving them a jumble of emotions. Y.O.G.A. teaches them strategies for calming these emotions."—Naomi Avery, 4th-grade teacher

The Y.O.G.A. program is just beginning its work to help improve school relations. It provides mindful lessons that empower students through building confidence as well as promoting tolerance, empathy, and compassion. This creates a more cohesive school environment. I am sure that as the program grows, so will the positive results we see in students and staff.

In October 2018, the Chemung County Sunshine Rotary Club awarded $500 to Parley Coburn's Y.O.G.A. program based on its innovative way to help students. With the money, I was able to buy many items to enhance the program, including stethoscopes for mindfully listening to your heartbeat, and *Be Mindful: Card Deck for Teens* by Gina M. Biegel to help foster mindful community circle discussions.

New Professional Opportunities to Share What I'm Learning

Lastly, I am finding success professionally, sharing my knowledge in content. GST BOCES, our area's Board of Cooperative Educational Services, has asked that I teach a class to fellow teachers on implementing yoga and mindfulness for calmer classrooms and I was also invited by the New York Center for Teacher Development to be an online instructor to provide lessons for teachers everywhere on yoga and mindfulness. It is a graduate-level college course called Practicing Peace: Mindful Practices for a Calmer and More Connected Classroom and 46 people are taking it in its first run starting November 2019.

I have learned so much since the initial introduction of the Y.O.G.A. program. I have learned to never end with an energizing game or activity, even if it encompasses mindful components. Students are hard to settle down after they have been excited. The negative perception of some teachers may be reinforced if the students return to class too energized to focus on their work. Instead, I am incorporating elements that excite them and create interest in the concept at the beginning of the class. I want them to have fun in this program and be enthusiastic about coming to see me, looking forward to whatever new game or kinesthetic activity I've designed to promote mindful awareness.

I also know there needs to be time for quiet and calm in our practice. Lessons are absorbed in the body and mind in a calm setting. Each lesson ends with a brief three-minute meditation. Although every lesson needs to have fresh ideas, activities or concepts to keep them interested and engaged, we have the most success when I employ four components in every lesson, like a formula or recipe. The four foundational pieces of Y.O.G.A. provide structure kids crave for stability. My foundations are:

1. Begin with breathing techniques
2. Practice asanas (yoga poses) and sequences of asanas
3. Include a mindful activity
4. Practice a meditation/closing.

I've been asked if I use the word 'meditation' when teaching, as some teachers try to avoid this word in schools. I haven't had any issues using it so far. I explain that meditation is just a practice to allow our minds to rest so that we can think more clearly and be better focused, much like our bodies have more energy and are better able to be active after we get enough rest.

Even though I employ all four foundational pillars in every lesson for every grade level, I do not give them equal weight in terms of time. I vary this according to the needs of the students. Third graders need more movement and love to practice asanas. We spend more time doing physical activities in these classes. On the opposite end of the spectrum, most older kids do not enjoy the poses; this may be since they are beginning puberty and are feeling self-conscious. We may do some light stretches or cool arm balances like crow, but then spend the remaining time with the mindfulness lesson and meditation.

Another thing I have discovered is that if I use a chiming sound, I can more quickly and efficiently transition to the next foundational element of our practice. I make a game out of it. "How many chimes will it take you to settle, quiet, and focus?" They try to get as few chimes as possible. This also promotes teamwork. Prior to figuring this out, I was waiting, and waiting, and waiting. They love to talk to each other or get squirmy and unfocused during transitions. I tried to look calm, but it annoyed me sometimes. Being mindful of my own annoyance, I began playing around with different ways to transition them. This has worked very well even with the most difficult classes.

In 2019, I began offering Parent Academies one evening a month in which I teach parents about the benefits of mindfulness. In our sessions, I help families learn the same tools and strategies their children are being taught to promote calming and self-regulation. Through the Parent Academies, we are helping unite our community school with a culture of kindness and caring. Parent Academies are voluntary, so interested families attend. We are working to build more interest by promoting on the district website.

Unifying the School

I believe the most important thing I have learned is that it will be an ongoing process. New questions will arise which will require careful thought. I am human and will make mistakes. If I am mindfully aware of the students and their energy, then I will be open-minded enough to adjust and adapt the program to their present-moment needs and interests. I will continue to learn, read, research and develop my own practices.

I was asked by my principal to develop lessons that were based on themes such as friendship, generosity, gratitude, and forgiveness. By using one theme per month, I am able to present important social-emotional concepts to students in a profound way. Additionally, it helps unify our school. We are using common language and all students are being exposed to similar experiences. For example, I created posters featuring breathing techniques, affirmations, and simple yoga poses students could refer to when feeling uncomfortable emotions such as anger, frustration or sadness.

I am also writing lessons specifically for each grade level based on their most important or foundational English Language Arts text. It was energizing to re-read the texts with a yoga/mindfulness mindset in addition to a Common Core mindset. I believe writing lessons from this perspective lends itself to powerful opportunities to connect curriculum with personal learning goals. If we can infuse mindful lessons into existing required curricula, it will promote mindfulness in the classroom without making it feel like yet another additional task teachers have been burdened with.

To grow the practice of mindfulness in an educational setting, we need to be offering mindfulness training to teachers as part of their professional development options. A person cannot teach what they don't know. It is also essential that teachers have easy access to mindfulness training for their own health and wellness. For instance, each month at our staff meetings I speak briefly about one new tactic, skill or mindful practice teachers can implement into their own classrooms.

Additionally, I facilitated a book study over the summer on Patricia A. Jennings' book, *Mindfulness for Teachers: Simple Skills for Peace and Productivity in the Classroom.* I have also designed a course called Breathe and Calm which focuses on teaching local area teachers yoga and mindful techniques they can adapt and modify to meet their classroom needs. The course has run four times in the last year at our local area BOCES.

If we were to see more mindful initiations in schools, it might prove to help the dreary statistics of teachers leaving the profession before five years are up. Another thing that would help is incorporating mindfulness training in college teacher training courses. People just coming into the education profession would be better prepared for the difficult reality of trying to manage an entire classroom with 25 or more different personalities, experiences, and temperaments, while still teaching curriculum in an efficient and effective way.

Mindfulness is a gift to yourself. It provides a person the opportunity to come out of the chatter in their head and to get to know themselves and their truth in a kind, compassionate way. When one can accept who they are, they will be able to more clearly choose a path that feels right for them. So many wonderful results can happen from practicing mindfulness: you can become calmer and at peace with yourself; you can learn to trust yourself; you can learn to forgive yourself and others for mistakes. Forgiveness is like taking an antidote to the toxic effects of holding onto hate, worry, or sadness.

Mindfulness is also a grounding practice. My yoga teacher always says, "We root to rise." I think this is a beautiful way of saying that to branch out and reach for new challenges or achieve our goals, we must first be centered, balanced and focused. Mindfulness grounds and stabilizes us, allowing us the opportunity to grow.

CHAPTER 24

Drop Everything and Move

Kathy Flaminio, MSW, LGSW, RYT-200

Founder, 1000 Petals LLC and Move Mindfully

with **Sarah Singleton** and **Jon Bonneville**

Sky Oaks Elementary, Burnsville, MN, ISD 191

I will never forget the day an 8th grader looked at me after doing a mindful movement practice and stated, "What is this?" I asked, "What is what?" And she replied, "This feeling inside me. I am so relaxed." And with tears in her eyes, she shared, "But my life is a mess." I explained, "It is not messy deep inside and you just touched that part of you. You now have a tool to go back there anytime you want." It truly was a miracle moment. She realized that no matter what comes her way, she has the capacity to breathe through it using mindfulness practices. Deep inside, life isn't days, weeks, months, or years. It is moments, and in that moment that student experienced something that would change the trajectory of her life.

MY NAME IS KATHY FLAMINIO AND IN 2007 I HAD BEEN a school social worker in Minneapolis public schools for over 14 years, was teaching fitness and yoga in my community, and was feeling really burnt out. Behavior referrals and suspensions were on the rise, youth hospitalization and day treatment referrals were increasing, and staff turnover was at the highest ever. I was extremely passionate about my work, but felt I was never reaching my students in a way that was truly meaningful and sustainable.

I knew we had to try something drastically different—then came a defining moment. One day in total exasperation, I looked at the group of 5th-grade girls I was leading and stated quite assertively, "We are done talking. We are going to do yoga!" Giggles of excitement filled the room as the girls got fully engaged in sharing all the movement they wanted to learn. I, in turn, got to expand their experience and share some movement and breathing practices that could help them when feeling stressed, worried or sad.

I started to go into classrooms at Jefferson Elementary and demonstrate simple breathing techniques, yoga-based movement, and rest strategies. Within a few months, we started seeing changes we had never seen before. Students were beginning to internalize these practices and then generalize them into their classrooms and homes.

Within a year, I applied for a sabbatical with a colleague, Julie Hurtubise, an occupational therapist. We were granted a year to research what was going on in schools around the country with mindfulness, yoga and mental health. We met the Yoga Calm® founders, Jim and Lynea Gillen, and we immediately made a plan for them to come to train twenty of our educators. In the next two years of learning and studying with the Gillens, we became Yoga Calm Certified instructors and trainers.

During those two years, we trained over one thousand educators. Many of the teachers and support staff were from Minneapolis Public Schools where teachers were paid to attend the trainings and then do action research on their implementation in their classrooms and therapeutic settings. It was a win-win for everyone.

We started to see results such as:

- Time on task increased from 2 minutes to 30 minutes during Drop Everything and Read
- Behavior referrals decreased from 14 to 2 per week in a 4th-grade classroom
- Classroom volume decreased by 19 decibels
- A speech clinician noted auditory comprehension improved
- Teachers noted that transitions went more smoothly

After these two years, I decided to leave the schools to begin my business, 1000 Petals LLC, where I could begin to bring this work to other school districts, hospitals, and juvenile service centers. To date, we have trained over 30,000 educators, therapists, parents and related service providers.

Integration into Existing Frameworks

While doing our trainings in the community and in various school districts, we realized that staff needed more hands-on support as well as tools to integrate these practices into their school settings. We began offering on-site customized training to help integrate these tools into their existing frameworks of PBIS (Positive Behavior Interventions and Support) and MTSS (Multi-Tiered System of Support).

Here are a few examples of how schools added mindfulness to their MTSS:

For Tier 1 interventions:

- All-school mindful breathing and/or movement during morning announcements
- Organize parent nights to share strategies with families
- All-staff workshops

For Tier 2 interventions:

- Design both calming and releasing areas in your classroom where students can reset as needed
- Add scheduled movement and mindfulness breaks throughout the day
- Have students begin to lead the movement and write their own rest scripts

For Tier 3 one-on-one interventions:

- Mindfulness and Movement routines for individual students, providing photo visuals
- Mindfulness and Movement routines (morning, homework, bedtime) for home

We also began to demonstrate how mindfulness and mindful movement could be incorporated into Responsive Classroom® structures of Morning Meeting, Restorative Circles, Zones of Regulation,® and Conscious Discipline.® For example, a Responsive Classroom meeting could start with the chime and breathing before greetings, and then transition into movement and sharing. Morning Meeting can end with the morning message and a short rest time to be ready for whatever comes next.

The mindfulness practices do not have to be another initiative school districts take on; they can be practices that support existing frameworks and structures. We also began to implement coaching and teaching side-by-side with teachers, which increased fidelity and sustainability.

Move Mindfully® Products and Residencies

As we began presenting workshops, I realized that there was a disconnect between the ideal implementation of these practices and the reality of the classroom setting. Teachers felt like they needed more support and modeling to be able to make these practices sustainable. From this need, we developed the Move Mindfully® Residency and products to support the work.

Sites tailor these practices to their unique environments from Pre-K to High School. The Residencies bring 1000 Petals instructors into a site for five weeks where they are partnered in classrooms with teachers to guide students through simple mindfulness, movement and SEL practices. Instructor and teacher work as a team to co-teach and plan strategies for embedding these practices throughout the day.

During the sessions, we work through a variety of self-regulation strategies for staff and youth, and present simple and accessible interventions. For example:

If anxious, try these three activities:

- Hand Tracing
- Eagle
- Head on Desk

If high energy, try these three movements:

- Down Dog
- Plank
- Child's Pose

Research from the University of Minnesota

Research is important and we had a unique opportunity to have our program studied by Laura Potter, a doctoral student in the Educational Psychology Department at the University of Minnesota. Her dissertation was titled *Training Educators to Implement Mindfulness-Based Interventions: Evaluating the Effects of In-Service and Coaching on Intervention Fidelity* (Potter, 2018) and examined the extent to which educators could implement the Yoga Calm® program with fidelity in response to in-service training alone, as well as in response to additional coaching. The study found that when a small group of educators (n= 15) was provided with Yoga Calm's high-quality, high-dosage (24 hours in total) in-service trainings, the educators demonstrated high levels of adherence to the core components of Yoga Calm when leading lessons in their classrooms (90% adherence on average, SD = 10%).

Notably, these results diverge from the broader research on effective professional development, which indicates that even the most well-designed workshops need to be supplemented by coaching or ongoing assistance to result in high levels of fidelity (Joyce & Showers, 2008). In this same dissertation paper, four educators who demonstrated lower fidelity levels after in-service training alone were additionally provided with six weeks of 1000 Petals on-site, individualized coaching. Results from a multiple-baseline design study indicated that the coaching led to an improvement in fidelity outcomes for all four educators.

Taken together, these results indicate that a two-tiered approach to professional development may be a useful strategy for school districts when implementing programs such as Yoga Calm and Move Mindfully. If most educators participate in a high quality, high-dosage in-service training and can demonstrate positive fidelity outcomes, then it could be that only a few educators would require additional coaching to demonstrate intervention fidelity.

Additionally, this study provided evidence that the specific training strategies used by Yoga Calm (both in-service and coaching) result in high levels of intervention fidelity for educators. See the full paper for a discussion on limitations of the study, additional factors that may have led to the positive fidelity outcomes, and suggestions for further research on this topic (https://conservancy.umn.edu /handle/11299/200271).

Working with Sky Oaks Elementary

One of the schools we have worked closely with is Sky Oaks Elementary. Sky Oaks is a Title 1, Pre-K through 5th-grade school in Burnsville, Minnesota, a vibrant and highly diverse community with 70% of students receiving free and reduced lunches. Transformation began with two passionate teachers, Sarah Singleton and Katy Prugh Ploehn, and a supportive principal, Jon Bonneville, saying yes to our partnership. In the first year, three classrooms had a 5-week residency and got the tools to bring this to their students. The results were exciting, but the reach and access were limited to a small group of students and teachers.

The Building Leadership Team became committed to bringing it to the ENTIRE school: staff, students, and parents. During the second year, we weren't able to secure funding so we continued to have the three classrooms use the practices and tools. In the third year, we were able to use Title 1 funds and State Health Improvement Grants (SHIP) to create an all-school roll out. This included providing Move Mindfully® Residencies in all classrooms and consultation for Title 1 teachers, special education, specialists and social workers. The grant monies allowed several staff to become certified in Yoga Calm® and then co-design with 1000 Petals an on-site training for all staff including paraprofessionals, specialists, school-based mental health practitioners, cultural liaisons, lunchroom staff, clerical staff, and parent advocates.

The day-long training with follow-up Residencies allowed staff to be supported in integrating these practices as part of their school day. Every classroom participated in a 5-week Residency with a 1000 Petal staff member trained in Yoga Calm. Every person working at Sky Oaks was given the books and tools necessary to utilize mindfulness for themselves and with the students that they encountered daily. There are card decks, glitter balls, Hoberman spheres, chimes, and Move Mindfully® movement posters in every room, and even some hallways throughout the school.

1000 Petals also offered on-site consulting with grade-level teams, counselors, and special education staff to strategize how these tools might be used with specific students. Classroom design and environment were also examined to create mindful, therapeutic environments for staff and students. 1000 Petals staff came back several times throughout the school year at staff meetings to continue the learning for the whole staff.

We planned a family night in October which included dinner, a raffle, and a demonstration of a mindfulness/movement class. Students co-led strategies they were using at school and led routines to use at home for homework and bedtime. This family night was one of their highest turnouts with 280 people in attendance. The evening was experienced in three languages—English, Spanish and Somali.

There was a second family night in March, that was attended by over 100 people, many who did not attend the Fall session. It was incredible to see families practicing mindfulness together and to hear how their children were bringing the practice home with them.

A Fun Way to Learn Move Mindfully Routines

Also during the month of March, the school designed a program called "Drop Everything and Move." During the four weeks of March, they focused on the Move Mindfully Routines: Focusing, Centering, Engaging, and Releasing. Each week was a new routine, at a new time during the school day. The times were chosen based on office referral data, at times with high levels of students out of the classroom due to behaviors. For example, in the first week of March, the Focusing routine was practiced at 10:00 am every day. The staff was given the full routine and times a few days in advance. Every day at 10:00 am the principal came over the loudspeaker, greeted the school, instructed everyone to get into their stretch spots, rang the chime, and began the routine.

It was a cumulative practice: Monday, everyone practiced the first 3 steps of the routine, Tuesday was the review of steps 1–3 and adding steps 4–5, and this continued all week until, by Friday, everyone in the building was practicing the whole routine. What was beautiful about the practice was, no matter where the students and staff were in the building, they stopped everything and did the routine as a whole school community. There were people in the hallway, cafeteria, classrooms, and nurse's office all doing the same mindfulness and movement practice at the same time.

In order to have a little fun, the PTO purchased twenty $5 gift cards that teachers and staff could win for taking a picture of their participation and posting on Twitter or SeeSaw for parents and the community to enjoy. Every day after the routine, the principal drew a winner's name over the loudspeaker. The students were excited to have their pictures taken showing the moves they could do and they cheered for all of the winners. During this month, the school felt like EVERYONE was involved and excited. Results from the year showed that the mindfulness and movement had a positive impact on staff and students alike.

From our work with many schools, we know these practices improve both student and staff well-being. The most impactful part of each school transformation is staff presence. Students feel "felt" and understood when mindfulness is made a priority during the school day, and they feel that they matter to the school community. We see this happen every day—in magical moments where love is actualized and students feel a sense of connection, safety, and belonging. They discover deep inside that they matter—and they have the tools to navigate life's joys and sorrows.

Potter, L. (2018). *Training educators to implement mindfulness-based interventions: Evaluating the effects of in-service and coaching on intervention fidelity.* Retrieved from http://hdl .handle.net/11299/200271

Joyce, B. R., & Showers, B. (2002). *Student achievement through staff development (3rd ed.).* Alexandria, VA: Association for Supervision and Curriculum Development.

CHAPTER 25

Fostering Culture in Middle School with Art, Humanities, and Mindfulness

Tim Iverson

Former Art and Humanities Teacher, Highview Middle School, New Brighton, MN, Board Member, Mindfulness in Education Network

I SIT ON MY PILLOW IN A QUIET ROOM, SURROUNDED BY SERENE FACES. Under me, the cool hardwood floors. Nearby, the tick of a clock. The instructor leads us gently through a tour of our minds, sharing insights to transform our lives. I have not known peace like this for decades. I am learning the practice of mindfulness, which helps me cope with what Jon Kabat-Zinn calls "the full catastrophe": aging parents, job stress, young children, feelings of depression and anxiety. Someone is finally showing me the owner's manual to my mind.

Fifteen years later, it's passing time at my busy middle school. After a bathroom break, I step into the hallway. I hear a dull roar that I've heard before. My ears perk up, my heart beats faster. Glancing down the hall, I see students shouting and gathering around two girls sprawled on the floor, fighting. Within seconds I am trying to separate them. A dean and a police officer arrive. One shouts, "Breathe!" as we hold tightly to one student, trying to keep her from continuing the scuffle. For a precious few moments, we all stop, just breathing in and out. A moment of stillness—the fight is over.

I step back in my room and have to move right into another class. No break for me; 25 faces look at me intently, wondering why I am walking in late. I notice my racing heart and heavy breathing. I tell the group that I need a brain break and they know what I mean. I ring the bell and we move right into silence. For a few moments, I take care of myself, noticing and calming my revved-up nervous system. I regain my balance and the class begins. My mindfulness training has kicked in again, enabling me to move forward and continue with our lesson.

The Building Leadership Votes for Brain Breaks

I recently retired after 30 years in public education as an arts and humanities teacher at Highview Middle School in New Brighton, Minnesota, a suburb of Minneapolis. My initial training was in 2001, with an 8-week course in Mindfulness-Based Stress Reduction, taught by Michael O'Neal in Minneapolis. In 2008, nearly 7 years after my own introduction to mindfulness, I gave an after school workshop for staff and began my unofficial role as a mindfulness leader.

The response among teachers was so positive that I was asked to provide in-person trainings and short, guided recordings which teachers could use on their computers. Not long after, our building leadership team voted to implement a school-wide mindfulness break, also called a brain break, which continues as of this writing.

I began recording brief audios on my computer and sharing them online with staff, about 2–4 minutes each, always keeping my students' capacities in mind. In addition, I created printed versions of some of the essential practices for teachers who wanted to read them themselves or have students do so. My principal at the time gave me extra prep time and I used it to the full, recording audios, writing scripts, sending emails, and later on, sharing Youtube clips. Here's a script I wrote, called "Body, Sound, Gratitude":

> *Sit upright but be relaxed . . . let your shoulders relax, let your hands rest on the table or on your lap . . . Bring your hands out in front of you, and press your palms together tightly . . . feel the tension in your arms and hands . . . hold this for a few seconds . . . and let go . . . feel the relaxation permeate your arms and hands . . . now scrunch up your face, and hold that for a couple of seconds . . . and then let go . . . explore the feelings of relaxation in the face. . . . Now let's bring our attention to our breath . . . feeling the breath as it enters and leaves the body . . . no need to force it or be any different than it is . . . just noticing the in and out breathing. . . .*
>
> *Now we will listen for the bell (ring bell). . . . If your mind wanders, just notice that, and bring it back to the bell . . . notice how the tone varies and begins to fade. . . . When it completely disappears, raise your hand . . . (allow for some silence here) Now just let your attention rest on other sounds . . . notice how some come and go quickly, while others are continuous. . . . Some are near, some are far away . . . (brief pause)*

Finally, let go of sounds, and bring to mind one thing that you are grateful for—use a mental picture or words and just dwell on that for a few moments . . . maybe it's a friend or your favorite food . . . it can be very simple . . . just focus on that image for a few moments . . . Notice how you are feeling now as we dwell on feelings of gratitude, and begin to close this practice . . . (Extension: you may wish to ask students to share out what they are grateful for, or what they noticed during the practice . . . remember, we are just noticing, not judging responses)

The brain break time of day varied by grade level, but essentially was about 5 minutes in the middle of the day. Teachers had the freedom to choose which audios to use, although I made suggestions as to which ones to implement. But many staff used shorter practices throughout the day.

Many teachers were very happy with the audios, as it removed the burden of another prep for them, and many could practice, and learn, along with the students. I also initiated a book study for interested staff, for a more in-depth experience. Our first book was Linda Lantieri's *Building Emotional Intelligence*. Another title we used was Chris Willard's *Growing Up Mindful*. I even made small cards and posters for teachers to use as reminders.

Over time, several teachers became strong supporters and we had a core group developing. I began sharing leadership responsibilities with teachers who had extra training, namely Tara Hupton and Marina Kuperman, who provided invaluable support. I continued to provide guidance, practice opportunities, and resources to my staff until my final year.

The Miracle of Mindfulness

Mindfulness in education is not a cure-all or a magic bullet. There will always be challenges to work with. But it's a powerful tool-perhaps even a miracle as Thich Nhat Hanh calls it. When I have students ask me for a brain break or to ring the bell, because they need a moment of stillness in their lives, that is a miracle. When I see young people with eyes closed, learning to work with their own minds, that too is a miracle. When a former student stops in my room after school to tell me how much meditation has helped him, and when that same student leads me in a meditation, that is a miracle too.

As a teenager in the 1970s, I didn't have the tools to deal with the intense anxiety I experienced. I coped in the best way I could, "white-knuckling it" as they say. Although I did a little yoga in college, it wasn't until my wife took a mindfulness class at the suggestion of her doctor, and recommended it to me, that the practice left the realm of reading *about* mindfulness and became very real.

Over time I began sharing practices in my classroom, and as an art and humanities teacher, there was wonderful overlap with mindfulness. Art is about engaging the senses, especially sight and touch. Studying the contours of shapes, color mixing, and theory, the notion of *seeing* versus *looking*—all are aspects of mindful awareness.

Students drew pictures from careful observation and also drew from memory. We made circular enso brush paintings. In my humanities classes, we read poems mindfully, using the method of Lectio Divina—slow, deep reading. In our aesthetics unit, we visualized places that brought us joy. We looked at the painting *The Death of Socrates* by David and noticed the various emotions portrayed by the artist. We registered the way different artworks affected our internal experience. Our concept of mindfulness was expansive and included a wide swath of human experience. We took the Socratic injunction to *know thyself* very seriously.

Deep Looking

A "go-to" practice was to have my students copy the following quote, attributed to Leonardo da Vinci, "The artist sees what others only catch a glimpse of." To me that's the perfect definition of mindfulness—seeing more, feeling more, observing more. To facilitate *deep looking* you don't need to be an art teacher, although you might need to practice a few times to get the feel of it. Here are a few simple steps to get you started:

1. Select a painting, drawing or photograph—an ambiguous image or one with several figures in a story setting works well.

2. To begin, have the class settle, maybe take a few deep breaths or moments of silence.

3. Direct them to *just look* at the image and without talking, just drink in as much detail as they can. You can vary this from a few seconds to a few minutes. If their mind wanders away, direct them to bring it back.

4. Then ask students to share what they notice; go around the room to mine responses. Stress a "just the facts" approach at this stage: no stories, judgments or inferences yet. What would a camera capture?

5. Then ask, "What questions do you have about the image?" Again, go around the room and field their questions, maybe recording them on a wall or poster-sized paper. It's okay not to know all the answers to their questions; just acknowledge them in a receptive, non-judgemental way. After all the questions have been taken, you might want to answer some, if you can, or make it an assignment to research later.

6. Finally, you can ask them, "What do you think the artist was trying to say with this work?" or "What do you think the artist's intention was in making this?" Keep your attitude one of curiosity and inquiry; avoid clinging to the "right" or official interpretation of the image—leave that to the experts. Be more interested in what *they* think.

Mindfulness Becomes Part of Our School Culture

Since mindfulness is ideally a voluntary practice, it has to be handled with sensitivity in a school setting. I did tread carefully, especially as I began to bring the practice to my colleagues. Teachers are overwhelmed with initiatives and often have to implement several new ideas every fall—from technology to curriculum and classroom management. Although some argue that mindfulness is not another add-on for teachers, it can feel that way.

The trainings I've organized have always been voluntary and easy-going with a focus on the needs of the teachers themselves. This in itself seems healing. I keep in mind the suffering of my colleagues; even the best endure pain, either physical or emotional or both. Teachers are asked to do a nearly impossible job and any compassion we can offer them is welcome.

At my school, we also offered a variety of mindfulness practices instead of implementing one set curriculum. There are pluses and minuses to each approach and our teachers liked the variety. Practices were short and simple using secular language. I used terms like stress reduction, emotional intelligence, self-awareness, self-regulation, and of course, mindfulness.

I continued my own training by going to conferences put on by the Mindfulness in Education Network (MiEN) on the east coast. Inspired by the teachings of Thich Nhat Hanh, MiEN brings together educators and researchers from all over the world who are implementing mindfulness in their workplaces. I also took online classes through Mindful Schools and inspired a couple of colleagues to do the same. Another teacher in our building completed her master's program focusing on mindfulness in education. Another set a digital bell on his computer to go off frequently which reminded him to breathe. Teachers told me that the brain breaks were just as important for them as they were for their students. Our practice wasn't perfect, but mindfulness has definitely become a part of our school culture.

Handling Staff Turnover and Student Resistance

Every fall we had new teachers who knew nothing about mindfulness, much less being mindfulness practitioners. For newcomers, we offered training and resources and encouraged very simple ways to get started in their classrooms, like taking some deep breaths or having a few moments of silence. Then, as teachers got more comfortable, they could begin exploring the longer practices and other resources.

A significant challenge for teachers is that some students are resistant. I found little difficulty with short practices, like listening to the sound of a bell, a few deep breaths or looking around the room for colors in an "I spy" way. Longer practices or movement practices, on the other hand, could elicit groans or sometimes outright refusal. Let's face it. We often have resistance in our own minds. Why wouldn't we encounter resistance in 30 other minds, especially teenage minds?

If we think of a class as a collective mind, resistance is entirely normal and to be expected. I usually allowed it to be there and continued on with the practice. In some cases, I would stop and remind the class what we were doing and why. At other times, I spoke to students privately about their behavior to find out what was going on with them. I tried to stay calm and to inquire.

Occasionally, I noticed anger or frustration arising in me and made that my object of mindfulness. I remembered that ultimately mindfulness is *not about a particular result*, even calmness. It's about noticing what's happening, even if that is very unpleasant in the moment. We often can't control others, in spite of our best efforts, and it's no different with mindfulness. We can only control our reaction. Often that is all I would focus on.

Relevancy and Respect

It's important to establish a rationale for sharing mindfulness with kids. Let students know up-front why they will be doing this. What are the benefits to them, or to the world? You might focus on the way mindfulness reduces stress in the brain and body, or how mindfulness is used by famous athletes to enhance focus and performance. An excellent video I shared was the Tedx talk by AnneMarie Rossi, entitled "Why aren't we teaching you mindfulness?" We had lots of discussions about the triune brain and I often had students sketch pictures of that model. We talked about the dangers of being distracted and how mindfulness can increase your present-moment awareness.

For formal brain break time, our default expectation was silence. We asked students to respect the right of others to some quiet time or to follow the practice if they chose. They had the option to sketch, read or practice along with me. Occasionally, I allowed students to sit in the hallway during brain break time if the silence was difficult for them.

When a practice isn't working for a group, I don't hesitate to switch things up when needed: move, go outside . . . do another practice like relaxation or gratitude.

In my art classes, we often paused for a bell or looked at an image to discuss it from multiple perspectives (mindful seeing). At times we did paired listening.

Teachers will no doubt rely on studies and scientific findings to support the implementation of mindfulness in their classrooms, but reams of data aren't the main reason teachers are adopting these practices. They will continue because they feel the benefits themselves and see it in their classes. Molly, a dean at our school, and now a principal, wrote me the following note after her experience with mindfulness:

> *Dear Tim,*
>
> *It has been a joy to work with you and you have given me a career-changing, life-changing gift. Thank you for being my mindfulness mentor. Your work on this topic is beyond extraordinary. Thank you for all that you do for students and staff. You are a pioneer and I am so lucky to have crossed paths with you.*

In the last years of my career, I was gratified with requests to speak at other schools, as well as at teacher meetings and conferences. With the emerging focus on mental health in schools, mindfulness is taking its place as an essential, non-sectarian practice available to all. I look forward to continuing to be a part of this movement, as it seeks to increase joy, self-awareness, and the easing of suffering.

CHAPTER 26

The Times Are a Changin'

Karen Hunnicutt

International Baccalaureate Teacher, Allen High School, Allen, TX

I HAVE TAUGHT FOR ALMOST TWENTY-FIVE YEARS, with most of the time being at Allen High School in Allen, Texas, in what I consider to be the best job a person could have. At the end of the spring semester in 2019, I was sitting in the office with a new addition to our administrative team, Jennifer Fuller, a passionate doctoral student who is completing her dissertation over the importance of mindfulness in education. We were discussing ways we could incorporate mindfulness in meaningful ways in the curriculum and showcase ways that teachers already use SEL in their classrooms. As we sat together, I smiled, and thought of Bob Dylan's 1964 song, "The Times They Are a Changin'."

This change has taken time. In 2016, I sat in the office of our Associate Principal, Jackie Schornick, crying. She listened as I outlined my concerns about students' stress. Although she is very busy, she quietly listened, and at the end of my filibuster, simply asked me, "Do you have a suggestion?" I did. I told her about Mindfulness-Based Stress Reduction (MBSR) and how these techniques were being adapted for teens by an instructor named Gina Biegel, founder of Stressed Teens. I asked if I could take her 10-week course called Mindfulness-Based Stress Reduction for Teens (MBSR-T) and utilize the training in the class I teach. Jackie said yes and paid for me to enroll.

In that same year another change was made, the hiring of Dr. Jason Johnston as the head principal, setting the wheels in motion for even more amazing things. He and Jackie Schornick, I refer to them as the Dynamic Duo, started bringing a number of positive modifications to Allen High School. There were many innovations with staff, house principals, opportunities for students, and professional learning teams. The times were a changin', but I was hoping for more in regards to students' social emotional well being.

When Change Isn't Happening Quick Enough

Fast forward to the beginning of the 2018–2019 school year. Our Crisis Counselor, Jennifer Atencio, and a House Principal, Jennifer Fuller, met with me about some of my concerns with students' well being. They know my dedication to helping students learn the skills to better cope with the many stressors in life they face (and will face). They reminded me that they shared the same goal. They also reminded me that our district was focused on preparing students academically and socially.

The changes were coming, but they were not coming as quickly as I wanted . . . and this is when I began to implement the tools Gina taught me. From my MBSR-T class, I remembered the questions to ask myself: Am I taking in the good, am I using my senses to be more mindful, am I showing gratitude for all the opportunities I have at Allen High School, am I breathing, am I anchoring into the moment, have I taken a break with the 3 B's (Body, Breathe, Begin), am I spending time in nature, am I taking care of myself, am I listening to uplifting music?

Gina taught me a lot that I was passing along to my students, and I had to remember to apply these same principles to my life. So that's what I did. I began seeing my situation with "new eyes" like I learned from Gina.

One thing I'm grateful for is being able to volunteer for Patriot Paws, an organization that pairs service dogs free of charge with disabled veterans. I have seen these dogs change lives. When I went to an International Baccalaureate (IB) training in New Mexico in 2016, I had Anne, one of the service dogs with me. In one of the small shops, I met a woman and her son with special needs; I estimate he was in his early 30s. She asked if he could meet Anne, and I said, "Of course." After they sat down together, I noticed we were blocking the walk-through area, so I had Anne wave goodbye to the young man. Anne started to wave, and I said "Bye" to the mother and her son.

As I was doing this, the mother said not to worry about having the dog wave goodbye, letting me know her son had been mute since birth. Since it was too late for me to stop Anne's wave, I just let her wave goodbye. It was at that moment that the young man said, "Bye." Time stood still and the mother and I stared at each other along with everyone else in the shop who overheard our conversation. There were no words to say. We shared that eternal moment of the young man saying his first word.

These dogs positively impact lives daily and I am currently working with the 20th dog to attend Allen High School. Dr. Johnston and Jackie Schornick have been very supportive of this program as well as another where I facilitate making sandwiches with my students. Every week, a diverse group of students joins me in making sandwiches for the homeless that I then deliver to downtown Dallas.

We have around 100 students volunteer on any given Friday and deliver around 700 sandwiches each week.

Three words started this project, "Are you housed?" A homeless man asked me this question around five years ago when I attended a homeless church. I answered that I was housed and asked him if he was. He told me that he was not, but he would be soon. I had taken my house, health, and safety for granted. I decided I was going to do what I could to help those who were not housed.

That is when Friday Sandwiches began. At the end of the school year, four of the seniors said they are going to start the same type of peanut butter and jelly making groups at their colleges to deliver to the homeless. It's interesting how sometimes change arrives and we take it for granted or fail to notice it. . . .

What Are You Doing to Help Kids Like Me?

Coming back to 2019, Jennifer Fuller began a Wellness Team and over 30 teachers eagerly signed up to be a part of it. She then asked Dr. Johnston if part of this group could be trained in MBSR-T to promote positivity among the teachers to pass along to their students, and he said yes.

Around this time, an officer in the Student Council asked me in the hallway, "What are you doing to help kids like me?" When I saw the pain in her eyes, I asked her to stop by my room so I could talk to her in more depth. After learning a little about her life and the anxiety she felt most days, I gave her a biodot, which works like a mood ring to monitor her physical reactions to stress. I then explained briefly about the concepts of the autonomic nervous system, neuroplasticity, and integration through mindfulness. I also wrote down some of Gina's activities from the MBSR-T course that she could try at home.

Soon after, I spoke to the Student Council to let them know our plan to train teachers to better help students learn mindfulness skills. The student officer with anxiety had already tried some of the activities and was finding benefits. At the presentation to the Student Council, I discussed the idea of training a group of teachers in MBSR-T to give them the skills to better help students. The Student Council was so excited that they decided to pay for the MBSR-T courses for the ten teachers!

As we finished out the 2018–19 school year, Allen ISD began a new initiative issuing the following statement: "Allen ISD will be expanding its counseling and student support programs next year through a new district-wide Social-Emotional Learning (SEL) initiative. Four different SEL programs will be rolled out starting in August 2019. The overall goal will be to help students understand and manage their emotions, set and achieve positive goals, feel and show empathy for others, establish and maintain positive relationships and make responsible decisions."

These programs are overseen by Cheryl Loving, our Director of Counseling whose name is a metaphor for the example she sets daily.

In the spring, some of my students decided to begin The Mindfulness Club, which meets once a month promoting wellness among the students at Allen High School. Meditation Mondays also started; students and teachers gather with me before and after school and we spent five minutes breathing and being present in the moment. It is a great way to start the week.

On the last day of school, the Student Council officer told me she had given a presentation in her class on the benefits of mindfulness. She said she was doing well, smiled, and said, "Thank you."

Tears of Gratitude

During the summer, the district paid for over 70 of our counselors, teachers, and staff to be trained in MBSR-T. After reading this on our school's website in May, I went back to Jackie Schornick's office and cried again. This time, the tears weren't out of sadness or frustration; they were out of gratitude.

The times are a changin', and I am thankful for the opportunity to teach at Allen High School and have the best job in the world with such inspirational students. I learn from the students as they learn from me. I start each IB Theory of Knowledge class with a short mindfulness activity. My students have also:
- created a gratitude tree,
- written letters to their future selves,
- ate mindfully together,
- practiced active listening,
- created songs inspired by their favorite quotes,
- brought awareness to the moment by Paying Attention With their Senses (PAWS),
- journaled about positive people in their lives,
- volunteered in the community picking up trash, and
- walked to raise money for Alzheimer's Awareness after one of my students shared that his mom had early-onset Alzheimer's Disease.

Many of these and other activities were learned from the MBSR-T course.

I'd like the biggest takeaway from my story to be this: when you're getting stuck and feel the times are not a changin' quick enough, take Gina Biegel's advice and see the situation anew. I call this looking through my *perspectiscope*—seeing the situation from as many perspectives as possible. Continue to live a life of mindfulness and appreciation, look for the positives, and seek out school mindfulness champions.

I am frequently referred to as the "Dog Lady" or "Peanut Butter Lady." Both of these bring a smile to my face and help me to remember that the times are a changin' at AHS. It is a journey, and though we are not where we want to be yet, we are well on our way—thanks to the key people mentioned above, and many more— to making a positive and lasting change in Allen, Texas.

CHAPTER 27

Why Well-Being, Teacher Identity, and Mindfulness Matter

Matt Dewar, EdD

Well-Being Coordinator, Lake Forest High School, IL, Author, *The Mindful Breathing Workbook for Teens*, Past President, COSEM

*Matt's chapter is an adapted transcript of an interview with Tracy Heilers on December 15, 2019. Search "Interview with Matt Dewar" on YouTube to watch the full interview.

What does your role as Well-Being Coordinator entail at your high school and how did you come to be in this role at your school?

THE WELL-BEING COORDINATOR POSITION AT LAKE FOREST HIGH SCHOOL grew out of the recognition that we needed to do more to address the social and emotional needs of our students and staff. And we needed someone who specifically looked at those needs and created meaningful experiences and resources to most effectively and successfully address those needs.

I liked that Dr. Holland's—our principal's—vision for this work was never about creating a program; it was about always keeping in mind and responding to the changing needs of students and staff, and that's the first thing we really agreed on: Going the way of program development was probably not in our best interest.

The first thing that came out of this position and approach entailed looking at different trends in well-being within the school—for both staff and students. And right away, pretty universally, everyone in the building identified stress and anxiety as the number one obstacle to their health and well-being.

And so then it was about identifying meaningful experiences, interventions, and resources that could address those issues. And as I explained at the keynote at the conference, I've been practicing mindfulness personally for almost 20 years, and it's something that has been very meaningful for me—and effective. I talked to Dr. Holland about that and how mindfulness might benefit our students and staff as well, and so with her approval, I got certified to teach mindfulness.

We initially used mindfulness with an AP Calculus class. It was just a pilot with three sections right before AP exams. We did six weeks of it, twice a week leading up to the exams, and then we conducted a basic assessment after. Every single student who took the assessment—I think it was 77 kids—they all said it was meaningful, valuable, they wanted more, they wish they had had it earlier, it helped them emotionally, and it helped them academically.

And so right there, we got immediate feedback, and then it kind of just took off in our district from that point, and it's evolved into a number of different things—and my position has also evolved into a number of different things as mindfulness has gained traction.

How many years have you been in this role? And what are your week-to-week and year-to-year responsibilities?

I've been in the position for five years, since 2015–2016, and we've been exploring mindfulness for four years. There really is no week-to-week in terms of responsibilities—some weeks I am just stacked with meetings with instructional directors talking about integrating SEL into their department's curriculum or into new course work that's emerging for the following year, doing mindfulness drop-ins for teachers, or leading mindfulness experiences before school for teachers or for students.

It ebbs and flows. When you start hitting times of the year when people get stressed out, I'm in high demand. It's kind of a feast or famine schedule, and I don't think that's necessarily ideal, but it's human nature to tend to be reactive and not proactive. Ideally, it would be great if we could be more proactive, and I think in general, we're moving in that direction as a district.

Year-to-year is more focused. Specifically, this year, my goal is to look at the competencies of self-awareness and self-management and talk to instructional directors about how these competencies are already implicitly in the curriculum of a given department—identifying where they naturally show up within courses.

This is kind of a tangent, but it's related—one of the things that teachers will get anxious about and push back about is that they think SEL is taking on new stuff, and they already feel overwhelmed, and there's no doubt that there is an aspect to that, about SEL—that it does mean at some point, taking on more stuff. I think it's dishonest to say that it doesn't entail that at some point, but it doesn't have to start there. It can start by simply identifying the things that are already there in the curriculum.

By the end of this year, I want to have all of the different departments be able to articulate and map out for freshman and sophomore courses where the competencies of self-awareness and self-management show up. How do we talk about them? How can we improve the way we talk about them and integrate them? And then,

I'm anticipating that next year, we will be looking at junior and senior courses as well as taking freshman and sophomore courses to the next level, asking where the gaps are for some courses, and where these competencies really aren't showing up.

You led a session at our inaugural conference about your Wellness for Life course. Share with us about it.

Wellness for Life is a course we offer for all incoming freshmen. It originally started as an optional pilot course, where parents could sign their kids up by choice. It was so popular and we realized that it was so effective in emphasizing SEL, that we made it mandatory five years ago. So now, all freshmen take Wellness for Life.

It's a year-long course that has both health and PE, fulfilling the state credit for both classes, but it goes above and beyond the requirements of health and PE, and it really intensively looks at social-emotional intelligence, and how do we become self-aware, how do we self-manage—how can we self-manage more successfully.

The course has been very effective, and it's so effective that we're looking now to continue the momentum into sophomore year, into junior year, etc. And one more fixture of that class is that upper-class students are TAs (teacher assistants). They are really involved in the course. To this end, when I taught the course, and we were exploring a particularly important issue like making good decisions under the duress of peer pressure, I would lean on the TAs to talk about what this actually looked like in real-time.

I trusted my TAs enough where I would excuse myself from the class and the TAs would take that topic, and it was planned in advance that they were going to do this, and they would speak to the freshmen in that class about real issues, and the decisions that are being made, and the values that are at stake. It's so much more powerful for a freshman to hear it from juniors and seniors who they look up to, then me.

Share about any resistance you've met from the educators regarding mindfulness.

There really hasn't been resistance because, again, we're not taking a programmatic approach, forcing people to do things they might not be ready for or comfortable with. One of the things about "programs" is that they're often heavy-handed, and they superimpose things onto people who maybe aren't ready to operate in that way. And if folks are forced to do things they don't yet understand, then they're just going through the motions—and if you're just going through the motions, students see that. They know if you believe something, and they know if you're just mindlessly going through the motions.

It's so important to not be heavy-handed; it's so important to try to always think about and believe that people want to be well, and if you keep putting out quality experiences, more and more people are going to be impacted, and more and more people are going to be interested. I think that's the right approach. At least it's been the right approach in our school because when I look back to four years ago, for example, to when we were just starting mindfulness interventions, the teacher's classrooms who I visit now are different.

Every year new teachers are coming into the fold, and they're doing so because they're hearing from colleagues that something was helpful for their students, and then they think, "Maybe I'll give this a shot." So they reach out, and we sit down and we talk and I say, "Hey, I can make this whatever you want it to be. I can come in for 15 minutes before an exam, just to help everyone calm down, or I can come in for 45 minutes and address a particular issue you're having in your class." Because it's not a program, I have the flexibility to meet them where they are, and I can tailor my services to the needs of a particular teacher and classroom.

So there hasn't been pushback because I think the approach has been fundamentally inclusive from the beginning, and because it's been inclusive and because it's been patient, because we're not running to get somewhere fast, we've got a nice, steady pace going, more and more people are coming on board over time. In my experience, that's the best approach.

From your keynote at our inaugural conference, I know you have developed a really great professional development model for your school; share about that.

Three years ago we created a professional development model that has three components: teacher identity, teacher well-being, and classroom experiences. That progression might seem counter-intuitive, but all the research on school-wide well-being is now showing that if you want to move the needle, you've got to start with teachers. Why? Because for most schools, teachers are the enduring culture. Administrators come and go, students come and go, parents come and go, but teachers remain. Since they're there for the longest period of time, they—collectively—make up the culture, the atmosphere of a school.

If you really want to change the culture of a school, you have to start by changing the consciousness of the teachers—and that takes time. The pace of an administrator is often more swift and urgent than the pace of a teacher. And that's often because the spans of time that they're operating within are different. Administrators know they've got maybe five years, and in those five years, they have to do something of value, and so they're going to push—they're running a sprint. And then you have teachers, for example, in my district—they're going be there for 35 years—so they're moving at a totally different pace.

I think this is so important for administrators and teachers to hear. They both get frustrated with each other because they're fundamentally operating at different paces. Administrators get frustrated with teachers that they're not onboard fast enough, but they have to understand that when they leave, teachers are still there —and that's really important to recognize. They're still there with the next batch of kids, and once those kids leave, and the parents with them, those teachers are still there. It's not that teachers aren't moving, it's that they're moving at a different pace because the nature of their game—the time span of their career in a given place—is just different. And so I think in many instances for administrators, it's in their best interest to take a breath and slow down.

I'm not saying teachers don't need to be pushed, but you need to understand what it's like to be a teacher—and that they're in the trenches, every day, and that they're concretely dealing with in real-time the issues that administrators are dealing with in the abstract. It's really important to recognize that there's a fundamental difference there.

What is covered in those three components of the professional development model?

I believe there's a false intuition that professional development should start with the technical aspects of teaching. I've seen, and I'm sure administrators see all the time, that providing teachers with the most sound instructional practices and framework and curricula doesn't guarantee successful learning and classroom experiences.

And so, as much as we want to reduce teaching to a science and a paint-by-number profession, it's not. Just because you can make a paint-by-number painting, doesn't mean you're an artist, and just because you can implement a bunch of instructional best practices and theory, doesn't mean you're a good teacher. There's a whole that's larger than the instructional parts, and that whole is the identity of the teacher— how they understand who they are and how that is translated and communicated in their instructional space. You teach with who and how you are—more than with any instructional technique or method or curriculum. When we walk into an instructional space, we can't hide who we are because the way teach is an extension of expression of our self-understanding. You cannot outperform your identity.

And I'm not saying that teaching isn't a science, or that there aren't scientific aspects of instruction, and that there aren't best practices, but good teaching isn't reducible to those things. You can have all of those things and still have an empty educational experience, an ineffective educational experience.

And what it comes down to is that teachers aren't given enough time or space to think about who they are and *why* they teach—because we all forget at some point in our career. We might have started our careers so motivated, wanting to change the world, wanting to do all these wonderful things, but the bottom line is—teaching is a grind. And it gets the best of every single one of us at some point. And when it does, and you get tired and you get burned out, you lose perspective, and you forget why you're doing what you're doing. And you just show up. And when you just show up, it destroys student learning and this whole project of education.

And so, starting the professional development model with teacher identity is essential. It's also validating to the teacher because teachers often feel that they're marginalized and abstracted. This is the source of most teacher negativity—they feel that their individuality in some way is not being appropriately regarded. And so, when you create a professional development model that says your identity, who you are, is the most important thing, you breathe life back into a teacher—and sometimes you remind them of what they once distinctly and vividly knew and have forgotten over time. You have to resuscitate that . . . you have to revive that . . . and wake up that self-actualizing tendency at the heart of every teacher.

There are parts of ourselves that fall asleep. It doesn't mean we're bad or whatever . . . it's just life. Life is a grind. Teachers internalize everything because we care so much about our students. There's so much in the teaching profession that is outside of our control, and we're reminded of that every day—and yet we care so much in an environment where we have so little control. That's not a good combination for personal health and life balance.

Many teachers will grind, and they don't realize that if they just took time to recharge and value self-care, that they would be doing their work more effectively and more efficiently. But we have this false belief that we can't take care of ourselves —that it's a luxury—and we just need to put our head down and grind. But when you do that, and you go into survival mode, you're not doing anything well, you're not helping anyone, and you're especially not helping yourself. And so by honoring and valuing self-care, and self-care protocols, and creating some sort of practice of self-care, you're actually ensuring that you're going to be taking better care of the young people you oversee.

And then once we have that identity piece, that well-being piece, up and running and thriving, or at least just up and running, hopefully thriving, then we can ask: How do I take that identity, and that sense of well-being, and channel it into my work as a professional in an educational space? That's when it makes sense to look at the most effective instructional tools, strategies, and approaches. But so much of professional development, again, just starts here, and it ignores those first two domains. When PD ignores a teacher's identity and well-being, it's empty and doomed to failure. We're people before we're professionals, so all "professional" development should be personal development at its core.

Also in your keynote, you talked about how stress is a distorted relationship with time, and how mindfulness can help with that. How is that related to our self-care?

As human beings, time is our most valuable resource, yet we act as if it were a renewable resource. It's our most valuable resource, and yet we constantly act as if it were renewable, and we waste it. We wish it away, we watch it pass, and we fill it with things that don't necessarily represent how valuable our time actually is.

Never before in human history have we been so able to indefinitely live in a state of denial and distraction—and it's now actually possible to spend the majority of a life completely distracted from what life actually is. I first became aware of this as a teenager, watching my grandfather and being with him in his final months and weeks and days. It was just gripping—to see someone realize that so much of their life had been spent without actually understanding or honoring the value of time.

What ends up happening, which I think is the biggest symptom of our time, that's associated with stress and anxiety, is an oppressive sense of time scarcity. We forget what we value—or we forget how important time is, and because we forget how important time is, we end up filling it with all sorts of things that are perfunctory and peripheral and not as urgent as we think. When you forget about what you value, everything becomes important. And when everything becomes important, everything stands forth as if it needs to be urgently addressed. We have technologies and all sorts of things that just play into this phenomenon neurobiologically. We think: I have to respond to this text, I have to write this email, I have to do this, whatever it is, right now.

And so we string these random moments together day after day, week after week, month after month, year after year. And your life just becomes entropy—there's no focus. Sören Kierkegaard, the philosopher said, "Purity of heart is to will one thing." How many of us will one thing? So many of us are willing a thousand things at once, and we're trying to do them all in a given day. This ends up leading to the self-perpetuating cycle of the lost sense of value. Everything becomes important because there's no underlying value hierarchy. Sooner or later you realize you're not getting done what you need to get done, and so now you've got to hurry to get things done . . . and then there's not enough time to do it! This is how everyone's life works . . . running around, like my mom used to say, "Like a chicken with its head cut off."

How do we interrupt this craziness? Well, if you're not doing anything, then you're just going where the current is going. And the current of modern-day life

—if you're living with the norm—means you're going somewhere you don't want to go, which means you have to, at some point, fight the current.

What would your life look like if you led with your strongest sense of value? What would your life look like if you actually honored and lived in accordance with what is most important? That doesn't mean being perfect, but it just means, more often than not, you fall back on and lean into your values, and you know that they're there, you know that they support you, and you know where they're ultimately leading you.

If you look at the etymology of "mindfulness," it comes from a Sanskrit word that means "to remember." And implicit in the idea of remembering is the recognition that we forget. And so, mindfulness then becomes this practice of remembering, of coming back to what we forget—which is our deepest sense of value, our sense of the sanctity of the present. If you're patient, there's nothing more life-affirming than the gifts of stillness and silence unfolding in the present.

As so, mindfulness is remembering our better nature, and it's remembering that life and our self-care are a journey—and that we are always in the process of becoming who we are. And that process invites us to be actively involved with it. I think that's a huge piece—it's the reason why I call it a *journey* of self-care. The journey means we're not at our destination; we're in this process of becoming—and that becoming needs our awareness, it needs our attention, it needs our skills. *We're actively fashioning our lives as we live them.* That's the most important thing. When we talk about well-being, we're talking about a life where you're actively involved in your own journey and constantly remembering to come back to what's most important.

CHAPTER 28

Creating Compassionate Learning Spaces

Tina Raspanti, MEd, CAPP

Love Warrior, Curious Learner, and Educator, Mt. Lebanon School District, Pittsburgh, PA, Founder of Building Compassionate Learning Communities Project, CARE Facilitator, CREATE for Education, Board Member, COSEM

WHEN I WAS IN HIGH SCHOOL, AS PART OF A FINAL PROJECT for my Sociology class, I visited our local juvenile detention center. I went to college with the naivety of youth—wanting to save the world—and started studying social work. Soon after, I switched my major to psychology, then switched again to education hoping to teach psychology in high school. Close to 30 years later and with the wisdom of living, I know, I'm not "saving" anyone. After teaching in two states, three districts and more than seven different preps, I now teach AP Psychology and Positive Psychology.

I went through many years of my life with the problematic view of, "I'll be happy when . . . ." I'll be happy when I graduate from college, I'll be happy when I get married, I'll be happy when I get a job, I'll be happy when I have kids. And so on, and so on. Of course, we know this is a myth. When I turned 30, an epiphany occurred; I knew that my happiness would never be found from the external factors of the world; instead, I needed to look inward—and that work continues.

After I began the AP Psychology program at my high school, I became curious about meditation and mindfulness. I would teach a little on it in our States of Conscious Unit, but plateaued in my curiosity for a while. Then, as I was going through my divorce, I read Elizabeth Gilbert's book *Eat, Pray, Love*. I too wanted to travel the world and get to know myself. I spent a summer practicing with what at the time I thought was meditation. I would sit and try to empty my mind, but of course, I failed at this day after day after day until finally, I quit.

But that itch—that curiosity—still lingered and I began reading more and started asking questions and listening to wise teachers. Along the way, I learned better definitions and practices, and I learned that I would never "empty" my mind. Instead, I began and continue to practice a form of what I consider mental training—focusing my attention in a purposeful way. Something that is a lifelong learning process and practice. I've learned teachers are all around me, including the one in the mirror.

Resources from Wisdom 2.0

In 2014, I felt a calling to attend a conference called Wisdom 2.0 in San Francisco. Quite honestly I wasn't completely sure what the conference was about; I knew it had to do with the mind-body connection, technology, and business. Many of the authors of the books I was reading or work I was following were speaking at this conference. They included Brother David Steindl-Rast, Jon Kabat-Zinn, Sharon Salzberg, Eckhart Tolle, and Arianna Huffington.

I was introduced to people and organizations that to this day continue to impact my learning, the course I teach, and programming within my district. Dr. Dan Siegel is a psychiatrist, researcher, and author. I incorporated his book *Brainstorm: The Power and Purpose of the Teenage Brain* into the Positive Psychology course. Dr. Michael Gervais is a sports psychologist and mental trainer for the Seattle Seahawks. I am a loyal follower of his Finding Mastery Podcast and I have created two projects for my classes rooted in his work. I learned of and from Dr. Shefali Tsabary, Dr. Larry Rosen, and many more. I discovered a new startup, Inner Explorer, an online program for mindfulness in schools. Today, all ten of the schools in my district have access to Inner Explorer.

In my district and my town, I felt somewhat alone on my journey, but at Wisdom 2.0, I found my tribe. I have gone back twice and connected with more people and resources that I have brought back to my district, including George Mumford, the author of *The Mindful Athlete* and a profound teacher, and the Holistic Life Foundation, a Baltimore based non-profit that provides yoga and mindfulness to individuals.

We use MyIntent as a student-led making project at our school. MyIntent was created by Chris Pan and its mission is to be a catalyst for meaningful conversations and positive action. They encourage us to choose a word of intention, then they create bracelets and necklaces as a primer for focusing daily on our word. Hundreds of students and staff members have participated.

Finally, seven of our sports teams used the Lucid mental training app, and Andrew Zimmermann of Lucid visited our district and worked with our teams on multiple occasions. I hold immense gratitude for all that Wisdom 2.0 has given to me and continues to impact my learning.

Creating a New Elective

As I continued to listen, read and learn, I knew I wanted to share my learning with my students, other teachers, and administrators that I worked with. That began with a new elective that I created. Much debate occurred over what to call this course; the curriculum committee eventually approved Intro to Positive Psychology. I started teaching the course in 2013, the fall before I attended that first Wisdom 2.0 conference, and it continues to evolve.

To summarize, the course I teach is rooted in mental well-being through social-emotional skills and tools such as mindfulness. We study the neuroscience of adolescence, emotions, relationships, meaning, accomplishments, resilience, character strengths, and other factors related to mental well-being. We incorporate the CASEL model, practicing tools to help us increase our self-awareness, self-regulation, social awareness and responsible decision making. We consider bias and equity and how our awareness of these, or lack thereof, impact our journeys and our interactions with others in our life.

We spend time recognizing that every human being has a story and the importance of respecting other's perspectives and experiences. We practice mindfulness regularly and discuss how this impacts the aforementioned topics. I love the class, can you tell?! Each year it's a little different. For example, this year students wrote their own personal philosophies, using the model put forth by Dr. Michael Gervais and Pete Carroll in their online and live educational platform called Compete to Create. And, we have a board filled with "Mumfordisms'" as George Mumford's wisdom continues to influence my teaching.

In the spring of 2016, I took a sabbatical where I completed a Certificate in Positive Psychology through the Flourishing Center and a year-long teacher training course with the fantastic organization—Courage of Care. I also did a workshop with George Mumford and took a Mindful Schools course. I was reading and trying to absorb all that I could.

In that same year, I trained in and am now a facilitator for CARE (Cultivating Awareness and Resilience in Education). CARE offers teachers and administrators tools and resources for reducing stress, preventing burnout, enlivening teaching and helping students thrive socially, emotionally and academically. It is a social emotional learning professional development program for adults.

Building Compassionate Learning Communities

In 2015, I attended the Greater Good Science Center's Summer SEL Teacher Institute. I saw great work happening in California and other major US cities, but I lived in Pittsburgh—at that point, no one was talking about SEL in my town. I went back and began what was the first of many conversations over the past four years with my superintendent, Dr. Tim Steinhauer. He invited me to design, present and coordinate the upcoming summer two-day workshop for his leadership team.

Our focus was on mental well-being and self-care. We invited Krishna Pendyala, founder of the nonprofit Mindful Nation to speak at it. The organization is named after Congressman Tim Ryan's book *A Mindful Nation: How a Simple Practice Can Help Us Reduce Stress, Improve Performance, and Recapture the American Spirit.* We also invited local Carnegie Mellon scientist, researcher, and professor Dr. David Creswell to speak at the leadership workshop. Dr. Creswell has been an influential teacher—meeting with me, guiding me and allowing me to learn from him. Congressman Ryan is from nearby Niles, Ohio, and graciously agreed to be our keynote speaker for the district convocation that same year. There was electricity, people were curious.

For the next two years, we continued to learn, slowly moving forward. By the spring of 2018, more people were talking about mindfulness and social emotional learning in Pittsburgh. I wanted to share with them even just a small portion of the people, organizations, and practitioners that I encountered on my own path. I started to gather a team of friends and wrote and received a grant from the Grable Foundation.

This was the beginning of what became the Building Compassionate Learning Communities Conference held in October 2018. We had over 300 attendees from more than 85 different school districts, universities, and community organizations. Please visit our website at bclctogether.org to learn more about our speakers, presenters and phenomenal team. Following the conference, we transitioned to the BCLC Project, providing free and low-cost professional development opportunities to educators.

Moving the Needle

After the conference, I contemplated on what was next. How do we make a real impact in a system? At the conference, Dr. Mark Greenberg, Edna Peterson Bennett Endowed Chair in Prevention Research at Penn State University, and co-founding member of CASEL, spoke to the importance of having administrators and principals as key factors to incorporating SEL at the building level.* Between Greenberg's talk and information I learned through Courage of Care, I believe for a system to be successful, it needs to take a whole systems approach, meaning providing training and education to every part of an organization. In the case of a public school, this would include the school board, the administrative team, teachers, all staff, parents, community members, and students.

Imposter Syndrome sometimes creeps into my mind—who am I to be doing this work? I work to shift that self-talk, sit with the discomfort, and walk through it. My first teacher, my dad, to this day encourages me to ask for what I want or what I need. He would say the worst you'll get is a no, and you won't lose anything by simply asking. And so I keep trying, keep moving forward.

Peaceful, Safe Spaces—Our MinDen

All schools should be a place where students feel safe. Students thrive when they feel cared for, safe, and respected. With the support of our building principal, Brian McFeeley, we created an advisory team, comprised of students, teachers, and administrators to create a student-driven space. During one of our first meetings, we assessed who the stakeholders were that might access the room and why they might want to have such a space. Surprisingly, when we stepped back and looked at the responses, there were some commonalities between the students, teachers, and administrators. It was validating to witness.

We wanted the MinDen to be a collaborative project for all members of our school community. Art students and teachers created a mural, woodshop students and teachers built movable storage, fashion art students and teachers sewed cushions, and interior design students helped to design the space. Science students added plants and other living elements to the room. Countless volunteers included staff, students and people both inside and outside of our community.

Students and staff recognized the need for a peaceful, quiet space to be able to decompress and recharge for learning throughout the day. This space is open for students to visit during their study halls, to take a mindfulness or yoga class during their lunch periods, to hear speakers, and to host student-led meetings. We asked staff members to donate books that inspired them and write a note inside. We have a gratitude corner where visitors can write notes of gratitude on postcards to staff and fellow students. The postcards contain student artwork.

We also have a stack of YOU MATTER cards; our district participates in the You Matter Marathon each November and throughout the year. It is a marathon of connection, created by my friend Cheryl Rice (youmattermarathon.com). We also offer after-school/evening programs to parents and community members in these spaces. We believe the in-service activities, programming, and events held in these spaces throughout the district and community will increase SEL literacy. By growing these skills, we empower and welcome all stakeholders into more compassionate learning communities and we are strengthening mental well-being.

Re-Centering/Learning/Disrupting

Over the past year, I have felt an undercurrent, something that was missing from what I had been learning, a shift that needed to occur. It began with the work I had started learning through Courage of Care and Dr. Brooke Lavelle. Mindfulness is an individual practice *and* it's relational, powerful, and can be transformational. My friend of over twenty years, Michelle King (@LrningInstigatr), has been a guiding light in my learning, asking me tough questions, encouraging me to sit with the discomfort I mentioned a little earlier, and reminding me that my life is my practice.

I read a powerful piece in the April 2019 ASCD Education Update by Yale professor Dr. Dena Simmons (@DenaSimmons), "Why We Can't Afford Whitewashed Social Emotional Learning." I had been following Simmons for a while on Twitter. Believe it or not, I have learned a great deal from educational leaders on twitter, such as Kelly Wickham Hurst (@mochamomma), Christina Torres (@biblio_phile), Tricia Ebarvia (@triciaebarvia), and Teresa Stoupas (@StoupasTeresa), just to name a few.

I have read incredibly impactful books by Meena Srinivasan, Zaretta Hammond, Ijeoma Oluo, Bryan Stevenson, Michelle Alexander, and Dr. Bettina Love. What have I learned? We must do no harm as we work to bring mindfulness and SEL programming to schools and that I/we need to be culturally responsive in the way we approach our work. None of these programs replace the need to continue to address issues of inequity that exist within educational systems.

If I could dream into the future for a district, I would wish all staff would receive training in mindfulness, social emotional learning, bias, equity, trauma-informed practices, and cultural responsiveness. I would wish that all students would feel safe as they entered their school building, in every classroom, and all had equal resources and opportunities. I would wish that all students, staff and parents felt respected and valued. This would be a truly loving and compassionate learning community.

*Mahfouz, Julia, Greenberg, Mark T., & Rodriguez, Amanda. *Principals' Social and Emotional Competence: A Key Factor for Creating Caring Schools.* Penn State College of Health and Human Development, Edna Bennett Pierce Prevention and Research Center Brief. http://prevention.psu.edu/uploads/files/PSU-Principals-Brief-103119.pdf.

CHAPTER 29

Mindfulness and Contemplative Practices in Teacher Education Programs

Debra Vinci-Minogue, EdD

Associate Professor and Director of Teacher Development Programs, Dominican University, River Forest, IL, Board Member, COSEM

MY LIFE SIGNIFICANTLY CHANGED ON TUESDAY, JUNE 12, 2017. It began like every other day with a long commute to work. As I drove, I remember feeling out-of-sorts and nervous, but I had no idea where the feelings of unease were coming from. By the time I arrived at the university, I was light-headed and felt as if I was going to pass out. As the day progressed, my feelings of nervousness increased, as well as my heart-rate. I felt trapped and unable to sit still, but did not know what was causing these strong sensations. My husband was out of town so I went to my parents' house for fear of being alone. I kept thinking, "What is happening to me?"

Fear, insomnia, restlessness, rapid heartbeat, lack of appetite, inability to concentrate, and hyper-emotionality were my reality for the next three months. To say that I was scared is putting it mildly; I was terrified that I would not get my life back. The rest of that summer, I became my mother's little child again and I felt like one. Afraid of being alone, my husband dropped me off at my parents' house before leaving for work and picked me up on his way home.

I followed my mom's routine and while running errands one day, I purchased the book *The Untethered Soul* by Michael Singer. I think I was drawn to the title since that is exactly how I was feeling, *untethered.* I must admit that the book frightened me a little, no, a lot. It got me thinking about all of the ways I had been neglecting my inner self. It was also my introduction to mindfulness, and drawn to it, I started reading about this fascinating term. I signed up for a mindful yoga class and an online Mindfulness-Based Stress Reduction program.

I was able to work from home during that summer and with help from my angel support network: my mom, dad, husband, sisters, friends, and doctors, I slowly healed and was able to begin the fall 2017 semester. I realize how fortunate I was to have had such a strong support system. It was that realization that led me to want to help others who may not have help or to reach others before they "break down" by offering mindfulness practices.

The entire time I was going through my frightening episode, I wondered "How are other people going through with their lives; how did I function before this?" I now look back on that time as both a terror and a blessing. My inner self needed to tell me something and I am still listening for new messages from it. I am now a passionate student of mindfulness enrolled in the Mindfulness Meditation Teacher Certification Program offered through Sounds True with teachers Jack Kornfield and Tara Brach. Two questions continue to linger in my mind, "How many other people are going through a similar, terrifying life-changing episode and how can I help them?"

Stressed Pre-Service Teachers Become Stressed Teachers

It was quite by accident that I started implementing mindfulness into my courses for pre-service teachers (teachers in training). I teach at a small, Catholic, liberal arts university in a suburb outside of Chicago. One day, before my Introduction to Education class, I noticed that students were unusually loud and agitated. I overheard comments like I'm so stressed out, I have so much to do, and this is too much. I sensed the stress in the room, felt that I needed to do something, and asked my students if they wanted to try a short 5–7 minute sit practice, a secular term for meditation. They loved it and asked if we could do it again on a regular basis. This was the start of mindfulness in the teacher education program.

There are many reasons why it is so important to incorporate mindfulness practices into teacher education programs. Among them, it is our obligation as educators to help our students succeed on every level, including wellness. Youth in our nation are under more stress than ever before. According to a 2018 survey conducted by the American Psychological Association, Generation Z, America's youngest adults aged 15–21, are most likely to report poor mental health. Young people are dealing with gun violence, immigration, sexual harassment and more, and most are not equipped with the tools to cope with the stress of modern living. In comes mindfulness. If students are not healthy in both mind and body, they cannot hope to succeed overall.

David Hawkins (2018) a widely-known authority in the fields of consciousness research and spirituality, suggests that meaningful learning experiences rely on three interdependent facets: 1) *it*, the content of teaching; 2) *thou*, who is being taught; and 3) *I*, who is teaching. Offering opportunities for contemplation in teacher education allows teacher reflection that deepens content knowledge, relationships with students, and self-awareness or the *I*, as teacher.

Much of what is focused on in teacher education programs is intellectual development. Teachers need content knowledge and to be able to convey that knowledge to students, but there is also a great need to develop and foster an inner knowing that relates to emotions and intuition. Because teachers are in the business of human interaction, it makes logical sense that teacher education programs offer learning opportunities that involve exploring the realm of one's inner self in relation to classrooms and students. Teachers must be allowed to access their inner selves through mindfulness practices and contemplative experiences. I have heard this quote many times; I am not sure who said it, but it is true, "Happy teachers equal happy students."

Integrating Mindfulness into Core Curriculum

Over the last two years, I've integrated mindfulness practices into two core courses in the Teacher Education Program. The courses are Introduction to Education and Diversity in Education. Both courses are required by all students who seek teacher certification. The Introduction course is the first course in the sequence and the Diversity course is typically taken during the second semester of the second year in the program. Both courses are 15 weeks and I begin integrating mindfulness practices during the first week of each course.

The mindfulness practices in the Introduction course are based on the traditional Mindfulness-Based Stress Reduction Program created by Jon Kabat-Zinn. In a 15 week semester, I introduce a new mindfulness topic every two or three weeks (observing thoughts, gratitude, observing breath or senses, loving-kindness) and students are invited to practice the concepts both in and outside of class; it is always invitational and not required. A typical class session begins with a sit practice, where I lead a guided meditation that lasts approximately 5–7 minutes. The meditation typically focuses on breath, gratitude, sounds, or loving-kindness, all recommended topics for beginner mindfulness practices.

Mindfulness practices and topics included in the Introduction to Education course:
- Introduction to mindfulness (what is mindfulness, etc.)
- Focus on breath sit practice
- Mindful eating, driving, brushing teeth, etc.
- Loving-kindness sit practice
- Movement meditation

Contemplative practices and topics included in the Diversity in Education course:
- Journaling
- Lectio Divina

- Deep listening
- Perspective-taking

Contemplative practices can be modified for any level and for most subject areas. These are just a few examples; others and more information regarding contemplative practices can be found at the Center for Contemplative Mind in Society (CMind) website, contemplativemind.org.

Journals are used in the Diversity course as a way for students to express exactly what they were experiencing while practicing mindfulness. Prompts are usually provided to help students stay present with the writing task at hand. Example prompts include:

- Recognize any feelings or thoughts that emerge; what are these emotions or thoughts that are present?
- Can you sit with them without judgment, just allowing them to be here? Write anything that comes to mind.
- Make a list of the people or things in your life who/that you are grateful for. Make time to "hang out" and thank them. Try to be mindful of these people and things—not taking them for granted.
- What does unconditional love look like for you?
- What would you do if you loved yourself unconditionally? How can you act on these things to make this a reality?
- Name a compassionate thing that you have done to support another person recently. How can you be more compassionate to yourself?

For those not familiar with Lectio Divina, it is an ancient practice of divine reading. Traditionally, Lectio Divina has four separate steps: read, meditate, pray, and contemplate. It has been adapted for use in secular classrooms as a contemplative practice and the steps can be modified as follows: read, reflect, respond, and remain.

An example of how this can be used is to start by selecting the text. I use many poems by Mark Nepo, an award-winning poet, teacher, and storyteller. The text should be read aloud slowly and displayed on a screen or given to students individually. After the first reading, students should be given time to reflect on the passage and are asked the question, "What word or words speak or stand out to you?" There are no correct or incorrect responses in Lectio Divina, it is non-evaluative. It allows students the space to connect and find meaning in the text for themselves, allowing for first-person inquiry.

After the first reflection, the text should be read again slowly, then students are asked to reflect on the passage and share what words or phrases stand out to them. The third reading of the text is done aloud and students are asked to rest or remain in the text, contemplating what they have just experienced. Sometimes I ask students to act on the text by writing a letter to themselves about what they just learned, or a similar activity that involves students taking some type of action based on what they discovered about themselves in the recently read text.

Perspective-taking mostly occurs during discussions about current events in education. Students are asked to consider the multiple perspectives that exist surrounding issues, particularly controversial issues. An activity that I borrowed from a colleague involves rock painting. Each student is given a rock with the instructions to paint a face on the rock and create an identity for the "rock pupil" that is different from your own. Students are asked to bring their rock pupils to every class session to remind them that they will be teaching students who are different from them and that they must consider the multiple perspectives of all individuals in the classroom. The activity was taken from the chapter "Rock, Rock! Who's There" by Mary-Ann Mitchell-Pellett (Mitchell-Pellett, 2018).

The majority of students in both courses participate and are fully engaged in the process throughout the semester. I do not mind when students chose not to participate because as I mentioned previously, mindfulness should be invitational and not forced. What could prove challenging are negative comments about or disruptive behavior during mindfulness practices. Thankfully, the few students who chose not to participate were respectful and engaged quietly in alternative activities.

We Have to Know It Before We Can Teach It

At the end of each semester, students were offered an opportunity to express their thoughts about the mindfulness practices they had engaged in during the semester. The overall response was positive. Most indicated that they enjoyed and looked forward to the sit practices in class and mentioned that our sit practice was the only time that they slowed down. I received a card at the end of the spring 2018 semester from a student who had been rather difficult in class. In it, she thanked me for introducing her to mindfulness and wrote she plans to practice on her own. I cannot describe the joy I felt in reading that card. I have placed the card in my "happy" folder. A happy folder is where I save notes, cards, and letters that are meaningful. It is always uplifting to go back and read through the positive notes.

I should mention that many students came to speak with me individually about mindfulness and indicated that they would like to continue practicing. Many have expressed an interest in having a mindfulness organization on campus and I am exploring that possibility.

One important thing that needs to be mentioned when incorporating mindfulness practices into any classroom situation—we have to know it before we can teach it. As stated by Barbezat and Bush (2014), "With contemplative practices, it is even more important to be soundly grounded in the practice, since practice affects not only how students inquire and learn, but also how teachers teach and how they act in the world." Incorporating mindfulness practices in teacher education programs allows pre-service teachers to begin their own practices and become grounded in them before they teach them to their own students.

With the increasing demands being made on teachers in our society, along with the alarming increase in levels of low mental health reported in youth, it is logical and appropriate to offer "a curriculum that incorporates the development of resiliency, coping, and well-being" (Hall et al., 2018) in teacher education programs. Imagine a world where every teacher is trained in mindfulness as well as how to integrate it into their classrooms. This can be realized by implementing mindfulness practices and contemplative pedagogy into teacher education programs. If we expect teachers to work with diverse learners, in an ever-changing educational landscape, we need to equip them with balanced teacher education that prepares them to be authentic, having integrity–possessing self-awareness, practicing empathy, seeking justice, being open to new ideas—all while fostering their intellectual development.

Mindfulness and contemplative pedagogy can deepen this work affording opportunities for pre-service teachers to explore their inner selves and their relationship to their environment. By implementing such practices into programs, teachers will have been introduced to and will have practiced a multitude of deep-learning experiences and reflective practices that they will be able to share with their own students in P-12 classrooms.

American Psychological Association. (2018). *Stress in America, Generation Z.* Retrieved from *https://www.apa.org.*

Barbezat, D. P., & Bush, M. (2014). *Contemplative practices in higher education: Powerful methods to transform teaching and learning.* San Francisco, CA: Jossey-Bass.

Byrnes, K., Dalton, J. E., & Dorman, E. H. (2018). *Cultivating a culture of learning: Contemplative practices, pedagogy, and research in education.* Lanham, MD: Rowman & Littlefield.

Center for Contemplative Mind in Society (The). *www.contemplativemind.org.*

Palmer, P., & Zajonc, A. (2010). *The heart of higher education: A call to renewal, transforming the academy through collegial conversations.* San Francisco, CA: Jossey-Bass.

Singer, M. A. (2007). *The Untethered Soul: The journey beyond yourself.* Oakland, CA: New Harbinger Publications.

PART 4

INTEGRATE

MINDFULNESS

DISTRICTWIDE

AND BEYOND

Creating a Districtwide Culture of Mindfulness with a SEL Mindfulness Specialist

James Butler, MEd

Austin ISD SEL Mindfulness Specialist, 2014 Austin ISD Teacher of the Year, Founder, Mindful Classrooms, Author, *Mindful Classrooms*

IN MY HEART AND SOUL, I AM A TEACHER. My first job was teaching kindergarten at Winn Elementary in the Austin Independent School District, a long way from my home in Cleveland, Ohio. Those six years changed my life in the best possible way. I was so connected with my students and their families and still remain connected, attending countless high school and college graduations of my former kindergarten students.

Relationships matter in the classroom. If I am going to reach my students academically, I need to connect with them and their families. It was even more important that I learn from my students and their families since we shared different lived experiences. I'm White and the majority of my students were African American and Latinx. Our connections led to quality learning opportunities.

In 2009, with an itch to teach abroad and immerse myself in another culture to learn and grow as a person, I decided to volunteer as a high school English and math teacher in Namibia, a country in Southern Africa. I used that same teaching philosophy of building relationships and trust. It was a longer process at Mangetti Combined School as they had never had a volunteer teacher at their school, as it was very remote. While teaching in Namibia, I started to implement some very basic mindfulness strategies with my students to help us deal with stress.

A Personal Challenge Leads to Mindful Growth

When I returned to the States in 2010 and was teaching kindergarten again, I became aware of a shift in how I was interacting with my students. I still deeply cared for them, but I noticed that I was more impatient. I realized that I was struggling personally and I was taking some of it out on my students. I needed help.

I went to therapy and was diagnosed with PTSD (post-traumatic stress disorder) from severe trauma experienced in my childhood. I was dealing with depression and anxiety and my therapist encouraged me to explore mindfulness as a means to help me manage triggers and everyday struggles.

I started exploring basic breathing and stretching practices and found a kids yoga video on YouTube called The Sun Dance by Bari Koral. We used it in class every day. My students loved that video as they got to bark during downward dog and hiss like a snake during cobra pose, and I loved it because I could use the time to focus deeply on my breathing and get centered for my students.

I noticed my patience growing and I was able to see my students in an entirely different light. I saw the root of behaviors rather than just the behavior itself. I was able to more clearly implement the H-A-L-T method of inquiry, which is a strategy that allows you to more fully understand behavior and where stress is coming from. I would ask myself if my student was hungry, angry, lonely or tired to see how I could best support them when they were having a difficult time with strong emotions.

In 2011, I switched schools to teach Pre-K. I continued with the daily mindfulness practice, but started expanding my work with my students as I learned more. I taught my four and five-year-olds about how mindfulness impacts our brain, specifically the amygdala, hippocampus, and prefrontal cortex. They loved the practices and learning about how they were making their brains stronger. I would even have students say to me, "Mr. Butler, my amygdala is going crazy right now; I need to do some mindful breathing." It was amazing.

In 2014, I had the immense honor of being named Teacher of the Year for the Austin Independent School District, a district with 129 schools and over 6,000 teachers. As a result, I was given many opportunities to speak with the superintendent and other decision-makers in the district. I spoke frequently about my mindfulness practices with my students and Dr. Paul Cruz, our superintendent, showed great interest. I wrote a 36-week guide for teaching mindfulness every day in the school year for my Pre-K colleagues and shared it with Dr. Cruz. He was so interested that he asked me to pilot the program in the district.

Stepping Out of My Comfort Zone to Teach Teachers

I was stunned, honored and terrified all at the same time. I was used to teaching four, five, and six-year-olds, and now I was going to have to teach teachers. I trained 20 teachers at the start of the 2015 school year and word spread. I was asked to lead trainings after school throughout the district and by the end of the school year, my 36-week mindfulness guide was being used in over 400 classrooms. The interest in mindfulness was so great that an SEL Mindfulness Specialist position was created in 2016, a position I have held since that time. The mindfulness guide that I created turned into the book *Mindful Classrooms: Daily 5-Minute Practices to Support Social-Emotional Learning*.

In my role as the SEL Mindfulness Specialist, I am responsible for supporting social and emotional learning in all of the schools and with district staff. It's been an incredibly gratifying experience full of learning and growing as there's been no model for me to follow. To my knowledge, I was the first and only public school mindfulness specialist in the entire country. I've also had the honor and privilege of founding Mindful Classrooms, an organization that travels the world sharing mindfulness with schools and districts based on my experience using mindfulness in the classroom. I'm grateful for this opportunity to share my successes and missteps along the way and hope it serves as a learning experience for you.

Caring and Connecting Deeply With Oneself and With Students

Teaching is hard. In Austin, which is growing exponentially, low teacher pay makes it very challenging. Some teachers have two jobs, which creates even more fatigue. I understand the struggles of being a teacher and the need for self-care. I am passionate about sharing how mindfulness helped me through my struggles with depression and anxiety.

The main focus of every professional learning experience that I lead is on the adult. We always want to know what to do with students because we're teachers and we want to support them. That's great, but if we're constantly ignoring our own needs, we're not going to be our best selves for our students. As the saying goes, "You can't pour from an empty cup." I learned this the hard way. I cared deeply for my students, but I was ignoring my own needs. I was struggling personally and my cup ran empty. Mindfulness helped me fill my cup and be my best self for my students. That's why I use that as the main focus for all mindfulness professional learning experiences I share.

Connecting deeply with oneself can lead to connecting more deeply with students. I've learned much from Zaretta Hammond's book *Culturally Responsive Teaching and the Brain*. This proved to be extremely helpful when my culture and lived experience was different from my students and their families. As a White teacher teaching mostly Black and Brown students, I occasionally caused harm because I wasn't aware of how my words and actions could impact others. It didn't matter that my intentions were coming from a good place if the impact was negative. Through mindfulness practice, I've learned to be more aware of my own culture and how that impacts how I move through the world.

Mindfulness is a way of raising awareness, both self-awareness, and social awareness. In our country, the vast majority of our teachers are White. Students of color are being disproportionately disciplined which creates a school-to-prison pipeline. I don't believe that all White teachers are intentionally trying to do this, but I do believe that we can use mindfulness as a tool to raise awareness about this issue. Just as I used the H-A-L-T method of inquiry with my students as a means to truly listen to them, I believe we need to pause and recognize that, as Zaretta Hammond says, "Culture is the way that every brain makes sense of the world."

My Mentors, Training and Personal Practice

In 2014, I was given an opportunity to attend any professional learning experience in the country and I chose the Bridging the Hearts and Minds of Youth Conference at the University of California, San Diego. I went two years in a row and had the honor of learning from people like J.G. Larochette, George Mumford, Jim Gillen, Dr. Kristin Neff, and many others. That conference piqued my interest in learning about mindfulness and I started reading books like *The Mindful Athlete* by George Mumford and *Teach Breathe Learn* by Meena Srinivasan. I am currently reading *Mindful of Race: Transforming Racism from the Inside Out* by Ruth King.

In 2018–2019, I completed a 200-hour yoga certification that had a trauma-informed, or healing-centered lens, as my mentor Shawn Kent prefers to call it. It was a rich learning experience and I learned more about the science behind mindfulness, especially its impact on the nervous system. I've known it to be helpful, but now I can explain and share different breathing and movement exercises that can either up-regulate or down-regulate our nervous system, depending on what's needed in that particular moment.

Shawn has been an incredible teacher, mentor, and friend over the past few years. One of my favorite quotes from Shawn concerning neuroplasticity was, "Every time I do something, I am training myself to do it better." When he said that a light bulb lit up in my mind and heart; I realized that I became so good at negative self-talk because I did it ALL THE TIME. I was training myself to be a professional at negative self-talk! As I started to practice positive self-talk with daily self-affirmations in my journal, I've noticed a significant increase in my self-esteem.

In addition to Shawn Kent, I've had the honor of learning from every one of my colleagues in the AISD Social & Emotional Learning Department, Dr. Angela Rose Black, Solomon Masala, my partner Lindsey Wineholt and every former student that I'm still in touch with, which is quite a few from all over the world. I'm full of gratitude for all the amazing people that I get to learn from and with.

With the help of all of the above, my personal mindfulness practice has slowly grown and solidified. It really took hold when I started using the five minutes waiting for my morning coffee to brew to focus on my breath. I realized that normally during that time I was on my phone checking email or social media and not doing anything productive. So I sat down while the timer was set and focused on my breathing instead of my phone. Those five minutes are now very worthwhile and have a positive impact on my whole day.

Time Scarcity, Religious Fears and Desires for Quick Fixes

Teachers have so many responsibilities that adding anything else to their plates is overwhelming. When sharing about mindfulness, I stress *integration* as opposed to *addition*— integrating mindfulness into already established routines, rather than adding something else to an already hectic schedule. When I was in the classroom, I integrated mindfulness into our morning circle time, similar to Morning Meeting and community building, and it was only for five minutes each day.

Again, integration as opposed to addition. That's been a very useful strategy for getting teachers to develop a personal and professional practice. I explain that my personal practice has expanded slowly over the years and if teachers want to do that, they can find what works best for them. But the initial buy-in is far greater when integration is the focus.

When I first started sharing mindfulness, my focus was on using it in the classroom. I shared how mindfulness helped me personally, but the focus would quickly shift to how to use it in the classroom. I soon realized that teachers were trying to use it as a quick fix for behavior problems. But it wasn't working because they had little or no practice of their own. Kids are brilliant and see through adults who try to teach them things that they don't fully believe. They can also sense when teachers are trying to use mindfulness inauthentically and for the wrong reasons.

I have been proactive to ensure that the mindfulness we practice is secular and that we honor all faiths and beliefs. Even so, fears have arisen, mostly from Christians. In those instances, we listen to the concerns and assure the families that the practices are research-based ways to help students be more self-aware which leads to more learning and better relationships with peers and adults. We strive to be proactive and even have letters to parents translated into six languages with a statement from our superintendent supporting mindfulness in schools and explaining some of the science behind it and how it's truly beneficial for students' academic, social and emotional learning. I've shared this at the end of my chapter.

That being said, it's also important to recognize the roots of mindfulness so as not to appropriate it. I've always acknowledged the origins of mindfulness in Hinduism and Buddhism and am still learning and growing with how to best recognize the roots of mindfulness and honor all belief systems.

Starting Goals and Shifts in Strategy

My goal in my first year as the SEL Mindfulness Specialist was to ensure that mindfulness was happening in all 129 schools in one way or another. I drove all over the city that year going to schools, leading lessons in classrooms, leading professional development at faculty meetings, leading sessions with families, etc. By the end of the year, all of the schools had mindfulness happening in some form or another, through the counselors, teachers and parent support specialists.

Through annual surveys, more than 95% of staff state that mindfulness is helpful to them, both personally and professionally. A key to that year was keeping my "teacher hat" on which allowed me to connect with teachers on a deeper level. Often the people who come into schools to talk about education haven't actually been teachers. Teaching is a special profession and the connection between teachers is strong. I used that connection when sharing about mindfulness and how helpful it can be with the stresses of being a teacher, as well as the stress inside the classroom.

After that first year, I decided to shift my strategy and focus more on hosting professional learning opportunities. Teachers who were interested in deepening their mindfulness practice would sign up on our learning platform and attend a half or full-day training at a district location. This allowed me to reach the mindfulness champions on campuses and in departments throughout the district. We have a series titled Mindfulness 101, 201 and 301 and we're starting more individualized mindfulness courses such as Mindfulness in the Arts, Mindfulness in Nature, Mindfulness and Unconscious Bias, Mindfulness in Sports, etc.

It has been a very helpful model to tap into different interests among staff members in the district. My favorite professional learning opportunities are our mindfulness retreats where we get volunteers from the community to teach mindfulness-related classes to teachers and other staff for free on a Saturday. They are set up similar to a conference with a keynote and then three different 45-minute sessions for AISD staff members to attend. We've had anywhere from 6–8 different classes for staff to choose from that range from yoga to drumming to Capoeira to meditation to singing bowls and more. It's an incredible opportunity for self-care and teachers get professional learning credit too!

Race and Awareness of How We Move Through the World

I will always be learning and growing. I used to be very goal-oriented and focused on the destination, and I still have goals, but I am much more focused on the journey. One thing that I'm learning is to be careful and explicit about the benefits and potential harms of mindfulness. This summer, I had the honor and privilege of attending an amazing institute led by Dr. Angela Rose Black titled Disrupting Systemic Whiteness in the Mindfulness Movement. It was the most profound professional learning experience I've ever attended.

To be honest, I went with the intention of learning strategies that I could use to help my White colleagues and family members realize how their words and actions cause harm to people of color and left with a deeper personal understanding of how I need to be more aware of how I move through the world. It wasn't a shaming experience, but an incredible experience full of growth. "Make the covert, overt" is something that Dr. Black said that stuck with me regarding sharing my own experiences with how mindfulness helped me understand my biases, especially implicit ones, and how to move forward so I don't act on those biases like I once did.

In addition to authentic conversations about my own growth and learning, I'm collaborating with the AISD Cultural Proficiency and Inclusiveness Department to make their powerful professional development titled Isolating Race a prerequisite for some advanced mindfulness PDs. This will allow us all to have common language and understanding when we discuss race and the racial dynamics in our school district. If we're not careful, mindfulness can also be used as a tool to oppress marginalized populations of students. I don't believe this happens with ill intent, but by focusing on what mindfulness is (a tool to help increase self and social awareness, etc.) and what mindfulness is not (a tool to get kids to be quiet, comply, etc.), we can share mindfulness in extremely powerful ways.

I strongly believe that mindfulness is a tool that can help us disrupt the school-to-prison pipeline and educational injustices that happen to our students of color every day. It can help the adults realize their biases, take a pause, and then act in a way that more clearly aligns with helping each individual student succeed based on what they need in that moment to be successful. It looks different for every student, and culture plays a significant role—so adult social-awareness is crucial. And mindfulness can help our students find their power and their voice to speak up when they or peers are not being heard or seen. It can provide a tool to stay as clear-minded as possible during difficult situations. This is why I'm trying to be as overt as possible with regards to mindfulness and it's connections to social justice during professional learning opportunities in our district.

Focus on Learning and Growing

I am an educator at my core and in my soul and that's how I share mindfulness. In order for mindfulness to grow in schools, we need to have teachers, staff, and administrators who are leading the charge. Folks from outside the classroom can be sharing information and teaching educator leaders, but true growth and sustainability come from within. The world of education, unfortunately, has too many people from the outside trying to dictate what happens in classrooms when they've never stepped foot in one as an adult.

Putting our focus and attention on teacher mindfulness champions is how mindfulness will grow and spread in our schools improving self-awareness, self-management and social awareness throughout. I hope my story as an educator first, and mindfulness practitioner second, will further validate the need to empower our teachers and school staff to be the true leaders in this work.

I also hope that sharing about my struggles inspires you to be authentic and vulnerable with yourself and others so we can use mindfulness as a tool to lift each other up. Difficult topics like race and mental health should be discussed more openly. I strongly believe that the stigma behind talking about these issues makes them more severe and divisive. I've been through a lot in my life. I've made mistakes and caused harm, but I'm focusing on learning and growing. Mindfulness has helped me in so many ways, but most importantly it's helped me learn so much about myself, which in turn has allowed me to learn more deeply about others, and ultimately to grow into a person that I'm proud to be: a teacher, a listener, and a learner.

A Letter to Start Communication with Families

It's important to communicate to caregivers what is happening in your class and school, and mindfulness is no different. To give you an example of what a beginning communication can look like, I'll end by sharing Austin ISD's letter to families.

> Dear Families,
>
> I am excited to share that we will be practicing some mindfulness in our class this year. Mindfulness is about being present, paying attention to our surroundings and our minds without getting carried away by it. It also focuses on being curious and kind to ourselves and others. These secular activities are endorsed by our Superintendent, Dr. Paul Cruz. The activities (mostly breathing and stretching) help calm and focus students, both mentally and physically, so they can focus on their schoolwork and build solid inter- and intra-personal skills. Research shows that mindfulness can improve memory and comprehension, build empathy and allow people to deal with difficult situations in a more effective way. If you're interested, I am more than happy to share resources

with you about using similar practices at home. Please let us know if you have any questions.

I have been inspired by the research presented that shows the positive effects of secular mindfulness in schools. Mindfulness allows time for reflection while reducing stress and anxiety. Learning how to relax and concentrate on the task at hand is important and worthwhile for students, teachers, and even superintendents. I'm hopeful for mindfulness to be implemented in AISD, and I want to encourage everyone to reflect on the importance of having a proper balance.—Dr. Paul Cruz, Superintendent

CHAPTER 31

Mindfulness and Positive Psychology Coaching Districtwide

Cindy Goldberg, MEd, CAPP, MMT

**Former CSD Mindfulness Coach and Teacher, Philadelphia, PA,
Mindfulness Educational Consultant, Author, *Penelope's Headache***

MINDFULNESS AND POSITIVE PSYCHOLOGY ARE CHANGING the way we teach today. Teachers who feel calm and happy can be far more effective than those who feel stressed and exhausted. The growing demands on our educators have made these two overlapping fields a necessity in classrooms, not a luxury. Educators who are able to utilize their strengths, a positive mindset, and an ability to pause in the midst of whatever arises have the tools to create an environment conducive to social, emotional and academic growth.

With the fast pace of our lives, our thoughts and our attention spans, and slowing down to listen, learn and study are becoming more and more difficult. Stress is affecting every age, including our youngest students. We desperately need something to counter our stressed-out lives and those of our students.

For me, that something began when I discovered positive psychology and mindfulness. I practiced mindfulness on and off for 20 years, but when I enrolled in the Flourishing Center's Certification in Applied Positive Psychology program, my mindset expanded. While traditional psychology focuses on what is wrong with people, positive psychology discovers what's right and helps people to feel better by focusing on and enhancing a person's innate strengths. Interventions include evidence-based activities, which when done systematically, can help a person feel better about life. I was always an optimistic person, but now science gave a name and research to how I felt and taught.

Feeling passionate about what I had learned, I introduced positive psychology to my own 2nd-grade classroom at Cheltenham School District. I embedded interventions into our day. Writing was part of the curriculum, so writing about three good things became part of our daily routine. The mechanics of good letter writing was a 2nd-grade goal, so writing gratitude letters, and then calling and reading them to the recipient wasn't a stretch. Mindful breathing, my favorite intervention, became our strategy for learning to settle, self-regulate and focus.

In addition to writing and meditating, we also reframed our negative thoughts, created vision boards, learned about the parts of the brain and made glitter jars. Many activities followed that taught my students how to understand and manage their stress. My seven-year-old students loved the interventions and I decided to set my own positive psychology goal of bringing my successes to a larger population— my school district.

Creating a Curriculum and Coaching the Whole District

Luckily, I worked for a district that embraced positive psychology. They funded 25 other educators to get certified and hoped we could influence the rest of the district. It was a great idea; however, there was no plan for how to proceed. I decided to make it my mission to share what I knew with my superintendent. He needed to hear the statistics and learn that the strategies were working in my classroom. After a year of trying to get his attention, I made my mantra, "If it doesn't open, it's not my door." I spoke to everyone I could and finally, by way of an accidental encounter, I got my appointment.

We sat down and talked about mental health statistics, teacher burnout and the stress levels of all stakeholders in our district. He listened and within two weeks I became the Mindfulness/Positive Psychology Coach for a public school district. It was a one year position and a first in Pennsylvania. With no guidance or program in place, I reached out to all staff members and offered six-week sessions in their classrooms to teach mindfulness interlaced with positive psychology. I researched best practices and used a combination of strategies I found, in addition to my own.

I immediately encountered apprehension throughout the schools. Teachers thought that this would be one more thing they needed to add to their mounting responsibilities. In actuality, it equated to one less thing. When mindfulness is embedded into a classroom, self-regulation, focus and calm result. The classroom ends up having fewer behavior issues, off-task problems and angry feelings. As I modeled, and teachers adopted the techniques, they became invested.

I began with people I knew well and within weeks there wasn't enough time to be in every class that requested me. I created curricula for grades K–2, 3–5, 6–8 and high school by modifying what I had learned. I would spend six weeks in each teacher's room. Teachers didn't need to do anything but participate—they got to take a breath and practice mindfulness with us. No computers, no grading papers. It was their time to just be. My hope was that they would embed this into their classrooms when I left.

Students, beginning in kindergarten, learned the science of the brain and how to use their breath, their body and their senses to be in control. They quickly felt the benefits and shared what they learned with their families.

Each 35-minute lesson began with a breathing practice, contained a positive psychology intervention and included an informal mindfulness practice. We also had time to reflect on when and how they practiced in their own lives. Most importantly, every lesson was fun. We got to balance peacock feathers, use bubbles and eat marshmallows along with many other formal and informal activities.

Students learned about their brains and began to understand what was happening when they became angry, stressed or felt insecure. The word amygdala became part of their everyday vocabulary. I would often hear about children's amygdalas instead of their anger. They discovered how to use their prefrontal cortex to calm down.

Every child and teacher received blue dot stickers to use as reminders to take a breath instead of reacting. I put mine on my steering wheel, my cell phone and my computer—places where my reactions were most likely to be triggered. I hung large blue dots throughout the district to remind us all.

Students loved the lessons, but more importantly, continued the practices at home and in their classrooms when I was gone. My goal was to no longer be needed, hoping that mindfulness would become part of the culture of their classrooms.

Sustainable Change Through Professional Development

Another facet of my position was to lead a group of teachers in bringing sustainable change to their buildings. One fun way we created positivity was to use the Character Strengths Survey on viacharacter.org and post our top five strengths on our email and websites to encourage others to discover their strengths. During professional development days, teachers and administrators were also given time to take the survey to learn and use their top five strengths.

Faculty meetings allotted at least five minutes to an intervention around positivity, engagement, meaning, relationship building or achievement from the PERMA model of positive psychology. According to Dr. Martin Seligman, one of the founders of Positive Psychology, there are five evidence-based avenues that contribute to a person's well-being and levels of happiness. Positivity is about optimism and feeling good. Engagement is doing things that are fulfilling that we are good at and enjoy doing. Relationship is concerned with our ability to connect with and get along with others. Meaning allows us to feel as though we have a purpose in our lives and are part of something. Achievement is about setting realistic goals and feeling the success associated with accomplishing them. Each is a pathway to well-being and makes up the PERMA model.

Each team created activities in their building that embraced positive psychology. Administrators, teachers, and staff began to see that this was not just something new, but was something that works. We worked together to bring well-being to the entire district staff. Each month we offered well-being workshops including Soul Collage, yoga, watercolor, Reiki and more. We tried to show teachers how much they were appreciated by creating notes along with tea, hugs and Kind bars. A gratitude tree went from school to school so that staff could show what they were grateful for by decorating the branches. We tried other fun interventions in our buildings. Several offered before and after school meditation periods.

Other Coaching Highlights

We also offered parenting workshops based on the book *The Strength Switch* by Lea Waters. They got to experience mindful breathing first-hand, as they identified their own strengths and discussed their children.

In our middle school, mindfulness was available daily for 30 minutes during Homeroom period. We had a special space to meditate, use a variety of mindfulness interventions and strategies, and reflect on what was working. This daily experience was rewarding to me because watching students go from reactive to thoughtful was an example of what can happen with inspired action.

Students from the middle school and high school culminated their year by visiting our four elementary schools and facilitating mindfulness and positive psychology activities with their younger peers. This "vertical learning" helped all ages as they worked together mindfully.

Finally, my position allowed me to create a district mindfulness website with resources for teachers, parents, and students. They could benefit from ready-to-use lesson plans, books, articles, videos, TED Talks and a variety of other materials.

At the end of two years in this position, more than half of the elementary classes had their own mindful spaces, 90 teachers had mindful toolkits, 50 had three-tone chimes and three schools had mindful rooms, all of which are being used. Sadly, budget cuts led to the elimination of several positions including mine. Happily, I can say that with over 2,000 students and hundreds of teachers learning mindfulness and positive psychology interventions, they now have the tools that they need.

As mindfulness practitioners know, to reap the benefits they will need to continue to apply their practice. My own mindfulness teacher once told me something that I have learned to be true, "We can plant the seeds, however, we will rarely see the beautiful flowers that grow." As for me, I've decided to continue this work with other districts, schools, and classrooms, as a COSEM chapter coordinator in Southeastern Pennsylvania and as a consultant in my community.

Below I share a sampling of interventions I used during my tenure as Mindfulness/Positive Psychology Coach. To see photos of them in action, you can view my tweets on Twitter@cindygoldberg13.

A Sampling of Mindfulness and Positive Psychology Interventions

Three Good Things

Write down three things that went well for you over the last 24 hours. Tell what they were and how you contributed to them happening.

Gratitude Letter

Write a thank you letter to someone who did something for you or to whom you are grateful. Be sure to include details. Call that person and read the letter to them.

Strength Spotting

Watch *The Science of Character* at letitripple.org/films/science-of-character and spot the trait that is most like you. For teens and adults, take the VIA Character Strengths survey at viacharacter.org and list your top five. Create a top five collage.

String Breathing

Each person gets a 12 inch piece of string to hold taut with both hands. On the inhale, the string ends are brought to meet as the hands meet. On the exhale, the hands return to the original taut position. Repeat at least three times.

Balancing

Each participant is given a peacock feather. They are instructed to quiet their mind and place the feather on their finger as they balance the feather with full concentration.

Flipping Thoughts

Write down a negative thought or worry that you have on a piece of colored paper. Be as specific as you can be. Use a small handheld shredder to "get rid of" that thought. Take a new paper and rewrite/flip the thought into a positive. Keep the new paper.

Growth Mindset

Change the way your students speak, by teaching the word 'yet' and the ways you can improve. For example, change "I can't read this" to "I can't read this yet. I can keep practicing until I get better at reading difficult words." As educators, we can speak keeping growth mindset language in mind. Instead of saying, "You are so smart" say, "You worked really hard at writing this paragraph and it shows."

CHAPTER 32

Moving Toward Equity with Mindfulness-Based Education

Lillie Huddleston, PhD

Executive Director of Equity and Student Support, City Schools of Decatur, GA

I GREW UP IN A FAMILY OF EDUCATORS AND I LISTENED to my parents share their experiences of living in the segregated South. During that time, education was viewed as the route to the American dream. While some of the educators I experienced were inspiring and loving, there were also those who made hurtful comments about my potential and that of other students who looked like me. I was driven to be a part of creating a community that nurtured, celebrated, and educated all students across racial and cultural differences.

I started my career in education as a music teacher. As an elementary chorus teacher, I had the opportunity to connect with every student in the school. I learned first-hand about the stressors that families faced to provide opportunities for their children while navigating the personal and societal challenges. In addition to providing the much needed creative and intellectual outlet music education offers, I was interested in learning ways to address some of the social and emotional issues that created barriers for some of my students. This prompted me to leave the classroom to pursue a graduate degree in School Psychology.

During my graduate studies, I was introduced to yoga and meditation. I discovered that mindfulness was an ideal practice to help me focus and relieve stress. I later learned that mindfulness was a tool to help me cope with racial microaggressions I experienced in my personal and professional life. I was particularly drawn to the teachings of Thich Nhat Hanh and angel Kyodo Williams. These teachings helped me begin the process of racial healing and informed my passion for creating space for people to collaborate and build meaningful connections across racial and cultural differences.

After completing my graduate studies, I learned about a position that incorporated all aspects of my professional experience. It was also aligned with my purpose to educate others and remove barriers to equitable outcomes for students who have been historically pushed to the margins in the public education system. The City Schools of Decatur was making a public commitment to eliminating disproportionate outcomes and closing achievement and opportunity gaps based on race. When I learned of the position, I was excited by the opportunity to address the inequities in an effort to help the district realize its vision of *"building the foundation for ALL children to be their best, achieve their dreams, and make the world a better place."* As a Black woman, who was born and raised in the South, I understood deeply the challenges associated with tackling racial inequity in education. The potential benefit to underserved students and families far outweighed the risk of facing the uncharted territory of addressing racial equity in public education.

I was hired as Equity Director for the City Schools of Decatur in the summer of 2017. The city is comprised of 4.7 miles surrounded by the metropolitan Atlanta area. The district includes ten schools (1 high school, 1 middle school, 2 upper elementary schools, 5 lower elementary schools, and 1 early learning center) and approximately 6000 students. Over the years the demographics have shifted and the city has faced some of the same challenges we see across the country including lack of affordable housing, gentrification, and racial inequity in education. While the district has been known for its high-quality educational programming for many years, it has been clear that the benefits have not been reaped by all students, particularly students of color. The district leaders were determined to tackle this issue and created the Equity Department and identified racial equity as a strategic priority for the 2017–2018 school year.

When researching best practices for promoting educational equity, I learned that mindfulness has been successfully implemented in school settings as an alternative to punitive discipline and to help teachers cope with stress. I also learned that mindfulness was one of the recommended strategies to interrupt and reduce implicit bias.

Developing a Plan to Address Inequitable Outcomes

It was important for me to understand the experiences of the school community before developing an action plan to address racial inequity. I worked with a consultant firm to conduct a mixed-method needs assessment to gain input from staff members, parents, and students. The results suggested that there was a need for professional learning related to cultural humility and culturally responsive education. The findings also highlighted that changes were needed in policies and procedures across the district to promote equitable outcomes.

In addition to guiding the district's equity efforts for all students and staff, I was a part of a team charged with developing a plan to prevent disproportionate discipline outcomes based on race for students receiving special education programming. Our theory of change is that beliefs drive behavior and behavior determines outcomes. In other words, if we can change our underlying beliefs we can change the way we work with underserved students and change their educational outcomes. This requires an inside-out approach where educators and administrators focus on self-awareness as the first step to reducing implicit bias and making connections across differences. I immediately thought about mindfulness as an option to incorporate a focus on self-awareness as well as personal and professional growth. It was clear that both students and teachers needed tools to reduce stress and to promote positive social interactions.

I reached out to Theo Koffler, the founder of Mindfulness Without Borders, and she connected me to Leah Gardiner. At the time, Leah was the Director of Partnerships and Lead Trainer. Theo explained that their evidence-based programs were secular in nature and designed to help students and teachers alike to strengthen their social and emotional health.

Their philosophy, like ours, was grounded in the belief that when people understand and value the experience of others, they create a culture of understanding, support, and collaboration. Their program sought to encourage young people to discover their unique talents, as well as appreciate the differences and diversity in others. With time and practice, participants would be ambassadors for human kindness, across all dimensions of identity differences.

In the Fall of 2017, Leah facilitated an on-site certification program for school administrators, teachers, and support staff. The experiential and interactive training taught the techniques and best practices to successfully bring their evidence-based program to our school community. We learned secular mindfulness practices and how to lead them. The curriculum featured strategies to pay attention to the present moment with a non-judgmental quality of mind, as well as to observe our thoughts, emotions and body sensations while they were happening. We also learned how to facilitate large and small group discussions using the dialogue prompts that were carefully crafted for age-appropriate discussions to help students build on their inner wisdom.

In addition to the curriculum, Leah had incredible vision for improving our school culture at large. She highlighted the importance of self-care and self-compassion and suggested that we work toward including everyone in the school community in our mindfulness practices. After all, while working in education is one of the most rewarding professions, it can also be deeply stressful. Thanks to Mindfulness Without Borders' holistic approach, we began to bring more members of the educational community into the conversation.

Piloting the Program with Students

The next step was to pilot the program with students. Though we worked to promote equity in the whole district, we decided to start with high school students with a focus on 9th and 10th-grade students. The school discipline data suggested that there were disproportionate discipline outcomes with a pattern of Black students being a greater risk for suspension and expulsion. Similarly, we identified gaps with achievement and attendance based on race. Parent and student interviews, also suggested that students of color did not feel connected to the school. I hypothesized that this lack of connectedness and belonging played a role in the disparate educational outcomes for Black students.

I wanted to provide tools for our students to manage stress and build positive connections with staff and administrators. That said, the district's priority and my personal goals remained the same: to create educational equity for all students with a focus on eliminating barriers for students of color.

Since diversity and inclusivity start in the classroom, it became apparent that accessing an educational program in which all students feel their perspectives are equally valued and respected was key to creating a successful learning environment. Our top priority was to eliminate opportunity gaps and meet the academic needs of students who have been historically underserved.

As a result, we were looking for a program that provided a safe learning space where all students could share their experiences and learn from the perspectives of others. It was the Mindfulness Ambassador Program for youth, developed by Mindfulness Without Borders, that became an important piece of the puzzle to support the challenges faced.

Shifting Away from Punitive Discipline

The research that we conducted on discipline and behavior management suggested that it would be possible to address behavioral issues using evidence-based mindfulness practices. We designed the intervention with mindfulness instruction to reach students with multiple discipline referrals, inconsistent attendance records, and limited course completion.

Given that few schools in our area were implementing this type of programming, we were cautiously optimistic. We were pleased to learn that there were immediate palpable benefits. Together with their highly-skilled facilitators and much hard work on behalf of our school team, we begin to see shifts in the way students participating in the intervention viewed themselves. We also noticed improved connections with staff members and a shift in the ways in which students with a history of persistent disciplinary concerns were viewed by the community. As one of our amazing facilitators stated:

"The ability to engage with students on a one-on-one basis has been an absolute game-changer for students. We've been able to have conversations that focus on goal setting not just for academics but also for their personal lives. Having someone in the building that they can come to for non-contingent engagement offers them the opportunity to share and build a trusting relationship geared toward their success. Our successes became clear at the end of the year as we saw student data shift toward stronger school and life success."

While the initial results of the pilot were promising, it is important to note that changing from punitive to proactive strategies is challenging and school staff members need a great deal of ongoing training and support as they shift to a more innovated restorative approach.

My fear was that we would default to habitual actions when faced with difficult situations, as approaching these challenges differently did not come naturally to everyone at first. However, over time, the skills we gained offered new ways of responding to and thinking about challenging behaviors. We learned that conflict is about opposition—between individuals, groups, or one's own thoughts and feelings—and that every behavior is a form of communication.

When students are non-compliant, they are seeking to meet an underlying need it is our job to listen to them, to figure out what is being communicated and to make them feel like valued human beings. We also must look holistically at students and provide support for those who have experienced trauma and other stressors that might impede their ability to access educational opportunities. Through the implementation of this pilot, we learned that thriving at school requires creativity and compassion: a balance between the consuming nature of a school day and the necessity to find well-being and purpose within it.

The Missing Piece in Our Education System: Mindfulness-Based SEL

Practicing mindfulness helped us develop the tools to increase self-awareness, better manage stress, cope with anxiety, and foster deep connections in the community and at school. Students who participated in the pilot felt listened to, valued and respected. We were able to make strides toward creating a school environment where all students feel safe, seen, and successful. Next, we want to expand the program to more students to remove barriers and create opportunities for student success. We also have plans to integrate a focus on mindfulness into our broader district focus on character development.

There are so many stories and so many different ways that the Mindfulness Ambassador Program touched the lives of our school community. I feel strongly that one of the missing pieces in our education system is mindfulness-based social and emotional learning programs. Having witnessed this program in action, I am convinced that schools, like ours, can become more peaceful and more equitable learning environments.

Clearly, not all human beings have the same start in life and many students face barriers to learning that come from outside the school environment. However, when we offer students the resources to build social and emotional competence and how to stop, breathe, and connect with their feelings, we can equip them with the tools they need to build resilience and navigate the challenges they face. Programs like the Mindfulness Ambassador Program can help transform school culture and student behavior. Many educators agree that equity in education should be a national priority, and for those of us who have seen it, mindfulness-based practices, as well as social and emotional learning, can be an integral part of the solution.

CHAPTER 33

Peace of Mind: Conflict Resolution with Mindfulness and Neuroscience

Linda Ryden

**Peace Teacher, Lafayette Elementary School, Washington DC,
Founder, Peace of Mind, Inc.**

with Cheryl Cole Dodwell and Madeleine Sagebiel

Peace of Mind, Inc.

I AM A CERTIFIED TEACHER AND HAD BEEN TEACHING conflict resolution to elementary school children in Washington DC for five years when I suddenly realized I was doing it all wrong. My "Peace Classes" were engaging and fun, my methods were inspired by some of the best curricula on conflict resolution, and many of the kids that I was teaching actually used the skills I had taught them in their daily lives. It all looked good.

But day after day I would see children being sent to the office for fighting at recess. Some of these kids would go straight from my classroom, where we had been role-playing how to work out a conflict, to the playground, where they would get into a fight over who goes first on the swings. When I asked the kids why they didn't use the conflict resolution skills they had just practiced, they usually looked at me blankly and shrugged their shoulders. Occasionally someone would say, "I was just too mad. I couldn't think straight." I was at a loss.

So I went back to the experts. I looked through more books and more curricula to see what was missing. I realized that what I needed to be teaching my kids was how to calm down. But how? The conflict resolution resources I read would often start with Step 1 Calm Down, Step 2. . . . . But there was no explanation in Step 1! How do you calm down? And how do you teach kids to calm down? Telling someone who is angry to "calm down" doesn't work. Telling someone who is angry to take a deep breath doesn't work either. So what could I do?

After doing some research, I started to focus on mindfulness. I was not a meditator back then and it was not the buzzword back in 2011 that it is now. I had friends who meditated, but I was one of those "my mind is too busy to meditate" people. It seemed a little out of my comfort zone and something I simply wouldn't be able to do, but the more I read about mindfulness, the more I started to think that this was exactly the step that was missing from my conflict resolution lessons. I decided that if this was what my kids needed, then I needed to find out more.

So I spent a summer learning about mindfulness and most importantly starting my own practice. I read a lot of books and took Mindful Schools' Fundamentals online course. And it turned out I actually really liked it. I found that after a few weeks, I started to notice patterns in my thinking. I had always been a terrible worrier, but I started to be able to notice when I was going into a worrying spiral and catch myself, breathe, and try to refocus my thoughts. Then I would be able to decide if the worrying was useful. It never was. I started to find comfort in the pause that you can get from mindfulness practice, the moment of space between reaction and a response. I had a feeling that this would be very helpful for me as a teacher.

I was nervous, but with three whole months of experience under my belt, I dove in with my students in the fall semester. As I said, this was a long time ago and mindfulness still seemed pretty foreign. My colleagues thought I was crazy, and parents had a lot of questions, but I was used to that, I was the Peace Teacher after all. However, I was surprised and thrilled to find that the children loved it. My students experienced mindfulness as it is meant to be: a set of skills that we can learn to help us to focus better, to manage our emotions, to calm ourselves down, to become kinder and more compassionate.

I started using mindfulness as the foundation for conflict resolution with my students. We began each of our weekly Peace Classes with mindfulness practice, and then we'd continue with our social-emotional learning lessons about friendships, feelings, including people, listening, empathy, kindness and conflict resolution. After a few months. the difference was noticeable. The kids (from first to fifth grade) not only loved the mindfulness practices, but the lessons we learned from mindfulness were deepening all of our other work. We were starting to notice a change in our school climate. There were fewer fights and the kids seemed to be calmer.

Learning About the Brain: The Missing Piece

Although things were so much better, I still felt like something was missing. Even though I was grateful that mindfulness had helped my students recognize and regulate their anger, I still didn't understand what was really going on in the moment. Why weren't they able to think when they were angry? Why do we all make such poor choices when we are mad?

I don't remember exactly when I heard about the work of Dr. Daniel Siegel, but it was a moment that changed my life. I watched a video in which he teaches about the amygdala. The amygdala's job is to keep you safe and protect you from harm. When the amygdala senses that you're under attack, it takes over your brain. It shuts down the parts of your brain that think and remember-the prefrontal cortex and the hippocampus. It puts your brain into fight or flight mode, and in this mode, you can't think and you can't remember—all you can do is react.

It blew my mind. I suddenly remembered my students telling me that they didn't use their conflict resolution skills when they were angry because they just couldn't think. And now I knew why! They were right. They were describing exactly what was happening in their brains. They couldn't think in that moment. Their amygdalas had hijacked their brains in order to protect them and had turned off all memory of my lessons. It all made sense now.

I went back to school the following year armed with what I now believe are the two most powerful conflict resolution tools: mindfulness and neuroscience. Once I was able to teach my students what was happening in their brains when they were angry and how they could take care of their brains with mindful breathing, then working out the conflict was much easier. This little bit of brain science has been incredibly liberating for my students, and for me!

Now, instead of just focusing on how to de-escalate conflicts, we began to focus on how to prevent conflicts from escalating in the first place. The kids began to feel the anger in their bodies when it was small. They learned how to use breathing to calm the anger. I wasn't teaching the kids to ignore or suppress their anger, but rather giving them tools to manage it.

We started noticing kids using Take Five breathing, a breathing exercise in which you trace the outline of your fingers and take deep breaths as you go, and other mindfulness practices on the playground, during tests, even during little league baseball games. They really took to these practices. As one of my students says, "Mindfulness is so much more than just breathing in and breathing out. It's a mindset." My students would even teach these skills to their parents.

Becoming a Peace Teacher

What I learned about mindfulness really changed everything at my school. After a few months, we were able to close down our Refocus Room, the place where kids were sent when they got in trouble at recess because no one was going there anymore. After a year or two, what had started as a little experiment in my classroom became a schoolwide program.

As I said at the beginning of this chapter, I had been teaching conflict resolution for several years before I discovered mindfulness. I taught my first Peace Class in 2003, starting as a volunteer while my own children were there. I taught a few classes a week, but after a few months, parents and teachers started asking for more. For a few more years I worked part-time, gradually increasing the number of grades I was teaching. It was a risk for my then principal, Lynn Main, to make room in the schedule for an unusual class like mine, but this was back in the early 2000s when there was a little more flexibility in school. There was more room for innovation.

The big question was always how to fund my position as the Peace Teacher. The parents at my school really stepped up to the plate. After two years of volunteering my time, I applied for a small grant from our Home School Association (HSA). Each year I applied, and as my workload grew, their financial support grew. It was difficult working as a contractor with no benefits, but my outsider status gave me enormous room for creativity.

Once my work became full-time, the employer role became too burdensome for the HSA. At that point, I partnered with Minds Inc, a local mindfulness-focused nonprofit. Minds Inc contracted with the school and then paid me. Working with the HSA has taken constant communication with parents about the value of this work, but my students have been a terrific aid in the process, bringing home what they have learned and sharing the benefits with their families.

In 2018 I was hired officially by the District of Columbia Public Schools (DCPS) as the very first Peace Teacher! I owe a great debt to my current principal Dr. Carrie Broquard for this. She is under enormous pressure to use every minute of the school day for academics and somehow manages to continue to find space for Peace Class. In fact, when our school was renovated a few years ago the planning team created a room just for Peace Class. The Peace Room is a bright, beautiful open space where all 750-plus students take a weekly 45-minute Peace Class.

Mindful Mentors Program

Getting teachers interested and on board with this program has been challenging. I'd like to say that I told everyone about mindfulness and they all bought in immediately, but that's just not true. Several teachers at my school have taken to mindfulness and made it a part of their personal practice as well as part of the everyday life of their classroom. Many teachers are interested, but feel too busy to try to learn something new. Some are simply not convinced that this is important work. Again my students have been the best ambassadors for mindfulness.

Principal Broquard asks teachers to allow for two Mindful Moments a day in their classrooms. When teachers forget or are too busy, the kids are the ones to remind them about the Mindful Moments. They really seem to get how much the practices benefit them.

One way that I have tried to get more teachers interested in sharing the mindfulness practices with their students is through a program called Mindful Mentors. I have a group of fifth-grade students who visit younger-grade classrooms twice a week near the end of the day to lead a Mindful Moment. The mentors love the opportunity to be leaders in our school and the younger kids are inspired to do the mindfulness practices because they look up to the fifth graders.

I think the Mindful Mentors have been able to convince many teachers as well. It's always a work in progress, but as the research about the positive effects of mindfulness starts to grow and the importance of social-emotional learning starts to become more accepted and widespread, I'm starting to feel more confident that this work is here to stay.

> *"It's a really great experience for the littlest kids. Sometimes it is easier to learn from someone who was recently in the same position as you instead of listening to just another adult about something as different as Mindfulness."*—Peace of Mind Graduate

Making Mindfulness Part of School Culture

We have worked hard to infuse mindfulness and the concepts taught in Peace Class into every aspect of our school culture. For example, when Dr. Broquard wanted our school to adopt PBIS (Positive Behavioral Intervention and Supports), we formed a committee to figure out how to adapt it to our existing framework. We wanted to bring mindfulness to PBIS and bring in more intrinsic rather than extrinsic motivation to the program. Rather than relying solely on a list of school rules and external rewards to regulate students' behavior, we developed a set of guidelines based in mindfulness: Speak Mindfully, Act Mindfully, and Move Mindfully, or "SAMM."

Children are encouraged to notice where they are in the building—the library, the gym, the cafeteria—and then to ask themselves: How loudly should I talk? How quickly should I move? Students are asked to think about how they treat one another in every situation, and to ask: Could I be kind to the new student sitting alone? Could I help the child who just dropped their pencil box? This way they begin to be mindfully aware of what is happening around them and to make choices about how to behave accordingly in that moment. Asking students to use mindfulness skills to take responsibility for their actions is very empowering and has resulted in a significant difference in student self-regulation and school climate.

Another way that we have built peace and mindfulness into the fabric of our school is through Peace Club. Peace Club is an alternative recess program that I run in the Peace Room. Kids who are struggling to make friends or who feel overwhelmed by the crowded, noisy playground are invited to come to Peace Club at recess. There they can choose among quieter, cooperative games that help them to learn how to better navigate the social challenges under my supervision and one of our school counselors.

As the culture of the school has changed, new teachers and families are drawn to our school because of the Peace of Mind Program. A virtuous circle of culture now exists among both kids and staff. This did not happen overnight. It has taken time, patience, dedication and trust in the value of the work for our children. But the results are undeniable.

The Peace of Mind Curricula is Born

After several years our program started to get a bit of media attention. An article in *The Washington Post* in 2011 focused on how our program was helping to prevent bullying at our school, and I was asked to serve on a city-wide committee to create a new bullying prevention policy. More and more administrators, educators and parents started to hear about what we were doing at Lafayette Elementary. I was suddenly inundated with requests to visit my classroom. Everyone was asking, "How can I do what you're doing? I want to be a Peace Teacher too!"

I was thrilled that people were excited about what we were doing at Lafayette, but the answers weren't simple. I had created my own curriculum because there wasn't anything like it out there. There were good mindfulness options and good SEL curricula, but nothing that integrated the two with brain science and conflict resolution. While I loved meeting with people and telling them about what we were doing at Lafayette, it was becoming very challenging to manage. I teach full-time, which at our huge school means teaching 25 classes a week. I realized that I needed another way to share what we were doing.

I felt called to write a curriculum to support other educators in bringing this work to their kids, but I had no idea how to go about it. Luckily for me, Cheryl Dodwell entered the picture at that point. I told her about my dream of writing a curriculum and the growing acknowledgment of the value of integrating mindfulness and SEL. None of the rest of this story would have been possible if Cheryl hadn't agreed to bring her considerable experience in publishing, nonprofit management, mindfulness and body-mind-healing, writing and editing to the task of co-authoring the curriculum.

Cheryl and I worked together to define the philosophy and framework of what I was doing in the classroom, to identify the core practices we needed to share with children, to design the most effective lesson sequence, and to create practical, easy-to-use, effective guides for educators that would allow them to integrate mindfulness, kindness, SEL, brain science and conflict resolution in a set of weekly lessons that would serve children from PreK through Grade 5. Over the course of a year and a half, we distilled over 15 years of classroom experience into three curriculum guides and published the first two volumes of the *Peace of Mind Core Curricula* Series in 2016. We partnered with Counselor Jillian Diesner to adapt Peace of Mind for Early Childhood, and published our Core Curriculum for Early Childhood in 2017.

I couldn't have done this without partners as I was and still am teaching full-time. It feels critical that our work continues to be rooted in the classroom in our work with real kids. We funded this first part of our work ourselves as we believed so deeply in its potential.

Pilots and Research

Research backs up the value of teaching mindfulness in schools, and other studies confirm the benefits of teaching social and emotional learning lessons for student well-being. But our Peace of Mind approach was new—no one had yet studied the value of integrating mindfulness-based social and emotional learning for kids. What I have learned in over a decade of teaching this work to thousands of kids is that the combination of the two is transformative. Our next step was to find out: would *Peace of Mind* serve other schools equally as well as my own?

We launched our first pilot in 2015–2016 at a public school with similar demographics to my own, Horace Mann Elementary in Washington DC, to see whether the curriculum would have a positive impact in the hands of other teachers. Our pre- and post-surveys showed that both students and teachers perceived a strongly positive impact of the curriculum. Great news!

The next school year, 2016–2017, we ran a pilot in four more schools with a wide range of demographics and implementation methodologies. With funds earned from sales of curricula, we hired a researcher to help us develop our pre- and post-survey instruments and to analyze the results. Again, all promising. 100% of teachers said they would be very likely to teach *Peace of Mind* again and would recommend it to a colleague. To have this reflected back by educators we respect and admire gave us hope that what we were working so hard to share had value.

While we were running our pilot studies, word of mouth carried *Peace of Mind* around the country and the world, and schools in Washington D.C., our hometown, began to inquire and adopt the curriculum as well. We were even featured in a documentary about mindfulness called *A Joyful Mind*. This was the confirmation we needed to form our nonprofit organization, Peace of Mind Inc, with a mission of equipping and supporting educators to bring mindfulness-based SEL to their students. Cheryl is the Executive Director and we have an extraordinary Board of Directors and an engaged and connected Advisory group.

"Finding quality, accessible, purposeful resources that have an immediate and positive impact on learners is a school leader's persistent goal. This Peace of Mind Curriculum achieves that aim as it provides educators with a set of teacher-developed-and-tested lessons that build a foundation of respect for self and others."—Liz Whisnant, Principal of Horace Mann E.S., Washington DC

Stand-Out Elements

Our *Peace of Mind Curriculum* integrates the best practices in teaching mindfulness, brain science, social and emotional learning, and conflict resolution skills into one thoughtfully constructed, extensively field-tested weekly curriculum. We believe, based on our experience and that of our pilot schools, that *Peace of Mind* can be most effective as a long-term, comprehensive, whole-school program taught by counselors or teachers, facilitating deep connections between students and caring adults, a key factor in student well-being.

It's so important to us that the *Peace of Mind Curricula* is rooted in the classroom, has been written for teachers by teachers, and that every lesson has been tested and developed with our students for over a decade. Teacher developed lessons are what we want to use in our own classrooms and the kind of resource we are committed to sharing. Every lesson starts with mindfulness practice and moves on to incorporate social and emotional learning lessons, brain science, conflict resolution practice, and kindness pals.

Recognizing that this work is all about the practice rather than perfection, we've designed a spiral curriculum that helps students deepen their mindfulness practice and SEL and conflict resolution skills as they grow. We've tried to make it flexible, so it can be used by classroom teachers, specials teachers or counselors in 30 to 45-minute blocks that fit into a weekly schedule.

Most importantly, the lessons in *Peace of Mind* reflect our belief that mindfulness is the essential foundation for students' acquisition and mastery of social and emotional skills and conflict resolution tools. Teachers do not have to be mindfulness experts, but this curriculum is most successful when teachers commit to practicing along with their students. This is it in a nutshell—our offering to educators.

Storybooks that Share Lessons

Another way that we have worked to get our message out is through storybooks. In 2014 I wrote and illustrated a book called *Rosie's Brain* to introduce my students to mindfulness skills and the parts of the brain that help us manage anger and calm down: the amygdala, hippocampus, and prefrontal cortex. We published it independently and sold it through Amazon and on our website.

My next three books have been published by Tilbury House Publishers. With illustrator Shearry Malone, we have created *Henry is Kind, Sergio Sees the Good,* and *Tyaja Uses the THiNK Test.* Each of these stories comes directly from the experiences of my students and features real kids I've taught through the years. We feel strongly about the importance of representation in children's books and so each of our books features a very diverse cast of characters. These books give us an opportunity to share some of the lessons from the *Peace of Mind Curriculum* with a wider audience and also give parents a way to share these lessons with their children.

Training, Continued Innovation and a Call to Action

Because I teach full-time, we are limited in how much in-person training we're able to offer so we've had to get creative. We're guided by a simple practice: listen to educators and kids and see what we can do to leverage our limited resources to meet their needs. As we can't be there in person as much as we'd like, we created three online training courses including an Introduction to Mindfulness and Social and Emotional Learning, Getting Started with the *Peace of Mind Curriculum* and Teaching Neuroscience to Kids. We love hearing from educators about their experience with these courses.

We have also recently produced the *Peace of Mind Curriculum for Grades 4 and 5* —a new curriculum that features lessons focusing on some of my more recent work helping kids to use mindfulness to address implicit bias, stereotypes, and bullying.

We're excited to be widening our scope to include middle school too. We were asked by Principal Megan Vroman who is opening a brand new middle school in DC to write a *Peace of Mind Curriculum* for her 6th-grade students. There are few mindfulness-based SEL resources for middle school students and we are excited about piloting this curriculum with the wonderful staff at Ida B. Wells Middle School.

If you are a teacher, counselor, youth group leader, or parent, perhaps you are thinking "I'd like to be a Peace Teacher too!" If you are, that's wonderful—you can be! We hope that you will take the opportunity to experiment and be creative and perhaps make *Peace of Mind* your own. Your community needs what you have to offer and the world needs mindful, peaceful people now more than ever.

CHAPTER 34

The Ocean is Calling: Transform School Climate with a Focus on Wellness

Lindsey J. Frank, MEd, RYT-200

Climate and Social Emotional Learning Coach, Community Consolidated School District 59, IL COSEM Chapter Meeting Facilitator

Be generous with your time,
Go where others are afraid to go,
Give it all you've got,
And love what you do.

I WROTE MY LIFE MOTTO YEARS AGO FOR A COLLEGE ASSIGNMENT, but I never knew it would continue to be the guide for my decisions and an alignment check on my core values. My motto has supported me through times when fear crept in and has given me the courage to pour my heart into my work, especially when taking the leap into the realm of mindfulness within schools. Take a moment . . . a breath . . . do you have a motto? A vision? A guidepost? Pull your vision into your heart and let this be the time to create a fire for action.

Previous chapters of my life have been written through the lens of compassion; however, I used a narrow definition of compassion that only included others and negated my Self.

Getting to work at the crack of dawn, staying until the moon rose high.
Creating the most "perfect" lessons and preparing for impactful IEP meetings.
Bringing the large tubs of work home, only to be exhausted at the sight of a book.
. . . I loved my job, but something was not matching . . .
I was worn out, run-down, and was not my best self.
My heart, although strong, began beating to its own rhythm,
The emotional rollercoaster became the new norm,
And my memory was slipping away . . .
I realized that chronic stress was impacting my life and physical health . . .

This awareness brought me to where I am today, where I have begun writing through the lens of self-compassion and worthiness. I believe that all individuals, especially in education, deserve the gift of mindfulness. When self-awareness, self-care, and wellness are established within education, our learning community can reap the benefits. My calling has started a mindfulness ripple, beginning with the adults supporting each learner.

Noticing a Need for Wellness and Self-Care in My Learning Community

My love of learning has provided me with experiences to cherish and understand diverse perspectives, as well as the ability to connect with many people. I am the districtwide Climate and Social Emotional Learning Coach for Community Consolidated School District 59 (CCSD59) that serves fifteen schools across several Chicagoland northwest suburbs. This position was established in 2017, which simultaneously aligned with when I personally began my mindfulness journey.

Prior to instructional coaching, I was a special educator, an interventionist, a pre-algebra teacher, and a guided reading teacher. I have an endorsement for working with students developing language and have a master's degree in Educational Leadership in Administration and Supervision. I am certified in Restorative Practices, have completed online trainings through Mindful Schools, and became a certified wellness yoga instructor through Breathe for Change in December 2018. I also have a passion for music and art, my violin expresses words when words cannot be found.

CCSD59 is a suburban public school district that has about 6,600 students within a diverse setting; 56% of our learners come from a low-income household and 16% of our learners are receiving specialized services (Illinois Report Card, 2018–2019). CCSD59 is an innovative public school district that is committed to wellness, social and emotional learning as a learning community. In 2017, we were featured by Education First as a model district for our social and emotional learning practices. We are continuously refining our approach with students and staff to create an equitable, holistic, trauma-skilled environment.

As you read about my experience, I hope you are inspired to look back and re-evaluate your life while also looking forward to prioritizing the need for personal mindful practices for staff in a simple, organic, and effective approach.

As an instructional coach partnering alongside professionals and students from all walks of life, I have noticed a significant need for wellness and self-care across the board. Low morale has become lurking dark water that often stems from the illusive compassionate heart open to others . . . but closed to ourselves. With the constant need to help others, teachers become drained, and eventually, the dark water submerges their compassionate heart. We need to come together to create an ocean of possibilities starting with the self.

"Teaching holds a mirror to the soul. If I am willing to look in that mirror and not run from what I see, I have a chance to gain self-knowledge—and knowing myself is as crucial to good teaching as knowing my students and my subject" (Palmer, 2017, p. 3). We are mirrors of each other, and we reflect our own roses and thorns. However, if we have a high level of self-awareness we are able to recognize what we see in the reflection.

Our response can move us from reactive to proactive and can open us to become aware of our breath, body, emotions, and thoughts. Every moment is an opportunity to create a positive change. Mindfulness allows us to appreciate these moments with a clear conscious. My reflection portrays wellness and has ignited my passion, I see hidden potential and *hope*. When you look into the mirror, what do you see?

The Plan: Be The Ripple

"I alone cannot change the world,
but I can cast a stone across the waters to make many ripples."

Mother Teresa's quote is a centerpiece of our work as a Social and Emotional Learning Team. Mindfulness in the district started as a ripple; however, this endeavor cannot sustain itself with a sole leader. It needs an interconnected network of passionate partnerships. Wellness develops from an organic desire to become invested in a lifestyle. When professionals commit to weaving mindfulness into their lives and classrooms, I support them as a coaching colleague. Below are the phases that grew from the passion and interest of staff over the course of one school year.

Phase 1: Embody Mindfulness with Integrity (Be The Ripple)

When passion radiates from the heart, it is hard for others not to notice. For mindfulness to be successful, those sharing the gift need to be highly self-aware and integrate mindfulness into their lives. My day consists of tuning into my breath, integrating my affirmations, reflecting, and taking a few moments to just be. Every action and every word has the potential to become a micro-mindful moment. Staying present without judgment when working with staff allows them to take risks and see the power of the pause.

At work, I include ways to stay grounded and present, such as placing my hands on my abdomen to maintain breath awareness for listening, carrying a stone in my pocket as a tactile grounding focus, and inviting others to join me in taking collective breaths. As staff experience the impact themselves, their curiosity propels their desire for continued learning about how to be mindful. Integrity assures that mindfulness does not become just another "thing" on the teaching platter, but an integrated part of education. This is *the* most important phase; without embodiment, each of the other phases is subject to becoming washed away.

Phase 2: Create Opportunities for Adult Wellness (Get in the Boat)

As interest increases and staff embrace the importance of their own wellness, schools and districts need to provide wellness opportunities for staff to thread healthy choices into their profession. I established three main district-wide avenues for wellness. These avenues were derived from my passion and the needs staff expressed. I was paid through experience, and I gave time out of my heart in an effort to show that mindfulness has a place in education.

1. An open 10–20 minute morning mindfulness session for staff once a week. I led "Thoughtful Thursdays" at a school with one of my passionate coaching colleagues. This was a combination of various mindful practices for staff to experience, and it helped dismantle preconceptions, especially about how mindfulness is typically portrayed. We crafted a flyer that listed each opportunity and shared it using the district weekly communications and school-based postings.

Barriers: Having a locked-in time for the sessions; the before school session was based on the junior high early start (7:00 a.m.); it was held at one building on one side of the district boundaries; there were limitations of districtwide communications.

Lessons Learned: It would be powerful if each school or cluster of schools had access. My plan is to travel to designated schools to offer more accessible opportunities and to alternate before school and after school sessions. I recently developed a mindfulness website and plan to create videos for staff to experience the moments when it works best for them. I will work with the communications department to get an ongoing "Staff Wellness" section.

2. Once a month, a district-wide 30-minute mindful movement was offered for any staff prior to the Morale and Mindfulness Committee.

Barriers: This was only offered prior to the committee meeting; only early-release staff had access to attend; the location was at the central office.

Lessons Learned: I would like to offer these more frequently and on a rotation based at schools. I will form a committee of teachers who are already engaged in their own practices or who are certified yoga instructors to build up their skills to facilitate experiences at their buildings. This includes sharing digital resources as guidance.

3. Schools could request a one-hour wellness mindful movement session for staff during professional development.

Barriers: Keeping up with the increasing number of requests districtwide as one facilitator; union contract constraints to require sessions to be optional; having enough materials; inconsistent spaces.

Lessons Learned: I will be creating a system for schools to schedule and plan out their requests so I have an equitable approach. Also, I will be creating specific mindfulness options that schools can choose from to best meet the needs of staff members.

Each of these opportunities was to test the waters. Knowing that there may not be many attendees in these initial stages, I would tell myself, *"Even if one person shows up, it is worth it . . . you are making a difference in their life and the lives of their students."*

In the future, I would like to collaborate with school leaders to help them develop a personal practice. Leaders may then be inspired to share mindfulness with their staff, model mindfulness as another way to cultivate a compassionate school environment, and commit to wellness schoolwide. Could there be a mindful walking club? Can meetings start with a breath to increase oxygen and awareness? What mindful moments could be found? Additionally, I would like to host sessions to join families, the community, and the district together to experience and grow with mindfulness. It would be a proactive way to dispel misconceptions as we integrate mindfulness into classrooms.

Phase 3: Learn Together (Learn to Swim and Steer)

Learning allows staff to feel confident in their practice and forms a strong support system when swimming in the deep ocean. I created paths for staff to learn about mindfulness and to learn alongside each other.

- I developed the Morale and Mindfulness Committee that was inspired by Elena Aguilar's book, *Onward: Cultivating Emotional Resilience in Educators.* This committee was voluntary and open to any staff member in the district. The interest in the committee was phenomenal and it was one of the largest-attended committees throughout the school year. Perception surveys were provided to committee members to help determine the effectiveness of the supports. One of the committee members shared, *"This committee has opened up my eyes to the importance of mindfulness and the value of applying it in my life. I've become much more aware of how important it is to my overall well-being . . .*

I hope that I can have a positive influence on more people in my life as I continue on my journey."

- Personalized mindfulness coaching cycles were offered to administrators, staff and their students. This involved exploring mindfulness together and how it impacts them personally and professionally. It also involves modeling and co-teaching mindfulness wherever the staff member is comfortable. The learning cycle may start with just a few mindful breaths prior to a meeting, coaching into self-awareness when working with behaviors (focusing on the staff's response and needs), or it may be fully integrating it into the classroom climate.
- To build skills and experiences within mindfulness, I developed a learning series for establishing a mindful culture and practices. The learning was shared with interested staff over the summer and can be sectioned into learning sessions over the school year.

Phase 4: Grow a Network of Passionate Partnerships (Form Your Crew)

Mindfulness grows from a single ripple into many waves. Find the passionate partnerships within your school or district and use them to keep growing. I have entire buildings (staff-driven) within the district requesting to become a mindful school and I have teachers reaching out asking questions to learn more. Other staff members have shared their expertise and offer to grow others, and I even have had individuals outside of my district contacting me for insights and connections. Always be on the lookout for partnerships; the stronger the wave, the bigger the impact.

Phase 5: Patience, Persistence, and Presence (Ride the Waves)

With an organic approach, people jump in when they are ready. There are questions, doubts, misconceptions, and other components that will surface. As staff explore their own practice, they may find a lost treasure in the ocean and will be learning how to navigate their newfound territory. Be there, be present, and ride the waves together. Here are a few strategies to support this phase:

- Maintain the secularity within education; if mindfulness does not resonate with someone, connect it back to wellness. Breathing, moving, and self-awareness are all a part of wellness and are backed by science.
- Keep the definition of mindfulness accessible for all. My definition is: *Mindfulness is being fully present and aware of your breath, body, emotions, and thoughts with an attitude of curiosity, openness, and acceptance.* The definition you create becomes the glue within conversations. If there is doubt—stay open; if there is worry—stay curious; if there are distractions—stay present.
- Provide clarification for those who think mindfulness is synonymous with

calmness and have an aversion to it because of this belief. Let them know that being calm can be a byproduct, but mindfulness at its core is about the self-awareness; bring their attention back to the definition.

Phase 6: Reflection (Admire the Ocean and Go Deeper)

Mindfulness is an alluring abyss . . . there is no "end" in learning. Self-awareness becomes clearer in deeper water, but learning to dive takes time. Just as the ocean has depths that have been unexplored, so do each of us. Knowing this helps us support our learners and staff as they discover what is under their water.

Mentors, Square Squad and Community

This plan came to fruition because of the support systems, experiences, and mentors I've had along the way. I believe that every person and experience in my life have been mentors. Everything holds energy and a message to guide me towards the direction I need to go. As I have become increasingly present and aware, the guidance has been clearer. When a major question or decision crosses my path, I often get validation through my heart and notice the small signs around me.

Additionally, I have a "Square Squad" as Brené Brown calls it. These are core individuals in my life who support me and whose opinions serve as guidance. My Square Squad includes specific family members, friends, colleagues, supervisors, and mindfulness partners I have come to know. I also believe in growing the self through personal learning like books, professional learning networks, and other sources. Sometimes when I am feeling alone on my journey, these resources are my strongest guides.

I am thankful for my community at Breathe for Change (B4C, a yoga and wellness certification program developed by teachers for teachers) for fostering my skill sets, validating my voice, and becoming a source of encouragement. The gratitude I have for this training and awareness is beyond measure and has transformed my life and teaching. My B4C mentorship group and online community are always sharing and learning together well past our initial 200-hour in-person training. The growing amount of resources I add to my repertoire helps refine my practices for staying grounded when sharing with others. My district's response validated that wellness is a necessary investment in education. The ripples are ready to become a part of the inspiring ocean.

Moving Through Challenges with Mindfulness

All of these successes have come with challenges. The biggest resistances and fears I have faced have manifested through my ego and self-doubt, but this awareness has allowed me to break down my own barriers and grow. It is easy to freeze when my inner voice says things like, "You are not good enough." "You don't know what you are talking about, you are inexperienced—there are way more experienced mindfulness practitioners than you." "No one understands you." "What do *they* think? *They* think you are crazy, no one will listen to *you*." "They don't care." However, I have realized that as long as I embody my words, thoughts, and actions with the intention of integrity, the negative inner voice subsides.

Having the ability to mindfully challenge someone and support them through the process have been powerful experiences for me. There will always be an excuse of limited time, money, logistics, resources and opinions, but let these motivate us to move forward with courage and vulnerability. Don't let that inner critic stop you; you can do it!

Through my experiences, I have learned that this journey is an unending expedition of self-development. By discovering myself and my purpose, I am creating a space for others to do the same. Our work is never done. Maintaining a humble mindset, we can stay open to seeing our impact in the present moment. Being mindful is not separate from the daily life experience; it does not discriminate and there is no "one size fits all" approach.

Mindfulness is equitable and accessible to anyone, anywhere, anytime, at no cost. Every individual is equipped with the tools they need to bring their best self forward. I have seen and felt the positive influence first-hand and believe that this work is pivotal for every human being. The sooner each person has access to their true self, the sooner we can nurture strong relationships so that everyone can live a meaningful life based on love.

Vision, Hope, and Encouragement

Imagine a world where all individuals have solid social and emotional learning skills, a mindful lifestyle, and a restorative approach to relationships shifting our world from chaos to understanding. I am passionate about bringing this vision into reality. I am encouraged that mindfulness is becoming integrated into our school culture, but we have a long way to go to shatter the stigmas and biases to have lasting social change. Society places identities and judgments on anything that invites people to uncover their own identity. Children are labeled with an identity as they take their first breath and are taught that there is a right and a wrong. Choice, truth, and courage need to be illuminated so that we no longer fear ourselves or fear each other.

My hope is for young learners to gain mindful insights so they can move through life with a sense of joy knowing that they can solve any challenge that comes their way. When they fall, they can appreciate the ground as they get back up with a strong will. Our children are ripples impacting their own life's ocean. If each child is a ripple extending their love to their self and others, the ripples will one day come together as a wave so large that all people will be captivated by the deep beauty.

I encourage you and all education professionals to embrace mindfulness starting with yourself. It is tempting to jump right into bringing mindfulness to students, but is this really mindful? With the increased accessibility of mindfulness apps and other resources, it is easy for educators to continue to hide from their own self and miss out on many meaningful opportunities. You are worth it; whatever is good for children is good for adults and we must embody the practice if we are to share it with integrity.

Take a moment . . . a breath . . .
The ocean is calling, be the ripple . . . what are you waiting for?

Aguilar, E. (2018). *Onward: Cultivating emotional resilience in educators.* San Francisco, CA: Jossey-Bass.

Breathe for Change. (2019). *Changing the world one teacher at a time.* Retrieved from https://www.breatheforchange.com

Brown, B. (2018). *Dare to Lead: Brave work, tough conversations, whole heart.* New York, NY: Random House.

Education First. (2019). SEL for teachers: Community Consolidated School District 59. Retrieved from https://selforteachers.org/community-consolidated-school-district-59

Illinois School Report Card. (2018). Community Consolidated School District 59. Retrieved from https://www.illinoisreportcard.com

Palmer, P. (2017). *The courage to teach: Exploring the inner landscape of a teacher's life.* San Francisco, CA: Jossey-Bass.

CHAPTER 35

Incorporating Mindfulness into the Fabric of Our Lives in Brooklyn, New York

Una-Kariim A. Cross, MFA, MSED

Leader of Professional Learning and Facilitative Leadership in the New York City Department of Education, Writer, Speaker, Inspirer

Disclaimer: I am writing in my personal capacity. These are my personal views and not necessarily the views of the DOE.

IT WAS A BEAUTIFUL FALL DAY IN EARLY SEPTEMBER 2007. I was a wide-eyed, energetic and cautiously optimistic new teacher in the New York City Department of Education. I had been circling the blocks for over 15 minutes looking for parking. Each passing minute brought me moments closer to the possibility of being late, and it was important to be on time, period. Intuition told me not to park my car in front of Marcy Projects on this particular day. I reassured myself that parking here today would be fine. I checked my privilege, checked my surroundings, checked my car and headed for the door.

The school sat on Tompkins Avenue between Park and Myrtle. It was actually walking or biking distance from my apartment in Fort Greene, Brooklyn, but as teachers, we are prone to carrying many bags. Just days on the job, I had already become *that* new, bag-carrying teacher. I didn't want to arrive too sweaty or disheveled so I opted for driving until I got the hang of things.

The school building housed several schools including the high school where I worked at the time. The energy in the building was always vibrant, colorful and loud. I passed by security who were still giving me the once over. I was hyper-aware of myself in the space; they knew that I was green and I *felt* green, but like most newbies, I tried to mask it. Their thoughts of me likely echoed my own, "*Did I have what it takes to be an NYC educator?* Or more bluntly, "*Who is she and is she going to make it?*" Despite the dim lighting and equally dim common uniforms (khakis and a school-specific uniform top), the space was filled with the energy, uncertainty, anxiety and insecure bravado of Black and Brown youth.

As a new co-teacher under a relatively new principal, I was assigned to a cohort of 9th-grade students. I was in the classes with other classroom teachers to support the needs of all students by providing additional support. Most high-school educators understand what it means to teach or be assigned to teach 9th-grade children, and I was learning. Their minds and bodies vary in size and development; some are still relatively small, some very tall, some more quiet and reserved, some very loud. They are socially-emotionally vulnerable and extremely nervous and excited to be in high school.

Classroom teaching is an art and a science. It is a delicate practice of understanding developmental psychology and applying those understandings to the children under your care. This is coupled with building a learning environment that is safe and that fosters curiosity while building autonomy. There's a necessary adeptness required when learning about and managing multiple, youthful personalities in order to create a safe environment for teaching and learning with from 20–30 young people in a classroom. This is a skill that is cultivated and developed over time. The cohort to which I was assigned was no different. They were energetic and vibrant; young personalities with personalities in progress trying to find their place and their new identities as high-school students. The days were challenging; I taught with several different teachers and each classroom experience was a new adventure with the same students. Like my students, I too was anxious, excited and needing to find and establish myself and my identity as a teacher. What I observed about being in those classrooms in my early days of teaching was that the children needed a lot: a lot of love, a lot of attention, structure, freedom, to be seen, to be heard, to be safe. They wanted to learn, yet they needed more. The curriculum at times felt hit or miss; some students were focused and on-task and learning, some were questioning the purpose of any given lesson in any given discipline on any given day. I wanted to give the young people more, but was still working to understand their academic and social needs.

I was barely 10 days on the job at this time. Nothing, in particular, stands out about this particular day except the fact that it was the eve of one of the September Jewish Holidays. Having made it through another day, I was preparing to make my way to the exit and hovering by the office. As I was preparing to head for the doors, a neighborhood friend, Pop, called to give me a heads up about some 'trouble on the block.' He advised me to be careful and "get home safe." I was steps from the door when I began hearing chaos and sirens outside, moments later there was an announcement over the PA system; the school was on lockdown. When we were finally released, the block was transformed. Yellow police tape, police cars, and people lingering in the aftermath of whatever had transpired lined the streets and sidewalks. I walked in the direction of where I had parked my car which was surrounded by more police and people. I tried to play it cool while look-ing, quietly for my car. An officer emerged with "Ma'am can I help you?" Looking past him, still trying to identify my car, I replied with "Yeah, I'm looking for my car." He asked if I could describe it, I obliged. He stated, "We were looking for you." I finally looked him in the eyes. His body, which had been blocking my car, moved slightly, revealing my car, which had also been transformed.

The windshield was shattered and caved in where the body had landed. A bullet hole had gone through the passenger window and lodged in the passen-ger seat. If someone had been sitting there, the bullet would have gone through their chest. I walked around my car in awe of what I saw, more bullets and blood. This was the start of my career as a New York City educator and my first time being in such close proximity to gun violence. It was the practice of breathing and staying centered, taught to me early on by my parents, family members, and later, my dear friend Ann Segal, that allowed me to remain calm and present in this moment. Often Black and Hispanic children in inner-city schools are considered "at-risk." They are not *at risk*, they are *in danger*. We also have to consider the proximity to danger that teachers enter schools with. Who is arriving to teach and lead and what personal, domestic, and/or national trauma are they carrying?

When we think of children and teachers in proximity to gun violence, many peo-ple think of what we know now as school shootings. The shooting outside of the school made me think of my children and adults and our proximity to gun vio-lence. There are other types of violence to which some Black and Hispanic youth and adults are also subject. We are living in a time where we are in or close to dan-ger and it's terrifying; mindfulness and healing practices inclusive of and beyond yoga and restorative justice are required for youth and educators in these times. For some of the children and youth, proximity to violence was just another day in the neighborhood. After the shooting outside of the school, I realized that I hadn't truly been considering all of the possibilities that surrounded my students' lives. I had always considered myself open, careful and considerate, but this experience led me to deeper thinking about their humanity and what they might experience, prior to simply arriving at a school building each day. At this time, "Stop and Frisk" was also an active policy. How often do we truly consider the proximity to violence and the fact that many Black and Hispanic youth and adult lives are in danger?

Throughout the year, I would bear witness to more experiences that pierced my emotional core; specifically, the trauma that students carried and how those deep pains influenced their behavior in schools and in the classroom. In addition to con-templating my students' proximity to violence, I also began thinking about what it meant to be a young person of low-socioeconomic status and being Black or youth "of color" in schools.

Nothing New About Trauma and Poverty

The pain and trauma from being Black or Brown was something that was, and remains, real for some of our children. Sexual or gender self-identification, language, and being of a certain socio-economic status can add additional layers and/or barriers. This was, and is, also a reality for some educators. I began realizing that real pain and/or trauma lie just beneath the surface for any of us at any given time; that we were carrying that hurt into a common space: our schools. Those scars, experiences, and trauma manifest in numerous ways. For educators, pain may show up as exhaustion, anxiety, depression, apathy, frustration and more. Any of these feelings can lead to difficulty being sensitive, empathetic and mindful in relationship to youth and colleagues. For youth and high-school students specifically, the signs and symptoms of trauma are similar to those of adults—and additionally suicidal ideation, or worse—suicide. According to a recent report aired on CNN, "From 1991 to 2017, the rate of reported suicide attempts by African-American teens rose, especially the rate among Black boys, according to a study published Monday in the medical journal Pediatrics."

I completed the school year on Tompkins Avenue before heading to Brooklyn Community District 16 which at the time, and remains, a district with the highest concentration of Black students in the city of New York. The history of Community District 16 is rich and complex. District 16 is where I would spend the rest of my career as a classroom educator and eventually become a district-based coach (Teacher Team Leader).

As I entered a new school, my questions from my time at Tompkins Avenue remained: how do we, as educators, address the pains and traumas in youth and educators so that schools can be safe, holistic spaces of learning, ideas, joy, and curiosity? I wondered what I could do. I wondered why more wasn't being done–because none of this was new. Poverty was not new nor was the violence and chaos that comes with it. Educators and people who grew up in, or around, urban areas populated with Black people and people of color–we were all too familiar with many of the issues that plagued our communities. Yet, while the ancestral lineage of most Black Americans can be traced to Africa, much of our cultural connection to those centering ancient practices of storytelling, community dialogue, drumming, yoga, capoeira and more were no longer immediate "go-to" practices to solve our community challenges or center ourselves or our youth when challenges arose.

My students in my new high school were from many of the same neighborhoods and housing developments as my previous students. They and their families faced many of the same challenges—food insecurity, housing insecurity, and the violence and chaos that can come with poverty. As a result, there were many fights, tears, emotional outbursts, curse-outs and more. It was painful to experience and yet, many of the adults in the building were committed and determined to find ways to help our students and the school community heal.

A small group of us educators began asking ourselves what we could do. Only a few of us, at that time, shared the same socio-economic background as our children. We had cultural and linguistic commonalities in our slang, music, food, gestures and other understandings, but our experiences were vastly different from that of our students. We had close relationships with them, but they would occasionally remind us that "we weren't hood." All of that was okay, yet none of us were okay. It was clear that our children were hurting in ways that we could not touch, but we understood.

As practitioners charged with the care and education of emotionally-fragile young people who were also survivors, we were constantly reflective and were mindful of who we were in the space; we were mindful of our students and families. At this time, we were not naming our reflections and considerations as "mindfulness" as we know it today, but that's what it was. We were sans yoga mats and breathing techniques, but they would come years later. With family and friends as yoga teachers, including my mother, who is also a social worker, coupled with a southern upbringing on my mother's side, what we now call "mindfulness" was just part and parcel of my ways of being and my existence. Mindfulness in my family meant thoughtful consideration of self and others. Mindfulness meant reflection on actions and how they impacted others. Mindfulness meant pause and reflection, a deep thoughtfulness and awareness that was to ground and center myself in general and in relationship to others.

Culturally-Responsive Curriculum and Experiences as Mindfulness

At the height of the school-based troubles, one particular educator, George Davis, proposed a town hall. This was our initial foray into mindfulness. If we were to look at communities within cultures that fall within the African Diaspora, elders speaking with youth is ritual in some villages and tribes. The purpose of the town halls was to provide a safe, community space in the school to reflect and address community issues. A space for youth to talk it out. The town halls were primarily youth-led and facilitated by us, the educators. The incidents in the school slowly began decreasing; there was greater calm and during this time both youth and educators were able to take individual and collective sighs of relief. The youth responsiveness to the town halls seemed to indicate an openness and willingness to heal, and this was refreshing for all. Two of the questions that I began asking in town halls and later in my classroom were: How do we heal? How do we break cycles of pain and violence? We had no real concrete answers, but at least my students would hear me asking this question repeatedly, over the years. I hoped that they would continue asking this question of themselves in search of actionable answers.

As the need for town halls decreased, the other issues that impacted children's behavior and moods—from hunger to displacement—emerged. We continued working collectively to meet the varying needs of the students with what we had—human capital. We had children that we wanted to see succeed; we wanted emotional and physical safety and we wanted to lead by example while learning from the youth.

Looking back, the town hall was a mindful space for the youth and educators. We probably should have continued it as a space to address the other needs of the youth. Of course, it could have been more robust if we had the time, equipment (yoga mats, drums, chimes), and trained educators to shift from talking and reflection to meditation, drumming, yoga, or other practices that could have become a more comprehensive mindfulness experience for our youth at the time, but this was our start. Over time, we were able to collaboratively establish healthier ways of being for our school community. Simultaneously, while all of those things were going on, educator Dorothy Bauhoff was working with various community partners to get a school-based partnership with the Whitney Museum of Art. We were able to offer three art classes, which was essentially unheard of. We began developing curriculum-based learning excursions, using the city as a classroom, by visiting various historical sites, museums, cultural institutions and more. This again, was not mindfulness as we speak of it currently (which I will get to), but I mention this because art practice can be therapeutic and while none of our classes were distinctly labeled "Art Therapy" or "Mindfulness Through Art" it was clear that these classes were providing a space for calm, experimentation, inquiry and critique in a way that was drawing students in. The art classrooms were spaces for students to breathe, practice and reflect. And before mindfulness in schools, we had to utilize the resources that we had. Later, the school was blessed to begin having a local arts-educator and yoga practitioner, Monique Schubert, on board. I did not know then that Monique had deep connections to and trained at Kripalu. Monique began teaching yoga as an elective to students in the schools. Many of the students who participated loved it; some resisted or were too uncomfortable with the practice to stick with it. When possible, the school social worker would encourage or promote yoga as a safe place for restoration; it caught on and this opportunity became a part of the school culture.

Art Criticism, Responsive Literature and Classroom Routines as Mindfulness

Very early on in my classroom practice, I established a "Bad Day" policy. It meant from the moment the students crossed the line to enter the classroom, it was their responsibility to let me know if they were having a bad day. They had a choice to sit in one of the three "bad day seats" around the room. They had the opportunity to participate in their own way on this day. This was one of the practices that allowed me to be mindful of students as humans and model for students that everyone has a right to have a bad day—that we never know what any person is experiencing or going through, and that we can be considerate of that.

I also tried a practice that I learned from my dear friend and yoga practitioner, Ann Segal, which was to have students take a moment to sit quietly and set an intention for the class. This one took a little too much time, I wasn't consistent with it, and it led to more jokes and time wasted than I could afford.

Students would enter the classroom, share what type of day they were having, place their bags and coats on the back table—as the school had no lockers or place for students to store their belongings, get their folders and get started on the task. These routines worked amazingly for years. The expectations were clear and students felt safe. After a while, I began adding light music; I was celebrating the establishment of routines and thinking I was the most mindful educator, then I hit a major snag—my content was amiss. One semester, after noticing that many of my students had a very singular, media-based perception of themselves and Black culture, I decided to select a book for them to read that I thought would ground them in a sense of pride and history, and expand their cultural awareness beyond that which they had experienced from mass media and possibly in their own neighborhoods. It was a failed attempt at being both mindful and culturally relevant without asking the students what they needed. I realized that as considerate as I thought I was, there was always room for me to learn, especially from the youth. Context is most important as we are on this journey of mindfulness and cultural relevance in education. We must ask our students and adults what they need. I assumed, as adults often do, that if it worked for me, then it could work for them.

Over my years, my instructional practices became stronger as I learned about and studied Chris Emdin's 7 C's of Effective Teaching which, in short, are student-centered teaching methods. Incorporating these strategies allowed me to begin building a more robust student-centered and at times, student-led classroom. My students wanted art, music, and literature, but they wanted it to be more accessible. They wanted to see themselves in the people we studied and seeing themselves went beyond skin color and spoke to experiences and the vibrancy of life in art and literature. I began developing an art criticism and literature curriculum that did just that—the old and the new—from Langston Hughes to Chimamanda Ngozi Adichie, from Chinua Achebe to young adult coming of age stories of hyphenated-Americans.

Sadly, during my time as a teacher in this school, multiple public/national tragedies happened. The execution of Troy Davis, the murders of Michael Brown, Tamir Rice and Trayvon Martin, the hostile arrest and subsequent mysterious death of Sandra Bland, and the death of Eric Garner. They were becoming aware, agitated and vocal. Some were attending protests, many were making signs in protest. As most teachers, I was back in the saddle reworking my curriculum to be relevant, to expand their learning, while giving them space to speak and be heard. We all needed collective healing. So many incidents were happening that it felt like many of us were in triage, trying to pull together learning opportunities, while also feeling traumatized and grieving. We were trying to cobble stories of empowerment and hope. Fortunately, through our curricular-based learning trips, we were able to design and find lessons that could help our community deal and heal. One of our most profound learning experiences was a schoolwide trip to see a public art performance by Dread Scott. Through that experience, we formed a partnership with a local arts organization called MORE ART who published the writing of some of our students as they were moving through and processing the world around them. We were mindful practitioners using art and curriculum to heal our collective wounds.

The experiences shifted us and I was more mindful as I shifted my curriculum design. Students were thriving. They were laughing, learning and thoughtful. While we, of course, had our days, I was witnessing them growing and becoming. From shy, apprehensive and youthfully rambunctious, and at times uninterested–to emerging as autonomous, thoughtful, calm and curious researchers and student discussion leaders. I appreciated that we had collectively created a classroom community that was safe for learning, which was peaceful and sometimes "fun." We were having a great time. While curriculum and lesson development was still a significant lift, it became more exciting. I was adjusting and redesigning constantly with consideration of my students' needs and learning. Yet there was still something missing.

My time in the classroom had been mostly great, despite many of the usual challenges that come with teaching in the urban, under-resourced environment. I loved teaching, I loved my students, I loved seeing their growth, their discoveries, their autonomy. Yet life was taking a turn for me. I had a couple of personal setbacks, my family had suffered yet another major loss, and I had surgery. I was now carrying some pretty heavy scars into the classroom. My breathing was shallow, my patience was thin. I was burned out. It took a moment for me to admit it, but I realized I was no longer doing great at intentionally weaving mindfulness into the fabric of my daily practice. I felt it, my students felt it. I knew it was time to move on. At the end of that school year, I exited the classroom.

Mindful Leadership and a Director of Mindfulness Come to NYCDOE

In 2017, I stepped out of my role as a classroom teacher into my new role as a Teacher Leadership Coach in District 16. I met Rahesha Amon, then Superintendent for Community District 16, in early September. She exuded confidence, passion, and purpose. She was a leader with a vision for her district. She was working to cultivate what she titled "The Urban Garden" in that she was growing capacity and leadership skills in adults for the purpose of serving children and increasing student achievement. She had identified the challenges in her district and one of those challenges was the hurt, pain, and trauma that adults carried and how that impacted them and how it was likely informing how school leaders, teachers, and other adults showed up for children. Within my first month, Ms. Amon shared an article from Stanford Magazine titled "Chief Kindness Officers" in preparation for one of our district team meetings. I was pleasantly surprised and excited. The article spoke about an educator who was leading her students through meditation in class and cultivating compassion. The course was taught by Stanford School of Business by Professor Leah Weiss. Leading with mindfulness was one of Amon's charges for herself and all of us in the district office; she would later share the article with district principals to help frame their work or begin at least reflecting on what it meant or what skills are needed to become a mindful leader.

One of the keywords in the article and in Weiss' course was compassion. This became my new focus question, "How do we cultivate compassionate leadership?" I reflected on my choice to leave the classroom, wondering whether I was so exhausted that I was no longer as compassionate as I had previously been? I wondered how other educators and school leaders felt and I was immediately in support of and wanted to embody the call to action: Compassionate Leadership. I needed new tools. While I was excited about all that I was learning via my work in the district and district office, I wanted to extend and better develop my practice. I was modeling my professional development and leadership after Amon; I was using the same articles that she shared with us, but I needed a next step. By January of 2018, Ms. Amon shared an email with me from a man who I had not yet met, named Barnaby Spring. Spring was inviting district office members to attend the RISE program training at Kripalu; the title in the email stated that this was an offer to receive "Leadership Resilience Training." I read about Kripalu, its offerings and the RISE program and was ecstatic. I learned the New York City Department of Education was working with Kripalu. My desire to receive more tools was being answered in a way that I could never have possibly imagined 10 years earlier.

I was fully living Rumi's quote, "What you seek is seeking you." I had been wondering, working, collaborating and also manifesting this experience, and learning that I was now having fully in Community District 16.

Part of me was in disbelief, the other part of me replied ASAP before I lost the opportunity. I knew nothing of Barnaby Spring, but I liked his name! I attended RISE at Kripalu with Amon and another district leader, Alex Brunner. We learned techniques to manage stress and we practiced intentional breathing; none of this was completely new to me, but the fact we were being trained in order to develop strategies to turn-key these practices in our district was phenomenal. After the experience and training, I sent an email thanking Barnaby. Later, I met Barnaby in person. By then he had become the newly-appointed Director of Mindfulness for the New York City Department of Education, this work greenlighted by the NYCDOE Chancellor and supported by the Office of the First Deputy Chancellor, Cheryl Watson-Harris. Brunner had moved on to become a principal at the Brooklyn Brownstone School and had already reached out to Kripalu to schedule a RISE training for his staff. Amon and I would go on to begin developing a mindfulness plan for District 16 titled "Mindfulness Rooted in Tradition|Ancient Practices & Equity: Connecting Mindfulness to Excellence in Leadership, A Healing Vision with a Purpose. It was a long title as we wanted to be sure to language the key components of the plan.

In addition to the district mindfulness plan, Amon and I went on to co-facilitate workshops on mindfulness and leadership at the Coalition of Schools Educating Boys of Color (COSEBOC) conferences in Boston and Detroit; one of our hashtags was #healthehealers which spoke of school and classroom leaders as "healers" who are also in need of safe spaces to address their pain and trauma. And late spring 2019, Barnaby Spring, Rahesha Amon, David Forbes and I co-facilitated a dynamic and well-received mindfulness workshop at the largest NYC educator conference: EdxEd.

Although Rahesha and I are no longer in Community District 16, we are excited to continue this work. By incorporating mindfulness, storytelling, and other ancient practices into our lives and our current professional leadership work citywide, we continue breathing life into change. It starts with self, it starts with one person. Below is the plan that we created, which we started to implement in 2018 before she moved into her current role as Senior Executive Director of Leadership and Professional Learning in the Office of the First Deputy Chancellor for the NYC Department of Education.

The Plan: Mindfulness Rooted in Tradition

The District 16 mindfulness plan launched in 2018 and was designed to commence over four phases between through the year 2021. The plan was designed to align with the Four Priorities set forth by New York City Department of Education Chancellor Richard Carranza. The Four Priorities are: Accelerate Learning and Instruction, Create and Deepen Partnerships with Communities, Develop People and Advance Equity Now. Phase I of Mindfulness Rooted in Tradition, A Healing Vision with a Purpose addresses awareness, disproportionality, and implicit bias. As the district leader, Amon ensures that leaders in her district attend implicit bias trainings being offered by the NYCDOE Office of Equity and Access. We are ever mindful of the historical fragility of the district, the present state of the district, and its children. We want people to be able to identify and name those things that have been painful–from gentrification to high-suspension rates among youth of color—and begin to look within to become aware of what understandings and behaviors lead to actions that caused harm. Phase II is titled Identifying, Unpacking, Healing, and Storytelling. We have identified a number of key partners that we seek to tap, including Barnaby Spring and the Office of Equity and Access. Beyond that, we facilitate trainings for district school leaders that allow them to begin addressing and identifying the pain that they carry into our schools and districts so that they can begin the process of unpacking and healing.

Phase III of the plan is titled The Courage to Dive Deep into Curriculum and School Culture. We seek to provide training and support that will ensure that the curriculum in schools is rich and relevant and aligned. We want to ensure educators are aware of Chris Emdin's 7 C's and more, and we believe that our facilitators and partners will provide tools and training for school leaders to work with educators, creating more robust learning experiences through curriculum in ways that will reshape and redefine school culture in positive, more holistic ways.

Phase IV is titled Schools as Locations of Healing and Connections. During this phase, school leaders will present a capstone project that demonstrates their growth and learning through each phase. What they have discovered about themselves, and their communities, what new learnings and research led them to revisit, and how they can better build capacity in educators. Additionally, leaders will demonstrate how their school will implement each phase with updated curriculum and rubrics, more robust instructional goals and strategies, and plans for healing spaces within the building. Each school will be allowed to choose what tools they need– from yoga and meditation to drumming–to other ancient practices that align with the school's need.

Coming Full Circle: Reflections on My Journey So Far

As my time in District 16 came to a close, my learning and wonderings had come full circle. I had seen and experienced the pain and traumas of the children and adults in schools; all inclusive of my pains and traumas. I knew the deep historical trauma of being a person of the African Diaspora whose ancestors and culture were snatched from its roots and practices. I had been in schools with limited resources and limited ability to fully address the challenges we faced, but I would exit District 16 with tools, resources, a plan and a new network of people, including Barnaby Spring and the Office of Mindfulness, to begin working with school leaders and teachers to become more mindful, more centered and more able to access resources to meet the needs in classrooms and schools.

My greatest intention is to inspire and encourage, to weave acts of mindfulness into daily practice of youth and educators. And I personally seek to embody the compassion, grace, peace and human regard, and seemingly effortless practice in mindfulness that my maternal grandmother modeled. I seek to encourage educators and school leaders to expand into broader mindful practices that include yoga, meditation, and breathing while also considering the context and the needs of the youth and the adults in the building. I want to encourage educators and educational leaders to stand in their truth while finding ways to influence and lead with compassion. Moreover, I want schools to become places of thriving, joy, learning, *and* healing.

My purpose and passion in this work is working with adults to reconnect mind, body, and spirit through relevant ancient, mindful healing practices. At some point in my life, I began saying, "Hurt people, hurt people." I'm not sure where this quote came from and many people say it now, but as educators and educational leaders, with the precious lives of children before us, we cannot afford to be so hurt that we hurt other people. We have to address our pains and traumas so that we do not injure our students and so that we can be better collaborators with adults. We have to create safe spaces to support them in addressing and moving through their pains and trauma, and this is best done if we are working towards healing.

Along my journey so far, my actions have been informed by my experiences as an educator in New York City and the need for children and adults in urban schools to have healthy tools that lead to thriving, especially in spaces where people are just trying to survive. I have always asked my students if they knew what it meant to thrive; they didn't know, but they learned. They knew they needed to survive, but they also wanted to thrive.

My actions and introduction to a more intentional mindful practice and yoga were inspired by Ann Segal, photographer, and former yoga instructor, when I was in graduate school. Learning intention setting and meditation and practicing yoga with Ann supported all that my parents had instilled. Ann put me on to self-care, introduced me to Thai massage, acupuncture and making the holistic connections between my mother and family teachings. My mother introduced me to mental health care, meditation, and African dance. Both parents taught me strategies to center myself through breathing. My father was constantly reminding me to "stay on an even keel." Later in my early 20s, I was a part of a "New Age" group that introduced me to Tikkun Magazine, Pema Chodron's *Loving Kindness*, Shambhala Sun, leading me to learn about Shambhala Centers, and later the teachings of Jiddu Krishnamurti.

One of my learnings from this journey is that mindfulness and the approaches used must be flexible in order to meet the needs of the community. I also believe that every school should be able to have mindfulness and healing centers in them, especially schools whose community face daily aggressions and pain that can cause trauma.

Mindful leaders should inquire about what, if any, practices a school community uses to provide centering practices. If there are tools and strategies in place, then find ways to expand or build on those opportunities. When possible, schools or trainings should offer and/or encourage choice relative to the identified needs of the school. It would be okay for a school to have a yoga and meditation program, as well as African Drumming and/or Capoeira if that's what the school thought its community needed. I am excited to be a part of and bear witness to the New York City Department of Education's step into mindfulness in connection with the Chancellor's priorities. The largest school system in the country is taking a major step by emerging as a national leader in Mindfulness and Equity training, and the two are interconnected.

One of my next steps in education relative to mindfulness is to continue facilitating healing workshops and professional development opportunities. I also aim to explore how educators and school leaders can utilize art and art therapy as a healing practice. Some of the training I desire to lead will be specifically for adults whereby others will be intergenerational. I believe in the power of healing circles, art, and ancient practices as tools that allow people to begin unpacking the baggage and shedding the weight of trauma in order to truly become mindful.

I am glad that I stayed the course in my own practice and even in doing "what we could with what we had." I would eventually land at a place in my professional practice and my personal experience where the questions I asked and the issues with which I was concerned were being answered, and I, and the people in our school system, would have access to the tools needed to better support youth and educators. Please believe as Rumi says, "What you seek, is seeking you," and that we can all empower ourselves from within.

Center for Contemplative Mind in Society (The). www.contemplativemind.org.
The Power of Traditional African Healing Methods. (2016). www.chopra.com/article
/power-traditional-african-healing-methods

Asase Yaa Cultural Arts Foundation. www.asaseyaaent.org

The New York Mindful Capoeira Center. www.newyorkcapoeira.com

Harriet's Apothecary. www.harrietsapothecary.com

CHAPTER 36

Addressing Equity, Race, and Bias Beliefs in Chicago Public Schools

Cheryl D. Watkins, PhD

Chief of Schools, Chicago Public Schools, District 299

SOMEWHERE DURING MY ELEMENTARY SCHOOL YEARS, I realized that I loved school. Everything about school excited me: the chalk, the erasers, the desks, the uniforms...everything! In the summer, when vacation seemed short and activities appeared plentiful, for most, rain hindered outdoor fun. When other kids were singing "rain, rain, go away come again another day," I was wishing the opposite. I wanted the rain to pour during the summer. When it rained, my friends indulged me in my desire to play school on the back porch of our apartment building. They would come over and let me be the teacher and they would be the students and we would play school.

I was always the teacher, never a principal. I loved teachers and thought they were THE c-o-o-l-e-s-t. On that back porch, I emulated what I saw my teachers do so I had some props. I had a Pepsi bottle and scratch paper for notes. At that time, I thought that was what teachers did, drink Pepsi and pass notes to each other because that was what I saw my 5th-grade teacher do. It was her and several others who made me want to be a teacher. They not only loved me and the other students in the school, but they loved each other and helped to foster a true familial environment at the school. I took everything I learned from them and cataloged every educational moment.

Whenever I met someone and we engaged in a discussion about education, I took a little piece of that conversation and stored it away. In 2004, after soliciting the support of two teachers and two parents, I used every morsel I collected to put into a proposal to start my own school. In 2005, we were granted the school. I became the founding principal of Pershing West Middle School and those two teachers became the 4th-grade and 8th-grade reading and language arts teachers. We got busy identifying the best faculty and staff to support our efforts to "nurture a society of leaders" and hit the ground running. No stone was left unturned as we worked for eight years to provide a viable instructional environment conducive to learning and growth by teachers and students. Within the school and over the years, we were also able to amass numerous successes outside of the academic success for students we were realizing.

We had teachers who were recognized for their teaching capabilities: one Golden Apple Award Winner, one Golden Apple Teacher of Distinction and three D.R.I.V.E. Award winners (recognized locally from Chicago Public Schools). In 2008, I was recognized as one of two Milken Award Winners within the state of Illinois. Our 5th graders helped us to bring home the championship trophy for winning the very first district-wide ballroom dance competition. On paper and within the school, everything seemed to be moving in the right direction, but I still felt there was something missing. I couldn't quite put my finger on it, but I knew there was a piece missing to be whole. I began the search. I didn't know it would take me almost seven years to find what I was looking for, but when I found it, I labeled it the secret sauce for success.

Love and Logic

In 2005, the members of our design team and I launched a valiant effort to positively impact our school community. We searched for positive responses to address student misconduct. We landed on Love and Logic and made sure that we gave students ownership to address their conduct. I don't want you to think that we had a school filled with mischievous students, but we were addressing issues absent of the kindness we all wanted to see. With that approach, we gave students a choice about the positive response we expected to see.

In classrooms and in the halls of the building, it would not be uncommon to hear something like, "Would you like to take your seat now or do you need 30 more seconds?" That worked for a little while until one day when my not so pleasant response to a student's misconduct prompted two teachers to yell down the hall at me, "Hey, Cheryl. Was that love or logic?" Now I can laugh about that question, but the truth is that it condemned me. I wasn't embracing the concept fully because the situation warranted something different. Or so I believed.

Peer Jury

The Peer Jury (of students) was formed to serve as a listening entity for their peers. This group of students gave feedback and provided the next steps to help their peers to restore the peace in the classroom or with another individual that they had disrupted. Members of the Peer Jury would meet with students during their lunch periods and took complete responsibility for doing so. I served as the sponsor for the group and ultimately handed it over to the counselor. It was highly successful.

S-CASS

Pershing West Middle School, like other schools across the world, was faced with multiple reports of bullying. To address this, we created another group called S-CASS (Students Creating a Safer School) that made a public show of addressing bullying from various perspectives: the bully, the bullied, the bystander and the upstander. S-CASS allowed us to implement lunch table discussions so that students in various roles related to bullying could discuss their role in the bullying situation. This program encouraged a celebration of differences rather than an opportunity for them to be put down. Students encouraged each other to confront behavior that was "un-CASS-like."

During the Summer of 2007, Pershing West students participated in the making of a PSA (public service announcement) for the Children's Brain Research Foundation to address bullying across the country. We also had an opportunity to serve as panelists on Chicago Tonight with Phil Ponce. To further spread our message of mutual respect, we presented at conferences both locally and regionally and shared the books we used to lead discussions with students. S-CASS was featured on WTTW's "No More Bullies" and the students starred in a video on bullying.

The efforts we made to combat bullying had been successful in the past, but after our school participated in an assembly called Operation Respect, we made an even larger impact. At this assembly, students and adults heard Peter Yarrow, from Peter, Paul, and Mary, sing "If I Had a Hammer," which opened up a new meaning for the Operation Respect. The lessons we taught included Don't Laugh at Me and addressed being kind and respectful to those who appeared to be different. From that experience, at Pershing West, we adopted the mantra, "You respect me and I'll respect you."

Finding Kind

Finally, in 2012, to address specific issues related to girl-on-girl disrespect, we gathered the girls together for activities designed to expose the characteristics we were witnessing. We modified a "cross-the-line" activity we'd see on Oprah, and asked questions like, "If you've never been invited to a party, step up to the line; if you have been the victim of bullying, step up to the line; and if you've ever said anything negative about a classmate or friend, step up to the line." If we thought we knew the results and anticipated the impact of the activity, we were wrong.

The same day, we watched Finding Kind, a documentary that chronicled experiences with girls that shaped who they were. The interviewers met with girls across the country to hear their stories with the hope of helping others. The female staff and I planted ourselves in stations within the vast auditorium to listen to girls share their stories, just like they did in the documentary. We asked them to write "kind apologies" to the girls they had hurt. The activities of the day served as the primers for unpacking deep feelings and sparked the need for us to scramble to provide the supports, in the form of mentors and mentoring programs, the students needed. I listened to student after student and found myself wiping away tears alongside them.

While planning for the day, I failed to heed the advice of one of my teachers who told me that we were not prepared to sufficiently address what the girls had bottled up inside of them. She told me we needed more time and more adults. That teacher was the beneficiary of an apology from me that day. She was right; we were not ready. We were not ready for the experiences the girls would share that pierced our hearts. We heard comments such as, "I never thought I was good enough" or, "When I look in the mirror I don't like what I see so I tend to be mean to others because of that."

After the event took place, one of my sixth graders asked to speak with me. She wanted me to read what she had written down. Let me describe her to you. She was taller than the average sixth grader, around 5'9" and weighed a little over 150 pounds. Her hair flowed down her back, her smile was beautiful creating dimples deep enough to plant a garden inside. Her grades and test scores were exemplary and she was a pleasant young lady.

When she entered my office, I saw that she had a pink piece of paper with her and I recognized it as a "kind apology." This is what she said: "Ms. Watkins, thank you for today. I needed this more than you would know. May I read my apology to you?" I smiled and said, "Of course." She continued. "This apology is written to me. I'm sorry for not believing that I was beautiful. Please forgive me for not thinking I was smart enough. Please accept my apology. I won't allow that to happen again." She's in college now, excelling and being the wonderful young lady that everyone knew she would be. And, she is the reason I kept searching.

MindUP

The use of Love and Logic, S-CASS, Peer Jury and the institution of Finding Kind Day existed, in concert with one another, until late spring of 2012. Then I received an email from a psychologist associated with The Hawn Foundation and their mindfulness program, MindUP. I was curious about it and began the conversation with him about the content. This is when I learned about mindfulness, taking time to be aware of your surroundings and learning about how your brain works. Basically, MindUP was the way we supported our students in being resilient. I introduced the work of the Hawn Foundation to the teachers on the design team and we decided to investigate further. We received training in the summer to learn how the brain works and tells us how to respond to situations.

Pershing West began implementation during the 2012–2013 school year, each teacher free to engage in MindUP practices with their students daily utilizing what we learned in training. In 4th grade, I saw students taking ownership of deep breathing exercises during the transition from one subject to another. On one occasion, after the teacher ended the lesson with, "We're about to transition to math," a student stood up without provocation, went to the interactive whiteboard and pointed to the image of the brain displayed there. She reminded her classmates of what oxygen did to increase brain activity. I heard another student say, "It's time to center ourselves as we prepare for math. Let your mind make the switch from reading to math and prepare to learn." My mouth fell open and I silently applauded. The student was using the techniques that the staff learned in professional learning sessions.

In the upper grades, I noticed one teacher had allocated time in the schedule to engage students in reflection after MindUP instruction had taken place. Students pulled out their journals and began writing notes about what they learned and what they intended to do with the knowledge. Another teacher took time in the school day to focus and conduct calming exercises with the students. It helped students to self-regulate. She used language to cue students to use what they learned in previous sessions. They began and ended the day with a chime or bell that helped students to center themselves, to calm their bodies. I considered MindUP, and the engagement in mindful practices across the school, to be the secret sauce that helped put us over the top in all categories, including academics and responses to misconducts.

My Leadership Journey

Pershing West Middle School closed in 2013, but that didn't curtail my interest in the impact of mindful practices on students. Through its implementation at Pershing West, I saw the confidence of my students increase. I witnessed students with a newfound sense of leadership that was anchored in a self-assurance that wasn't always visible. I took what I knew about mindful practices to Network 11, also within Chicago Public Schools, and used them in my positions as both an Instructional Support Leader and Deputy Chief of Schools. Within this network of schools, located in the Englewood Community, I provided leadership support to 42 school principals and their assistant principals.

In this network, we engaged with both elementary and high school principals. It was during this time that I learned to anchor the opportunity to reflect on leadership practices with the use of texts such as *The Seven Habits of Highly Effective People* by Stephen Covey and *The Four Agreements* by Don Miguel Ruiz. Then and now I encourage school leaders to embrace the 7th Habit which says you must "Sharpen Your Saw." Typically, I also add "Guidepost 10" from Brene Brown's *Daring Greatly* which tells the reader to cultivate laughter, song, and dance in our lives. Connecting all of that, I contend that if we don't take care of ourselves, we are not fully capable of taking care of others. I stand on the practice of engaging school leaders during weekly newsletters and monthly administrator meetings with thoughtful questions to reflect on their work with students and the potential differences they make in their practices.

Since July of 2017, I have been the Network 13 Chief of Schools for 31 elementary schools in the Chicago Public Schools and responsible for the instructional achievement of more than 11,000 students. I know that mindful practices will do for them what it did for the more than 250 students at my school. The question I was faced with in the summer of 2018 was how to successfully introduce this effort to impact 56 school administrators, 700 teaching faculty, 300 aides and other support staff. I discovered the answer and it entails addressing the elephant in the room.

Year One: Encountering the Man in the Mirror

After attending a workshop on race and privilege during an institute for principals, assistant principals and administrators in the Chicago Public Schools, I realized that the efforts to bring mindful practices to students in my network of schools could only take place if every person associated with the students believed that the students could not only engage in some form of mindful practice, but that the students were going to be better because of them. The session gave me the push I needed to speak boldly about the change that needed to take place to see the academic opportunities presented to students that would make a difference in their lives.

I believe that if we, the adults working with students, don't use mindfulness to confront our biases, we will not be successful. In the well-known song by Michael Jackson, we hear the words, "If you wanna make the world a better place, take a look at yourself and then make a change." The words have become my personal mantra in the daily work that I do to support students, teachers, leaders, and schools. I have to be brave enough to confront my biases and courageous enough to share why I believe that all children should have equal access to programs and practices.

To accomplish this massive scale-up, I solicited the support of the social-emotional learning (SEL) specialist, an instructional support leader (ISL) and a principal from my network. We began designing activities to introduce the subject of bias associated with supporting students with individual learning plans (IEPs), those students living in temporary living situations (STLS), those individuals who identified as LGBTQ+ and those who were a minority. For more than a year, we delivered the sessions to principals, assistant principals, and school deans and asked them to reflect on and identify their biases. Further, we asked them to engage the teachers within their schools in these same, or similar activities. Here are some of the mindful activities we engaged them in:

Privilege Walk

Everyone stands up and moves into the line taped at the front of the room. Participants stand shoulder to shoulder in a line together. As steps are taken, this will become more critical. Several statements are read, and with each statement, participants are asked to take one step forward or one step backward. After all statements are read, participants engage in discussions about the outcome. Here are some example statements:

- If you are a white male, take one step forward.
- If you are a citizen of the United States, take one step forward.
- If your work holidays coincide with religious holidays that you celebrate, take one step backward.
- If English is your first language, take one step forward.
- If you took out loans for your education, take one step backward.
- If you attended private school or summer camp, take one step forward.
- If you, or someone in your immediate family, have visible or invisible disabilities take one step backward.

Gallery Walk with Proverbs, Quotes and Sayings on Race and Equity

Participants find a quote and stand next to it. They engage in conversation about how they connect to the quote. Here are some examples of quotes that could be used:

- "Children have never been very good at listening to their elders, but they have never failed to imitate them." James Baldwin
- "There is no greater agony than bearing an untold story inside you." Maya Angelou
- "A society grows great when old men plant trees whose shade they know they shall never sit in." Greek Proverb
- "The benefits you get become the debts you owe to others." Arabian Proverb

Inclusion and Equity Activity

Participants have five minutes to complete a free write based on the following prompts. When done, they engage in discussion with a partner. What similarities, if any, did you discover?

- Recall a time from your own schooling when you felt especially included, engaged, appreciated, and validated in the learning process.
- Recall a situation during your educational experience when you felt especially excluded, alienated, and invalidated from the learning process.

Race and Equity Data Reflection

Use data from your school or district to engage with others around four critical questions:

- What possible inequities are evident in this data? Racial, gender, disability, class, etc.
- Are these results reflective of your staff's commitment to equity?
- Is your staff more equitable because you lead them?
- What are you prepared to do to address how equity is impacting your student outcomes?

Equity Survey and Articles

In our sessions, each teacher, administrator or staff member also took a survey to use as a reflective tool. We adapted it from Gare's Employee Survey for Local Governments. I invite you to take it now, reflecting on each statement and answering with: don't know, strongly disagree, somewhat disagree, somewhat agree or strongly agree.

- I think it is valuable to examine and discuss the impacts of race on our work at our school.
- I have a basic understanding of concepts related to racial equity.
- I know how to identify examples of interpersonal/individual racism (i.e. using coded language, questioning someone's competence based on their race or ethnicity).
- I know how to identify examples of structural racism (i.e. people of color have been left out of wealth creation, home ownership as a result of centuries of structured racialized practices, police are likely to focus on certain areas of a city where there are predominantly African-American and Latino people etc.).
- I am comfortable talking about race and class as it relates to education.
- I create an environment where all students have equal opportunities to advance.
- I can set aside my own discomfort and fear of saying the wrong thing when talking about race.

- I am actively involved in advancing equity at my school.
- I treat and regard all students and families as equal, regardless of their: income level or social class . . . their disability . . . their immigration status or English language skills . . . their gender identity or sexual orientation . . . their religion or religious beliefs
- I feel equipped to participate in internal and external conversations around race.
- There are no visible social divisions or animosity among staff at my school based on race.
- I would become more prepared to advance racial equity if . . .
- Based on this survey, the needs of my colleagues to support race and equity are related to . . .
- My personal priority action steps are . . .

Here are some articles that we provided at the end of our sessions through online links for participants to review and continue their learning:

Davis-Doss, T. (2006). "I don't see color, kids are just kids." *Connections: The Journal of the National School Reform Faculty*, Fall, 10.

Delpit, L. (1988). The silenced dialogue: Power and pedagogy in educating other people's children. *Harvard Educational Review, 58*(3), 280–299.

Galloway, M. K., & Ishimaru, A. M. (2015). Radical recentering: Equity in educational leadership standards. *Educational Administration Quarterly*, 51(3), 372-408.

Kafele, B. (2019, February 17). School and classroom equity . . . a reflection of your humanity and a window to your soul. [Blog post]. Retrieved from http://www.principalkafelewrites.com/2019/02/school-classroom-equitya-reflection-of.html

Year Two and Beyond

I don't pretend to have everything figured out. In fact, if I am honest, and I am, I am attempting to build this mindful practice introductory plane as I am flying it. But, here is what I know and believe. In order to see success with the introduction and implementation of mindful practices in our network of 31 schools, with 68% African American and 29% Latinx students, we must address our biases at the same time. I also believe that individuals need to address their biases based on race, ethnicity, economic status, LGBTQ+, homeless status and/or IEP status prior to engaging in presenting mindfulness practices.

In some spaces, I have found that staff does not openly believe that children in these categories can benefit from mindful practices. I believe just the opposite . . . that they can and do because it was successful at my school. Pershing West Middle School was born out of a "newness" philosophy, with the butterfly as our mascot. Not believing in doing everything possible to impact student achievement was NOT an option.

Year one is over. It is now time to bring mindful practices to the forefront. Our students deserve to benefit from practices that allow them to build critical skills to improve their thinking and reduce anxious feelings. Within the network, we have several practices in place with a foundation of, or some aspect of mindfulness practices in place: Calm Classroom, Conscious Discipline, Morning Meetings, Leader in Me and Second Step. We even engage participants in a breathing exercise during professional development sessions to relieve the potential stress of the data we share.

Calm Classroom

Currently, there are five schools that use Calm Classroom where students engage in breathing techniques and where a conscious effort is made to anchor the school day in calmness. When entering the school in the morning, you will often hear a student or an adult over the intercom address the school population with messages such as, "Relax your mind and your body for instruction today. Be mindful of your actions as you go about your school day."

Conscious Discipline

After attending an informative session delivered by our SEL Specialist, we have one school within our network piloting Conscious Discipline. It is anchored in relationship building, the development and maintaining of classroom structures and deliberate SEL instruction. There is also a component that addresses breathing techniques. This program emphasizes self-awareness for student success.

Leader in Me

As a principal, Pershing West was a Leader in Me School. The 7 Habits Tree was painted on the wall when you entered the school. It was important for me to bring this resource to both Network 11 and Network 13. Currently, in Network 13, there are six schools with LIM status. Reflection on the 7 Habits is the cornerstone of the resource, but there is also a goal setting piece that fits in nicely with other practices in place at the schools.

Morning Meeting

Although it looks different at each school, seven of our schools engage in some type of morning gathering. One school conducts Monday Morning Mentoring where every student has an assigned mentoring group. There are mentors who provide the check-ins with students about their weekend and pressing issues. This is an "all hands on deck" moment where everyone, including the lunchroom manager, teachers, and counselors, conducts a group. At another school, Morning Meeting is more traditional and takes place in classrooms with homeroom teachers.

Two of our schools engage in weekly meetings with their school teams to check-in with them before the school day begins. A different grade band of teachers each week (either K–2, 3–5 or 6–8) leads the reflection and discussion at one school and at another school, before students enter, you will see teachers holding hands in a circle checking in with each other and reciting affirmations. And, one school focuses solely on their middle school students, anchoring their practices with attendance, homework completion or misconduct data provided by the classroom teacher or principal specifically related to them.

Second Step

In Network 13, more than 20 of our schools use Second Step with fidelity. In the younger grades, students are focused on being prepared to learn. They cite, "My eyes are watching, my ears are listening and my body is still." The focus on putting words to their feelings is critical to be successful with this practice. With older students, they are given the words to name and describe what they are experiencing and feeling. And, almost like MindUp, there are lessons on the brain and how it impacts their success.

At this time, two-thirds of our schools engaged in some type of mindful practice on a consistent basis. Because of the work we have been focused on with mindful practices and identifying our impact on achievement, there has been an improvement in both our misconduct/suspension data and academic achievement data. During the 2017–2018 school year, there were 453 suspensions issued within Network 13. At the close of the 2018–2019 school year, the number was reduced to 255 suspensions. The majority of students who received out of school suspensions were African American males who also were identified as having an IEP. We have placed a critical eye on students with IEPs to lessen their suspensions for the 2019–2020 school year.

As a network, we saw an increase in the percent of students who were reading on grade level from the 2017–2018 school to the 2018–2019 school year and a decrease for those on grade level in math. I am looking for our mindful practices to have an even larger impact on academic achievement.

If the adults are ready to face the "man in the mirror," then our students will be the recipients of that secret sauce that helped the students at Pershing West Middle School to be successful. If not, well, that just means there is more work to be done to get them there. In the meantime, I will continue to stay focused on leading the work that includes bringing new opportunities for mindful practices to students because they are the ones who deserve it and need it the most.

CHAPTER 37

Student Perspectives and Educator Support in Suburban and Rural Illinois

Miriam Ojaghi

SEL Consultant, Dekalb Regional Office of Education, Founder, Resilient Mind Consulting, Board Member, COSEM

MY NAME IS MIRIAM (MIMI) OJAGHI AND I AM currently a social emotional learning consultant at the Dekalb Regional Office of Education in rural Illinois and the founder of Resilient Mind Consulting. I came to mindfulness through a CD. I had been teaching middle school for three years and was struggling with a particularly challenging group of students (we've all had *that* class).

At the same time, having grown up with an alcoholic father and a mentally ill mother, I was navigating the fallout of the habits and behaviors we can adopt in these circumstances, all while trying to support my divorced parents as they battled cancer. I had trouble sleeping and was exhausted because my brain felt like a gerbil on an exercise wheel that could not stop thinking. My counselor recommended I try the strategy of wearing a rubber band and snapping my wrist with it each time I found myself lost in thought. That sounded entirely unpleasant and I wasn't interested in being a masochist, so, instead, I started listening to a mindfulness CD.

I don't recall how I came across the CD, but I remember popping it into my stereo for my 20-minute commute to school which, despite the safety concerns, felt like the only time I had available. The CD had four, fifteen-minute sessions and the first one was just about noticing our thoughts and letting them pass. This was a novel concept to me and one that helped shift my perspective as I started to realize how much I was perpetuating my own misery by marinating in my thinking. I listened to the CD with some consistency and found it beneficial, but didn't pursue mindfulness much further until several years later.

Research with Underrepresented Minorities Pursuing STEM Degrees

Fast forward 15 years where, as a university instructor pursuing my doctorate in Leadership in Curriculum and Instruction, I studied the intersection of mindfulness and education. So many of these endeavors require us to look back and recognize our journey and I realized that as a Persian American woman, I have always been keenly aware of race and gender and its impact on my own life experience, especially at school. Additionally, because I was also deeply interested in, but also intimidated by pursuing science as a career, I grew up to be cognizant of the underrepresentation of minorities and women in STEM (Science, Technology, Engineering, and Math).

As a well-intentioned educator who had benefited personally from dabbling in mindfulness, I set out to learn more and prove how mindfulness could "fix" under-represented minorities so they could persist and succeed in the challenging pursuit of STEM. But as my research evolved, I realized my understanding of the issue was informed by complex and problematic assumptions and stereotypes rooted in a deficit model that required a counter-narrative. As a result, I was compelled to pursue the students' perspectives about their experiences.

Eager to hear their stories, I conducted student interviews which yielded detailed examples of educational disparities such as inadequate access to academic resources, disproportionate numbers of behavior referrals, and predatory college recruit-ment practices that ran counter to the deficiency narrative of education focused on "at-risk" students. My frustration, anger, and shame grew as I came to realize that despite my intention to be proactive as an educator, I had been an unwitting participant in a social structure that perpetuated some of the very injustices I had set out to rectify when I pursued teaching as a profession.

In fact, research suggests programs designed to support minorities in STEM that have applied a deficiency model have potentially marginalized minority stu-dents *even further.* In their examination of national trends documented in Project STEP-UP, a longitudinal study of the experiences of underrepresented minori-ties (URM) in ten public research universities, Linley and George-Jackson (2013) the critical difference between a deficiency model of URM STEM education that emphasizes enrollment, funding and "catching students up" in contrast with a dif-ference model which considers structural, cultural, and climate issues related to race on campuses across the nation. Noting this difference, they contend that "pro-grams that seek to *repair* students rather than *initiate institutional change* will fail to contribute to the social change that is needed to include and advance underrep-resented students in STEM fields." (p.100).

Thus, the complexity of the experience of underrepresented minority students in the American education system requires critical and intentional consideration of numerous factors, particularly with regard to the mindfulness movement which is lacking in diversity itself. In an effort to recognize and possibly address some of these issues, I introduced Koru Mindfulness training exclusively to URM students pursuing STEM degrees.

Assumptions About Mindfulness are Revealed

I chose Koru Mindfulness because, at the time, it was one of the only programs designed for college students or "emerging adults" that was also manualized, an important element in research, much of which was critical of the "replicability" of mindfulness research thus far. Recognizing the unique circumstances of college students who were in a transitional state between adolescence and adulthood, Koru took a pragmatic approach that required consistent practice with a somewhat minimal time commitment. The program was delivered in hourly sessions for four weeks and students agreed to attend all four weeks while also practicing mindfulness for a minimum of ten minutes a day during those four weeks. Additionally, all resources were being made available including the log, timer, and recordings of all meditation practices taught in the course, a particularly appealing feature to young practitioners.

I began by interviewing students before any mindfulness instruction, again midway through, and then after all coursework was completed. In addition to building relationships with students, I learned about the role mindfulness came to play in their lives, as well as the sense of community and belonging they developed as part of both their personal lives and academic experiences.

A total of 11 students enrolled in the first course and included Black male and female students, several Latina students, and two Muslim American students. Although the class was focused on the experiences of Latinx and Black students, two female, Muslim students, one from India and one from Palestine, who wore the traditional headdress, or hijab, also asked to enroll. Because these young women wore the hijab, and therefore, announced their faith and religious affiliation, they were a visible minority at this small Midwestern university and, were therefore interviewed as a point of comparison with the perspectives of those minorities who are traditionally underrepresented.

I was interested in understanding what stereotypes students had about mindfulness and meditation as well as their academic experiences prior to enrollment in college. During their interviews students revealed several assumptions. Importantly, they shared their beliefs that meditation was a religion that was primarily practiced by white people or "hippies who did yoga." Few had had any previous experience with the exception of one young Black woman who had been exposed to some brief mindfulness practices as part of the yoga segment of a health class.

Some were concerned that it would detract from, or compromise, their own religious beliefs and practices and were pleasantly surprised when, after the study, they found being mindful had actually increased their religious intentionality, "Because of mindfulness I realized I was actually racing through prayer just to get it over with!" Others shared that taking time to sit and "do nothing" seemed indulgent and would be frowned upon by family members, particularly when these students had numerous household responsibilities sometimes in multigenerational living arrangements.

With regard to academics, students revealed that they hadn't had access to important opportunities like rigorous AP or honors classes, or hadn't had the support to succeed in those classes if they were offered. Most did not feel that school prioritized college attendance for them, and a Black male spoke about having numerous substitutes for his entire year of chemistry, as well as an emphasis on playing sports rather than worrying about academics. One young Latina had never seen a microscope in any of her high school science classes and therefore, didn't understand how to use one in college causing her anxiety that resulted in doubting her chosen major of biology.

These were very different experiences from the two Muslim women who observed and spoke about the significant educational differences they had experienced including the intense expectations and pressures of enrolling in AP courses and pursuing challenging fields of study. Students also reflected upon how their lived experiences, including being first-generation students unfamiliar with college expectations, made college attendance and success challenging, and many admitted they struggled to feel that they belonged anywhere on campus and especially in STEM classes, particularly when they were one of a handful, if not the only, minority students in the class.

Mindfulness Class Creates a Sense of Community and Belonging

Our weekly, hour-long sessions met at lunchtime in a campus museum that was serene and somewhat removed from the main campus. While the students came to know one another and looked forward to visiting, class time was primarily focused on the Koru lessons and practice of different mindfulness techniques. Because it was during lunchtime, students were encouraged to bring their lunches and I also provided snacks and beverages. Each class included a check-in session followed by a brief lesson on the basic tenets of mindfulness and then instruction and practice of techniques such as the body scan and mindful eating.

Encouragingly, mindfulness class presented a unique opportunity where students felt a sense of community with their fellow Koru students who helped them navigate and process their experiences as URM students in college STEM programs. Several students discussed how the mindfulness techniques affected them in multiple ways and, more specifically, in their ability to cope with anxiety and stress. For example, all students discussed how they utilized different calming or focusing techniques before exams, during classes, or while studying. They also provided examples of how they applied the teaching of impermanence, the idea that all experiences and sensations are temporary and will, therefore, come and go when they found themselves ruminating or dwelling on circumstances that were beyond their control. As one student explained,

> "When getting stressed, I would kind of just stop and wait and just think about, like, what's happening now, should I really be this stressed out, or can I just take a step back and breathe? It's not that big of a deal. I don't have to worry so much about it and I've kind of been using that with finals and just with exams in general. More of, like, being in the moment like we talked about, as opposed to just thinking ahead and what do I need to get on this exam to get this grade, and things like that, which I always do."

Feeling a sense of belonging is not only an important motivating factor it is also an indicator of academic success and several students discussed how practicing mindfulness with a group of other minorities created an enhanced sense of belonging on campus. For example, students shared that it was helpful to know that others struggled with some of the same challenges in both their personal and academic lives. Participants, including Loo, who described the experience as "transformative" also explained how impactful it had been to be exclusively solicited to participate because they were minority students. In his role as perhaps the most enthusiastic participant, another student, a young Black man named Robert (pseudonym) explained how mindfulness contributed to his evolving experience and sense of belonging. As he shared,

> "It definitely helped me feel more belonging on campus because of the conversations that we had and seeing my experience is not just my own, other people have the same thoughts or have the same struggles, or even the same fears and doubts. And knowing that you recognized that made me feel that I had the power to go out and pursue things that I thought I could not pursue before. It's definitely an experience that helped me become a little bit more outspoken, especially on social issues. I mean in a lot of my classes, we don't really talk about social issues because I'm in all science classes, but when it came to just everyday conversations, I think I was a little bit more open to sharing my opinions and not feeling like I'm going to get bashed or someone's going to condemn me for it."

In his final interview at the conclusion of the course, Robert also described the increased awareness and attention to detail he developed through mindfulness as akin to having "superpowers." Like other participants, Robert expressed being pleasantly surprised that something so seemingly simple could have such a significant impact on his life. Given their positive experiences, students felt strongly that this opportunity should be made available to others and convinced me to offer two more sessions. Though I did not conduct similar formal interviews, there was a general sense of fellowship and community in informal discussions and students said they benefited from learning mindfulness in a gathering of their peers.

SEL and Mindfulness Support from Dekalb Regional Office of Education

Today, as a certified Koru Mindfulness instructor and social-emotional learning consultant with the DeKalb Regional Office of Education, I offer professional development support to eight rural school districts. Although they represent a unique demographic, they have not been immune to the nationwide trends of increasingly rigorous academic demands, the opioid crisis, and rising mental health concerns among both teachers and students. While I have met a handful of teachers who have introduced mindfulness in their classrooms, I am most often invited to present an introductory overview at teacher institute days or work with grade-level teams primarily as a follow up to presentations on trauma or the Illinois Social Emotional Learning Standards.

Thus far, with about a year at the ROE, teachers have been primarily interested in learning strategies—that they then proceed to implement inconsistently as something students can do before a test or in a moment of crisis, rather than a more holistic, proactive approach. For example, one frustrated teacher who was attending a second presentation told me, "I tried that hand breathing when a kid was freaking out, but it didn't work." Stumped initially, I asked if the teacher had provided any consistent practice opportunities *prior to* the crisis. Her response, one all too common in education, was that she had not had time to do so.

Unfortunately, unless we are intentional in shifting this paradigm, most teachers, few of whom are mindfulness practitioners themselves, struggle with making time for something they see as interfering with the delivery of academic content they feel compelled to "cover."

Despite these systemic challenges, the growing neuroscientific evidence, coupled with increasingly challenging behavior issues in the classroom are resulting in increasing inquiry and efforts to understand the multifaceted complexity of addressing social and emotional learning. Recently, after spending time with teachers at one middle school, the 8th-grade team introduced some basic mindfulness practices. All four teachers reported being surprised by student candor about the severe anxiety and stress they were experiencing and how helpful the mindfulness strategies had been. They reported that students asked for the opportunity to implement mindfulness regularly. As a result, I was invited back for further support in embedding SEL and mindfulness in the classroom including strategizing with teachers, sharing resources and research, and serving as a "guest" instructor in multiple classrooms.

In my tenure at the ROE, I have come to realize how critical it is that we first educate and support teachers by offering multiple opportunities to experience what we mean when we ask, or in some cases, mandate, that they teach SEL and mindfulness. As is often the case, teachers have been handed SEL standards and charged with implementation, often with minimal "one and done" training and resources. This has lead to teacher frustration and resentment that has translated to the perception of SEL as "one more thing to do" rather than a beneficial resource embedded in the fabric of the classroom for teachers and students alike.

This is not Another "Sit and Get": Teacher Wellness and Self-Care

In an effort to acknowledge the importance of teacher wellness, our office also hosts a teacher "spirit" day before the start of the school year focused on health, wellness, and yes, even fun! We solicit community organizations for donations of food and prizes and offer a variety of activities. This year, teachers chose from sessions on how to grow microgreens, self-care, laughter yoga, music and art projects, mindfulness, guided nature walks, martial arts and, perhaps the most popular of all, puppy therapy.

While some, particularly middle and high school teachers, are dismissive of what they term the "touchy-feely" nature of this day and other SEL initiatives, Dr. Kristen Neff's extensive research on self-care shows that as humans, touching and feeling are particularly meaningful modes of communication. This was a useful counter-narrative to offer recently when a principal mocked a neighboring school for what was perceived as a weakness in requesting training on secondary trauma for teachers.

Importantly, every educator I spoke with informally expressed gratitude for the opportunity to have fun and practice wellness exercises with their colleagues rather than the traditional "sit and get" professional development that is a hallmark of education. Seeing joyful teachers together was an important reminder that many are first responders who address issues of poverty, violence, and other trauma that exact a toll on their mental and physical well-being. It will serve us well to acknowledge that educator emotional resilience, or lack thereof, is a critical determinant of the classroom climate.

The challenges faced by teachers are increasingly evident in the costs associated with teacher burnout including, but not limited to, medical leave and teacher training and retention, not to mention the impact on students, emotionally and academically. As a result, my present emphasis is on the importance of teacher familiarity with and practice of social and emotional learning, including mindfulness, before any discussion of classroom implementation occurs.

To that end, I have supported my consultation responsibilities by starting a DeKalb Chapter of COSEM. While I was hesitant to commit to "one more thing" myself, I have found the community of educators who attend to be supportive, appreciative and understanding rather than burdensome. So far, our monthly meetings have provided the opportunity to develop and strengthen our practice while learning about new mindfulness techniques and what does and doesn't work in the classroom.

Our meetings start at 4:30 and are about an hour and a half; they start with introductions and a welcoming practice, then we discuss a topic based on resources such as books and trainings. This is followed by sharing of personal practice and experience, and networking. As classrooms become increasingly more complex, there is growing interest in mindfulness and teachers have said they value the supportive community we have cultivated.

Go To Practices and Diligence in our Stewardship of Mindfulness

To date, mindfulness advocates in schools have promoted the practice as a resource for learning important social and emotional skills such as self-awareness and self-management. However, the emphasis on data in education is increasingly calling for evidence of successful implementation as reflected by the quantifiable measurement of important, but secondary by-products such as disciplinary referrals and test scores. As educators navigate this "new normal," we must be diligent in our stewardship of mindfulness to ensure that the implementation is not misappropriated by efforts to "fix" what is seen as deficient or problematic behavior without addressing systemic issues including antiquated teaching methods, implicit biases, and excessive standardization and assessment.

Furthermore, in order to ensure sustainable implementation of mindfulness, it is important first to train and gain the support of teachers. Having done so, successful adoption in schools should be voluntary and introduced as a practice done *with* rather than *to* students. Finally, in an effort to capture the complexity of the context in which it is practiced, it is essential that we remember to solicit the experiences of the students themselves, especially when some of those voices have been traditionally marginalized.

In my work presenting to a variety of participants ranging in age from 5 to 75 with whom I don't have any established relationship, I have come to rely on a few "go-to" strategies that have proven most effective for our short time together. Here are the details for a few of them.

Body Scan

I start my presentation with a brief three to five-minute body scan. Participants are invited to sit with their eyes closed as I guide them to anchor their attention in their breath and/or their body. I explain that we close our eyes to limit sensory input and that if their mind wanders as is normal for it to do, to simply notice and return their attention to the breath without judgment. I then start at the feet and work my way up the body until we reach the top of the head.

I do not require anyone to participate if they would prefer not to. Instead, I acknowledge that closing one's eyes and sitting still in silence can be a vulnerable experience. As a result, I ask that they simply gaze at the table or the floor in front of them out of courtesy to those who are closing their eyes. I used to get upset when students would giggle or fidget and now I've come to understand this is often the result of discomfort so I let it run its course if it happens, and then remind them to respect others who are interested in participating and direct them to doodle, read, or sit quietly.

Ice Cube Activity

A strategy I learned at the inaugural Educating Mindfully Conference in 2019 involves ice cubes. Participants are invited to close their eyes, place a piece of ice in their hands, and notice the sensations they feel. They are then guided to observe the discomfort with curiosity and intention rather than the judgment to which they might be accustomed. When they have held the ice for a few minutes and finally put it down, students are invited to discuss the experience and inevitably recognize that while unpleasant, the pain is both temporary and bearable. The simple but memorable activity is used to introduce the notion of impermanence and remind them that they are strong and resilient and though they are suffering, eventually the suffering ceases and they move on.

Hoberman Sphere

Younger students enjoy learning about breathing with the Hoberman Sphere. After I demonstrate inhaling and exhaling by expanding and contracting the sphere, students are inevitably engaged and eager to participate. Eventually, we pass the sphere around and students take turns leading the group in paying attention as they synchronize their breath with the sphere.

Passing a Cup of Water

The last strategy I'll share here that I have found to be useful involves a cup of water. Participants are invited to form a circle and then directed to pass a cup of water around to one person at a time paying attention to the weight, temperature, and texture of the cup as it comes to them. After the cup has made it around the entire circle, they repeat the activity, this time with their eyes closed. Participants are keenly focused on paying attention to sensory cues and intentional awareness, and often remark that they weren't thinking about anything else and enjoyed the break from their mental chatter.

This activity can also be used to introduce impermanence as even if the water spills, it eventually evaporates and sometimes our anticipation and thinking of what might happen is far worse than the problem, in this case, getting wet. Depending on the group, the activity can also be modified by filling the cup with cotton balls or marsh-mallows and working their way up to water as they train their focus and attention.

An Important Reminder

Finally, I always remind all participants that, ultimately, we are exploring the mind and they should always be cautious and intentional when doing so. To paraphrase one young person, we shouldn't invite anyone to explore their mind unless we are prepared to support them as they possibly face difficult and potentially even disturbing experiences.

I am regularly humbled by and grateful for the impact mindfulness has had on my own life. I feel fortunate to have had the honor and privilege of participating in a movement that, I believe, will transform our experience as living beings, and I am optimistic about the future, at least most of the time, as a result of this experience. Wherever you may be on this journey, I wish you peace, strength, and resilience.

Linley, J. L., & George-Jackson, C. E. (2013). Addressing underrepresentation in STEM fields through undergraduate interventions. *New Directions for Student Services, 144*, 97–102. doi:10.1002/ss.20073

CHAPTER 38

Working Together in Delaware to Create a Trauma-Informed State

Teri B. Lawler

Education Associate for Trauma-Informed Practices and SEL, Delaware Department of Education

Jess Weaver

Program Associate, Pure Edge, Inc.

Chi Kim

CEO, Pure Edge, Inc.

THERE IS NOTHING LIKE THE EXCITEMENT OF A NEW SCHOOL YEAR! Magic is in the air and the adrenaline is electrifying. There is the instant colliding of energy between the old and the new. There are the newly graduated and the newly hired exchanging smiles and ideas with the seasoned and inspired. There are renovated school buildings and freshly decorated classrooms to replace the dust and disarray of the summer clean-up from the weeks prior. Most importantly, there is the anticipation of renewed relationships and re-imagined dreams.

Schools, at their core, are dream factories; and the starting school year ushers in the opportunity to give birth to new dreams. Write the vision and make it plain. If you fail to plan, you plan to fail. This is the time to set goals and reach for the stars. So regardless of whether your mission statement aims to leave no child behind or race to the top, the ultimate plan is for every student to succeed no matter what the investment—and I'm not talking about money. Real educators trade with a currency held together by love and sweat equity. They are committed and don't hold anything back. They go in—ALL IN!

Unfortunately, in 2010, this idyllic description only existed on the vision board posted in my home's kitchen. My back-to-school reality was pretty heavy and hopeless. There was a thickness in the air as teachers huddled to discuss summer happenings.

Administrative changes promised to pave the way for yet another *new* mission statement. A number of colleagues found escape in job offers at *higher-performing* schools. Undoubtedly, many others considered leaving, but clung to the audacious hope for a high-quality education for the students we would serve. For us, this was an issue of social justice and our school community was immersed in the struggle.

Schools have always been in the struggle as they typically have provided the landscape or battleground for achievement and economic success for those who are disadvantaged and disenfranchised. For students from urban communities, in particular, education represents so much more than the acquisition of reading, writing, and arithmetic skills. Schools function as community hubs for information and access. Education represents the opportunity to level the playing field with the soft skills, code-switching, as well as book knowledge required to be successful in life. For these reasons, educators must make the most of every minute of every day because *these minutes* are a down payment on their students' futures—and every dollar counts!

I was a school psychologist in Red Clay Consolidated School District in Wilmington, Delaware. I was assigned to serve the Stanton Middle School community and while I was new to this school I was not *brand* new. I had spent over 20 years in the same school district and worked at this particular school building early in my career—many years prior. I was actually excited to return as the plan was for me to transition to middle school alongside the new 6th-grade class—all of us recently graduated from the elementary school where I served for 7 years prior.

At the elementary school, we had forged a trail of successes. We had piloted a thriving multidisciplinary team model that focused on the needs of the whole child and developed wraparound services to support children in the school and community. We had experimented with the development of in-house assessments for early identification of vulnerable students that encompassed more than office disciplinary referrals (ODRs) and used those assessments to create school-based normative samples of behavior. We had established intervention strategies that blended behavioral and instructional supports. We had also invested more than 2 years collaborating with a team of district and community partners to open school-based health centers to meet the physical and emotional needs of our students and their families. The initial plan included employing what was learned from these experiences to facilitate a similar process to develop the first school-based health center at a local middle school.

Lasting Transformation Starts From Within

The prospect of getting this project off the ground was exciting, but it quickly became apparent that there were many competing priorities to tackle. The school was different than I remembered and different from where I had been. The first of many lightbulb moments included the observation that schools are microsystems and no two schools are the same. They all have different personalities, temperaments, and rhythms. As such, they deserve so much better than *cookie-cutter, one-size-fits-all* solutions. Next, was the notion that the most committed attempts toward problem analysis and solutions would come from within the school walls rather than from outside of them. Real and lasting transformation starts within, right?

Who would be more invested in bringing about lasting change than the people living and breathing in that school community? There are so many models for this concept—whether looking to our faith communities, counseling and 12-step programs, or one of my television favorites at the time, *The Biggest Loser*. Lasting change comes from intense self-study and reflection. You cannot change what you won't confront. To borrow a phrase from the '90s singing group, En Vogue, "*Free your mind and the rest will follow.*" Now was the opportunity to apply that real-life change strategy in the school setting.

Another hidden obstacle that caught me unaware was my own physical and mental exhaustion. I loved my work, but there always seemed to be too much to do and never enough time. As the changing leaves ushered us into fall, I found myself on autopilot, existing on caffeinated beverages and take-out meals. Weeks went by when I did not even turn on my stove or oven. I joked that I did not miss any meals, but I was saddened to see another of my personal passions—cooking—sacrificed to my work.

Community tensions and threats of violence frequently spilled into the school. There was one crisis call after another and it took everything that I had physically and mentally to get through each day. Worn out, but pushing through the pain, had become the name of my work game. By my assessment and report, however, I was doing fine. "Fine" was a word that I knew well and used often, but I wasn't fine, and it never dawned on me that I wasn't fine, although I am certain that others could see it. In my mind, all I needed was the upcoming Thanksgiving break to catch up on some rest so I could actually be what I professed—fine.

My daughter, Erin, flew home from college. Swamped at work and hoping to redeem some time, I made an airport shuttle reservation to have her dropped off at my school. On our drive home, my cell phone rang and it was my mother calling from Virginia. Her voice cracked as she started the difficult conversation. She shared that my uncle, her brother, had passed away. She solemnly stated, "He had gone home to be with the Lord." That was her phrase akin to my "fine." We had heard this too many times in the preceding 10 years as we coped with the changing dynamic of our family.

Our close-knit clan had suffered the loss of my maternal grandfather and endured the lengthy illnesses and slow transitions of two uncles previously. My heart ached for my widowed aunt and fatherless cousins. I ached for my grandmother who would have to bury another child. I ached for my mother who had to cope with a gone playmate and brother. I ached for everyone else, but I didn't allow myself the space to grieve for me.

Once I gathered the details and inquired about the well-being of my loved ones, my focus shifted to making plans to journey south for the memorial services. I drove in silence with a whirlwind of noise in my head. The car had become my safe place over the years. This was the place that cocooned me from the turmoil of the day and transported me to the safety of home. As my seat warmed, I could feel the warmth of tears streaming down my cheeks. My daughter's whisper brought me back to the car, "Are you okay, Mom?" I quickly prepared my typical response, but before I could spew it out, she followed up her question with a shocking observation: "Your face doesn't move. I haven't seen your face move . . . not when you laugh or when you cry. How can you do that? You're so good at hiding your emotions."

The words hit me hard and the jolt forced me to think. When did I stop moving my face? When did I get too busy to own and acknowledge my feelings? In what other ways was I betraying my heart? These questions resurfaced over and over again as the days of our holiday break slipped away. I surmised that there were other disconnects in my life. I ruminated over their origins and the fuel that sustained them. I realized that I was living out my own personal Still Face Experiment and it had likely started many years before.

Exposure to the Tragedies Impacting Vulnerable Communities

While in graduate school, I studied the relationship between emotions, temperament, and attachment at the University of Delaware's Human Emotions Laboratory. I worked under the tutelage of Dr. Carroll Izard, a larger-than-life scholar in the field who was eager to mentor his students to do developmental research that could be applied to real life. There, our team was trained to decode the muscles of the face that were involved in the formation of facial expressions.

In the lab, we videotaped interactions between mothers and infants as they developed into childhood, assessing subtle movements in the eye, nose, and mouth areas to make inferences about the quality of their relationships. It was in this environment that I learned about the Still Face Experiment, a procedure developed by Dr. Ed Tronick in 1978, where a mother faces her baby and is asked to hold a still face in which she does not react to the baby's behaviors. The baby's responses to the mother's stillness are observed. In general, babies tend to become agitated by failed attempts to evoke reactions from their mothers.

My time in the lab was both exhilarating and gratifying, but that was only one aspect of my training. During this time, I also had multiple clinical rotations where I was required to provide individual and family counseling to children and families in crisis. My clinical training rotations were my first real exposure to the tragedies that impact children and families living in poverty and vulnerable communities. I'm a southern girl at heart and my parents raised me to live by the Golden Rule. That said, I can hold a conversation with anybody. I was an excellent listener and a clear problem-solver so I demonstrated an easy proficiency when sorting out the problems presented during therapy sessions.

My challenge was that I absorbed the pain of many of the clients that I saw as if it were my own. My heart broke at every session and by the end of my clinic rotations, I could barely breathe. Some of my clients were court-involved and had been separated from their loved ones. Most were drowning in adversities that impaired their school functioning and social relationships. I found myself frequently tearing up in anticipation of appointments. I worried so much about my clients and their families between sessions that it interrupted my sleep. For these reasons, I created distance from their experiences by training my face to stay still and not display the horrors that I felt inside.

Using the 3Rs to Build Resilience and Regulation

The time that I spent reflecting following Thanksgiving of 2010 showed me that there were obviously other traces of my attempts to anesthetize and disconnect myself from the struggles of life that were swirling around me. I had apparently adopted this and other coping mechanisms to fortify myself when things got hard or overwhelming at home, too. I comforted myself with food and preferred to read or watch television rather than spend time with friends. What I knew for sure was that it was absolutely unnatural to cease feeling and I did not want to continue like that in my personal life or my work. I was certain that I could be more valuable by feeling with others without letting the hurts consume me or those around me. That way, we could shift to productive, collaborative problem-solving.

I have two great professional loves that have become my lifeline: reading and research. These are my go-to strategies for processing and problem-solving. I use both regularly in my life for engaging in a practice that I have coined the 3Rs—refocusing, retooling, and returning with new learning. I have been a voracious reader for as long as I can remember. I used to get in trouble as a child for reading with a flashlight under the covers after my bedtime. No surprise, then, that I turned to bibliotherapy to explore my new self-discovery.

Eager for change, I started reading about the mind-body connection and cognitive and behavioral techniques that I could integrate to build resilience. The more

I learned, the more questions arose, and all of this new knowledge was triangulated, through reflection, to build capacity in my life and ultimately my work. I have discovered that reflection is much needed, but often missing from the hustle and bustle of a typical workday. It is sacrificed because of limited time, but I believe if practiced regularly, it has the capacity to make our work more efficient and buy us more time for productivity.

During this time, I discovered the amazing work of Dr. Bruce Perry and Dr. Bessel van der Kolk. They are separately renowned theorists and researchers. Each has focused his work on creating real-life therapeutic applications for children and adults. Both posit that strategies for calming the brain can be paired to enhance therapeutic interventions and maximize opportunities for healing. I participated in Dr. Perry's Neurosequential Model of Education (NME) boot camp and year-long coaching experience with his colleague, Steve Graner, to learn how to create developmental maps of the brain and intervention protocols of patterned, repetitive movements to remediate developmental weaknesses resulting from trauma and toxic stress.

I also read Dr. van der Kolk's book, *The Body Keeps the Score*. In it, he talks about how frightening experiences can activate the amygdala and throw the body into a debilitating fight, flight, or freeze modes that make it hard for those affected to move beyond their pain. I learned that our capacity to cope can be overwhelmed. This does not mean that we are weak or victims. Stress can render any of us paralyzed, detached, and with restricted reasoning and problem-solving. This was a real epiphany for me because somewhere down the line I had told myself that I didn't need anybody's help. I was the Lone Ranger. I was my own superhero and savior. I never took a break and even chastised myself for being a slacker when deadlines from too many commitments caught up with me.

Not only did the information that I learned about stress seem relevant for me, but it seemed to also address many of the challenges that I had observed over the years with the children, youth, and families with whom I worked. Frequently, I watched students leave their classrooms to visit my office to apply my 3R's to their situations. With my support, they would REFOCUS after frustrations, RETOOL by practicing coping strategies, and RETURN to class in hopes of applying these skills. I even incorporated social scenarios and descriptions into our practice time together to assure that students expanded their repertoires of response options from which to choose so they could satisfy the demands of any challenging situations.

Regretfully, they seemed to return to classes and get stuck in the same old destructive behavior cycles and get ejected from classes again. However, applying the brain science to these interactions helped me understand and refine my support methods. You see, when my students and I worked together, they were able to access their prefrontal cortexes for thinking, reasoning, and choosing appropriate behavior responses because their brains were in calm and alert-for-learning states. When caught in the moment of perceived physical, psychological or emotional threat, their midbrains took over, preventing them from accessing the strategies that we had so carefully practiced. By integrating mindfulness, deep breathing, and strategies to calm and when necessary energize the brain, I was able to support students and myself in creating more awareness for productive problem-solving.

Assessing with SBIRT and Supporting with Mindful Protocols

I started using mindfulness and deep breathing to ground my body at the start and end of each school day, especially during the workweek. I realized early on that we all breathed very shallowly, and sometimes even panted, depending on what was happening throughout the day. I found these discoveries so valuable that I began using them throughout the whole day to maintain my own regulation and productivity. I saw such benefit that I also started using the breathing and mindfulness strategies in my work with students. Students would request deep breathing during check-in and check-out. We committed afterschool professional development and grade-level learning communities to the study of the brain and stress' impact on behavior. We began to experiment with other rhythmic, patterned, and repetitive movements like clapping and foot-tapping sequences and even walking to introduce more regulation opportunities.

As a school psychologist, I was trained to use screening and assessment to inform intervention strategies and progress monitoring for positive outcomes. Many of our school assessment processes have historically been used for diagnosis and identification for special education services. However, I began to recognize that our assessment practices also had the potential to inform health promotion and prevention. So I adapted the SBIRT (Screening, Brief Intervention, and Referral to Treatment) protocol from the community mental health and substance abuse arena to apply to my work in youth development and student support.

The SBIRT protocol uses screening and progress monitoring of the individual's response to a brief intervention before referring to more intensive and potentially restrictive interventions and treatments. I had struggled to identify supports that were socially valid, but also reduced the time that students needed to spend outside of the learning setting. The implementation of SBIRT would allow us to assess vulnerability early and support students with mindfulness and deep breathing as a universal strategy for building self-regulation in anticipation of achieving "brain-ready" calm states for learning and building coping skills.

Since mindfulness and deep breathing are portable tools that students could use anywhere, a benefit is less time out of class. We even identified a number of free and low-cost apps that students could use right on their cell phones or tablets whether in school or at home and in the community. Recognizing the value of physical activity to strengthen the networks of the brain, our support team mapped out walking trails throughout the first floor of the school. There was an exercise bike placed outside my office. We experimented with weighted vests, rocking chairs, standing desks, and stability balls. We paired bean bag tosses with math facts and vocabulary drills to strengthen the corpus callosum, connecting the left and right hemispheres of the brain.

I supported the students in identifying sensory strategies and mindful movement protocols that they could employ proactively to calm or energize their brains. Eventually, we included coloring and journaling and even established designated toolkits or areas of the classroom where students could refocus and retool themselves and return to productivity. Students were empowered to collaborate with their teachers to prescribe appropriate "doses" of mindful activities that could be alternated throughout the day to maintain their regulation.

When students did visit the support center, the support staff encouraged them to employ my 3Rs. Recognizing that behavior reactions did not take place in a vacuum, once regulated through mindfulness and movement, we supported the evaluation of what happened in their bodies prior to challenging situations, gave voice to physical and emotional triggers, and realized the power available through breathing and staying connected.

Change Model Applied Throughout the State

In the 7 years that followed, the climate of our middle school changed. There were strong, supportive relationships between students and adults. Adults were committed to staying regulated and worked to co-regulate with students, and classroom instruction was planned to provide "doses" of brain calming and energizing activities. In 2014, Stanton Middle School was awarded the Golden Psi by the American Psychological Association. The award celebrates one school annually that best exemplifies the integration of academic and behavioral supports in its service delivery framework. We were invited to share our learnings around the state and eventually became a model for other schools and with the support of several community partners founded the Delaware Compassionate Schools Learning Collaborative.

Our early frustrations had sparked innovation. We went on to learn about Adverse Childhood Experiences (ACEs) and the way adversity can rewire the brain. We agreed with Aristotle's assertion that educating the mind without educating the heart is no education at all. We changed the lens with which we viewed behavior and evaluated the underlying messages that behaviors were intended to communicate. We recognized that our students were probably showing dissociative responses and we focused on building trust and attachment to facilitate school engagement.

Almost concurrently, the Center for Disease Control and Prevention (CDC) came to our area to study youth gun violence. This created another exciting opportunity for me and I became part of a group called the Wilmington Community Advisory Council (WCAC). With the support of Casey Family Programs, I was commissioned to write a startup guide documenting our school work which was adapted by the WCAC for use in creating multi-tiered support systems for community centers.

I also started conducting professional development through the Compassionate Schools Learning Collaborative to share learnings and resources with educators and other youth-serving organizations. In 2016, we developed a partnership with the Office of the Child Advocate and conducted four Saturday trainings: Nurture, Nature and Neurons; Strategies to Build Resilience; Educator Self-Care; and It's Hot in Here: Self-Regulation Strategies for Students and Staff. In a two-year period, our efforts impacted over 4,000 of our state's educators. Shortly thereafter, the Office of Innovation and Improvement was added to our state's Department of Education.

Becoming a Trauma-Informed State with the Help of Pure Edge, Inc.

In October 2018, Governor John Carney signed an executive order declaring Delaware a trauma-informed state. The Department of Education was the first state agency to create a position to lead that work, and I was the person who earned the opportunity to jump in and expand the work throughout the state. With mixed but visible emotions, I left my safety net at Stanton Middle School to assume the role of Delaware's first Education Associate for Trauma-Informed Practices and Social and Emotional Learning. It's a long title and a huge undertaking for a single person. However, with my mindfulness practices in tow, I set out to scale the changes that we had facilitated at Stanton throughout the entire state. My learning curve has been super steep, but I have committed to working smart, collaborating often, and pacing myself for sustainable growth.

One of my earliest assignments was to write the strategic plan for my work. It was an honor to bring intentionality to the vision and mission of whole-child development. The work has been conceptualized to strengthen collaborations across all youth-serving sectors so there is support wrapped around students in every environment that they function. Our state strategy realizes the prevalence of adversity, recognizes the plasticity of the brain, and relies on social and emotional learning (SEL) as universal practices to build relationships and strengthen attachments. We are participating in CASEL's Collaborating States Initiative (CSI) and writing SEL competency guidance for birth to adulthood.

The CASEL work has come with an unlimited number of benefits including access to national experts for technical assistance. As a result, our state leaders were introduced to the work of Pure Edge, Inc. (PEI) and CEO, Chi Kim. We discovered an immediate harmony between their work and ours. Pure Edge's passion for starting with the heart was compelling enough to be integrated into our strategic plan. I feel strongly that incorporating mindfulness as a universal practice in our schools supports social and emotional learning. No real learning can take place without the regulation of the brain and behavior, and that is exactly what we have found mindfulness to do.

The Department of Education partnered with PEI to host the first three-day, *Culture of Care* summit and an all-day session for educators around educator well-being. We have adapted their curriculum for early childhood education certification. PEI also introduced the Headspace app to our state's educators in hopes of having everyone from transportation specialists to building leaders develop a mindfulness practice to improve regulation and self-care. Educators and support staff report feeling more hopeful and engaged. I have received so many emails about what they have learned and how understanding basic neuroscience and mindfulness practices have impacted them personally and professionally.

Pure Edge, Inc. is a private operating foundation that provides direct service to school districts and nonprofit education organizations through professional development and strategy thought partnership. PEI also provides grants to national organizations that advance the work of whole-child development and social, emotional, and academic development. PEI's Pure Power Curriculum has been researched in two independent studies: a randomized control trial by Long Island University and a Stanford University multidisciplinary study, which studied the neurobiological impact of the curriculum.

The Stanford study was the largest of its kind and a multidisciplinary look into how yoga and mindfulness impact student performance and well-being. Details at: http://med.stanford.edu/elspap/innovationanddissemination.html.

Long Island University studied 112 students in a New York City public high school. The results showed that compared to PE classes, participation in yoga classes improves academic performance in urban high school students. Details at: http://pureedgeinc.org/wpcontent/uploads/2016/09/hagins_2016_effect_of _yoga_on_academic_performance.pdf

In 2016, Pure Edge CEO Chi Kim met Dr. Mark Greenberg, who holds the Bennett Endowed Chair in Prevention Research in Penn State's College of Health and Human Development and is Emeritus Professor and Founding Director of the Edna Bennett Pierce Prevention Research Center. At the time, Dr. Greenberg was working on a research brief for the Robert Wood Johnson Foundation on the impact of teacher stress and burnout, which has become a prevalent concern in the world of education. It was after learning about Dr. Greenberg's research and the impact of stress on the nation's most important workforce that PEI dedicated itself to working with districts and state agencies to support educator self-care first, before following up with supports for learners.

Taking care of the educators who care for learners is vital to creating a lasting culture of care. When educators are equipped and empowered to care for themselves, they show up as better versions of themselves for learners. They also model social and emotional skills in their classrooms, demonstrating self-regulation and fostering positive relationships between themselves and their learners.

PEI's core belief is that all educators and learners deserve to be taught strategies that help combat stress and support the development of social, emotional, and academic learning competencies. In order to make these tools as accessible as possible, the Pure Power curriculum and all other online resources are free for educators and available in English and Spanish. Educators often implement the curriculum and "breathe, most, rest" strategies in their classrooms, as well as use them in support of their own self-care. From 2017 to 2019, PEI served over 30,000 adults at in-person trainings. The team continues to focus on supporting the health and wellness of those who serve young people.

Focus on the Positives and Measure What You Value

I am often asked how we created buy-in, particularly during the early days of implementation. I have to admit there were a number of hurdles as not all of my colleagues were thrilled with our new way of being. There were definitely challenges as many colleagues suffered from initiative fatigue, quipped that we were being "soft" on students, and resisted change. It was especially hard for our more-seasoned educators and school administrators who had become accustomed to strict, zero-tolerance practices. Thus, there was some pushback when shifting from more punitive models to developmentally-respectful practices that embodied grace and reconciliation. I had to adjust my lens when interpreting adult behavior just as I had to understand the students. I came to realize that many of my peers were stressed and even burnt out and that state restricts your curiosity and problem-solving. This helped me develop a mindful awareness of different perspectives and not judge them so I could show compassion when faced with resistance.

Instead of responding to naysayers, we focused on celebrating early adopters who achieved success with building relationships and gaining the support of students who had demonstrated more challenging and maladaptive behaviors. We focused less on creating buy-in and more on celebrating the commitment of colleagues to transforming our school culture and climate with mindfulness practices to enhance our own wellness and self-care, as well as to create safe and supportive systems for our students. When we observed the slightest inroads or open doors, we squeezed in a book study or short video to expand thinking and reinforce concepts.

It was also important to acknowledge the history of our team. We had experienced a great deal of distress over the years as we were called to support our school community through the transition of multiple school leaders and a variety of initiatives. I began to recognize the observed resistance as fear and I combatted the fear with deep professional learning. We hosted monthly workshops on child development, the impact of trauma on the brain, and strategies to build resilience. We met in professional learning communities (PLCs) monthly to discuss student support strategies and to problem solve collaboratively with grade-level teams. We also used book studies to expand our knowledge and created mini-experiments to test the practical applications of the concepts that we were learning.

I developed assessment strategies to measure what we valued. We also measured the fidelity of implementation for interventions that were mapped directly to those assessments. As we learned that relationships were the number one mediator for trauma and toxic stress, we made building supportive relationships a priority. We valued relationships and as a common practice measured students' assessments of supportive relationships with adults. We also expected that being more regulated through mindfulness practices would increase daily opportunities for students to strengthen attachments in the school environment.

We employed a simple strategy of posting every student's name and having adults place dots beside every individual with whom they maintained positive relationships. After two years of engaging in this practice, we even went so far as to have students place dots beside the names of adults to whom they felt positively connected. Anyone who could not identify at least two supportive connections was targeted for relationship-building interventions. On average, we maintained an 89–95% rate of connection based on students' reports of supportive relationships in the building. Since positive relationships were valued and prioritized, we grew to become a school that was viewed as so safe and supportive that parents started applying for school choice to have their children attend our school.

Working Together for True School Improvement

While there is lots of great information about transforming school culture and climate, I believe that the pairing of mindfulness practices, physical movement, and brain regulation strategies with skill-building has the ability to change the game for student support and school-based therapeutic service delivery. I found it impossible to experience the benefits of a personal mindfulness practice without sharing it with others. The benefits are so great that you cannot keep it to yourself. When new staff and students joined our school, they acclimated quickly to our way of being and what started as work eventually became a way of life.

Delaware taking on trauma at a state level has been an incredible achievement. We seek to build capacity within the Department of Education, but also to create professional learning opportunities that inspire districts to take mindfulness on and make it an integral part of their own practices. We realized it doesn't just stop with us. Schools cannot do this work alone. We have to partner with every organization that supports kids and families to intentionally shift the culture of all systems that impact our community. We want to engage our afterschool programs and community centers, all educators—including administrators, clerical staff, bus drivers and facilities and school nutrition employees.

We are aiming for a collective impact that includes hospital systems, churches, and faith-based organizations and anyone else who impacts the lives of our students. We are working to provide professional learning on trauma awareness for all of those organizations. The hope is that all of this work is coordinated through the Department of Education. We have to involve everyone in order to layer supports around children and families. The fact that this is the direction we are headed tells us that our goals are being reached and that we can continue to create new, bolder ones with the ultimate goal of building stronger children, one school community at a time.

Personally, I learned that I did not have to detach, but could actually engage and live in the power of my breath during challenging times. I did not have to dissociate and numb my feelings, but could embrace my life and my work with my whole heart and expressive face during tough times. While I am truly a work in progress, I have embraced the concept of awareness without judgment and this has made all the difference for me. I have shared this with students and colleagues to see us become a more kind, forgiving, and grateful school community. That, to me, is authentic school improvement.

CHAPTER 39

Meditations on the Emergence of Mindfulness in the Western Model of Education

Barnaby Spring

Director, Mindfulness in Education, Office of the First Deputy Chancellor, New York City Department of Education

Disclaimer: I am writing in my personal capacity. These are my personal views and not necessarily the views of the DOE.

IN THE NEW YORK CITY DEPARTMENT OF EDUCATION, mindfulness has been emerging over the past forty to sixty years via the dedicated work of professional educators, state and city licensed pedagogues, who, through their own tireless devotion, commitment and innovative expertise have been adapting the technique of meditation to secular, educational environments.

Mindfulness in the western model of education is not a revolution, a movement, an initiative, a rollout, a mandate, a panacea and it is not, certainly not, a sudden spiritual awakening in the form of any religion, nor is it, at this point, a covert operation of the dark state to develop obedient, compliant members of a capitalist state. These are just a few of the concerns that mindfulness in education, having emerged enough in our western mind to have some legs of its own, is now willingly embracing, considering, debunking, responding to, and if required, adapting itself to in the arena of discourse, discussion, and debate.

As the Director of Mindfulness in Education in the Office of the First Deputy Chancellor (OFDC) in the New York City Department of Education (NYCDOE), I am compelled to jump right into the current issues. An emerging, maturing field of study must be able to face and respond, mindfully, critically, if it actually is the very thing that many are beginning to realize it might be: a necessary emergence in a time of glocal (local and global) emergency.

Before I tell the story of mindfulness in education in the NYCDOE, I must first confirm the fervent times we are living through in the NYCDOE, in New York City. You see, we have a Chancellor, Richard Carranza, who has mindfully, courageously challenged our city and rallied our NYCDOE team around four public education priorities: Accelerate Learning and Instruction, Partner with Communities, Develop People and Advance Equity Now. These might be condensed into one thing, one simple goal he has offered after his initial listening tour conducted shortly after joining us. As gently and firmly as possible, he has invited the citizens – and the youth as well—of NYC to take more meaningful and urgent steps around desegregating the most segregated public education system in the country in one of the most internationally progressive cities in the world. One might simply pause and take a mindful moment around that.

A Director of Mindfulness in Education in a public education system? Honestly, how did this happen?! The answer to that lies in another example of mindful leadership, not only of our Chancellor, but also in the person of First Deputy Chancellor, Cheryl Watson-Harris. I met our 1st Dep. Chancellor when she came to the NYCDOE to lead one of the borough-wide city offices as an Executive Director.

In 2015 at the first "meet and greet" of the Brooklyn South team, I met our Cheryl Watson-Harris, recently arrived back to her hometown of Brooklyn from the Boston Public School system. It was exciting to meet Cheryl as she brought a leadership style that was inclusive, empowering and distributive. She encouraged her team to share our ideas for initiatives that would align with the current chancellor, Carmen Farina's, leadership focus.

Our Appreciative Inquiry Approach

I suggested to Cheryl that we take a look at something I believed was far more widespread throughout the city than we realized: the way mindfulness and yoga strategies were being implemented and developed in schools that addressed not only the social and emotional needs of students, but also positively impacted on their academic and student leadership needs. Cheryl agreed and said get to it.

This was not the first time I had advocated for mindfulness and yoga in the NYC-DOE. Over my career in the NYCDOE, I have been a teacher of adolescent and adult women attending schools on Rikers Island; I have taught middle and high school students in an alternative to incarceration school; served as a dean of students in an alternative high school, a principal in two high schools, and a principal advisor. During that time, I became a certified yoga and mindfulness teacher. I had a yoga and meditation practice. When I was invited by the principal of the alternative high school to become the dean of students, we agreed that my offering a yoga and mindfulness class for students would be a great idea. In my first high school as principal, I taught a yoga class . . . and yet . . . the demands of being a school administrator even in a small school are massive and, for the time being, I had to let go of any efforts to bring this work into education.

In my new role working under Cheryl Watson-Harris as the Executive Director of the Brooklyn South Field Support Center, I teamed up with colleagues on the student services team to figure out how best to proceed with our inquiry around the current state of mindfulness and yoga in our schools. Greg Bowen, Director of Student Services in Brooklyn South and Kevin Rank, a high school counseling manager, were two of the main members of a team of colleagues that whole-heartedly supported this work. I must admit, even then, there were a couple of members on our student services team who had no idea what mindfulness was. Cheryl supported our work by making sure all members of our team had access to trainings on mindfulness in education.

We reached out to Dr. David Forbes, teaching at Brooklyn College. We knew Dr. Forbes had written on mindfulness in education and had been introducing mindfulness to students studying to be school counselors in their education program as a student support strategy. He remains a critical advisor to our ongoing work.

In a month we realized, within the catchment area of the 186 schools of Brooklyn South, mindfulness existed in a number of schools, PreK to 12, on a continuum of beginning to advanced. They ranged from those not knowing and wanting to learn what mindfulness is; to schools that were in the process of implementing mindfulness programs; to those that were looking to expand their programs; to those that had been in place for ten years or more, concrete exemplars of effective "showcase school" level programs for mindfulness and yoga.

This was not that big of a surprise. New York City is a megatropolis. We have schools that are progressive, parochial, and traditional—literally, no two schools in the NYCDOE are alike. Besides, you know New Yokers!! We have pre-existing assumptions about EVERYTHING!! :-) The big surprise that slowly dawned on us was that if the number of schools in one portion of one borough of Brooklyn was this engaged with mindfulness and yoga on so many levels, what might we expect to find throughout the city?!!

The continuum of the existence of mindfulness and yoga programs in Brooklyn South seemed to be in direct proportion to the continuum of understanding around what mindfulness is and what it is not. Some schools had teachers who had taken mindfulness trainings from organizations like Mindful Schools. Many schools had teachers who were certified yoga instructors via one of the many yoga organizations in New York City that provided support. It seemed yoga was fully accepted into schools—prior to mindfulness—with mindfulness as an aspect of that practice, with certified yoga teachers and their students and families engaged in learning and practicing yoga.

The most immediate question for our team in Brooklyn South was: How shall we respond mindfully to this emergence of mindfulness in our schools? We couldn't call it a "rollout" because it was already happening. We could not refer to it as an initiative. Educators had already taken initiative in the form of our incredibly resourceful and committed educators and school leaders who were following and attuned to the research, the evidence, the arguments that were beginning to come out in the press and in scientific studies around meditation and, of course, mindfulness. Also, schools and school leaders have a degree of autonomy in how they identify school needs relative to engaging vendor licensed yoga and mindfulness training supports.

We took an appreciative inquiry approach. We committed ourselves to giving and gathering information. We developed an introductory presentation on mindfulness in education and started providing professional learning opportunities to districts of schools in Brooklyn South and to larger borough-wide student services manager meetings. I reported to Cheryl Watson-Harris that I was beginning to feel like Glenda the Good Witch in the *Wizard of Oz* who was saying, "You can come out now. The danger is gone."

Schools were literally coming out of the woodwork, inviting us to see their mindfulness rooms, to observe a mindfulness or yoga class that was part of school programming. I met veteran principals who had taken mindfulness trainings to support themselves as school leaders. It's important to note: in 2016 educators and school leaders doing this work were and are veteran educators and leaders. They tend to be highly competent in their instructional fields, highly aware of and sensitive to the need to address potential misperceptions around mindfulness, meditation, and yoga. For this reason, they understand the importance of introducing this work to families and students in ways that articulate and confirm a secular, pedagogical and developmentally appropriate grounding.

This is interesting to compare to the yoga/mindfulness in education presentations we were asked to provide to all of our new teachers in each borough at the start of the 2019-2020 school year. At each session, in each borough, our presenters reported feedback and follow up inquiries by brand new educators who were letting us know they were already certified yoga teachers and had been introduced to mindfulness in education in their higher education programs.

As we continued to learn about the emergence of mindfulness in the NYCDOE, we saw that the most successful schools had been skillful in bringing this work initially to their staff, providing them with time and space to investigate this work for themselves. As professionally experienced and licensed pedagogues, they were able to make effective modifications to these mindfulness and yoga strategies that were developmentally appropriate. In parent meetings and school curriculum nights, in back-packed letters home—when those teachers were ready to integrate this work into their curriculum or into their programming—they were explicit in providing all necessary information on mindfulness and yoga in education, in their school communities.

They were also very clear on how mindfulness in public education, given all of its varied origins, is a secularized, holistic approach to developing overall health, and wellness as well as resilience, readiness for learning in ways that were scientifically researched, evidence-based and transformative. There was no official city-wide position from the Central Office on mindfulness in education other than it not be sectarian. There was, rather, an explicit trust and expectation that school leaders—knowing their communities, educational city, state and federal guidelines; and working in collaboration with the school leadership team, the leadership cabinet and teams of educators—would be sure to assess the need, the viability and best way to introduce the strategies of mindfulness and yoga to all stakeholders in their communities.

Moving Slow to Move Fast

During this process, there was another issue that was becoming increasingly clear to us. Mindfulness and yoga in public education must be articulated transparently, and delivered with an expectation of accountability as a secular practice. At no time, ever, must any student or staff be expected to learn or practice yoga or mindfulness if they feel uncomfortable doing so for religious or other reasons. Organizations that were unable to clarify and/or modify questionable or potentially controversial activities seeking to introduce mindfulness into public education should not be engaged. Certainly, we wanted all adult members of our communities—senior leadership, parents, teachers, elected officials—to know what mindfulness is and the benefits of mindfulness; how and why it was emerging in schools in various ways.

Our rationale was that, as an emerging field of study, with serious implications for how students learn, grow, relate to the workings of their brains, nerve, skeletal, muscular, respiratory systems, etc., we needed to "move slow to move fast" in order to make sure that we had the capacity in place, at least in Brooklyn South, to address any misperceptions or concerns of parents or teachers as to the intentionally secular nature of these strategies.

We needed to be prepared to address misperceptions and questions of this work and to respond to any criticisms while also providing quality professional development to our schools. Most importantly, it was clear that a powerfully effective secular and pedagogically attuned approach to mindfulness and yoga was emerging, organically, from the institutional expertise of our own educators and had been for forty to sixty years via the ongoing refinement and application of these strategies in the public educational environment. From the very first months in Brooklyn

South, one could see the NYCDOE was realizing its own purely secular, culturally responsive, varied and individuated approaches to teaching mindfulness and yoga to ALL of our students.

What is Our Evidence of Impact?

What, in fact, is our evidence of impact—just the facts, sir—on how these mindfulness and yoga practices are improving student learning, student growth, teacher performance, and school leadership? Impact was and is the word!! There were certainly national studies coming out from various organizations and research groups providing the quantitative data indicating and, in many cases, confirming benefits of mindfulness related to self-regulation, sustained attention on a task, impact on anxiety and depression, lowering blood pressure, to name a few.

Key studies that immediately caught our eye were those done that actually included NYCDOE educators. Professor Patricia Jennings of The Curry School of Education at the University of Virginia had completed a study involving NYCDOE teachers that confirmed when educators practiced mindfulness strategies just for themselves, the quality of instruction increased. Who benefits from an increase in the quality of instruction? Our students!

https://news.virginia.edu/content/curry-study-reducing-teachers-stress-leads-higher-quality-classrooms

Teachers working in schools with supportive school leaders asserted the same outcomes for supporting student achievement, as well as the increased quality of their own professional performance by focusing on introducing mindfulness first to our urban educators as a strategy for stress-management. Our own educators were investigating and considering how these strategies might be modified and introduced to students and families in developmentally appropriate ways that naturally engaged parents in the process. Indeed, last year, one of our school districts, 34 schools, decided to embrace mindfulness as a district-wide initiative that would include each school having its own "Mindfulness Team" that would be trained via a four-day mindfulness intensive. Each team had three members: a student, a teacher, and a parent.

School after school told us the story of how mindfulness had changed the community culture, improved the quality of instruction, changed leadership mindsets and planning resulting in school improvement. Students in schools where experienced educators were introducing these strategies to them to support their overall health and well-being confirmed improvement across the board. We were hearing stories and reports of not only increased well-being in students, but a positive impact on their academic performance. Teachers, school counselors, deans of students, family assistants, school aides, special educators, para-professionals and athletic coaches reported on the usage and impact; families were coming to the school asking, offering, attending parent coordinator-facilitated mindfulness PDs.

Initially, we did not have the kinds of studies that are now emerging regularly, such as this one published by Harvard University that came out earlier this month (December 2019) on the impacts of mindfulness on student learning and professional performance in public education.

https://cepr.harvard.edu/news/bringing-mindfulness-classroom

Neither were we aware of studies such as this one that came out earlier in 2019 (October) around the impact of a study published in Mind, Brain and Education by Harvard, Yale and University of California researchers around impacts of mindfulness for middle school students.

http://exclusive.multibriefs.com/content/mindfulness-a-potential-life-boat-for-middle-school-students/education

However, even with the ongoing sharing of studies such as those above, nothing was more powerful, more evident, more convincing, or more vivid, authentic, as clearly articulated than the students' own reports of change, of discovery, of accomplishment in all areas of their educational lives. We continue to hear stories that confirm those studies above being told by our NYCDOE elementary, middle, high school students, parents, teachers, and school leaders.

Nothing is more powerful than to see students' teachers and school leaders standing behind them, nodding their heads, as they deliver these reports and stories. Nothing is more critical for public education servants to be mindful of than parents standing behind teachers, nodding their heads and asking when mindfulness/yoga programming would come to other schools and/or be made available to them as parents who want to be better, more mindful, "co-educators" at home.

School leaders and teachers know there is a holistic impact via the implementation of mindfulness and yoga programs. In NYCDOE Mindfulness/Yoga in Education, we are responding to the urgent need to show evidence of impact via specific measurement tools. In addition to those referenced in the studies above, we are currently working with psychometricians, learning about the measurement tools our own educators have developed in their schools to evaluate the impact of this work in quantitative ways relative to the key indicators that matter most to the decision-makers around funding streams in public education. Those areas include classroom-based behavior management issues, suspension rates, credit accumulation, attendance, increased scores on standardized tests; increased student and school community well being and resilience.

The list continues to grow as mindfulness strategies are being purposefully combined with social, emotional, academic and civic engagement instruction and professional development. Additionally, now that our superintendents throughout the city are increasingly requesting district-wide support for mindfulness in education training, we have a city-wide survey we hope to engage them with to get a sense of the current number of existing mindfulness and yoga programs in our schools and the teachers providing these services.

High Expectations Around Quality and Alignment

As this awareness of the impact of mindfulness in our schools in Brooklyn South was initially confirmed, our team realized we needed to create spaces for our schools to come out of isolation around this "ground-up emergence" and into collaboration around this work. We became very busy in a short amount of time letting educators in our own borough support office know what was going on. We signed them up for trainings on mindfulness and supported a mindfulness group in our Brooklyn South office. As the trainings took root and word of mouth spread the message that our own citywide system—on a formal level—was becoming mindful of mindfulness and yoga in our schools, the call for mindfulness training and informational sessions increased as did the invitations from multiple schools to come and see what they were doing with mindfulness in their instructional programming.

Our response was immediate and positive. We believed it was our responsibility as Central administrators to be champions, thought-partners, and connectors to our schools wanting to either begin, deepen or refine the work they were doing around mindfulness and yoga in education. Instead of mandating high expectations, we focused on modeling high expectations around the quality and alignment of our own presentations, trainings, and resources provided and recommended to our schools. If we were going to start paying attention within our own system around what's really going on with mindfulness and yoga, we needed to be mindful in our response. This was no small task for a student services team, each member with specific workflows, and an increasing realization that we were actually becoming mindful of mindfulness within a small portion of a system as large as our own.

We began to look at the findings of multiple researchers, studying the products and services being offered to schools around mindfulness in education. We are lucky in New York City to have a number of outstanding outside providers working with our schools who have been taking the time and space to truly understand how our educators need to be supported in learning, and adapting these strategies in effective, secular, accessible, transparent ways. As a result of these informal and formal collaborations of individual educators, schools and even whole districts in the

NYCDOE, we know now we are clearly at a tipping point of actually accepting and taking action to cultivate the literal structures, processes and procedures of support that have emerged, again, over some time, within our own system in organic ways. The task given to us by both the Chancellor and First Depuy Chancellor is to begin to develop citywide structures of support or this work.

As we continued to investigate and learn from the stories that were being shared around the impact of mindfulness and yoga in our students' and teachers' lives, it was impossible not to make connections with our own personal paths. In the same way that learning and instruction are simultaneously professional and personal – so too is mindfulness. To connect our stories to mindfulness and to use mindfulness to excavate our stories goes hand in hand. I am aware that the editors have a specific request that we weave our own personal stories to how we became involved with this work and to share what I have been learning. This is good teaching practice.

Mindfulness, in and of itself, does not change you or me or anything. Mindfulness makes it possible to increase one's awareness in order to pay and sustain attention to the change that is continuously happening so that you may respond more effectively. Mindfulness helps you to be more of what you already, inherently, are.

Naturally, in education, as students grow and learn, the matter of personal identity takes on greater importance. Who am I? What is my purpose? What do I believe? How do I want to be in the world? For me, in terms of my own personal story, I needed the strategy of mindfulness to have the capacity to sit with, in, accept, understand, forgive, heal and glean various skills and capacities that came as the outcomes of my learning and growth.

Like many who emerge from family origins of adverse childhood experiences (ACE), I entered early adulthood struggling to process the too much too-much-ness of dangerous and harmful people, places and things I had been exposed to. In these cases, sometimes the best one can do, in the absence of a solid sense of identity, at the beginning of a journey of healing and extricating oneself from the traumatic childhood, is to take a drink of water from the ancient well of one's story. Telling one's story can be and is a powerful medicine (the narrative cure) and highly regarded as a mindfulness practice in its own right. If you listen mindfully to someone's story, you can learn a great deal about them in a very short amount of time. It's also possible that your own mindful attention of another in the process of telling their story can be one of humanity's organic lifelines from one being to another.

Resilience Develops Around Self-Awareness, Acceptance, and Understanding

I had lost my family at a young age, had been severely abused both prior to and after the demise of that vital unit, and institutionalized in a home for boys where I experienced an existence that was like a combination of Lord of the Flies and Little Lord Fauntleroy. I lived the pain of loss, the pain of physical attack, sexual abuse, emotional rejection by one's own parents, and, worst of all, the all-pervasive psychic loss of place, space, domain, and sovereignty. I had been nipped in the bud.

From the age of ten to eighteen I grew up with other abandoned, abused and neglected youth; boys of all races, creeds, and walks of life; and became the Mayor of Father Flanagan's Boys Home, Boys Town, Nebraska in my sophomore year of high school. Upon graduation, I received a full scholarship to Cornell University's College Scholar Honors Program where my exit thesis was on the Relation of Technique in the Experimental Sciences and the Creative Arts. I had access to a law scholarship if I wished to pursue that, but I decided to study the technique of the stage actor and earned an M.F.A. under the tutelage of William Esper who was running the Acting Conservatory Program at the Mason Gross School of the Arts.

As an ACE survivor, it was only a short time before the deeper issues of post-traumatic stress syndrome (PTSD)—which could somehow be made more workable, more acceptable for me within the world of acting and drama—began to make themselves known.

I was lucky as a freshly-minted actor from a well-known acting conservatory to be signed to an agent, to be sent on auditions, and to actually be cast in some off-off-Broadway and regional theater productions. One would be amazed at how an actor's unresolved issues combined with simply reacting to others' behaviors in powerful, expressive ways can be considered "impressive," "skillful," "natural talent' when seen in the context of troubled, struggling characters. Some success combined with unaddressed PTSD and an increasing realization that I needed to get help, led me almost immediately from graduate school into a self-designed course of study around my own early-time-in-my-life story that was supported by rigorous psychotherapy and a willingness to truly go to any lengths to be healed from "what was ailing me."

Like many young creative, curious people in New York City, more interested in being life-long learners than worrying specifically about career or making money, I was learning how one might excavate one's own story for gems of enduring understandings. These realizations and the discussions, movies, relationships, failures/successes became the ground for my own understanding of how mindfulness emerges and lives in all kinds of situations; and in some cases, is simply a byproduct of telling and living out from our stories and into the world.

My own understanding of mindfulness was taking root in me when I moved from the container of an M.F.A. program to living in New York City. Therapy increased my capacity to pay attention on purpose in a particular way to what I really felt about various experiences in my life—that were increasingly less about the past and more about the present—that somehow led to my seeing them in different ways. A kind of resilience was developing in me around self-awareness, acceptance, and understanding.

I became increasingly curious around the experiences of my own childhood that had never had the full opportunity to be processed, considered, reflected on . . . responded to. I was firmly rooted in the amygdala area of my brain, of threat and attack, fight or flight or freeze. It became more and more interesting to sit with whatever I was experiencing, to write about it, to read other writers, to work on characters and simply sit with the words they spoke and pay attention to what arose in my mind without judging.

Informal Pathways of Mindfulness

A critical aspect of the emergence of mindfulness in education is that, on the one hand, there is the mindfulness technique, a way of practicing mindfulness meditation that, in its own right, helps one to regulate one's thoughts, emotions, and physical sensations. This is what many people think when they think about mindfulness.

On the other hand, there are all of the very things we are doing now—many of the creative arts, many of the crafts we engage in, any of the sense-based activities that, when done in a mindful way, become a mindfulness practice in their own right! These, of course, are the informal aspect of mindfulness: a walk in a park, watching a sunset, preparing a meal, playing a musical instrument, dancing, playing a sport. Activities that when done in less automaticity-based ways—in ways where we are being just slightly more intentional around noticing, appreciating, pausing, extending, stretching a moment out, lingering in a moment in the midst of the action itself—are enhanced, made more vivid—when we simply allow ourselves to become mindful.

There is also, and perhaps most important for our times, the space that human beings can inhabit together as a result of practicing, embodying, mindfulness. Much of the healing we must come to terms with as a wounded people, a wounded planet is the call to heal together, in public, and in ways that require us to have the courage, humility, and grace to inhabit our common spaces, ourselves and the diverse realities of one another through empathy and emotional intelligence. As adults many of us have lost the capacity to be with one another, particularly "the other"; the other we perceive as different, strange, unknown to us. This is where the resilience to be and stay with one another in difficult times, in difficult processes, can be nurtured by mindfulness. We might find the courage to pause together and ask, "What is really going on here?"

Having these moments of "pause" to reflect, in my early adult life, were opportunities that reminded me (or, as Toni Morrison described in her Beloved, "rememoried" me) of moments in my childhood when I had somehow found the same pause—the same gap, whether circumstances were good, bad, happy or sad—where I could rest a bit in the midst of the situation; and linger there a while, breathe in the eye of whatever the domestic hurricane I would find myself in. I now know, in my own community of what I refer to as the "nipped in the bud club," this is not so uncommon for traumatized children, whether in touch with their situation or not: to instinctively seek out or, in some cases, accidentally stumble into these moments of informal mindfulness if she or he is lucky. Those moments where it seems as if the silence and stillness and the rhythm of heartbeat and breath send a message of hope that this too shall pass. This is where resilience was born in me and I know it is the same place where resilience is born in our most struggling and disengaged students.

My early informal meditation was meditation without becoming "aware" of the rhythm of heart or breath; it was meditation without becoming aware of the "suffering" of life. On the other hand, even as I've tried to qualify here to some degree in terms of my own experience, as I reflect back, what brought me to "accidental" moments of meditation were usually based on struggles or difficult situations I was having in my life that would thoroughly exhaust me. It was also meditation without a conscious sense of generating compassion for others, even if it may have been emerging. I did not know that a wave of unease would rise, fall, rise, fall again. I just experienced it.

I did not know or understand the benefits of meditation, but my body knew. My brain knew. A child often stumbles into meditation as great scientists and artists stumble into their discoveries and inspirations. Amanda J. Moreno of the Erikson Institute, in researching the impact of mindfulness in the lives of children, says that "mindfulness teaches without instructing." When I heard her say that in an interview, I realized what had been happening, informally, in my childhood. I was falling, awkwardly, in the gaps of my life into moments of meditation, and "abandoned," "neglected," "traumatized" . . . whatever . . . I was also learning how to become friends with myself, my experience, without anyone or anything "teaching" me to.

I was making connections between reading, therapy, reflection, sitting still, waiting, being silent, paying attention . . . that kept on working for . . . and "on" me in the sense that lifting weights works on the muscles of a weight-lifter. I could sense a change in myself that somehow was making it possible for me to "stay with," to face difficult challenges, etc. In some ways, mindfulness is a healthy practice like working out in the gym or an important aspect of hygiene—like a toothbrush and dental floss for the brain.

A Humbling and Healing Time

No one was talking about "mindfulness" in my neck of the woods in the mid-'80s. It was by the renowned and recently passed acting mentor, William Esper, in a three-year acting conservatory at Rutgers University, that I was introduced, formally, to the idea and practice of meditation. All beginning actors in his conservatory program at the Mason Gross School of Art had to read a book *Zen and the Art of Archery*.

Esper knew what the great Russian artist Konstantin Stanislavsky knew. He used meditation as part of the actor's craft to relax and inhabit characters to be brought to life, to be lived through truthfully in imaginary circumstances. Stanislavsky was famous for actually formalizing the incredibly elusive technique of acting from an informal process into a formal one. I believe there is a relationship, as powerful as the relationship of meditation and the various religions that claim it as their own, for moral and other reasons, between meditation and the arts that is, if you will, "older than god."

In the early to mid-'90s, I had logged about ten years as a professional actor/playwright, which was marked by a deep and life-changing relationship and mentorship as a student of Wynn Handman, founder and director of The American Place Theater. During this time I would work at my word processing supervisor job, do regional and off-Broadway theater, spots on film, television and spend the rest of my hours at Wynn's Carnegie Hall studio with other actors, toiling away in his famous scene-study class.

Wynn encouraged me to create and perform my own material. I did. Once I had enough materials he produced my play, a one-man show at the American Place Theater, an off-Broadway theater in NYC. It was my expectation this work would turn me into a movie star. Instead of Hollywood knocking on my door, I was noticing that more and more NYCDOE students were attending the shows, accompanied by their teachers. I was curious to know about the reason for these trips to see the show. Educators and principals explained to me that the adverse childhood experiences (simply called child abuse then) faced by the characters I was portraying were relative to the lives of their students. I was offering something that was empowering them to know they were not alone in their own private struggles. My road was not pointing to Hollywood but to public education.

After performances, I found myself increasingly engaged in conversations with students, teachers, and principals. I saw and heard in the expressed responses of kids and NYCDOE educators there was something in my story that radiated out far more to urban youth than it did to Hollywood. The teachers told me I had something to offer. The fact that young people identified with the work was initially baffling to me . . . and disappointing if I am going to be completely transparent. After all, this was supposed to make me a "STAR"!! This was a humble and healing time for me with these young theater-goers.

I learned that my trauma-drama was not so terminally unique. I realized, going back to my meditation practice, that if I could learn how to be disappointed in life, I would have achieved something far greater than becoming a star. Again, sitting, stillness, cultivating awareness, acceptance . . . and then . . . seeing how it all came and left . . . provided me with a level of resilience I had never had before in my life. It also seemed to ignite a level of creative thinking that was taking me back to my exciting years at Cornell. I had an idea!!

If I was going to pursue a position as a teacher in the NYCDOE, I needed to find a way to offer something that had meaning for me or I'd soon turn into one of the living dead. I saw what happened to folks who became teachers because they felt it was the only option they had. I knew there were "career" teachers too. I felt intimidated by those folks. What could I offer that I actually knew something about? What could I do that would move me through the dangers and pitfalls of the bureaucratic, western model of education that had never been on my list of possible career choices? Was there a way to be as excited about teaching urban youth and working alongside public educators as I had been as an actor?

Something to Offer Urban Youth: Rooting Pedagogy in Story

You don't live in a home for boys for eight years and not have something to offer urban youth. Also, while I was leaving the acting profession as a pursuit, the actual profession of acting was not leaving me. What was it that I had learned about acting, about telling your story, about personal narrative and oral history that had helped me to extricate myself to some degree from the oblivion of my childhood? Sitting, breathing with these questions, noticing what arose without judging it, began to give me some answers.

Friends told me I'd never get a job as a drama-performing arts licensed instructor, "The DOE needs math teachers, science teachers. You won't get a job for years." I worked as a word processing supervisor at an investment banking firm that was encouraging me to look into their training program. Instead of taking them up on that offer, I arranged to only work weekends and the rest of the week I lived frugally in Sharon, Connecticut where I started reading tons of books on education and coming up with ideas. I realized that, for better or worse, telling my story, writing about it, acting about it, listening to the stories of others—this had done an awful lot to help me move out of my personal hell and into identification with others in ways that made me feel connected to community.

Even though I had not yet met Dr. Robert Coles of Harvard University, his books were some of the books I was reading. One of those books was *Teaching and the Moral Imagination*. We were fortunate to meet when he became interested in my work with students as an educator in the NYCDOE and came to NYC to interview me about my work. We shared stories around working with at-risk youth (I would call them at-promise today). Dr. Coles' work with the young Ruby Bridges supporting her in the integration of her experience crossing the picket line to attend school, with children in crisis around the world, and his insights into teaching and youth made a deep impact on my own views around teaching—particularly in the areas of culturally responsive teaching and teaching that is rooted in relationships of trust and confidence. Robert Coles taught me as much about the power of mindfulness, awareness and paying attention as any meditation or mindfulness teacher has. He taught me about the power of a meditation rooted in story, of a mindfulness rooted in paying attention to the story of the "other."

I learned from Robert Coles and this learning was deepened in me by the work of Christopher Emdin, that a living and effective pedagogy or curriculum needs to be rooted in story. Coles talked to me about what his own mentor, William Carlos Williams, had told him about the importance of listening to the stories that his patients had to tell him about themselves and their illnesses. Coles wrote in *The Call of Stories*, "The people who come to see us bring us their stories. They hope they tell them well enough so that we understand the truth of their lives. They hope we know how to interpret their stories correctly. We have to remember that what we hear is their story."

I created a curriculum for "at-risk youth" (the popular term to use at that time) based on oral history, personal narrative and storytelling. I was ready to get back to NYC full time and I had a plan.

I looked up the name and phone number of the superintendent of schools in Manhattan because all of my time was spent in Manhattan when I was auditioning. This time I wasn't looking for plays, I was trying to find names of NYCDOE superintendents. Granger Ward! I called him on the phone and told him I would be greatly honored if I could get his feedback on a curriculum I had written. I had some cache from having had my play mentioned in a national periodical and he knew about it. He was flattered. I was prepared. When we met, he said he liked the curriculum. He asked me if this was something I wanted to teach. I said yes.

He then leaned back in his chair, fairly sure of his next statement. "I imagine you know which school you want to teach this in." He was surprised when I said I only wanted to teach this curriculum to kids who nobody else wanted to teach. He smiled. "Would you work on Rikers Island?" "I live in Jackson Heights." For folks not familiar with Queens in NYC, Jackson Heights is as close as you can get to Rikers Island before you actually live there. Teacher colleagues with security placards would pick me up and drive me across a bridge straight to the facility I taught in. Door to door service. I started my career in the NYCDOE at the Rose M. Singer Center, Correctional Facility for Adolescent and Adult Women, Rikers Island.

Mindfulness for the New Teacher in Education

I began teaching predominantly girls and women of color who exploded into my classroom at the Rikers Island Correctional Facility. I had only started learning about meditation. At that time the late Barbara Ford was principal of this school. We connected instantly and she became an instant mentor. She encouraged me to investigate how what I was learning about mindfulness would support my first days as an educator.

Let's be clear, this was no slacking kind of school leader. Principal Ford looked at me with all my ambition, my newly created "STORYQUEST," a curriculum to support students via storytelling, personal narrative, and oral history, that I had created and been hired for. She saw my eager face and realized I had no clue whatsoever around what I was about to experience. I did not know what it meant to criminalize a girl of color, to adultify her, to marginalize her. Those lessons were standing in line, waiting for me. I was determined to employ my newly discovered and developing mindfulness practice in my work with my students.

I began to notice that there were thoughts, feelings and even physical sensations (fearful ones) in reaction to what I was experiencing as I sat and began to learn among my students as the conditions were clear: I would have to learn first before anything educational could happen. We now call this an essential aspect of culturally responsive education: to learn from the students first about who they are, how they are. I confess, the conditions would not allow for anything but this kind of approach, and mindfulness served me well.

There were thoughts I would notice about the moment to moment situation and then there was what was right in front of my nose. Did I want to choose the narrative that I, a white male in a white male supremacist society, was scrambling to manufacture as fast I could in my mind about who, what, where, why, how these human beings were? Or did I want to notice those thoughts and come back to the present moment? I could pay attention to what arose in the present moment without judging or I could rest in the self-serving narrative of myself as a "woke" white male (before the term was being bandied about) who was some kind of knight in shining armor.

I stayed in the moment. Human beings in any kind of circumstances are never stupid, never innately unintelligent on instinctual levels. Those students could see I was staying in that moment because they could see the authentic impact of what I saw and realized as I sat with them. They knew the difference between an educator who was on a self-serving "mission" and one who was simply going to stay and pay attention.

Would I stay there and risk having my heart broken by what I saw? I did and, subsequently, my knowledge and understanding of how life goes for some of our most vulnerable students changed dramatically. I saw girls around 16, 17, 18. They were in many ways much younger than their chronological ages as they had not been allowed by any kind of safe, nurturing environment whatsoever to emerge in accordance with their being. In other ways, they were far older, far wiser, far more experienced than either they or I realized. Then the older students, the women ranging in age from 30 to 65 (in some cases) who were participating in a special program called STEP, would join the young ladies in class.

My whole world was being "flipped." That's when the basic instruction around mindfulness that I had been learning kicked in: simply allowing myself to breathe, to stay relaxed, to feel my feet on the floor, my spine uplifted, noticing my thoughts, feelings, physical sensations, breathing, not reacting, not judging, open chest, not slouched or sitting as if I'm trying to puff myself up, eyes taking in the whole space. Staying. I found that following my breath both relaxed my body and kept me in the present moment. I found that being in the present moment was somehow contagious. The kids and the adults could tell the difference between authenticity and automaticity. As I became more authentic by simply being there—they sure weren't going to be taking any "lessons" from me, not yet—we all became less automatic and we all began to pay attention to what was happening in the room.

In about two weeks, after some very hilarious questions about, "Mister, what are you doing?" I realized that by simply staying attentive and not reacting, staying available but not judging, staying in control of myself and letting go of control of the classroom . . . I had become the anchor of calm in that space.

Having been a teacher, a dean of students, a principal and in the work for well over thirty years, I know the first big hurdle for any new teacher is classroom management. Mindfulness was helping me, in the very moment-to-moment process of the work, to actually see how my own awareness of thoughts, feelings and physical sensations impacted our capacity as a group in the space to cultivate a calm, focused, safe environment. Students have a visceral sense of when a teacher has accepted what she or he can and cannot control via some kind of power dynamic in a classroom.

The simple fact that mindfulness, before teaching my students how to self-regulate, was teaching ME how to self-regulate—communicated a powerful message to my students. A message around my own acceptance of a power dynamic around who's in charge, who's not in charge and an even more honest question, "Who's really in charge here?" Being able to live in that question moved our unspoken conversation about power from "who has it" to how can we each take responsibility for the power we each have in ways that do not cause harm to ourselves or others.

What Mindfulness Is and Is Not

Mindfulness is not what most people think it is. It certainly is not a religion. Certainly not a way to escape the "misery" of reality and go to a happy place. Certainly not a way to ensure the compliance and obedience of the worker. It's not a panacea, not a silver bullet and not going to solve our problems.

I offer that mindfulness in education is a holistic and democratic technique for the cultivation of common sense as it is expressed in eight interdependent, fluid domains: Decide, Learn, Practice, Investigate, Report, Listen, Discuss, Integrate.

I see Social Mindfulness as a mindfulness that encompasses a scope and sequence—that can cover where mindfulness actually is now in our schools—from PreK to 12th grades. A social mindfulness that develops a student's capacity to become mindful of self, mindful of others and mindful of man-made (governments, laws, rules, etc) as well as nature's structure, processes, and systems (the natural laws articulated by the sciences) that, in and of themselves, if not mindfully responded to, can impede the overall health and well being of all. Implications for this social mindfulness include mindfulness and social justice, mindfulness and bias, mindfulness and climate crisis.

"But Mr. Director of Mindfulness—mindfulness is not reflection." I agree. Mindfulness is to reflection as a bookcase is to a book. "Mindfulness is not paying attention." Agreed, mindfulness is to paying attention as a bookcase is to one of the pieces of wood that is needed to make the bookcase. "Hey, mindfulness is NOT social emotional learning!!!" Could not agree with you more. Again, mindfulness is to all the SEL strategies, curricula, branded programs as a bookcase is to larger collections of books and bunches of binders that sit on shelves. Mindfulness can't sit on a shelf. It's only there to help us become aware of, accept and, perhaps, take action around what's on the shelf.

That is all to say: Mindfulness is not something you do "instead of." Mindfulness is not "another thing" you have to do. Mindfulness is what a healthy, vibrant, nurtured mind naturally does when it is not suffering from too many wheels spinning in the head; when it is not being so stimulated by the glocal world of technology, complexity, etc., that the only thing it can do is react with a kind of toxic automaticity. Mindfulness is what a PreK student in one of our schools does when she wakes up in the middle of the night and, instead of waking up needing-their-sleep adults, is able to put herself back to sleep again by counting her breath or doing a simple body scan.

Mindfulness is what the middle school "bully" becomes aware of when he realizes one day that even though he knows he's a bully, he just noticed a thought or a feeling or both—that made him realize he does not want to be a bully. He IS a bully and he DOES NOT WANT to be a bully. He brings this situation to his mindfulness teacher and is taught about the brain and that his bullying is not his fault, but is his responsibility and he can do something about it. He can take more responsibility by practicing mindfulness and noticing that when thoughts of bullying arise, he is not those thoughts and does not have to react to them. He can respond. He can respond in a way that empowers him. In a way that shocks his mother into wanting to know how or why her son has been transformed into a kind big brother.

No big miracle here. A child was provided with the time and space to realize that this was not something he wanted to do. Mindfulness is the thing that is helping both adults and children deal with our nation's big Pink Elephant in the room: unresolved adverse childhood experiences, or ACEs. Watch the film *Resilience* and you will see what I mean. If, as is popularly said, "Culture eats strategy for breakfast," then mindfulness is the thing that gives me the humility to offer that it is equally true that, "Trauma eats culture for breakfast, lunch, dinner and midnight snacks."

How to respond mindfully to this emergence of mindfulness in education? First, don't interfere, but rather, champion, cultivate, support mindfulness that is already in our schools. Don't try to pigeon-hole mindfulness as something that should exist within your own professional wheel-house. One of the primary purposes of mindfulness is to assist one in dealing with all the wheels in the wheel-house between one's ears—those spinning wheels and habits that, as Dr. Ellen Langer of Harvard University has pointed out, keep us in a world of mindless automaticity approximately 95% of the time.

Yes, there are guidelines: no religion, no proselytizing. Understand that this is an emerging and not an established field, and at this point why would you risk controversy or having the truly secular work of your colleagues in public education be conflated with approaches that are either controversial, that rely far more on promotion of their product, than on authentic attraction rooted in sound, thorough scientific research.

Don't just talk about it: do it. Don't do it if you think this is some kind of volun-told or mandate or expectation. It will not work that way. Learn and understand the meaning of an opt-in model, start with the educators first. Then engage all adult members of the community. Engage does not mean "make them practice mindfulness." Engage means inform, invite, show, provide, be responsible to, be willing to collaborate and modify where needed . . . and embody this practice.

Mindfulness as an Ally to Democracy

What follows is where I am currently calling from—in my own riding of the wave of the emergence of mindfulness in my own culture, in my own liquid, liminal, times as a public servant.

C. Wright Mills argued 50 years ago that one important measure of the demise of vibrant democracy and the corresponding impoverishment of political life can be found in the increasing inability of a society to translate private struggles to broader public issues. (Giroux, *The Spectacle of Illiteracy and the Crisis of Democracy*, C. Wright Mills, *The Sociological Imagination*).

Mindfulness in education, in a democracy . . . or perhaps in any form of society, culture, government . . . supports the private citizen in responding effectively to one's personal struggle via the cultivation of the awareness of things one might put down and things one might pick up to change the causes and conditions of that struggle to improve the quality of one's direct, valid experience of life. Mindfulness then offers itself as an ally to the practitioner in the acceptance of the discomfort risked and felt when one purposefully decides to step out of one's perceived comfort zone of self-involvement and into the perceived discomfort of the "other" only to discover and confirm a common humanity, in a shared existence, around a struggle that one holds and has in common with the other.

Together, both might find community with any number of other private citizens who seek public spaces to confirm struggles that, once private, are not private anymore, but of the community—defined and confirmed in the common, public space inhabited by citizens from all walks of life, all races, creeds, genders, etc. These are now no longer "struggles," but issues that the community of "others"—who realize their differences, similarities, and inseparability via the broader public issues they must face together—must organize around together, must take mindful action around together for the greater good, the greater community of people.

I see, emerging in public education, from the ongoing discourse, discussion, and debate around a social and secular mindfulness; a societal technique that might ensure the awareness and identification of one's personal struggle with the struggle of the "other"—supporting sustained critical thinking and reflection that nurtures the development of the simple, accessible communication required for articulation and understanding of critical public issues, while simultaneously cultivating the necessary resilience—both in the individual and in the community—to become engaged with one's own condition, the condition of one's own community—and to take public, skillfully organized and transformative action for the good of a whole and healed society.

Currently Underway and Visions for the Future

We are a large city. Large? Around 1800 schools serving approximately 1.1 million students. Humongous!! I have been in this position since August 2018, for approximately a year and a half, and we still have schools coming to us to see if it's true that the NYCDOE is formally embracing mindfulness in education. We are still in the process of discovering and celebrating outstanding mindfulness and yoga programs in our schools.

I proudly offer a few bullet points highlighting activities around this work that are currently underway and/or in place:

- Establishing and building capacity of borough citywide office-based Mindfulness Leads to provide introductory presentations to schools on professional development days and during Parent/Teacher meetings.
- Offering citywide CTLE credit-granting professional learning opportunities in the form of 4-day Mindfulness Intensives, facilitated by borough citywide office-based teams to ensure opportunities for NYCDOE teachers and school leaders to investigate this work.
- Developing borough-based partnerships with higher education, elected officials and senior leadership in the NYCDOE to develop special programs targeting new teachers in teacher training programs, crisis and de-escalation management, trauma-informed mindfulness and mindfulness for the development of professional and leadership performance as well as mindfulness for college/career readiness resilience to get into college, stay in college and finish college.
- Expanding services of our NYCDOE Mindfulness@Work Employee Resource Group throughout the city.
- Developing an "in-house" Yoga and Mindfulness Teacher Training Program, Yoga Alliance Approved that provides yoga teaching training programs to NYCDOE educators.

The cost savings on this in-house initiative is clear. Teachers who pay multiple thousands dollars on yoga teacher trainings that they bring back to the classroom will now be offered these trainings as part of their work in the NYCDOE. We will be graduating our first cohort of Yoga Alliance, NYCDOE certified Yoga and Mindfulness teachers this month. Educators have been reaching out to us both from the NYCDOE and around the country to say how important this is to them. Our goal is to develop a structure that will eventually serve the whole city. A Yoga/Mindfulness in Education Academy providing a hub/space for ongoing professional development, investigation of relative areas of contemplative, somatic and practices that address social justice, implicit bias and deepen the city's commitment to culturally responsive, STEM and social, emotional learning.

Another key aspect of this structure is that it will be responsible for convening and facilitating ongoing seminars, conferences and opportunities for discourse, discussion and debate with a common mission to develop and refine the highest quality secular approach to mindfulness and yoga in education that addresses issues such as LGBTQ needs, the decolonization of mindfulness, special needs of students, multiple language learners and our families.

Finally, most recently, a group of NYCDOE principals from a new initiative for principal leadership development—the Grey Fellows—reached out to have a meeting. This fellows program focuses on how school leaders who are looking at the bigger picture might collaborate to be change agents in our system in the future. They notified us that they had all been not only attending the mindfulness trainings we were offering, but had taken these practices back to and implemented them in their schools. Based on what they were seeing and hearing in their own schools, they had decided—a group of principals—that they wanted to collaborate on taking the work of mindfulness in education further throughout the five boroughs of our city. When this kind of school leadership finds its own way into the work, and in ways that clearly indicate not only impact but vision . . . BINGO!

It's Not About Me . . . It's About We

In the NYCDOE, because we have been inspired by our leadership to simultaneously be champions of children and equity warriors, we need as much mindfulness as we can muster and no one needs mindfulness more than the Director of Mindfulness. The fact that many of our city leaders and our own Chancellor Carranza are supportive of the cultivation of mindfulness in our school system is a given circumstance that many of my colleagues across the nation do not enjoy.

I cannot possibly shout out ALL of my own colleagues in the Office of the First Deputy Chancellor and Student Support Services Teams and throughout the NYC-DOE who are cultivating this work in our city. However: Dr. Jo Ann Benoit, Greg Bowen, Dr. Debra Lamb, Kevin Dantzler, Lottie Almonte, Steven Strull and Beverly Logan are as much a part of my personal story around the emergence of this work as are all of my students and the many other professionals to whom I apologize for not naming here.

There is not enough space to list all the names of Senior Leadership, District Superintendents, BCO-based personnel, Central leadership, and principals and, most of all, the hard-working and unseen educators of the past and currently in the NYCDOE providing highly effective mindfulness and yoga supports to their school communities. Which is a shame because these are the people we must continue to seek out, learn from, champion, empower, and engage in becoming the leaders of this work when we step down.

We are only at the very beginning of becoming mindful of mindfulness and yoga in the NYCDOE. There is a positive sense of urgency around the window of opportunity provided to us by our Chancellor, the 1st Deputy Chancellor and our city-wide Supportive Environment Framework as developed under the leadership of LaShawn Robinson, Deputy Chancellor for School Climate and Wellness and her team to implement, develop, deepen and refine these interdependent and holistic approaches that are rooted in the national imperative to advance equity now.

It is clear that all credit for this work of becoming mindful around mindfulness in education as well as responding, professionally, to an emerging field of study in its own right goes to all those who simply choose to pay attention. It is the great French philosopher, Simone Weil, who said, "The most generous thing one human being can give to another, is their attention." It is the current fierce writer, Adrienne Maree Brown, who wrote in her work, *Emergent Strategies*, that, "What we pay attention to grows." I am not the only one in the NYCDOE paying attention to mindfulness in education. There are many came who before me, many doing the work now and many who will be doing it after.

Thank you to Coalition of Schools Educating Mindfully for this call for submissions to help us all pay attention to mindfulness emerging in our nation, our world.

CHAPTER 40

Mindfulness as an Equity Tool: You Cannot Teach What You Do Not Embody

Tovi C. Scruggs-Hussein

Former Principal of San Lorenzo High School, Oakland, CA, Educational Leader & Healer, SELf-Transformation for School-Transformation, President and CA Chapter Coordinator, COSEM

"All meaningful and lasting change begins on the inside."—Martin Luther King, Jr.

I have been an educational leader for over 20 years and a meditation practitioner for over 25 years, having experienced 4 week-long silent retreats and multiple day-long silent retreats. My love and dedication to silence, mindfulness, self-growth/mastery, and leadership development are vast. I met COSEM founder Tracy Heilers via their Facebook group. I was deeply impressed with the energy and spirit of the organization and simply wanted to support their inaugural conference by buying a t-shirt, so I reached out to Tracy on Facebook.

It was synchronistic timing because Tracy had set the intention to bring more racial diversity to COSEM's leadership team, as well as learn more about mindfulness's role in educational equity. After reading my educational leadership services website, Tracy reached out and we found our intentions aligned. Soon after, Tracy invited me to be the 2019–2020 president, a role that I am honored to hold. The organization's mission and leadership are deeply aligned with my own values and beliefs—about the powerful role we play in educating *all* children more mindfully—and about educators being the source of the learning and expertise.

Because Tracy is a vortex of inspired action and COSEM was so new when I came on board, I knew I wanted to contribute my expertise in a way that was deeply meaningful and aligned to both of our intentions: bringing an equity lens to the work and especially supporting the inner-work of the adults in order to best serve *all* students more mindfully and with greater inclusion. Although shaking in my boots from fear of never having led webinars or podcasts, I offered to begin the

COSEM Equity-Based Conversation Series, where I facilitate equity topics related to our inner-work, racial healing, mindfulness, and culturally-responsive teaching and learning. It is a brave, safe space and a contribution I am proud to offer.

Tracy invited me to write a journey-based chapter for this book incorporating portions of one of my signature workshops that I have been teaching since 2016: Mindfulness as an Equity Tool. So, as I do at the start of all of my workshops, I invite you to keep an open mind, suspend judgment, and lean into discomfort as you read this chapter.

My Early Beginnings of Developing Emotional Intelligence Through Meditation

I was introduced to meditation for personal growth and development just after college. I needed to heal from the death of my mother several years earlier, strained family relationships, and answer the calling to cultivate the strength to create the life of purpose I felt in my heart I was destined for. It was then, in 1993, that I cultivated a consistent, daily meditation practice that fuels me to this day. This was shortly before I started teaching at San Lorenzo High School, which is located less than 10 miles from Oakland, California, a large Bay Area city where I have lived for over 20 years.

After two years of using meditation for what I thought were purely personal reasons, I felt integration happening. I was already recognizing the power of a meditation practice for *professional* reasons and I knew I was onto something that felt absolutely healing, magical and critical to my well-being and service in working in our challenging educational system.

From my own lived experience, I know and can attest that meditation has improved my way-of-being and efficacy as an educational leader, making it possible to avoid union grievances, calm irate parents with ease, lead and teach for equity, shift the culture and climate of an entire urban school site, and increase educational outcomes. To me, meditating means you are getting into your own head, your own heart, and your own psyche. There is no better way of developing self-awareness... and self-awareness is the most critical foundation for emotional intelligence... and emotional intelligence, through self-awareness, is the essential key to developing an equity lens.

We cannot cultivate a deep sense of emotional intelligence and embodiment to respond to all of the varied groups we serve including students, parents, administration, district leaders (and the list goes on), and deal with all of the variables that face us in our day without an enhanced sense of self. Research shows you cannot develop a great sense of self without spending time with YOU. It is being with "self" and paying attention to "awareness" that develops "self-awareness." Most of us don't spend time with ourselves in a way that creates an awareness. Being alone does not automatically create self-awareness because you are usually alone and doing a task or activity versus just "being"—spending time with your inner landscape and paying deep attention to what you are feeling and giving yourself the time to explore WHY you're feeling it. This level of our inner-work is absolutely key to our work as educators, and especially as school leaders and leaders of equity.

We want our students to realize their greatest potential, and we want to help them to do that, but first, we must do that for ourselves. Oftentimes we are not present enough to what we are doing in any given moment, burdened with distraction, multi-tasking and having flurried thoughts about what happened or what is going to happen. Mindfulness is the umbrella under which meditation is included; for school educators, it is about being present so you can be your optimum self and show up as the best leader you can be so that you can support and serve others.

Emotional intelligence, mindfulness, and meditation help us to realize our greatest potential, living from the inside-out. My intention with this chapter is to make the case that to develop our emotional intelligence as leaders, it is imperative that we meditate regularly. There are many types of mindfulness activities and forms of meditation, but what I'll be referring to here falls into a family of mental training practices designed to familiarize us, the practitioner, with our own mental processes and the awareness that arises from that, and then how this awareness that arises from the stillness and silence of our be-ing guides us in being acutely aware of the dynamic aspects of our thoughts, beliefs, and feelings.

Courage to Create My Own Path

San Lorenzo High looked very much like many of the schools in our nation with mostly white teachers and the demographics of the students, mostly of color, not reflected in most staff. In 1996–97, after 3 years of teaching there, the first wave of high-stakes testing came out and conversations quickly started to become, "Well, THOSE kids are bringing down our test scores; well, if THOSE kids had these kinds of parents; well if THOSE kids could do xyz, then our school wouldn't look like zyx." The conversation was not feeling good and to be blunt, it was feeling racist. This disrupted my schema, as there I was with leaders and colleagues whom I loved dearly and who I knew loved me dearly. They cared about our school, cared about our families, and cared about our students. I'm talking about people who are still my dear friends and colleagues to this day, 25 years later. How could they be talking about kids who looked like me in this painful way? I wanted to get angry because I was angry.

Yet, at the same time, my own self-awareness and growing emotional capacity for goodness were allowing me to stay centered in a key truth: my colleagues are not racist, but there is a cultural disconnect happening. It was showing up as an emotional disconnect when we talked about how our work was related to equity, and how race needed to be part of the conversation. We could be more successful in our jobs. Not having these conversations in a way that was helping our students was preventing us from being more successful in our work, killing my spirit, and contributing to racial fatigue far too early in my career.

I felt destined to create deep change and one day, while leaving a staff meeting that, again, caused my spirit to ache, I departed with a colleague who has now been my sista-friend for over 20 years, Sharon Parker, science teacher extraordinaire. We were walking down the hall, feeling frustrated and longing for a system that recognized the greatness of all children, especially Black children. I remember our words, "We can't go on like this. Did you hear what she said? Did you hear what he said? I wish I would have said. I really wanted to say. . . . We should just start our own school! We couldn't possibly do any worse than what is happening now! We know we could do it better with better conditions and intentions." We actually paused, looked at each other—and in some strange, synchronistic moment, it felt very possible and viable. And we said "yes" to the calling and to each other.

We took frustration and replaced it with courage. We took courage and allowed it to fuel discipline, dedication, and creativity. We envisioned a school where the greatness of our children and our families could be recognized, valued and acknowledged in every moment. We envisioned creating the counter-narrative. We envisioned ASA Academy & Community Science Center. And the name said it all: "ASA" (pronounced "ah-sah") means "life is given" in Arabic and we knew that at our school, at ASA, life—a better chance at a quality life in our country—would be given to our children, our families, and all who served them. ASA was a STEM-focused school with strong humanities. It was fully STEM-focused for youth of color before it was "trendy" and we meditated together as an entire school community *every* morning before that became "trendy."

After four years of planning 2–3 nights a week, a few sista-girl planning retreats, several fundraisers, and an "angel loan" of $250,000, Sharon and I had our own nonprofit and private school with a community science center in the heart of Oakland. We opened our doors in 2002 with 4 students, eventually growing to a new building and close to 100 students in grades 6–12. It was like a Howard University for middle and high schoolers; we were fully accredited by WASC (school governance for California) and our high school courses were a-g certified (college-approved for the UC/CSU systems of California). Private schools are not mandated to do this, but we were a Black private school which meant we had to be sure to go above and beyond to prove our worth in a society that says so. We ran ASA for 8 years until the economic downturn of 2008–09 caused us to close.

At ASA, there was no achievement gap; there was no struggle to be well or feel good, and the teachers were *diverse*, which was key to reinforcing my belief that if teachers are skillful and truly believe in the learner's success, then students can achieve and thrive; the intention and belief must be there. I was heartbroken and upset when our doors closed with our Graduating Class of 2009, whom we had since they were 6th and 7th graders. I was feeling so emotionally conflicted about going back to public education, to a school system that had broken my spirit. How could I go back to a system that had teachers and friends of mine talking about kids that looked like me in ways that didn't feel good?

Back in the Game

When ASA closed, I spent a year tending to my restoration and healing. I was physically and emotionally exhausted, and the thought of entering the job market after 8 years of entrepreneurship felt daunting and even more exhausting. Plus, I was committed to not returning to a system that was failing so many children of color. It was not at all a glamorous year. I barely had any money and hosted tutoring and workshops in my church to supplement my unemployment checks. Really rough year, yet one of the most creative, inspirational and restorative of my life.

In 2010, I was recruited to serve the YMCA as Executive Director of Urban Services for the East Bay developing educational programs for them. I thought it was the perfect job for me, not having to go to a dysfunctional traditional school setting, still being connected to urban youth and education, and being highly creative to design educational programming for youth of color. Only two months into the role though, I kept hearing my heart share, "This is not a school. This doesn't feel right. This is not who I am or where I belong." I had to remind myself that being "off" my path was critical to gaining clarity that my path in school-based education was my true path. It was this realization that gave me the strength, courage, and wisdom for the game-changing opportunity that was to come next.

One afternoon in 2012, I get a call from a mentor in San Lorenzo USD and she says, "Guess what? The principalship at San Lorenzo High just opened up." While I cringe at the possibility, I also get very excited about the possibility of returning to where I started as a 22-year old teacher. I had been out of public education for 10 years and A LOT had changed. I compete against 7 candidates, all white (6 men and 1 woman), and I get the position. Almost 15 years later, I am now the principal of the same school where I first started teaching!

I land the job the day before school starts. By twelve o'clock noon, I am getting introduced to my staff, the majority of whom were friendly faces, and I have only 15 minutes to launch into a school year with inspirational leadership. Internally, I have to reconcile that everything "in place" for the school year to begin is not of my own creation, mindset or leadership, yet I was on a mission. This was my chance to take all that I had learned while outside of the system, including my resilience and leadership development, and bring it to scale inside the system to increase positive outcomes for students of color.

I realize how happy I am to be back with folks who I love and care about—and they are happy too. But now I'm the principal . . . and shockingly, I immediately feel like I am in the Twilight Zone. The demographics of both staff and students had not changed, the data had not changed . . . and worst of all, the conversations had not changed. After all this time, it was still about why Black and Brown kids are not excelling in the same ways as our Asian and White kids. I ask them, "Why are we still having this conversation? I left because of this conversation! What are we going to do about it?"

Again, the internal part of me is saying, "These are people who *care*. These are outstanding teachers; they are skilled and have the strategies and know-how to teach. I've been in their classrooms." Not only that, they are good and caring people. All the good stuff. So what was the real issue? I was perplexed and concerned. As I tried to unearth the source of our failure in our data, I was targeted as "an angry black woman" for being upset about the data, but honestly, I couldn't be a principal and have my name attached to that kind of data. In my mind, I had pictures of the kids and families attached to "that data." That data had dreams, hopes, aspirations. That data had a valuable life attached to it.

SELf-Transformation for School-Transformation

(Adult Social Emotional Learning of the "self" in order to create inner transformation that results in school transformation.)

Reflecting on how I was going to stay in this education game with my sanity, sense of efficacy and health intact, I decided to go on a week-long silent retreat. As I knew from attending them before, it was a powerful way to grow and deepen with dedicated time to just BE. And to be fully transparent, the question that I was going to sit with was, "God, what do I need to do to get these white people to listen to me so that our kids can do well?" By about day 3 or 4 of no talking, just meditating for about 15 hours a day, I am sitting on my mat and I start crying. As I am crying, I am getting the answer to my question. Of course, it doesn't make it true for you— unless it is—as it is my experience.

The answer that I got was: It must be painful for white people, who love teaching, to go in day after day, busting their butts working hard to get only subpar results and then be chastised for it—to carry a sense of failure in their work, day after day, and not really know what to do about it, or where to go to talk about it. It was a HUGE answer. And it wasn't only the words, but it was the feeling of deep pain in my heart and in my body. I felt the pain of not doing a job you felt called to do well. It hurt. Feeling this pain increased my compassion, a way-of-being that I had not fully embodied previously.

Right after that first a-ha moment, came the next one: It wasn't about them not listening to me, it was about what I needed to change in ME to make it so my voice could be heard by them. And, then, how could I get white people to then make enough of a change to make enough of a difference?

At the time, I had no idea, but during my "sit" three critical parts of my brain were getting activated. The insula is the interior part of your brain and it triggers empathy and compassion; it's connected to your heart and triggers the feeling of love, the feeling of the connection. This means we are designed/hardwired *to be connectors* with each other—to be more humane and compassionate! It's our conditioning that creates disconnection, which happens on an intellectual level, not a heart level. Knowing the insula is triggering empathy and compassion means equity work is deeply about our own humanity of empathy and compassion. I call it the "lovely insula" and this is what happened when I got the message to have a changing message and to be more compassionate with my teachers at SLz.

The beauty of it is that when you are meditating, all of this is happening unconsciously on a physiological and neurological level. I will not belabor the science, as there is plenty of research to substantiate this. Yet, I will highlight that meditation benefits our brains to "rewire" in greater emotional balance and less reactivity via the amygdala, supports greater executive function via the prefrontal cortex, and increases our empathy and compassion via the insula. I find great comfort in knowing that I don't have to work hard to be my best self via meditation, I simply show up for myself, my leadership, and those I serve by meditating. Our brains are designed to do this and support us in being our most optimum selves. And whether we want it to or not, this is happening; this is our body's natural regenerative and restorative response to sitting still and becoming more self-aware.

By continuing to work on ourselves, the self-awareness and the empathy in all of us will grow because it's really all about the *connection* needing to be cultivated. It's not about the color, it's not about that. It's truly about the connection, but we have to start to have open, honest conversations with ourselves first. Then, we can grow and have the needed conversations with each other. We can learn together.

I've been doing equity work long enough to know that many of us, especially white people, get scared to talk about race because it often doesn't go well or folks don't want to be dinged for saying something racist. But we ALL have a lot of racist stuff going on in our minds and hearts no matter what color we are.

I returned from that retreat a new, better leader. The three "answers" I received would profoundly shift my entire approach and way-of-being related to my leadership and equity work. I was speaking and leading with greater compassion. My new way-of-being was just what we needed for me to lead my team with success, care, and skillfulness to utilize new strategies and increase achievement. It wasn't only about me looking *out* but about me looking *in* and prioritizing the time to do so.

I'll tell a story that is hard for me to share, but I tell it because I need people to get what I am saying, to know that they are not alone when it comes to racialized bias, and that bias is not about white people being biased, but about us *all* being biased. When I was at San Lorenzo High as a second-year teacher, I had an Asian boy and I will never forget this. I had only 25 students in my health class, which was not a hard class to do well in. I remember consciously making a choice, a decision to dismiss him, because, due to my upbringing, I felt like he was going to be fine and that he didn't need my help.

Why would I hold that thought? Stereotypes, a blatant stereotype, and a form of racism. Because of that thought, I didn't give him any extra attention all semester. That was my own bias. Oh, the power of it! It took me time to get in touch with my own psyche and my own emotions and then the courage to own the ugliness of a belief I held—my own implicit bias about Asian students that I acted out very explicitly. That's the hard truth that we often don't like to name because it's so painful: whether explicit or implicit, our biases create the same effects, yielding the same hurtful outcomes that result in the "gaps" we try to rationalize away.

Changing the Game

The comforting thing about meditation is that you can sit all by yourself and nobody knows what's going through your mind, through your heart, through your body. It's your own, very personal and protected experience. It's a private time to be raw and unfiltered with yourself . . . and then have the courage to admit to what you are witnessing, becoming aware of, and choosing to be or do differently as a result. You can have all the racist thoughts that you want to have, working out all of the biases that you want to work out in private. That was the other message I got on my retreat.

The insights from my meditation retreat changed the whole game. So much so, that I knew that I had to also begin to teach adults about the power of meditation and stop being afraid to bring it to my campus schoolwide with greater intention. We implemented such deep change that all of our discipline referrals went down, our suspension rates went down, classroom referrals went down, students roaming the halls were almost nil, numbers of kids of color in AP classes went up, the number of students on honor roll went up, the number of students with perfect attendance went up, the staff was happier. Our culture and climate shifted so much that district leaders were coming and asking in disbelief, "What happened here?" Things were so different in feeling tone—in the energy that we were starting to carry as a staff and a collective holding of our students—it was palpable.

Our data improved so greatly in just a year and a half that I got an award, for both the strategies used and the results gained in such a short period of time. Strategies ranged from creating more connection on campus simply by saying "hello" to each other, to bringing in Inner Explorer for a 30-minute mindfulness talk to teachers— to "give permission" that mindfulness was okay to practice with your students other than only my voice saying so. We also had an intentionally-aligned advisory period held by one of the most cohesive departments, and created schoolwide quarterly awards for academic recognition at spirit rallies. We galvanized Student Council and school clubs behind common messages and got all teachers to agree to a list of about 20 common systems to be used.

Plus, I did away with our school's brand of "Rebel Pride" and replaced that message with "Rebel Love." Consistently, I would also tell students what they needed to hear most: that I loved them. In fact, telling them, "I love you" was how I opened my first school assembly as principal, in the gym with over 1500 students. It took us about 6 months to recalibrate and reap the rewards of what became lovingly known as "The Rebel Way." What I also learned along the way is that much of what I had done intuitively was trauma-informed and supported that strand of our work as educators. There's so much more to share on the process and strategies; that's a whole other chapter or workshop!

I left San Lorenzo High with the Class of 2016; the class I started with as freshman. We were graduating together. I felt strongly that it was time to take much of what I had learned to scale, and I wanted to impact education even more deeply by supporting and cultivating leadership development for our leaders and teachers, particularly in the areas that had impacted me most: personal growth (Adult SEL), equity and racial healing, trauma and resilience healing, and emotional intelligence via meditation. Also, unfortunately, the new district leadership and I were not fully aligned.

While at San Lorenzo High, I was a veteran educator and site leader, having been a principal in one form or another for over 15 years. The traditional professional development being offered to me was not resonating or intellectually stimulating for what I knew was needed to lead in our ever-changing landscape. I had to search for the professional development that would best groom me as a leader, as well as benefit my school's achievement. Remember, my teachers were good teachers and many were great teachers; we needed the support of adult SEL to go from good to great and great to excellent. With this awareness and conviction, I embarked on several certifications to support me in supporting my own leadership development and self-transformation that I knew were keys to unlocking the challenges of school transformation, including an Integral Coaching Certification via New Ventures West in 2013 and Search Inside Yourself Emotional Intelligence Certification in 2015.

In 2016, I was invited to co-design and co-teach a course at Mills College called Trauma-Informed Leadership with an Equity Lens. There was also an educational nonprofit organization, Partners in School Innovation, that believed in what I had to offer to create equitable school transformation and improve the outcomes for students of color. There, I was hired as Regional Executive Director of California. It was a breath of fresh air to be part of the leadership team of an organization aligned to what I deeply believe to be true: that if we give staff time to talk about and address equity issues, then this intentional, highly transformative time will result in improved outcomes for those we serve. I knew I hit the jackpot in what was next for me in the journey.

At Partners in School Innovation, my CEO and one of my favorite equity leaders, Dr. Derek Mitchell, often says, "We are *all* in this ocean of equity work–and if we are all in this ocean of equity work, then it means we are *all* getting wet." So it needs to be reinforced that not only white people need this work and this framing. That is not the case—we all need this practice of self-awareness. We all have biases that we carry about people, and we work with too many people to not be in touch with our biases. This is precisely why I am so passionate about this, why it is so important, and why I do all I can to spread this message and teach mindfulness as an equity tool.

I continued my personal and professional development in 2018 with Niroga Institute's Dynamic Mindfulness Instructor Certification and in 2019 with Brené Brown's Dare to Lead Instructor Certification. In 2019, I shifted from working for Partners in School Innovation to, again, going out on my own. I feel like the field of education is now ready for what I have to offer: "SELf-Transformation for School-Transformation," where integral self-mastery is the focus to have professional development for educators that is centered on Adult Social Emotional Learning of the "self" in order to create inner transformation that results in school transformation. And, of course, much of this is with an emphasis on equity and healing at the core.

Awareness of What is Arising Right Now

Many people say meditation is difficult and they have to try too hard, but it's not about trying or efforting. Meditation is about becoming more aware and allowing for that awareness to arise and be observed with care and non-judgment. It's about what I call "A.W.A.R-ing:" Awareness of What is Arising Right now-ing.

For me, meditation is the gateway to our inside-out work or our inner-work. Meditation serves as a vehicle to connect to our biases and our self-awareness. Here is my framework of how I approach this work (I usually have a visual to go with this—with these next items around a circle and with a double arrow between them; you can find it on my website at ticiess.com):

> We have our lens of how we view the world—
>
> which informs our values, beliefs, and assumptions—
>
> which determines our interactions and expectations of others—
>
> which influences how we be and do.

What is critical here is that whatever lens we observe with determines what shows up in our work, and what plays out in our classrooms and in our lives. Around our lens, is our conditioning—and it is HUGE in our biases. We are all at the whim of the conditioning of our families, of our culture, of our society, and the epigenetic piece that plays into that. We have these layers of conditioning that govern our thought patterns and govern our behaviors.

Our conditioning is the stereotypes, the societal ideas, and what we learn about "those people," what our parents may have taught us about "those people." What is freeing about this is that we can identify that our biases do not make us "bad people." We get our conditioning honestly, thus, there is nothing to be ashamed of. A lot of times when we talk about racism or racist beliefs we learned from our families, that is all it is. It's not true racism originating by us.

It's really a belief or something based on our conditioning that is impacting our lens of how we view the world which causes the above cycle of: informing our values, beliefs and assumptions which determines our interactions and expectations of others, which impacts how we be and do because that is the lens we are using. And using this lens projects to the experience that we create. Imagine conditioning like an onion and how you can peel back thin layers of an onion only to find more until you get to the center. That is what it is like to peel back layers of conditioning, seemingly never ending.

We are not responsible for all of our conditioning, but we ARE responsible for how it makes us behave. We are also responsible for the process of our A.W.A.R-ing. Self-awareness from meditation allows us to tap into that conditioning. And remember, it allows us to do it in private, free of public shame, free of the fear of being called a racist, free of other's intrusions into our own very personal process. And in this process, in the identification, comes our release of the conditioning, and then comes our healing. When we slow ourselves down with that training, becoming aware and present, then we are in a moment of power within ourselves.

Biases are Malleable: Explore & Unlearn What is Getting in the Way

A bias is by nature a judgment or behavior that results in subtle cognitive processes. The judgment often arises when our brain does what it is most conditioned to do: make meaning. But it makes meaning out of the conditioning of our own biases, implicit or otherwise. If the bias is an implicit attitude and stereotype, then it is operating at a level below our own awareness like a computer virus. Our work is to shine a light through increased self-awareness so that we are not acting out an implicit bias below our awareness. The good news is that biases are malleable which means they are changeable. They can be unlearned because they are learned.

Let's go back to my example with my Asian student. I can go back and trace where I learned it—studying the "model minority" in college, and what I learned supported my experience and my view. But I had to get that real and aware with myself to unearth that harmful bias-virus. In the moment, you can't intellectualize the actions that come from the bias; you have an autopilot reaction. But like I did, you can spend time with mindfulness practices developing greater self-awareness and emotional rigor, which leads to being able to intellectualize the bias.

Taking the analogy further: There's nothing wrong with the software (strategies), it's our own hardware (our minds) that needs the fixing so the software can run. It's like having a virus (bias) on the computer . . . nothing will run as well until the hardware is cleaned up and the virus is deleted. Emotional intelligence and self-awareness delete our bias-virus! And the virus can come back . . . so each day, the computer has software that will scan for viruses to ensure the smooth running for the day. That "scan" is our daily meditation practice. It's using what I call SELF-WARE.

Going into more detail: Action is based on the emotion that is triggered by the judgment you make that stems from the bias—the action itself was from the bias AND the emotion. In milliseconds your brain has a thought, then a judgment, then an emotion, then you act out of habit and without interruption. It is compulsion that results from habitual choice. The practice of meditation allows us to be so self-aware that we can move from compulsion to choice, catching the trigger of the thought and choosing a different response. If we do self-awareness training through meditation and other mindfulness practices, then we are putting ourselves in the place of greatest potential to stop the bias.

Here are the three key experiential steps for de-biasing your thoughts around kids who may not be like you and/or that you are challenged by:

1. Set your intention to want to unearth whatever bias you are holding. And this is totally personal—you don't have to share a word about it.

2. Then give it some attention. Giving it "attention" is two-fold. First, you want to "sit" with it and allow it to show up to be examined in some way, without overthinking or judging it; just being with it. Second, you want it to be in the forefront of your present attention as you go through your day-to-day activities so that you can see how, when, and under what circumstances it may show up. Again, you notice this and do not judge it. This noticing increases your awareness of it as you aim to be more mindful of it to interrupt it.

3. Then practice acting against that bias until your interrupting it becomes embodied. The intention is to become savvy enough at your own self-awareness that you catch yourself in the act of possibly enacting your bias. As a result, you become more and more skillful in catching it before you act on it, allowing a different response to be chosen. This is critical because your bias is so deeply ingrained that it's virtually impossible for it to entirely go away. It can be reduced and interrupted, but will more than likely always have a place in your psyche.

To go back to my example one last time: I under-served the Asian student because of my own belief and my own conditioning, but it's not something that will happen again because I have done the inner work—setting the intention, meditating, reflecting and acting against the bias again and again. I am now hyper-sensitive to it. I will still have the biased thought again because it is a bias that I am used to holding; it lives in me, but it no longer guides me like a compulsion would. I will not act out on the bias, but instead I will choose to act more responsibly to bring honor to my own humanity and my profession. Once I think it, I will make the choice to behave differently, to overcompensate for conditioning that I am healing. That is what self-awareness does. That is what we want to have happen in our classrooms. Remember, "non-judgmentally"—don't be hard on yourself, work on yourself. We are all in the ocean getting wet.

Empathy and Compassion to Support Capacity-Building

Empathy and compassion play important roles to support us with our colleagues. Let us not get angry with each other for the biases that we are carrying. Let us share and be vulnerable and explore these biases together as a team so that our students who are struggling can do even better. As educators, we have or can easily get all of the necessary strategies, information, and content knowledge. It's our conditioning, our mindsets, our biases, that prevent all of what you know to do from working.

Educational leader Bill Dagget says, "Culture trumps strategy." Intuitively, I've chased after culture fiercely and first, wherever I have taught and led. Academic success has always become a natural by-product. Students and families felt loved, cared about, and held—and the teachers and the staff felt successful. They carried that feeling of being able to be successful into each day. Success became our self-fulfilling prophecy. That is what happened at ASA and it is what happened as part of The Rebel Way at San Lorenzo High.

Meditation and self-awareness work to breed compassion and empathy to support the capacity-building of doing equity work. If we are going to talk about equity, we have to get really comfortable with the discomfort of being with difficult emotions. We must have the courage to be there and stay engaged. Our mindfulness work, coupled with compassion, can lead us to be more effective leaders of equity so that we can lean in and have real conversations, emotional conversations, authentic race-based, gender-based conversations. This is how we shift the outcomes.

Inquiry and Implications for Our Work as Educators and Equity Leaders

My biggest question for the field of education right now is, "How can we teach what we do not embody?" I'm frustrated that mindfulness is being treated in some schools as something that is being done to kids and that teachers are feeling forced to do it in terms of social emotional learning (SEL)—when often the adults have not engaged in their own SEL. We are struggling with culturally-responsive teaching strategies due to the lack of inner-work around healing and our own equity work.

Words don't teach; only experience truly teaches. You can read all about mindfulness and you can hear all about it, but until you experience it yourself, it's all living in your intellect versus an embodiment experience that you can begin to speak to. We have to embody what we are talking about. We have to *be* the mindset or else our strategies will not work; they will be as futile as they have been for the last several decades because of user-error.

I'd like there to be a warning sign on all school mindfulness books and programs: "Beware—there is authenticity required before you go and 'do this.'" A lot of this is the work that WE have to look at for ourselves. Also, I am asserting that teacher preparation programs need to engage in Adult SEL for incoming educators and that it needs to be part of ongoing teacher professional development because we have to engage in that as adults.

If we are not embodying it, then we cannot bring it into our classroom. Our kids are coming to school with too much "stuff" and they are with us all day and we have to hold them. We have to build our own emotional capacity to hold them. People are studying it and reading it, but the application is not usually there. We can have strategies all day long, but the strategies without the embodiment will not yield the results to create the changes we need for more equitable education.

What I'm also asserting is that we have to approach great intellect with greater emotional rigor. Everyone is showing up so smart and brilliant that we need the emotional workout to be more rigorous in order to outsmart ourselves into healing and take the intellect out of it. This work is not about intellect, it's about emotional intelligence.

Bill George of Harvard Business School says, "The main case for meditation is that if you are fully present on the job, you will be more effective as a leader. You will make better decisions, and you will work better with other people." In education, these "people" are our stakeholders: board members, community members, alumni, teachers, parents, students—and I am sure you could expand on the list. That's a lot of people to be responsive to. That's a lot of people to be kind to. That's a lot of people to care for. And that's a lot of people to love, genuinely love, connect with. Yet, a lot of who we are and who we bring to the work gets in the way of how responsive we can be to those stakeholder groups, for whatever reason, explicit or implicit.

Remember that this is a journey, you are not ever going to get "there." And when we do our mindfulness work, all of the "sweet spots" of the brain, like the insula, will be getting activated . . . it's all happening on its own, you don't need to try or effort. Just be with it and ALLOW it to happen. Allow your own SELf-Transformation for School Transformation, our children are counting on it.

Call to Mindful, Inspired Action

We've given you a lot of words in this book, including some bias-busting support in my chapter, but the magic is in the practicing of it. It's embodying it and it's living it. When you apply the practices we've shared about this work, to all of the skills, strategies and content-knowledge that you already know and what we have learned from Zaretta Hammond, Sharroky Hollie, Baruti Kafele, Anthony Muhammad, Jeff Zwiers, Kate Kinsella, and numerous others who have offered both keen and culturally-responsive strategies . . . you put this "meditation magic" on it . . . five minutes each day . . . to set your tone and ground yourself in your own intentions and awareness before you jump into work . . . five magic, game-changing minutes . . . impreovement happens.

And, if you are really tapping into being more mindful for both your personal and professional lifestyles, you might also consider adding five more magic-minutes in the evening to process the day, practicing self-compassion for things that didn't go as planned and cultivating gratitude for those that did. Simply, live into your A.W.A.R-ing.

We, at COSEM, encourage all educators and students to "Commit to 1%" for their wellness by practicing mindfulness daily together for 10 minutes, which is approximately 1% of our waking day. This could be 10 minutes at the start of the day or spread throughout in shorter segments at times of transition. Teachers and students are equally stressed these days from the basics of modern living. And, of course, we must acknowledge the trauma with adverse life experiences that many have faced along with teacher wellness issues. What is key is that mindfulness practices, like meditation, have been research-based and scientifically proven to serve as an antidote. So, you are invited to join our "Commit to 1%" Campaign at educatingmindfully.org/commit.

Parents, school staff and kids ALL need the benefits of mindfulness to thrive so it makes sense to learn and practice *together*. Beyond personal benefits, it bonds those practicing together in a special way, especially when you take the time after practicing to reflect as a community. COSEM's goal is to make mental hygiene just as important as physical hygiene—"brushing our brain" with mindfulness just as common as brushing our teeth.

To conclude, as COSEM's National Board President, I want to personally thank COSEM founder Tracy Heilers for her clear vision, countless hours volunteered so far, and for her courage to launch Coalition of Schools Educating Mindfully. She is a testament to the impact that one person's inspired action can have. In the words of Brené Brown, "When one of us acts with courage, it inspires others to do the same. Courage is contagious." Yes, indeed, Tracy, your courage has been contagious!

On behalf of us all, I extend a deep bow of gratitude and say, "Thank you and we salute your courage." For me, working closely with Tracy, our amazing Board of Directors, and Advisory Team has been a joy in giving freely to the practice that has served me more fully than words can ever express. I have no doubt that the best is yet to come as we grow COSEM and express the vision and mission in ways that are meaningful to us. For more information on how to be more involved with COSEM, please visit educatingmindfully.org.

A Final Reflection

Barbara Larrivee, COSEM Board Member, Author, and Former Teacher Education Professor at Rhode Island College and California State University

Your head may be spinning with all the grand ideas shared in this book. You may be excited, yet overwhelmed, trying to digest the plethora of practices offered. And many of the considerations may have been outside of your awareness until enlightened by many of the authors' visions of a multidimensional perspective for bringing mindfulness to today's classrooms.

While more and more research is validating the impact of mindfulness-based and social-emotional learning practices for focusing attention, reducing the effects of stress, regulating emotional reactivity and promoting self-regulation, with a wider lens we can do so much more. Many of the practices presented here ask you to think beyond these important outcomes to simultaneously challenge your own biases to engage in culturally-responsive teaching practices that ensure an equitable, inclusive and safe learning climate. They call on you to be sensitive to adverse childhood experiences, utilize trauma-informed practices and employ non-punitive conflict resolution and behavior interventions.

Of the many valuable takeaways, we want to reiterate three messages consistently woven throughout this book:
- Start with your own practice.
- Make self-care a priority.
- Ensure practices you share with your students "stand the test of secularity" by using universal language and practices that have no connection to spiritual or religious beliefs.

20 Questions to Ask Yourself

As a way to assimilate and absorb all that is shared here, we invite you to take time to reflect on these questions to get you thinking more specifically about next steps to begin your own practice, and then bring it to your classroom and/or school. Or, if you've already started on your journey, consider how you might expand and enrich what you currently do.

First, examine your deepest values, pondering why you chose teaching in the first place asking yourself:

1. In addition to my academic goals, what other goals do I have for my students?
2. What student needs are not being addressed by my current teaching practices?
3. What situation or condition would I like to change or improve?
4. What values are most important for me to impart to my students?
5. How do I make these values evident in my teaching?

Next, after reading this book, thinking about all the ideas expressed in the many chapters ask yourself:

6. What was my most significant learning or insight?
7. What resonated the most with me?
8. What are some of the mindfulness practices that "stuck" that I want to try and share with my students?

It may be helpful to think about embarking on a practice on three levels: (1) your personal practice, (2) practicing with your students, and (3) creating a "community of practice."

For your personal practice, ask yourself these questions:

9. Thinking about the sequence of my day, how can I carve out some time for my own self-care?

10. Can I incorporate practicing mindfulness into a routine part of my day, such as the beginning or end of the day, before or after a meal, or transitioning from my school life to my home life?

11. What avenues for practicing are best aligned with my learning style, personality and preferences?

For practicing with your students, consider these questions:

12. What am I already doing in my classroom that could be reframed as practicing mindfulness?

13. What could I give up that I'm currently doing to make time for practicing mindfulness?

14. Are there any activities in my teaching day that I could streamline to shorten to make room for practicing with my students?

15. How can I build a practice into transitions in the school day, like the beginning or end of the day or class period, or before or after recess or lunch?

16. Can I create a dedicated space to serve as a place where students can take a necessary break or I can send students as a non-punitive alternative to reflect on their behavior?

For creating a community of practice you can think locally or globally for your support network by asking yourself:

17. Do I want to become a member of COSEM (educatingmindfully.org/members) to receive the monthly newsletter to keep informed of all that's happening in mindfulness in education?

18. Should I get involved with my state chapter if there is one, or should I consider spearheading my own state chapter if my state doesn't have one?

19. Will I stay connected by joining COSEM's Facebook group, Mindfulness in Education Network's (MiEN) Listserv, or Association for Mindfulness in Education's (AME) Google Group?

20. Am I willing to seek out like-minded professionals in my school or district to share ideas and practices as well as concerns and potential solutions, or would I prefer to start by enlisting just a single colleague to be my "mindfulness buddy" so we can support each other?

One thing we've learned for sure—this work is better done with a network of supportive practitioners. And it is so much more inspiring and fulfilling to work together on this transformative journey.

Acknowledgments

Many thanks are in order and I want to start with Tim Iverson and Barbara Larrivee. They volunteered many, many hours to assist me in editing this volume. As drafts were submitted, we "divided and conquered" and worked closely with the authors to get just the right amount of story and substance in each chapter. The whole process was really fun—as each author had a very distinct voice and writing style—and our job was basically to let their voices shine within our loose book parameters—and in some cases just pull a little more out of them based on what we were seeing coming in from different authors and what we knew we wanted to cover in the book as a whole. They also helped me make key decisions about the book, such as book layout designer (thank you Dorie McClelland!) and what order the chapters should be in to create a nice flow.

The next big thanks goes to our Board. All of the actions of COSEM represent the field of mindfulness in education, and that can feel daunting at times—we have many people to "make proud." I want to be a servant to the field and I look to our all-educator Board for ideas and to ensure that all actions have integrity and align with our mission. My appreciation for their help in organizing the conference and with all of our other big and little tasks cannot be overstated.

I especially want to thank our current president Tovi Scruggs-Hussein who has helped me to grow as an educational organization leader. Before she joined our organization, equity was just a word I typed on our homepage, knowing theoretically that mindfulness can foster it, but not giving it much thought beyond a surface level. When viewing our inaugural conference promotional video, it was shockingly clear that it was a white suburban conference organized by a team lacking racial diversity. I acknowledged our starting spot and made an intention to have COSEM more fully value and embrace equity explicitly. Shortly after, I met Tovi, and she shared in her chapter some of the ways she has brought an equity lens to our mission. Tovi has supported the inner-work of myself and many other educators through COSEM already and I look forward to working closely with her for years to come.

The heart of our mission depends on our state chapter coordinators and meeting facilitators. These passionate educators are not only bringing mindfulness to their classrooms and schools but in some cases to whole school districts and communities. And we are asking them, on top of this and in their "spare" time, to connect educators in their area with educators in nearby areas, as well as with educators statewide as the number of mindful educators in their state grows. We so appreciate their inspired action as they "move slow to move fast" creating grassroots support networks and increasing the momentum of the movement, or emergence—as Barnaby Spring inspires us to call it.

Thank you, Barnaby, for lighting the fire within me to envision and then give birth to something much grander than I could have envisioned on my own. That is exactly what we want for our state and local chapters—to help each other expand further—both personally and professionally—than we could individually. And thank you to the organization and community leaders on our Advisory Team, who I call on regularly with questions and when feelings of doubt arise. I lean on your continued mentorship.

And of course, and most pertinent here, so many thanks to the chapter authors extraordinaire! When we put out our call for chapter proposals and asked specific organizations to partner with us on this project, I had no idea if the book would unfold as I had envisioned it or if it would even come together at all—I just trusted that something amazing would result—and it did. The whole process has been so rewarding! I thank you all for trusting my vision for your chapter and for the book as a whole, and for the courage to allow the world into your hearts and minds through our co-creation.

Thank you, everyone above and to many others, such as my husband Gary, for helping COSEM reach its fullest potential in your own very special way. And thank you readers for supporting our mission by purchasing this book. As COSEM's executive director, I would be remiss not to extend the opportunity for you to support and learn with us further through annual membership to our Mindful Learning Center. You'll have access to our growing video library including conference session recordings, past interviews and webinars, our Equity-Based Convo Series and more. Mindful Learning Center members also get discounts from our resource provider partners. Use code BOOK2020 for 20% off in 2020. Learn more at educatingmindfully.org/MLC.

We invite you to join our community at educatingmindfully.org/members. Members receive our monthly newsletter which shares the scoop of all things mindfulness in education, including educator video-shares, interviews, webinars, conversations on relevant topics, and mindfulness-based professional development listings from across the globe.

Love and appreciation.

—Tracy Heilers, Founder and Executive Director of Coalition of Schools Educating Mindfully

About the Contributors

1. Amy Saltzman M.D., is a holistic physician, mindfulness coach, scientist, wife, mother, devoted student of transformation, long-time athlete, and occasional poet. Her passion is supporting people in enhancing their well-being, experiencing joy, and finding flow. She is a pioneer in the field of mindfulness for youth. She offers in-person and online courses for teachers, counselors, allied professionals, athletes, and coaches. Stillquietplace.com; dramy@stillquietplace.com

2. Richard Brady is a mindfulness consultant (www.mindingyourlife.net) and a retired high school mathematics teacher. He was a founder and the first President of the Mindfulness in Education Network. In 2001 Richard was recognized by Thich Nhat Hanh as a teacher in his tradition with a special focus on cultivating mindfulness in young people. He is co-editor of *Tuning In: Mindfulness in Teaching and Learning.*

3. Elizabeth Kriynovich has been bringing mindfulness practices into the classroom since 2009, specifically passionate about supporting the needs of students with learning disabilities using mindfulness. She is a certified yoga teacher, leading workshops and presentations nationwide. She is a member of Wake Up Schools, a worldwide community of educators in the Thich Nhat Hanh/Plum Village tradition and also Board President of the Mindfulness in Education Network.

4. Laurie Grossman is an activist for social justice and educational equity. In her quest to make the world better for kids, she piloted bringing mindfulness into the classroom, co-founding Mindful Schools. As a team member of Inner Explorer, she is very happy bringing daily mindfulness practice to over a million kids. She, Angelina Alvarez, and 5th graders co-authored *How to Be Your Own Superhero in Times of Stress* and *Breath Friends Forever.* lgrossman@innerexplorer.org

5. Megan Sweet, Ed.D, in Educational Leadership, is a systems-thinker who has been in education for more than 25 years. She's been a teacher, school administrator, and school district leader. Her academic and professional interests rest mainly with how to create effective change in educational contexts. Megan serves as the Director of Training at Mindful Schools, a leader in mindfulness programming for educators. Megan is a published author, podcaster, and blogger.

6. Lynea Gillen, LPC, RYT, is an author, speaker, and pioneer in the field of health and wellness education for youth. From its development in a rural Oregon elementary school, her college-accredited Yoga Calm program (YogaCalm.org) is now used with tens of thousands of children each day in diverse settings, such as Head Start programs, urban classrooms, occupational therapy clinics, and psychiatric units at the Masonic Children's Hospital and the Mayo Clinic.

Jim Gillen, ERYT-500, has been practicing yoga and mindfulness meditation since 1973 and teaching yoga for over 22 years. He is the co-founder of Yoga Calm, co-author of *Yoga Calm for Children*, publisher at Three Pebble Press, and director of Still Moving Yoga studio in Portland, Oregon. Jim developed youth education programs for the National Science Foundation, published education articles, and taught at National Sports Center for the Disabled.

7. Dido Balla is an educator who started his career as a high school teacher in the inner city in Miami where he noticed that his students struggled because of extreme poverty, lack of socioeconomic support, and inability to regulate strong emotions. Today, Dido has trained thousands of students, parents, and educators, and his work with MindUP spans throughout the US and across multiple continents, reaching communities in places like Brazil and Jordan.

8. Theo Koffler, former corporate executive and founder of Mindfulness Without Borders, works passionately advocating for systemic change in education through mindfulness-based SEL programs for youth and their educators. In 2015, the Huffington Post recognized Mindfulness Without Borders for bringing meditation to the masses and providing meaningful and innovative solutions that will shape the next decade. mindfulnesswithoutborders.org and rethinkkit.org

9. Brendan Ozawa-de Silva, PhD, is Associate Director for SEE Learning at the Center for Contemplative Science and Compassion-Based Ethics at Emory University. He served as Associate Professor of Psychology and as Associate Director for the Center for Compassion, Integrity, and Secular Ethics at Life University. He researches various dimensions of prosocial emotions and their cultivation. He was founding Director of the Chillon Project.

10. Jersey Cosantino, MEd, a trans/non-binary educator, completed a graduate certificate in Mindfulness Studies from Lesley University. They are a doctoral student in Cultural Foundations of Education at Syracuse University. Research interests

include identifying the harmful impacts of binary ideologies, language, and systems in K-12 education settings on the identity evolution of non-binary students and staff, particularly those with disabilities. jersey.cosantino@gmail.com

Sara Bartolino Krachman is the Founder and Executive Director of Transforming Education, a nonprofit that supports schools and districts in fostering the development of the whole child. She is an author of many publications and toolkits that translate findings from neuroscience, psychology, and related disciplines into actionable guidance and strategies for K-12 educators. To learn more about Transforming Education, visit transformingeducation.org.

Akira Gutierrez Renzulli is a former early childhood educator and human development researcher from Miami. She has created resources especially for educators to help bring mindfulness to the classroom. Akira is currently training as a child and adolescent clinical psychologist and scientist—continuing to advance her work with educators, children, and families—at Florida International University. She can be reached at akira.gutierrez@gmail.com.

11. Jennifer Cohen Harper is an educator, author, and mother, working to support children in the development of strong inner resources. As the founder of Little Flower Yoga, Jennifer brings embodied mindfulness to schools nationwide. She has created many resources, including her most recent book, *Thank You Body, Thank You Heart: A Gratitude and Self Compassion Practice for Bedtime*, and a variety of card decks and activity books. littlefloweryoga.com

Traci Childress, MA, MEd, is Executive Director of Saint Mary's Nursery School in Philadelphia. She has taught in the USA, Mexico, the Czech Republic, and Germany. She is co-founder of the Children's Community School and is co-editor of *Best Practices for Yoga in Schools*. Her passion is developing processes for community reflection, inquiry, and empowerment to support school communities and organizations.

Catherine Cook-Cottone is a Professor in the Department of Counseling, School, and Educational Psychology at the University at Buffalo, where she teaches courses on mindful therapy, yoga for health and healing, self-care and service, eating disorder prevention and treatment, and counseling with children and adolescents. She is an author and presents nationally and internationally and her research focuses on embodied self-regulation and psychosocial disorders.

12. Monica Claridge is an elementary physical education teacher in Kodiak, Alaska. After receiving training from Mindful Schools, she started including a mindful minute at the end of her physical education classes. This evolved into teaching weekly mindfulness lessons to her students as well as sharing the practice with the staff at her school and throughout the district and the community at large.

13. Candice Lynn Davies is a Speech and Language Pathologist with over 30 years of experience in a variety of settings, including public education. She is a certified Art Educator, Director and owner of Integrity Movement Studio since 2004, which specializes in children, and the owner and Creative Director for DharmaDinos, yoga, and mindfulness education products for youth. Candice is a certified instructor with Mindful Schools.

14. Jennifer Haston-Maciejewski teaches in an alternative school in Greenfield, Indiana. After receiving training in yoga and mindfulness, she opened her own yoga studio and started a program called Stop.Breathe.Be. Her program focuses on restorative justice and replacing detentions and suspensions with a mindfulness program. She is currently training in wilderness therapy and hopes to bridge wilderness therapy and mindfulness together.

15. Michelle A. Martin is a 27-year veteran instructor, currently at Brebeuf Jesuit Preparatory School, where she teaches French and for-credit mindfulness courses. A proud graduate of Indiana State University, she holds two master's degrees in Educational Leadership, Curriculum and Instruction, and French and is an IMTA Certified Mindfulness Teacher, Professional Level. Her pride and joy are her son and two special needs dogs adopted from DINGO Team Rescue in Armenia.

16. Laura Bean's Mindful Literacy curriculum combines the best of SEL with reading and writing. She has practiced mindfulness for three decades and completed Mindful School's Mindful Educator Year-long Program in 2018. A published author with an MFA in Creative Writing, Laura's work has been featured in UC Berkeley's *Greater Good Science Center Magazine*. View videos of her work championing mindfulness and creative self-expression at MindfulLiteracy.com.

17. Jana York is a former Health Promotion Educator for the U.S. Army where she taught mindfulness. She took courses with Mindful Schools and Mindfulness in Schools Project to teach mindfulness to students K-12. Ms. York has taught students in Japan and Thailand. She has written a guidebook for teachers, parents and

counselors called *The Vowels of Mindfulness*. For information on the guidebook contact Jana York at Mindfullyyours@outlook.com.

18. Andrew Jordan Nance is the founder of Mindful Arts San Francisco and author of *Puppy Mind, Mindful Arts in the Classroom, The Lion in Me,* and *The Barefoot King.* He offers trainings and assemblies around the globe. His mindfulness education comes from Mindful Schools, Spirit Rock Meditation Center, Omega Insitute, and Esalen. A graduate of New York University's Tisch School of the Arts, he was Conservatory Director of San Francisco's New Conservatory Theatre Center.

19. Mary McCarter BS, RN, MEd, recently retired as a Certified School Nurse for over 20 years. Her students had medical, cognitive, behavioral and emotional challenges and she incorporated mindfulness and yoga into their daily care. She is a teacher in Hatha and Integrative Yoga Therapy and taught yoga in PE classes and mindfulness techniques to general classes. Through Quincy University, she developed and taught a Mindfulness for Educator Course to staff in her district.

20. Carla Tantillo Philibert, the founder of Mindful Practices, conducts professional development workshops across the globe. Carla is the author of *Cooling Down Your Classroom* and the *Everyday SEL* series, providing practical social-emotional learning and mindfulness solutions for early childhood to high school teachers. With more than 15 years of experience as a teacher and PD provider, Carla creates thoughtful and sustainable SEL curriculums for school districts.

21. Renee Metty is a former middle school emotional behavioral disorder teacher and preK-1st grade teacher in both Boston and Seattle. After training with Mindful Schools, she created one of the first mindfulness-based preschools in the country. She is a leadership development coach and consultant and brings mindfulness to parents, educators, schools, and organizations. Renee created a short film about mindfulness and early childhood education at vimeo.com/372526115.

22. Julie Chamberlain, MEd, MS in Counseling, has been a school counselor for 24 years and an educator for 27. She was a therapist in private practice, a trainer/consultant for the People Skills Institute and Human Development Consultation Services, and a facilitator for spiritual retreats. She is currently a mindfulness educator for Making Mindful Connections, LLC, and an adjunct professor for the College of William and Mary. She is VA State Chapter Coordinator for COSEM.

Erica Herrera, MSW, is in her fourth year as a school social worker at Tyler Elementary School and Marsteller Middle School, both in Prince William County, VA. She served as a housing counselor for a homeless shelter, grant writer, an Intensive Case Manager for Family Services, a high school English instructor, and a yoga instructor. She was the inspiration behind making Tyler Elementary a mindful school. She had taught mindful lessons and led mindful groups and clubs.

Jennifer Perilla, Post-Master's Certificate in Educational Leadership, MEd, is in her ninth year as principal of Tyler Elementary School in Gainesville, VA, where she also served as the assistant principal for three. She taught special education for seven years and was the Leadership Development Coordinator for the Office of Professional Development. She is a mindful educator and administrator, practicing mindfulness with each student, staff and parent interaction.

23. Jessica Janowsky is an NYS permanently certified teacher. She is currently teaching students to better self-regulate and calm themselves in the face of adversity through her program, Y.O.G.A. (Your Objectives Get Accomplished). She holds Certifications for Yoga Instructor, Children's Yoga Teacher, Trauma-Informed Yoga, and Stress Reduction, Calming Techniques, and Meditation. She is a health consultant at Yoga m.a.g.i.c. LLC. ultimatefitchick.com

24. Kathy Flaminio, LGSW, MSW, E-RYT-200, is founder of 1000 Petals and Move Mindfully and has trained 30,000+ individuals on how to integrate yoga-based movement, breathing techniques, and social/emotional skills into classroom and therapeutic settings. Kathy has 20+ years of experience as a social worker in regular and special education settings, is adjunct faculty for Saint Mary's University, and is American Council on Exercise, Yoga Alliance and Yoga Calm certified.

25. Tim Iverson is a former art and humanities teacher from Minnesota. After training in MBSR, he began sharing mindful practices with teachers and students in the Mounds View (MN) Public Schools and elsewhere. He currently serves on the board of the Mindfulness in Education Network (MiEN). In addition, Tim is an award-winning artist, and a former writer and contributing editor for The Artist's Magazine. Tim's blog: highviewtest.blogspot.com

26. Karen Hunnicutt is an IB Theory of Knowledge teacher at Allen High School in Texas. She is in her 24th year of teaching and has trained in MBSR-T with Gina Biegel of Stressed Teens. Karen is married to her high school sweetheart and best

friend, Eric. Karen volunteers for Patriot PAWS and is currently working with her 21st dog. Her goal is to help students believe in themselves as much as she believes in them.

27. Matt Dewar, EdD, is a teacher, learning facilitator, and well-being coordinator at Lake Forest High School. He speaks at and leads workshops and retreats for schools and organizations across the country. His work has been featured on TEDx, NPR, the National Wellness Institute, and Thrive Global. He is the author of *The Mindful Breathing Workbook for Teens* (2021) and *Education and Well-Being: An Ontological Inquiry* (2016). mattdewar.com

28. Tina Raspanti, MEd, CAPP, teaches AP Psychology and Positive Psychology at Mt. Lebanon School District in Pittsburgh, PA. She created a high school elective rooted in mental well-being, peak performance, SEL, and mindfulness. She is a CARE Facilitator for CREATE for Education and founded the Building Compassionate Learning Communities Project (bclctogether.org), educators fostering SEL, mindfulness, and resilience for all stakeholders in educational settings.

29. Debra Vinci-Minogue is an Associate Professor and Director of Teacher Development Programs at Dominican University in River Forest, IL. She currently implements mindfulness practices and contemplative pedagogy in both teacher education courses, as well as introductory French courses. Debra is seeking certification in the Mindfulness Meditation Teacher Certification Program (MMTCP) and serves on the Board of Directors for the COSEM.

30. James Butler is the SEL Mindfulness Specialist for the Austin Independent School District. He is the founder of Mindful Classrooms, educating schools on how to sustainably implement mindfulness into their daily routines, climate, and culture. For 14 years, he taught Pre-K and K. He wrote a mindfulness curriculum titled *Mindful Classrooms: 5 Minute Daily Practices to Support Social & Emotional Learning* with Free Spirit Publishing. mindfulclassrooms.com

31. Cindy Goldberg, MMT, CAPP, is a former teacher and Mindfulness/Positive Psychology Coach in PA where she brought both into the lives of thousands of students in public K-12 classrooms. She is now an educational consultant, workshop facilitator, COSEM State Chapter Coordinator, author of *Penelope's Headache,* and several articles including Chimes May Be an Answer (Mindful Leader, May 2019). mindfulnesswithcindy@gmail.com

32. Dr. Lillie Huddleston, Executive Director of Equity and Student Support for the City Schools of Decatur, GA, oversees the district's strategic efforts to close the racial achievement gap and promote educational equity. She leads the District Equity Team, which is devoted to increasing the capacity of school-based teams to address inequity related to discipline, academics, and school climate. Prior, she held faculty appointments at Georgia State University and Emory University.

33. Linda Ryden is the creator of the Peace of Mind program and the Peace Teacher at Lafayette Elementary in Washington, DC. Linda is the author of five volumes of curricula and four children's books published by Tilbury House. The Peace of Mind Curriculum, which integrates mindfulness with conflict resolution and SEL, is used at schools across the country and internationally.

Cheryl Dodwell is the co-author of the Peace of Mind Curricula for Grades 1–6, editor of the *Peace of Mind Core Curriculum for Early Childhood*. She also serves as Executive Director of Peace of Mind Inc., a nonprofit founded by Linda Ryden dedicated to the teaching of mindfulness-based social and emotional learning and conflict resolution in our schools. Cheryl brings experience in mindfulness, non-profit management, banking and healing arts to Peace of Mind.

Madeleine Sagebiel is originally from the Bay Area in California and graduated from Dickinson College with a B.A. in Sociology. She became interested in Peace of Mind and mindfulness in the classroom as a way to promote mental health at school. She is currently Peace of Mind's Communications and Research Intern.

34. Lindsey Frank, MEd, is a district-wide Climate and SEL Coach in IL reaching students from PreK to 8th Grade. She is a Learning Behavior Specialist, certified in Restorative Practices, a Certified Yoga Instructor (RYT 200) through Breathe for Change and has taken coursework through Mindful Schools. She has her Trauma-Informed Yoga Certification through Catherine Ashton's Yoga to Transform Trauma. She is also an IL chapter meeting facilitator for COSEM.

35. Una-Kariim A. Cross is a New York-based former English Language Arts and Art Criticism Teacher. She is a dynamic workshop facilitator, passionate about growing leadership capacity in youth and educators using mindful practices, inspiration, and storytelling. She serves as a leader of professional learning and facilitative leadership in the NYCDOE. She is also a published writer and photographer and has written about emerging and established contemporary artists.

36. Cheryl D. Watkins, PhD, will tell you that she summons the strength to do the ever-evolving work as an advocate for students from her parents. She credits them with anchoring her childhood in sacrifice, family, and truth. Dr. Watkins is an award-winning educator who has held many positions in education. She holds near and dear the opportunity to impact more than 11,000 students in her current position as a Chief of Schools within the Chicago Public Schools.

37. Miriam Ojaghi is the founder of Resilient Mind Consulting, a nonprofit dedicated to helping communities reach their full potential through the implementation of contemplative practices. She is a Board member of COSEM and an SEL Specialist for Dekalb Regional Office of Education in rural Illinois. She received her doctorate in Leadership in Curriculum and Instruction from Aurora University in 2017 and has completed trainings with Koru Mindfulness and Learning to Breathe.

38. Teri B. Lawler, Education Associate, Trauma-Informed Practices and Social and Emotional Learning, Delaware Dept. of Education, is an innovative school psychologist who is passionate about creating equity of opportunity for all children. Committed to translating research to practice to ensure the highest quality learnings inform daily school practices, she is a founding member, trainer, and curriculum architect at Delaware Compassionate Schools Learning Collaborative.

39. Barnaby Spring is an actor, artist, writer, educator, public speaker, activist, certified mindfulness and yoga teacher, educational theorist and currently serves as Director of Mindfulness in Education and Director of Student Services in the Office of the First Deputy Chancellor, in the New York City Department of Education. He has served in the NYCDOE since the mid-90s as a teacher, a Dean of Students, as high school principals and now in his current role.

40. Tovi Scruggs-Hussein is an author, healer, and award-winning educator with over 25 years of leadership, meditation, and school-transformation experience. She is on a mission to heal our schools through Adult SEL, Emotional Intelligence via Mindfulness, Equity/Racial Healing, and Trauma-Informed Resilience. Tovi cultivates conscious, connected, and courageous leaders world-wide. ticiess.com

Made in the USA
Monee, IL
11 June 2021